THE RURAL ENTREPRENEURS

A History of the Stock and Station Agent Industry in Australia and New Zealand

This richly illustrated book is a rare history of a uniquely Australasian institution, the stock and station agency. The stock and station agent was a respected and influential figure, coordinating farmers and connecting them to the outside world of banks, wool buyers, and government agencies in Australasia and overseas. Simon Ville examines the ways in which stock and station agents grew from their beginnings in the 1840s to offer a wide range of support services to remote and inexperienced farming communities. In the twentieth century, the leading agents expanded their range of activities and became some of Australasia's earliest nationwide firms and biggest businesses. After 150 years of development this quintessentially Australasian institution stands at the crossroads of the crisis now facing rural communities. *The Rural Entrepreneurs* provides new insights in understanding Australasia's rural history and economic and business development.

Simon Ville is a Reader in Economic History at the Australian National University. He has written extensively in major journals in the areas of economics, economic history, business, law, accounting, and Australasian history. His most recent books are *Transport and the Development of the European Economy, 1750–1918* (1990) and, as editor (with D. H. Aldcroft) *The European Economy, 1750–1914* (1994)

For Sue

THE RURAL ENTREPRENEURS
A History of the Stock and Station
Agent Industry
in Australia and New Zealand

SIMON VILLE

Australian National University

CAMBRIDGE UNIVERSITY PRESS
Cambridge, New York, Melbourne, Madrid, Cape Town, Singapore,
São Paulo, Delhi, Dubai, Tokyo

Cambridge University Press
The Edinburgh Building, Cambridge CB2 8RU, UK

Published in the United States of America by Cambridge University Press, New York

www.cambridge.org
Information on this title: www.cambridge.org/9780521125949

First published 2000
This digitally printed version 2009

A catalogue record for this publication is available from the British Library

National Library of Australia Cataloguing in Publication data
Ville, Simon P.
The rural entrepreneurs: a history of the stock and station agent
industry in Australia and New Zealand
Bibliography.
Includes index.
ISBN 0 521 64265 5
1. Stock and station agents – Australia – History. 2. Stock and station
agents – New Zealand – History. 3 Rural industries – Australia – Marketing –
History. 4. Rural industries – New Zealand – Marketing – History.
5. Entrepreneurship – Australia. 6. Entrepreneurship – New Zealand.
I. Title. II Title: A History of the stock and station agent industry in
Australia and New Zealand
338.108622

ISBN 978-0-521-64265-1 Hardback
ISBN 978-0-521-12594-9 Paperback

Publication of this work is supported by Elders Limited.

Contents

List of Figures, Tables, and Plates   viii
Preface   x
List of Abbreviations   xii

1 A QUINTESSENTIALLY AUSTRALASIAN INSTITUTION   1
The development background   1
Economic development and the farming sector   3
Economic characteristics and historical development of
    pastoralism in Australasia   7
The stock and station agent   14

2 THE DEVELOPMENT OF THE STOCK AND STATION
AGENT INDUSTRY   18
Birth of the stock and station agent industry   18
Service diversification   20
Incorporation   23
Leadership and concentration   27
National growth   39
International activities   45
Mergers and acquisitions   46
Product and market diversification   50
Rationalisation, amalgamation, and rebirth   52
Conclusion   55

3 THE FARMING COMMUNITY NETWORK   56
Network forms of organisation   56
Networks in the Australasian pastoral industry:
    some stylised models   58
Phase 1: rise of the monocentric network   60
Phase 2: the polycentric network   67
Phase 3: the decline of pastoral networks   71
Conclusion   72

4 FINANCIAL SERVICES   74
Demand for finance   74
Comparative finance provision   76
The development of agent lending   80
The financial structure of agents   86

Loan screening and contract design 91
Monitoring and enforcement 95
Lending margins and profitability 99
Conclusion 101

5 MARKETING SERVICES: LIVESTOCK, LAND, AND
PRODUCE 102
Marketing the farm 102
Livestock 105
Land 114
Produce, farm equipment, and household requirements 115
Conclusion 118

6 MARKETING SERVICES: WOOL CONSIGNMENT AND
BROKERAGE 119
Functions of wool marketing 119
Overseas consignment 120
The development of the Australasian wool auction 126
Improving the auction system 134
Charges, costs, and prices 137
Controlling the market 143
Innovation and deregulation 147
Conclusion 148

7 INFORMATION, ADVISORY, AND ADVOCACY SERVICES 150
The information problem 150
Information acquisition 153
Information dissemination 155
Some key developments 158
The farmer's advocate 161
Conclusion 163

8 ORGANISATIONAL STRUCTURES AND
ADMINISTRATIVE PRACTICES 164
The motives for organisational development 164
Patterns of hierarchical design 166
Patterns of operational design 176
Conclusion 188

9 INTER-ORGANISATIONAL RELATIONS:
COMPETITION, COOPERATION, AND COLLUSION
AMONG AGENCY FIRMS 189
Cooperative strategies 189
The limits of cooperation 192
Cooperative alliances and groupings 196
The cooperation contract 199
Conclusion 201

10 BUSINESS INTERMEDIATION AND RURAL
    ENTREPRENEURSHIP: THE ROLE OF THE STOCK
    AND STATION AGENT INDUSTRY   202
    Growth strategies and patterns   203
    Local and international networks   203
    Corporate capabilities   204
    Financial services   205
    Marketing services   205
    Adviser and spokesperson   206
    National differences   206
    Corporate leadership   207
    An assessment of pastoral services   207

Appendix: Principal Mergers   211
Notes   216
Bibliography   244
Index   251

Figures, Tables, and Plates

FIGURES

2.1	Sales by Australian woolbrokers, 1892–1981	31
2.2	Sales by New Zealand woolbrokers, 1909–1980	34
3.1	Service flows in agent-led pastoral network	59
3.2	Transaction map, *c.* 1860s	61
3.3	Transaction map, *c.* 1880s	64
3.4	Otago agent-led pastoral network by the 1880s	66
3.5	Transaction map, *c.* 1900s	68
3.6	Transaction map, *c.* 1920s	71
4.1	Agent lending in Australia, 1890–1988	81
4.2	Rural lending by leading Australasian agents, 1890–1939	82
4.3	Australian rural lending and agent profits, 1910–1939	84
4.4	New Zealand Loan and Mercantile Agency Co., 1865–1940	87
4.5	Murray Roberts, 1880–1908	88
4.6	Otago Farmers Cooperative Association, 1900–1940	90
8.1	Organisational design, 1871: remote control	167
8.2	Organisational design, 1901: departmentalisation and centralisation	168
8.3	Organisational design, 1931: regional divisionalisation and decentralisation	171
8.4	Organisational design, 1961: structural pluralism	175
A1	Elder Smith	211
A2	Goldsbrough Mort	212
A3	Elders	213
A4	Dalgety–NZLMA (Australia)	214
A5	Dalgety–NZLMA (New Zealand)	214
A6	NMA–Wright Stephenson	215

TABLES

2.1	Firm concentration levels in woolbroking	27
2.2	Market share of Australian woolbrokers	29

2.3   Market share of New Zealand woolbrokers 32
2.4   Australian branches of stock and station agents 35
2.5   Pastoral agents in top one hundred Australian companies 39
2.6   Regional spread of Australian woolbrokers 43
2.7   Regional spread of New Zealand woolbrokers 44
4.1   Lending ratios: loans as a share of assets, 1910–1930 83
5.1   Adelaide livestock sales, 1913–1952 106
6.1   Principal London wool consignors of Australasian wool 122
6.2   Local and overseas wool sales, 1881–1939 126
6.3   Wool-selling centres in Australia and New Zealand 127
6.4   Regional distribution of Australian wool sales 128
6.5   Regional distribution of New Zealand wool sales 129
6.6   Alternative marketing strategies 133

PLATES

2.1   Dalgety and Company Fiftieth Anniversary of Incorporation,
      1884–1934 25
2.2   Frederick Dalgety, 1817–1894 26
2.3   Sir Thomas Elder, 1816–1897 28
2.4   Goldsbrough's wool stores, Melbourne, 1911 35
2.5   Map of principal Australian branches and sub-branches
      of Dalgety, 1934 36
2.6   Map of principal New Zealand branches and sub-branches
      of Dalgety, 1934 37
2.7   New Zealand Loan and Mercantile Agency, Melbourne
      Wool and Grain Warehouses, 1889 38
2.8   Dalgety, warehouses, Melbourne, 1889 42
4.1   The burdens of the backcountry squatter, 1892 97
5.1   Glentanner Station, Canterbury, New Zealand 110
5.2   A stock and station agent's country office 112
5.3   A country saleyard 112
5.4   Livestock auctions in town and country 113
5.5   Elder, Smith & Co. – advertising material for supplementary
      sheep feed, 1930 117
6.1   A shearing shed 121
6.2   A bullock team transporting wool overland 124
6.3   Bales of wool awaiting shipment from Sydney 125
6.4   Classing wool at Dalgety's store 137
6.5   Buyers inspecting wool at the warehouse of Winchcombe
      Carson in Sydney 138
6.6   An Australian liner discharging wool at the South-
      West India Dock, London 141
7.1   'The strongest union in Australia' – cartoon 160

Preface

This book has been a long time coming. I first became interested in stock and station agents when I migrated from Britain to New Zealand in 1989. From what I could glean from several centennial company histories and general economic history texts they seemed to have played an important role in New Zealand's economic development. In discussing the industry with friends and colleagues I noted with interest the number of people whose uncle, father, or some other relation had worked for a stock and station firm. Yet, no one had written a study of the industry. On moving to Australia two years later I was struck by the same situation on this side of the Tasman. Aided by a Faculties Research Fund grant from the Australian National University in 1992 I established that there was plenty of extant archival material for such a study. Indeed, substantial evidence survived for just about all of the leading companies in both countries. An Australian Research Council grant enabled me to employ two research assistants to help me with the enormous task of investigation, James Bond and then Andrew Parnell. Latterly, my wife Sue Granger has aided me. I owe an inestimable debt to James, Andrew, and Sue whose careful and persistent support kept the project on course while I was deeply involved in management of the Department of Economic History at the Australian National University.

I am grateful for the support of many other people, particularly Michael Saclier, Emma Jolley and their team at the Noel Butlin Archives Centre, which remains a remarkable source of our national heritage and history. Staff at the University of Melbourne Archives, Fletcher Challenge Records Centre, National Library of New Zealand, and Hocken Archives have been very helpful during extended visits. Participants at seminars and conferences organised by the Universities of Glasgow, Reading, and Auckland, Australian National University, London School of Economics, and the Economic History Society of Australia and New Zealand have offered valuable comments and criticism. I am grateful to the Department of Economic History at the London School of Economics and the Department of Management at the University of Melbourne for giving me a quiet home in 1998–99 when I was busy writing. David Merrett, Gordon Boyce,

Steve Jones, and Kosmas Tsokhas have generously contributed their expertise through commenting on chapter drafts, discussing ideas, and sharing sources with me. Grant Fleming and I co-authored several articles on networks and loan contracts on which chapters 3 and 4 draw. Phillipa McGuinness, Peter Debus, and Paul Watt at Cambridge University Press have kindly supported the project and responded helpfully and promptly to my enquiries. I have benefited enormously from the published expertise of Alan Barnard and Noel Butlin on the subject. Barnard's unpublished notes and drafts deposited in the Noel Butlin Archives Centre have also helped me in the development of arguments and ideas.

My greatest debt is to my wife, Sue Granger, whose constancy and relentless support in research, reading, talking, and much more have kept me on track and allowed the story of this remarkable industry to be told. To her this book is dedicated.

Abbreviations

AE	Australian Estates
AFR	*Australian Financial Review*
AGPS	Australian Government Publishing Service
AIBR	*Australian Insurance and Banking Record*
AMA	Australasian Mortgage & Agency Company
AMLF	Australian Mortgage (later Mercantile) Loan & Finance Company
APR	*Australasian Pastoralists Review*
BA'sia	Bank of Australasia
BAWRA	British Australian Wool Realisation Appraisement
BNSW	Bank of New South Wales
BNZ	Bank of New Zealand
BNZMA	British New Zealand Mortgage and Agency Company
BSL	Bagot Shakes & Lewis
CBC	Commercial Banking Company of Sydney
CSIR	Council for Scientific and Industrial Research
DAWR	*Dalgety's Annual Wool Review*
DNZL	Dalgety New Zealand Loan
ES	Elders pre-1963
F & G	Farmers' & Graziers' Cooperative
GM	Goldsbrough Mort
HJD	Harrison, Jones & Devlin
ICI	Imperial Chemical Industries
JID	*Jobson's Investment Digest*
MR	Murray Roberts
MWBA	Melbourne Woolbrokers Association
NCWSB	National Council of Wool-Selling Brokers
NMA	National Mortgage and Agency Company
NZAL	New Zealand and Australian Land Company
NZLAAA	New Zealand Livestock Agents and Auctioneers Association
NZLMA	New Zealand Loan & Mercantile Agency
NZSSA	New Zealand Stock and Station Agents Association
NZWBA	New Zealand Woolbrokers Association

PGG	Pyne Gould Guinness
QIL	Queensland Investment & Land Company
RA	Redfern Alexander
SAFC	South Australian Farmers Cooperative
SAI	Scottish Australian Investment Company
SALM	South Australian Land & Mortgage Company
SM	Sanderson Murray
SWBA	Sydney Woolbrokers Association
UBA	Union Bank of Australia
UMA	Union Mortgage and Agency
WC	Winchcombe Carson
WNMA	Wrightson–NMA
WS	Wright Stephenson
WWBA	Wellington Woolbrokers Association

CHAPTER ONE

A Quintessentially Australasian Institution

THE DEVELOPMENT BACKGROUND

Australasia was one of the most rapidly developing regions of the world economy in the nineteenth century. In the half-century from 1820 Australia was the fastest growing economy among sixteen major nations measured by total and per capita real Gross Domestic Product (GDP); a list that included the United Kingdom, United States and Japan. New Zealand's per capita income level was probably larger even than that of Australia's by the mid-1860s and the greatest of any nation of reasonable size. By 1870–1913 Australia was still one of the fastest growing nations after Canada and the United States, and her per capita income remained amongst the highest. For the subsequent period, 1913–50, both total and per capita income growth suggest a relatively poor performance. Likewise, New Zealand's comparative position also declined in the late nineteenth century and particularly through the interwar period. In the decades since World War Two real GDP in both economies has grown rapidly in absolute and relative terms although per capita GDP has performed poorly relative to other major economies.[1]

Before 1810, however, the level of economic activity among European settlers had been very modest with about 12 000 people in Australia while New Zealand, not yet formally colonised by Britain, was home to a negligible population scattered across sealing and whaling stations.[2] By 1850 the Australian population had grown to about a third of a million and real GDP had expanded at a similar rate though with a slight improvement in per capita incomes. In spite of an economic depression in the 1840s the Australian colonial economies soon resumed their high growth rates. The New Zealand European population was a mere 26 000 in 1851.[3]

From the 1860s more detailed information is available indicating real product growth of 4 to 5 per cent per annum in the following three decades, including a growth per head of about 1.5 per cent. Growth rates were somewhat lower in the second half of this period than before the mid-1870s despite rising investment. A deterioration in performance from the mid-1870s is also suggested by a slower growth in labour productivity.[4] Per capita real incomes in New Zealand have been estimated by Hawke to have risen by about 1 per cent per annum in the second half of the nineteenth century. Substantial growth in the 1870s gave way to faltering progress, possibly slight contraction, in the 1880s and early 1890s before rising to much higher growth rates of about 3 per cent between 1896 and 1903. Rankin's more recent revisions, though, suggest higher per capita GDP levels by 1870 followed by more limited growth from thence to the 1890s.[5] An economic downturn also occurred in Australia in the first half of the 1890s that reduced real GDP by up to 20 per cent with per capita levels falling further.[6] It took at least a decade to resume pre-Depression levels of per capita GDP. The interwar period witnessed more years of crisis than of growth in both countries, with the period 1926–32 probably the nadir of progress. In New Zealand, for example, per capita real incomes fell by 10 to 20 per cent during the interwar years. The higher average growth rates after 1945 also concealed volatility. After real GDP growth rates of around 2 per cent per annum in the 1950s and 1960s, the collapse of the commodity price boom in the mid-1970s left the New Zealand economy growing at only 0.4 per cent. The more diversified Australian economy experienced slightly higher and more stable growth of nearly 3 per cent in the 1960s and 1970s before falling to 1.3 per cent in 1975–82.[7]

The causes and components of economic expansion are complex but some generalisations are accepted. The period 1820–50 is often known as the 'Pastoral Age' because of the dominance of the pastoral sector, gold discoveries played a vital role in the 1850s and 1860s, while development of the urban infrastructure and the construction of the railway system were increasingly important activities in the 1870s and 1880s. By World War One dairying and refrigeration had provided a further boost to GDP. Therefore, by the early twentieth century, the two economies had begun to modernise in several respects. Each had a broadening spectrum of productive sectors including some manufacturing and services, in addition, a few larger corporations were emerging and an active capital market was beginning to take shape.[8] However, these trends still had a long way to go, and it might be argued that the Australasian economies did not reach 'maturity' until after World War Two with the spread of large-scale enterprise across a wide range of industries.

A key aspect of economic expansion in the nineteenth century was the heavy reliance on international migration, trade and investment. Approximately 40 per cent of the increase in the Australian population, 1860–90, was due to net immigration compared with nearly 50 per cent for New Zealand.[9] Over the same period and continuing into the twentieth century the share of GDP accounted for by imports and exports rose periodically to as high as 25 to 30 per cent each for both countries.[10] The high foreign trade ratio was dominated by trade with Britain, particularly the export of primary products and natural resources, most notably wool, meat, dairy products, grain and gold. In 1888/90, for example, farm products accounted for 70 per cent of total Australian exports and minerals for 24 per cent. Wool exports alone have been estimated to account for up to two-thirds of total exports in some years.[11] Pastoral exports were more dominant in New Zealand and their share actually rose in the early twentieth century to over 90 per cent by the 1920s with the contraction of grain and gold exports. Sixty per cent of New Zealand's import and 79 per cent of her export trade was conducted with the United Kingdom, most of the rest being with the United States and the Australian colonies.[12] Capital imports, largely from Great Britain, periodically accounted for up to half of Australian gross domestic capital formation and 10 per cent of GDP.[13] From what is known about public debt, New Zealand relied at least as heavily on overseas borrowing from Britain, particularly during the boom of the 1870s initiated by the Vogel government.[14] The reliance of both countries on capital imports from Britain built up rising levels of debt servicing and profit repatriation by the late 1880s at a time of falling land and commodity prices.[15] In the course of the twentieth century the maturing and diversifying Australasian economies reduced their reliance on farming exports, and British buyers and investors.[16]

ECONOMIC DEVELOPMENT AND THE FARMING SECTOR

Even this cursory glance back at Australasia's development experience signifies the role of rural production, and the pastoral sector in particular, in shaping the pattern of growth and change. Besides the dominance over exports, investment, output, and employment all confirm the importance of wool, meat, and dairy products in Australasian economic development. Sectoral distributions of economic activity are difficult to measure before about 1850 although Butlin's estimates suggest the dominance of the pastoral sector, which accounted in some years for up to 40 per cent of a small GDP. Focusing on the period since the mid-nineteenth century reveals that farming's share of GDP was 17 per cent in 1861, rose to 19 per cent by 1913, and then fell to 13 per cent by 1939 by which time it had been surpassed by manufacturing, and trade and transport as the leading sector. Farming output fell to a mere 4 per cent of GDP by 1983. Figures are less accurate for New Zealand but suggest a larger and more dominant share for the sector of about a third by the interwar period, declining to around 10 per cent by the 1970s. The rural workforce was the largest group in 1891, accounting for more than a quarter of total employment in Australia, but fell to a fifth by 1939 behind more labour-intensive manu-facturing, trade and transport. By 1979 it constituted just 6 per cent of the workforce. Farming is confirmed as being more dominant in New Zealand, absorbing close to 35 per cent of the workforce in the mid-1890s, reducing to around 25 per cent after World War One though it remained the largest group throughout the interwar period. By the 1970s it employed about 12 per cent of the workforce.[17]

Most revealing, though, is farming's share of private capital formation, which in Australia was 31 per cent in 1861 before rising to more than 50 per cent in some years of the 1870s and 1880s. In New Zealand, capital formation in the sector also rose to around 50 per cent of private investment in some years of the 1870s. After the collapse of the mid-1890s its volume and share fell dramatically to around 10 to 20 per cent in Australia. The central importance of refrigeration in New Zealand explains a further upward movement in pastoral investment in the decade from the mid-1890s before falling sharply during the interwar period. In line with the other indicators, the sector's share of investment continued falling after 1945 in both countries.[18]

The fact that farming appears central to the pattern of economic progress in Australasia is not to assume that it was necessarily a critical driving force, although at certain periods this may well have been the case. Rostow argued that a particular sector or industry, known as a 'leading sector', might drive economic expansion through its 'spreading effects' or linkages to other potentially expansive areas of the economy.[19] Staple theory is a particular version of this approach, which emphasises the economic impact of the rapid export growth of a particular product normally derived from a surplus natural resource.[20] However, this theory reveals little about the supply-side response to such opportunities. Moreover, a dominant sector might possess few important linkages or, worse, 'crowd out' resources, such as capital and labour, away from potentially more productive areas of the economy. A downturn of that dominant sector might drag linked sectors into a spiral of negative growth.

Qualitative evidence regarding linkages might support the central position of farming in Australasian economic development in the nineteenth century. Tsokhas believes 'domestic multiplier effects' resulted from the role of woolgrowers as 'borrowers, investors, consumers, and employers'.[21] Farming activities induced investment in general purpose infrastructure such as roads, railways and ports, and business services such as finance and insurance. Bulky farm products provided two-way trading for international shipping which meant lower freight rates. Farmers sought the products of manufacturing industries, especially engineering, and the size of this demand encouraged the development of new skills and technologies. Looking downstream in the production process farm products were often the raw materials for developing secondary industries. More directly, refrigerated meat and dairy products stimulated manufacturing in primary processing activities. Farming profits additionally provided a source of investment for other expanding domestic industries.[22] It is more difficult to measure accurately the extent of such stimulation, how far the benefits were captured locally, and whether alternative investments in other potential growth sectors would have provided more extensive connections.

The significance of farming activity varied over time and between the two emerging nations. In the so-called Pastoral Age in Australia (1820–50) vast tracts of good quality, easily accessible, 'free' land were put to use and wool exports expanded at a rapid pace, multiplying 200 times and making them a 'powerful source of economic expansion'.[23] Pastoral farming was the first large-scale and sustained private sector activity by European settlers on both sides of the Tasman and provided much of the export income that made it possible to import capital equipment and facilitate the spread of economic activity from the middle decades of the nineteenth century. However, the direct linkages for the rest of the economy from simple pastoral activity before 1850, which required limited capital, technology or specific skills, were few.

By the last quarter of the nineteenth century pastoralism was widespread and continued to attract the dominant share of capital formation, but its relative contribution to GDP was reduced especially during the declining wool prices and rising indebtedness of the 1880s. This reflected more capital-intensive farming methods and the increased cost of farming more marginal and less accessible land. The rapid spread of the rabbit and dingo populations required investment in fencing and eradication measures. Refrigeration boosted the export of meat and dairy products but consumed a great deal of capital in the construction of freezing works and the development of suitable steamships. Dairying required capital-intensive factory production and thus helped to diversify the nature of economic activity. Thus, while farming occupied a large portion of capital investment, it also provided significant linkages to other emerging sectors. Indeed, extensions of secondary and tertiary production in New Zealand at the end of the nineteenth century were mostly related to farming output, such as the transport and processing of produce. Hawke confirms that primary processing was the fastest growing area of manufacturing between 1870 and 1910.[24] While pastoralism's share of economic activity declined in both countries during the twentieth century, the average benefit to the local economy increased through the relocation of produce markets, company ownership and management to Australasia, and the increasing reliance on local industry for farming equipment and inputs.

None the less the question of the slowing growth of GDP and declining international standing from the late nineteenth century, in spite of high investment rates, has dominated much thinking. Several prominent Australian economic historians have argued either that there was a general over-supply of capital from Britain (Coghlan) or that it was misdirected into housing, the railways, and pastoralism at the expense of manufacturing and arable agriculture (Butlin). Hawke takes a more optimistic view of the New Zealand economy. While indebtedness continued to increase, the additional goods and services this investment generated converted the long-term trend in the balance of trade from negative into positive from the mid-1880s, which expanded domestic sources for future investment. He notes that it was the proportion of investment in farming, rather than transport or urbanisation, that made New Zealand unusual among developing economies, but is more ambivalent as to whether this represented a misallocation of resources.[25]

Coghlan's notion of over-investment is not wholly convincing. The sustained expansion of farming output stimulated the demand for social overhead capital in the form of transport and housing as part of a natural process of economic development. Social investment accounts for rising levels of capital formation in the 1880s.[26] Returns on social overhead capital, however, take much longer to achieve than directly productive activities and are not easily measured as part of total product. In addition, rising export prices from the mid-1890s helped to reduce the impact of indebtedness. By way of comparison it should be noted that during the post-World War Two period Asian economies, such as Singapore and Hong Kong, have achieved rapid rates of economic growth and development by specifically attracting large volumes of foreign investment. This has provided those economies with additional output and much needed technological and entrepreneurial expertise. Australia today remains heavily dependent on capital imports. The current level of Australia's foreign indebtedness, which is equivalent to more than 40 per cent of national income, is not regarded as a problem by many economists.[27]

The debate about structural imbalance is more significant. Concentration of productive investment on pastoral output directed to the British market may have precipitated a longer and more serious Depression in the 1890s than might have occurred with a more diversified economic structure. Moreover, the nature of pastoralism is of high degrees of uncertainty through price volatility and low entry barriers, which together provide some understanding of the prolonged instability of these economies, particularly in the interwar period. Failure to broaden economic activity has led to criticism of governments, particularly during the interwar period, for placing too much faith in an upturn in the price and demand for farming exports and for lacking a clear industry policy.[28] On the other hand, some of the problems of the interwar period were externally generated, such as low export prices and the cessation of overseas borrowing, and governments did show some manufacturing vision. The economic structure had begun to diversify, a process which was extended after World War Two.

Rankin's national income estimates for New Zealand emphasise the interwar volatility, which he attributes to the country's 'narrowly structured economic development based on pastoral exports to the British market'.[29] His views provide a resonance of those of Simkin, writing forty years earlier about the period before World War One, who stressed the instability and uncertainty created by sectoral concentration.[30] Although there is no modern policy study for New Zealand that is comparable with Schedvin, the evidence suggests that attempts at economic diversification were, at best, limited. Among contemporaries W. B. Sutch was a vocal minority advocate of a more fully developed industry policy.[31]

While Australasia can claim a strong comparative advantage in the rural industries, the work of Michael Porter has alerted us to the fact that nations can achieve rapid economic development by alternatively fostering long-term competitive advantages in new high-growth industries.[32] Alfred Chandler has provided the principal historical application of these ideas in his studies of the rise of big business in the United States and Europe.[33]

He has argued that the rapid development of the United States economy since the mid-nineteenth century has been driven by the 'visible hand' of large, efficient corporations administered by well-organised tiers of professional managers. These firms have operated in new high-growth industries such as chemicals, oil and automobiles, and by investing extensively in the three 'prongs' of production, marketing and management have developed capabilities which have enabled them to sustain their initial advantages as 'prime-movers', or early leaders of their industry. Heavy commitments to research have helped them to diversify their production to yield economies of scope in addition to their size-based economies of scale. United States corporate and economy-wide success is contrasted with slower progress in Britain where firms often failed to make the three-pronged investment.

It is a matter for dispute how far Australia or New Zealand may have been able to diversify away from resource-based comparative advantages at an earlier stage to develop competitive advantages in the rapidly growing new technology industries of the late nineteenth century. The conditions faced by Australasian firms were quite different from those in Europe and North America. The smallness of the domestic market scattered across different colonies, and the remoteness from foreign markets and sources of technological change, distinguished Australasia from more advanced manufacturing nations and suggest that the economy's resources would not have been efficiently deployed in a broader strategy of industrialisation. Moreover, it is questionable whether foreign investment would have been attracted into alternative industries. British investors were attracted to the natural resource benefits of Australasia but may have been less convinced of manufacturing projects. If this were so, crowding out in the capital market was unlikely. The Australasian capital market was poorly developed in the nineteenth century and relied on special and privileged links which were mostly only well established in the rural industries.

Thus, it is possible to disagree with Butlin in that while structural imbalance, or sectoral concentration, existed to differing degrees in both economies before World War Two, this did not come at a high opportunity cost since there were few credible alternative paths of development. While there may have been excessive investment in pastoralism in the 1880s in response to the 1870s boom, over-expansion based on optimistic expectations is an endemic feature of private investment cycles irrespective of sector or nation.[34] None the less, there is still the problem of explaining why the flow of resources, especially capital, was diverted so extensively and persistently into pastoralism and how efficiently such resources were deployed.

ECONOMIC CHARACTERISTICS AND HISTORICAL DEVELOPMENT OF PASTORALISM IN AUSTRALASIA

Farming output in both countries was initially dominated by pastoral produce notably, wool, meat, and dairy products. Rabbit and sheep skins and tallow were also pastoral products, though of much less value. Agriculture, or crop production, was more modest before the twentieth century but included the growing of wheat, sugar, and flax. Some farmers also diversified into related rural industries such as stock breeding, timber, kauri gum, and horse-drawn contracting services.[35]

It was noted in the previous section that during Australia's so-called Pastoral Age (1820–50) wool output expanded rapidly and occupied a central position in total output and export from the colonies. A growth spurt occurred, particularly in the 1830s, with sheep numbers rising by an annual average of 22 per cent and wool exports 32 per cent by value. In the 1840s annual growth was still as high as 12 and 11 per cent respectively.[36] The availability of free and accessible coastal land and free convict labour facilitated this expansion. High British wool prices in the 1830s and rising long-term demand, together with the opportunity to sell livestock to new farmers, provided incentives on the demand side.

On closer inspection, however, the pastoral expansion was not so impressive. Progress provided few solid foundations for the long-term expansion of the industry. The minimal use of capital and technology reflected the view of many that their stay would be temporary, and helps explain the frequency of low or negative returns.[37] Simple nomadic herding, inadequate flock control, and inexperienced ex-convict overseers contributed to heavy stock losses and animals of poor quality. Although the merino sheep was introduced to Australia in 1797, expansion of suitable fine wool sheep breeds was delayed by the need for meat-producing herds and ignorance of breeding methods. These problems were compounded by high turnover rates resulting from a lack of experience and resources to deal with droughts, bushfires, bushranging, sheep rustling, pestilence, and periodically falling prices. Ignorance of the best farming practices used in Britain, such as preferred shearing times, was common and there was little attempt to develop techniques appropriate for local conditions such as fodder crops and artificial grasses. Even the Australian Agricultural Company herded sheep in damp conditions in spite of the existence of problems caused by this practice in Britain. It took the company at least sixteen years to achieve a reasonable level of fine wool production.[38]

It is hardly surprising that early progress was unimpressive, given the uncertainties associated with farming and the problems of settlement in colonial Australasia. Farming is subject to high degrees of instability. World output and prices fluctuate significantly from year to year due to vicissitudes in supply and demand. Fluctuations in farming activity have often run ahead of the main trade cycle, adding to uncertainty by making it more difficult to judge future trends.[39] Farmers are price-takers in a fragmented global market and therefore have little or no influence over price trends. In addition, it is very difficult to cut costs at times of falling prices. Farm equipment and land mortgages and maintenance are fixed, while variable costs may increase if farmers seek to raise output in years of poor prices. Climatic conditions, particularly drought and flood, can substantially reduce animal survival rates, crop size, and the consequent availability of feeds with the result that falls in output will continue over successive years. Thus, a production shortfall in a year of low world prices is particularly damaging for the farmer, and such uncertainties are best handled by offsetting the gains from good years against the losses from poor ones.

Remoteness and unfamiliarity with different economic, geological and climatic conditions were the predominant sources of uncertainty for Australasian settlement. Production cost structures were the reverse of those in Britain, with cheap and plentiful land but scarce and expensive capital and labour.[40] Australian growing conditions were also quite different from those in Britain, where severe and prolonged droughts were unknown. Even amongst those farmers not constrained by finance or thoughts of returning Home (that is, to Great Britain), sinking investments in soil improvements, the construction of working properties, and the purchase of equipment was risky until more was understood about the environment. International remoteness derived from Australasia's geographical location and the absence of regular shipping services. Local isolation was a reflection of the undeveloped infrastructure. Remoteness from other farming nations emphasised the difficulties of keeping up to date with best practice, while local isolation between farms slowed the development and diffusion of core knowledge of preferred local techniques. Appropriately skilled labour was also in short supply and finding seasonal labour for shearing and harvesting was difficult in the absence of an organised labour market.

By mid-century the challenges facing the farming community were increasing. The ending of transportation in the 1840s exacerbated labour problems as did the distraction of the gold rushes in the following decade. The boom in the English wool industry in the 1830s attracted many new and inexperienced settlers to Australia to take up farming. They included individuals from many walks of life, such as the military, law, the clergy, and commerce, who entered sheep farming on a small scale and had little previous experience.[41] Ignorance of business techniques, such as accounting and labour management, was common. New farmers increasingly had to settle on poorer quality and less accessible land away from the coast, which required a greater investment of time and money to bring it into effective use and to maintain. Geological conditions beyond the coastal fringes were less familiar to British settlers and greater inaccessibility meant higher transport and information costs and greater risks of produce damage.

Distance to market was also increasing with a rising share of output being sold in Britain by the 1860s. This required complex organisation of local transport, storage in port warehouses, loading vessels, unloading and delivery at the destination port. All of this had to be organised, insured, and financed prior to receipt of payment for the sale, at a time when slow and unpredictable sailing vessels dominated trade with Europe. Export also required careful attention to product quality to compete with respected European produce that had travelled much shorter distances to the market. Thus, knowledge of the latest breeding, herding, and produce handling practices designed to improve wool quality was vital. By mid-century Australian wool occupied a dominant place in the London market and, therefore, maintaining a high quality reputation was more important than in the earlier decades of the century when it was no more than a marginal supplement to European suppliers. Well organised marketing practices would also help the competitive position of Australian wool exports.

It has been suggested that the Australian pastoral industry was facing resource and market constraints by mid-century.[42] The constraint would have been serious if the methods of production and marketing of the early Pastoral Age had been maintained. In order to farm land which was less accessible, often less suitable, and no longer free, and generate from it high quality produce for sale in distant competitive markets, important improvements in the pastoral industry were needed. These changes principally involved farmers investing heavily in capital intensive farms, adopting the latest techniques, and finding an efficient way of consigning their produce to the market. Each of these requirements – finance, technical expertise, and marketing – lay beyond the capacity of all but the largest and most experienced of colonial farmers. Thus, it might be argued that by the middle of the nineteenth century the continued expansion of the leading sector, pastoralism, could not be sustained by the farmers alone but required additional specialist support.

Pastoralism naturally began somewhat later in New Zealand and was influenced by news of the Australian experience. Sheep were introduced to Canterbury, Marlborough, Wairarapa, and Hawke's Bay in the 1850s and 1860s partly in response to the migration of farmers from the slump in the Australian industry in the late 1840s and through the demand for meat from gold diggers. Sheep numbers increased rapidly from 2 to nearly 10 million during the 1860s.[43] Similar problems and challenges were encountered to those of the Australian colonies, including local remoteness, the growth of distant markets, poor or inappropriate animal breeds which suffered various diseases and produced low wool yields, farmer inexperience, and inadequate funding to develop efficient and fully capitalised farms.

Some important differences in geology and climate between Australia and New Zealand have affected the evolution of farming. In addition to the much smaller land mass than Australia, drought is uncommon in most areas of New Zealand where most areas have a temperate maritime climate. This has made for smaller but more stable levels of pastoral output. Serious droughts have been a regular occurrence in Australia with particularly severe and prolonged ones in the 1890s and 1960s. At such times both produce output and quality, together with livestock numbers, contracted sharply and farmer indebtedness rose equally dramatically.[44] Thus, while Australian wool exports fell by 34 per cent between 1896 and 1903, New Zealand's rose by 20 per cent.[45] Less land in New Zealand is located away from the coast than in Australia, although uneven terrain, together with many rivers and dense forests, has made inaccessibility a problem only a short distance inland. The very high degree of suitability of New

Zealand's climate and geology to pastoralism meant that arable agriculture was never as significant as in Australia, but dairying became very popular. It has also been suggested that Maoris served as effective shearers in many places thereby helping to overcome labour shortages. In Australia Aborigines were most commonly employed in the northern cattle industry from the second half of the nineteenth century.[46]

Therefore, by about the 1860s pastoralism on both sides of the Tasman had experienced a burst of growth but had not established the foundations for self-sustaining development, and faced challenges which had to be addressed if the considerable potential for long-term growth was to be met. The subsequent history of both Australia and New Zealand confirms that this potential was realised: as was shown, expanded farming production dominated the subsequent expansion of both economies. This expansion was accompanied by significant improvements in output quality and yields as farmers learnt best practice and modified techniques for local conditions. In New Zealand there was a doubling in the survival rates of lambs, of the amount and quality of wool yielded from a single sheep, and in the stock capacity of the land.[47] Breeds improved and diversified, and the incidence of disease was mitigated. As Australian settlement pushed westwards across New South Wales and Queensland in the 1870s and 1880s in response to buoyant demand and prices, farmers were brought on to poorer quality land that was more susceptible to drought. In order to reduce the risks of working in these areas farmers pioneered new techniques in relation to water conservation, soil improvement, and the development of appropriate sheep breeds.[48] In both countries seasonal labour needs were reduced by machine shearing which began in the 1880s and 1890s. Fencing also reduced labour requirements, addressed the rabbit and dingo problems, and encouraged experimentation and the adoption of new techniques. Farmers therefore faced a broadening range of technological and operational alternatives from which they had to choose and try to achieve a sensible balance of investment between, for example, improved pasture and more productive stock. These developments illustrate that farming had become more complex, requiring informed decision-making.

Smaller scale but intensive farming became an important feature in the last quarter of the nineteenth century. High land values and the expense of maintaining large estates during a period of high interest rates combined with the increasing capital intensity of farming methods encouraged the break-up of large estates from the 1870s. The financial problems of the 1890s added to the pressure for subdivision. Closer settlement was also consistent with the impact of dairying and refrigeration which required more intensive farming. The growing popularity of mixed farming provided manure for soils, fodder crops for animals, and a hedge against fluctuating prices. Official policy was heading in a similar direction. Land legislation in New South Wales in 1884 divided many existing leases.[49] In the 1890s the New Zealand government fostered subdivision and closer settlement, particularly through the Lands for Settlement Act of 1892, which authorised the government to spend £50 000 per annum in repurchasing land for closer settlement. Two years later the amount was increased to £250 000 and the government was given the power of compulsory purchase. In eleven years 176 south island properties were expropriated and divided into 3500 farms. Surviving large estates were, in practice, often farmed as separate units by different farmers.[50] The small family farm was to remain the typical unit of enterprise up to the 1950s.[51]

Profits had been high in the 1870s reflecting buoyant demand, but this was followed by falling land and wool prices in the 1880s. The crisis, however, was a factor behind the development of refrigerated meat and dairy exports. New Zealand responded quickly to technological developments in refrigeration and dominated the export of frozen lamb and mutton to Britain by the mid-1880s, with Australia catching up from the 1890s.[52] In contrast to wool exports, which required little additional activity after shearing, besides cleaning and classing, dairy and frozen meat involved greater processing. By 1891 there were twenty-one freezing works in New Zealand.[53] Dairying involved the use of new and relatively complex technology organised in factories and requiring significant additional investment. Dairying also encouraged the geographical expansion of pastoralism into higher rainfall areas that produced the lush grass better suited to cattle than sheep. These areas, which included South Auckland, Taranaki, the Waikato, and Northland, were recently acquired from the Maoris and titles needed to be resolved and the land cleared.[54] Such factors delayed the expansion of dairying until after 1900, cheese exports growing rapidly in the decade up to the end of World War One and butter in the following decade.[55] In Australia alternative diversification opportunities were pursued with the rapid expansion of wheat, sugar, and fruit production. The area sown under wheat rose from 5 million acres at the beginning of the twentieth century to 18 million (404 700 ha) by 1930–31, with yields at least doubling through increasing fertiliser applications. Sugar yields trebled in the 1920s.[56]

World Wars One and Two brought prosperity to the Australasian pastoral sector as high British demand for wool and foodstuffs resulted from the severing of alternative supplies. Moreover, the risks were mitigated by a bulk purchase agreement at fixed prices with the British government, which in addition took responsibility for freights and losses through enemy action. As Hawke noted: 'marketing had never been so easy and the prices paid were favourable'.[57]

The interwar environment, however, was very different. The challenges facing farmers changed from those associated with growth to ones of survival in the face of sustained adversity. Prices were lower and, like exchange rates, unstable.[58] Most marketing responsibilities were returned to the pastoral sector despite the establishment of several government agencies, including the Meat Export Control Board (1922) and the Dairy Export Control Board (1923) in New Zealand. Competition intensified, particularly from Argentina and Denmark, at a time when British incomes were falling. Substitute products, most notably margarine and synthetic textile fibres, were being developed and threatened to erode Australasia's resource-based comparative advantage.[59] This was an era of increasingly sophisticated mechanical technology whose application to farming required additional finance and appropriate expertise, including after-sales support. It also required the farmer to think more carefully about capital accounting procedures and the amortisation of major pieces of equipment. The introduction of the tractor in the 1920s was particularly important in expanding the range of farm machinery. Improved technology and a number of good seasons raised output. These two factors, taken with increased competition and lower demand, caused prices to fall; a trend exacerbated by the farmer's reaction of expanding output.[60]

The depth of the downturn occurred from around the end of the 1920s: in spite of increasing output and farm employment, gross pastoral (including dairy) income in New Zealand fell from $123 million in 1928/29 to $62 million in 1932/33. A recovery in prices and preferential treatment at the Ottawa Conference, which helped Australia and New Zealand increase their share of British imports at the expense of Argentina and Denmark, enabled incomes to rise to $103 million by 1935/36. Although this was a period of general price deflation these figures still represent extreme adversity for farmers. In Australia wool's share of total exports fell from 43 per cent in the 1920s to 35 per cent during 1929–32. Wheat also lost share although butter and meat exports gained slightly.[61]

The extent of suffering which lay behind these figures is reflected in evidence of rising indebtedness, contemporary correspondence, and the fact that some gave up on years of hard work and investment by walking off their farm. Others barely survived by enduring years of abstinence and hardship.[62] The policy of providing land for returning soldiers had exacerbated problems by introducing a new class of inexperienced farmers into low rainfall areas who made many mistakes and had borrowed against inflated postwar land values. Many were put on to newly irrigated land to work on undeveloped export products, conditions which would have, 'tested the most experienced and astute farmers'.[63]

Further changes after World War Two centred around the more rapid decline in relative importance of the pastoral (including dairying) sector. In Australia its share of exports fell from 67 per cent in 1953/54 to 41 per cent in 1967/68. In New Zealand farming incomes declined from about 30 per cent of GDP before World War Two to about 13 per cent by the mid-1970s.[64] Much of this relative decline reflected adverse movements in the terms of trade between sectors. Australia continued to supply a large share of international markets, including 40 per cent of world wool output in 1960.[65] Squeezed margins required larger farming units which benefited from scale economies based on new technologies.[66] As part of this process the smaller family farm has been under pressure through increased indebtedness and is being replaced by the consolidation of individual landholdings into larger, more capital intensive, and often vertically integrated, agri-businesses. As a result, the rural landscape is in a process of social, economic, and political change with the decline of communities populated by small family farms and their workforces.[67]

THE STOCK AND STATION AGENT

It is clear, therefore, that farming output has continued to dominate both economies until recently, its relative share contracting with the broadening of activity. This dominance has been achieved in the face of frequent new challenges for different groups and generations of farmers which, as we have seen, covered all aspects of farming business. While United States economic expansion was driven by large manufacturing corporations, with evolving internal capabilities, and manned by hierarchies of experienced executives, Australasian development was associated with a predominance of small family farming units of limited resources and experience.

It is the central contention of this book that this 'entrepreneurial gap' in Australasia's dominant economic sector was filled by a well organised group of intermediaries and business advisers commonly known as stock and station agents.[68] Drawing on a mixture of local and British resources and experience, they recognised the prospects for the long-term expansion of pastoralism at a time when its initial but unsustainable growth spurt threatened to peter out in the face of the many new challenges that were beyond the countenance of the average small-scale settler farmer. Agents fostered long-term and wide-ranging business relationships with farmers providing them with commercial, financial, technical, marketing, and general business services, which helped many farmers increase the quantity and quality of their output, improve the organisation of their farm in good times, and withstand insolvency pressures in bad.

The agent provided long-term finance against the purchase of property, equipment, and livestock, and short-term finance to cover the period from processing and shipment to final sale. He arranged the marketing of produce either locally or overseas, including transport, insurance, storage, presentation, final delivery, and the collection of payment. The farmer was provided with a wide range of technical, legal, and commercial information and advice on such matters as new techniques, animal breeds, land tenure regulations, and produce market trends. Farming inputs including raw materials, equipment, and stock were often supplied through the local agent as, quite often, were more general household needs. The agent was also a source of general business advice including the keeping of accounts. Finally, agents acted as powerful advocates with other groups and in political debate. In return for these services the agent received commissions, interest payments, and resale margins. Some services were offered at a zero price, including information and advice, as a means of building up long-term farmer–agent relationships based on mutual dependency and trust.

The earliest specialist stock and station agents emerged around the middle of the nineteenth century in Australia and a decade or so later in New Zealand. In the second half of the nineteenth century firms recognised the synergies of providing a full gamut of farming services. The financial collapses of the 1890s also led firms to diversify away from an emphasis on mortgage lending. In the twentieth century, market leaders emerged as national firms with competitive strategies and well-conceived organisational structures. They have been amongst the largest companies in both countries.

Thus, if there was an equivalent to the United States' large-scale industrial leaders in Australia's dominant economic sector it was the pastoral agency firms which developed strong competitive capabilities. They provided linkages to other sectors of the economy with their urban headquarters, industrial shareholdings, and regular contracting with finance, transport, insurance, processing, and equipment manufacturing firms. It was their efficient channels into otherwise primitive financial markets, in particular, which help answer the question raised earlier: that of why pastoralism continued to attract the lion's share of new investment. Studying the stock and station agent, therefore, provides a microeconomic dimension and explanation of why pastoralism dominated investment, and also allows us to assess how efficiently resources were allocated within this sector. Whether agents actually attracted too much investment in the first place, as Butlin implies, requires further macroeconomic analysis of the major alternative areas of expansion.

The role of agency firms has changed significantly since World War Two with farming incomes in decline, the large and independent agribusiness firm becoming more important, and greater government involvement in the industry. Other changes have included the increased availability of public information and reduced isolation through quicker and more efficient transport and communications. Each of these has impinged on the broad service role of the agents and has meant that farmers are better placed to contact service providers directly or include the function in their own integrated activities. Agents have simultaneously gone through a process of merger and diversification which has led them further away from farming connections and pastoral interests, and left the farmer with fewer specialist agents from which to choose.[69]

There is no doubt that the stock and station agent has been a legendary figure in local folklore, connected or related to many individuals and groups, a central figure embedded in rural settler communities, and about whom everyone has had a view.[70] This social perspective helps inform our understanding of the agent's role and importance in economic activities since trust, reputation, and personal connection were the vital lubricants in sustaining business relationships and networks. Although locally connected agency firms still survive, the postwar trend of large diverse corporations and agri-businesses has removed much of the local networking on which the farmer–agent relationship flourished and, with it, rural economy and society.

Relations between the two groups, farmers and agents, have not always been good. Some farmers believed they had been enslaved to the same agent and subject to collusive price fixing between firms. Conversely, a New Zealand agent, responding to some negative comments at a woolgrowers conference in 1920 noted: 'they use our brains, ask for and accept assistance in every way . . . and the only return we receive is abuse'.[71] None the less, many long-term cooperative relationships developed between individual farmers and their agents over the years.

Stock and station agents periodically faced competition from other organisations. Banks perceived the profit potential of the expanding pastoral sector, although the effectiveness of their lending policies was often constrained by lack of specialisation in this sector, and therefore inexperience and intermittency in dealing with farmers. Banks often lent indirectly to farmers through agents and developed close working relations with particular agents. More sustained competition came from farmer cooperatives towards the end of the nineteenth century. Most began as bulk purchasing organisations for farmers but developed many of the functions of stock and station agents. As a result their activities will be analysed in some detail in this book. Pastoral and agricultural societies provided information about new techniques and breeds. State marketing during and after World War One introduced a powerful competitor and regulator that had a major influence over the handling of the interwar debt crisis. Since 1945 a proliferation of government bodies impinged further on agent operations. The state also contributed to the development and diffusion of technical change in the industry, although Australasian governments have been compared unfavourably in this role with those of other nations, particularly Denmark.[72]

The importance of the stock and station agent has been acknowledged by contemporaries and historians. The wool enquiry committee of 1932 noted: 'the wool-selling brokers can be said to render excellent service to the producers'.[73] In his ground-breaking survey of Australian economic development in the second half of the nineteenth century, Butlin appears to suggest that agents contributed to 'faster and larger expansion of pastoral investment and . . . encouraged the flow of resources to this sector'. Barnard is equally supportive of the varied roles of the agent, particularly as 'the first link between the grower and the market'. New Zealand writers appear yet more emphatic. Gore emphasised the support provided by agents in both good times and bad, noting that 'no institution has stood the farmer in such good stead as his stock and station agent'.[74] There exists, however, no comparative or scholarly study of the stock and station agent industry in spite of its economic and social significance. Many writers have concentrated on the broad development of the Australasian economies and highlighted the significance of the pastoral sector. Studies of pastoralism have referred to the agents in merely general and brief terms, while individual company histories of several firms concentrate mostly on a chronology of specific facts.[75]

This omission from the literature is the more disappointing in light of the fact that the pastoral agent may have been unique to Australasia. Small-scale farming in Britain, for example, was often in the hands of tenant farmers who had recourse to the landlord on many matters. In addition, the British market was more localised, and since fewer farmers were starting from scratch they required less finance and technical advice. While it is possible to find agricultural intermediaries in various newly developing countries concentrating on primary production, these examples appear to relate to firms involved with finance or marketing as their principal task. None seem to have been involved in providing such a comprehensive range of services and over such a long period of time to the farmer.[76] The agencies were 'clearly an adaptation to local conditions', several aspects of Australasian development helping explain this institutional form.[77] International isolation made the farmer's tasks, such as marketing and the acquisition of information and equipment, particularly difficult in an age of poor communications. Local isolation as settlement moved inland augmented the problem. Distance also created problems of control of contractual behaviour by trading partners, and therefore a holistic approach covering all aspects of farming and encouraging commitment to a long-term trustworthy relationship was highly desirable. If not unique, stock and station agents were a quintessentially Australasian response to the particular historical and geographical circumstances.

CHAPTER TWO

The Development of the Stock and Station Agent Industry

The development of the stock and station agent industry has occurred in distinct phases. Provision of stock and station services originated with the early years of pastoral expansion from the 1830s and 1840s. The rapid expansion of wool production attracted specialist stock and station agent firms from various backgrounds by the 1850s. Recognising potential synergies, they diversified their range of pastoral services over the following decades. Incorporation from about the 1880s enabled agents to expand their activities and make more advances to new settlers. The financial and economic crises of the 1890s cleared out some smaller firms and encouraged others to develop national networks of branches as a preferred competitive tool to greater lending. By the turn of the century concentration levels were high in the industry, which contained many of Australia's and New Zealand's largest firms. Acquisitions and internal growth throughout the first half of the twentieth century extended the influence of the industry leaders. Initially between the wars, and more extensively after 1945, the firms diversified the range of goods they handled and the markets they served. The merger of the leading four companies into two dominant new firms in each country in the 1960s and 1970s recognised the problems of overcompetition and extended resources brought about by this policy and by changed economic circumstances.

BIRTH OF THE STOCK AND STATION AGENT INDUSTRY

Stock and station services were being provided to farmers by the time of the early growth of pastoralism in the 1830s and 1840s. Some of the many general mercantile houses common in the small embryonic economies of Australasia included one or more pastoral services amongst their activities, such as wool consignment, farm finance, and livestock sales. As wool production expanded around mid-century several of the leading trading houses saw specialisation in pastoral services as an opportunity to become

more efficient and combat increasing competition.[1] The benefits of specialisation included the accumulation of expertise, scale economies, and the
development of a profile and reputation.

Since wool was the dominant commodity in both countries it was here
that many specialist firms were first spawned, concentrating in particular
on woolbroking and the sale of livestock and property. Elders originated
in Adelaide in 1839, their initial activities centring on general merchanting
and commission business, then mining and transport, before concentrating
on the pastoral sector by the 1860s. The Melbourne firm of James Turner
began as importers and commission merchants in 1846 before specialising
in wool exports in the 1850s. Dalgety started as a general importing firm
in Melbourne in 1846, made a great deal of money from gold trading
during the Victorian boom of the early 1850s, before concentrating on wool
consignment for which the long-term prospects were much better.[2] Richard
Goldsbrough, another pioneer Melbourne agent, began as a wool classer
and broker in 1848. The extension of the specialist pastoral agent through
the 1860s can be seen from the evidence that in 1858 they handled 13 per
cent of the Victorian wool trade, rising to 40 per cent by 1870.[3] Thomas
Mort had established a general auctioneering business in Sydney in 1843
but by 1850 began to concentrate on auctioning wool, livestock, and
pastoral properties.

The mounting financial needs of the expanding pastoral industry
challenged these specialist colonial businesses, most of whom were small-
scale private firms unable to finance new settlers on to stations.[4] Such needs
were met initially by pastoral finance companies floated on the London
Stock Exchange to conduct business overseas as British free-standing
companies.[5] Prominent among them were Australian Mercantile Land and
Finance Company formed in 1863 and New Zealand Loan and Mercantile Agency Company in 1865, who raised finance at low rates of interest
on debenture stocks to relend to colonial settlers. Colonial business and
administrative interests, conscious of the financial needs of farmer settlers
and aware of the profit potential, initiated the companies. AMLF's
promoters included former colonial administrators Charles Nicholson and
Henry Young, and Geelong stock and station agent David Aitchison. The
NZLMA was initially a subsidiary of the Bank of New Zealand and its
colonial Board consisted of prominent business and financial figures in
New Zealand including John Logan Campbell and Josiah Clifton Firth.[6]

Later British settlement and economic expansion delayed the agent
industry in New Zealand by several decades. Specialist pastoral agents
emerged more often from the 1860s to 1880s. These included Wright
Stephenson who originated as general merchants in Dunedin in 1861 but
soon concentrated on livestock sales and woolbroking. Levins were amongst
the earliest general merchants in Wellington in 1841 and were handling wool
by 1848 as well as a good deal of liquor, but it was several decades before
they became pastoral specialists.[7] Gould began trading in Lyttelton in 1851
but did not specialise until the following decade. Williams & Kettle, from
commercial and agricultural backgrounds, set up as pastoral agents in

Hawke's Bay in 1885. Donald Reid, a local farmer and businessman, began a pastoral agency business in Dunedin in 1878. NZLMA commenced in New Zealand at the same time as in Australia in 1865, and with Dalgety quick to cross the Tasman in 1858, the emergence of strong local competitors in the tiny New Zealand economy of the mid-nineteenth century was delayed. Other powerful British entrants included Murray Roberts (1868) who were owned by London wool importers Sanderson Murray, and National Mortgage and Agency (1864) representing a mixture of British and colonial financial interests including the National Bank of New Zealand.[8]

Cooperatives appeared simultaneously in the two countries from about the 1880s. Most farmers' cooperatives began as bulk purchasing organisations but expanded their range of services. The stronger economic and political position of the farming community and the greater importance of dairying in New Zealand made the cooperatives more widespread and more powerful competitors there. The formation of the highly successful Hawke's Bay Farmers Cooperative Association in 1891, for example, caused local agents Williams & Kettle to convert immediately to the cooperative principle, selling shares only to farmers and giving rebates, in order to defend their market share. Most cooperatives were financially weaker than the private agent firms and lacked their entrepreneurial experience. However, by the 1920s accumulated experience, financial resources, and greater cooperation among closely settled farmers sharing meat freezing works and dairy factories made several cooperatives serious competitors.

SERVICE DIVERSIFICATION

While the diverse origins of the firms were reflected in their operations – London companies providing long-term finance, local agents consignment, and cooperatives farming supplies – each group recognised the synergies from diversifying their range of pastoral services. Initial specialisation in a function such as woolbroking or livestock auctions brought economies of scale, reputation, and expertise. Diversification across pastoral services, though, provided economies of scope from using the same or similar physical assets and customer information. Diversification produced information synergies through wider and more regular transactions with each farmer. Therefore, agents had greater client knowledge from which to make informed lending and consignment decisions and this enabled closer monitoring. Thus, 'transactions costs' were reduced by increasing the amount of business with existing clients in an atmosphere of more complete information.[9] Reputation and expertise in the pastoral industry were also extended. For the farmer, more business with a single intermediary reduced his transactions costs and increased the likelihood of receiving 'free' services such as technical and business advice.

As competition in the pastoral agent industry intensified in the late nineteenth century, wool consignment, lending, and livestock sales became virtual joint services: consignors increasingly provided at least short-term finance until the sale, while initial financial support for a farmer increased the probability of also handling his produce business. Thus, the London companies realised that not only could they lend at profit but they were well placed to take a share of the consignment business from the local private stock and station agents. Contrariwise, local firms soon appreciated that finance helped to extend their list of wool-consigning clients and the operation of a livestock auction raised their local profile.[10]

Thus, by about the 1880s Australian pastoral agents were diversifying their range of pastoral services although sometimes it took the shock of the 1890s crisis to precipitate a full service line. AMLF was initially a pastoral financier, diversified into consignment after the merger with Richard Gibbs in 1865, but did not sell wool in Australia until 1903, stations until at least 1904, nor livestock until the 1920s.[11] Most of the leading New Zealand firms such as NMA did not diversify fully until the early twentieth century. Pyne Gould Guinness achieved full diversification by their three-way merger in 1919. The mix of service bundles was never identical, some firms retaining or developing a stronger interest in one area or another, but the convergence and commonalities have been sufficient to talk of a single stock and station agent industry.

As an alternative growth strategy, vertical integration provided some transaction and information economies similar to those discussed above. Many pastoral agents integrated backwards into station ownership and farm management in the 1880s and 1890s, including Murray Roberts, Gould, Dalgety, NZLMA, Goldsbrough Mort, and AMLF, but had begun withdrawing by the early twentieth century.[12] Murray Roberts' station operations existed largely to supply wool to the mills of their parent firm, Sanderson Murray, and by 1908 they had replaced these interests with wider pastoral services.

More typically, AMLF and Gould's farm ownership and management resulted from loan defaults and foreclosures particularly in 1890–91 and 1898–99. Like many firms, Gould were reluctant recipients of pastoral properties, the result of poor farmer management and adverse economic conditions, and disposed of them at the earliest opportunity.[13] NZLMA sold their stations in drought-affected areas after the experiences of the 1890s.[14] Dalgety was one of the first firms to discharge its properties and use the proceeds to expand its agency activities.[15] Although AMLF included station ownership as a company objective in 1903, within a few years the policy was relegated in favour of an expansion of agency services. In anticipation of heavy land taxes for large landowners they sold off further properties in 1909–11 and by 1924 their stations yielded only 6000 bales of wool compared with total volume at their sales of 168 000.[16] Goldsbrough Mort also preferred agency functions, noting in 1924 that while short-term growing prospects were good, uncertainty over land tenure laws and the possibility of further subdivision policies cast a longer-term shadow.[17] Elders was one of several companies whose station ownership derived partly from the farming backgrounds of senior partners and founders. Conflicting interests, disputes over company policy, and incorporation diminished this practice, and firms took steps to prevent officers from owning or leasing properties.[18] Company involvement in farming activities also resulted from estate management for absentees, although this declined as most farmers became resident settlers. Agents sometimes invested their reserves in pastoral enterprises though consols and government debentures were more common.[19]

Forward vertical integration into such areas as shipping, primary processing, or textile manufacture was less common. Where it did occur the intention was mostly to provide venture capital to develop new areas of farming production or infrastructure such as slaughtering and freezing works, railway lines, dairy factories, and stud farms. NMA was actively involved in refrigeration companies but ultimately decided it was 'outside the ordinary activities of the company'.[20] Williams & Kettle were partners in Richardson's, a coastal shipping and lightering company based in Hawke's Bay, whose small regional economy lacked sufficient trade-supporting services in the nineteenth century. A second motive was to regard vertical integration as a strategic investment, designed to obtain preferential terms, such as in freight bookings, to prevent competitors assuming undue influence over these downstream services, to influence their smooth functioning, and to improve access to information sources. Such investments additionally facilitated local agency and handling work for the firm, and were commonly found in shipping firms although Elders also invested in several stevedoring companies.[21] Mutual inter-locking investments were also used as bonding devices to secure both up and downstream links between companies. Wright Stephenson invested in Ross and Glendinning, pastoralists and textile manufacturers, as part of extensive arrangements between the two firms, which enabled Wright Stephenson to sell them wool if they had a shortage or auction any wool surplus to their production needs.

Thus, while backward and forward vertical integration did occur they were not typical strategies for pastoral agents for much of their history. Vertical integration did not yield scale and scope economies, or joint products, and informational synergies were limited. It required different forms of expertise in forward integration, while backward integration implied either a concentration of risks in a few large estates or significant problems of coordination between the managers of many smaller dispersed farms. Instead, the agents learned to make limited upstream strategic investments, in the form of loans, in many farms, which yielded trading commissions and a say in their operation without high investment and coordination costs.[22] Not infrequently, these were farms developed on land and properties sold by the companies themselves as part of the process of subdivision.[23] Furthermore, avoiding integration portrayed the stock and station agent as a separate intermediary closely tied with the farmer's inter-ests rather than a competitor, and thereby helped to develop loyal trust-based farmer–agent relations.[24]

Some businesses overextended their interests beyond the pastoral sector before 1900. At this early stage of the industry's development there were few economic advantages from broader unrelated diversification aside from risk-spreading. Thomas Mort and Henry Holt were energetic diversifiers and experimentalists across many sectors who had been active in the early pastoral industry but lost ground to other firms that diversified within the industry. However, the merger with Richard Goldsbrough in 1888 and their subsequent expansion of pastoral services secured Mort's future success as a pastoral agent.[25] William Sloane had been a successful Melbourne stock and station agent in the early years of the industry. The company was floated as Union Mortgage and Agency Company in 1884 and set about acquiring other prospering pastoral agents including James Turner, and M. D. Synott. In the course of its expansion it diversified into sugar milling and vertically integrated into pastoral ownership.[26] UMA hit serious trouble in the 1890s and restructured itself with Australian Estates as its farm-owning subsidiary and eventual owner in 1902. Australian Estates survived until its acquisition by Colonial Sugar Refining Company in 1975 but had soon lost ground to those firms that concentrated on pastoral services as their growth path.

Service diversification within the industry, therefore, was a common policy of all of the leading pastoral agent firms and provided prime-mover advantages for firms like Dalgety. Equipped with all the benefits discussed above the firms spearheaded expansion into newly settled areas and business with new farmers coming on to the land through subdivision. Some of the pastoral finance companies that failed to follow the diversification path, such as New Zealand Trust and Loan, and Queensland Investment Land Mortgage and Agency Company, on the other hand, lost their competitive edge.

INCORPORATION

Acts passed in Australia and New Zealand in the 1860s and 1870s followed landmark British legislation of 1855–62 liberalising company law.[27] A simple registration procedure and a minimal number of shareholders enabled firms to incorporate and thus benefit from limited liability, separate legal personality, and free share transferability. For an industry like the stock and station agent, characterised by cyclical instability and large numbers of debtors, limited liability and the right to sue in the company's name were important benefits. On the other hand, incorporation might lead to loss of control and greater regulatory demands, including more extensive disclosure requirements. Such issues were of concern to agents who jealously guarded their closely managed firms and valued secrecy in an information-intense industry. In most cases, therefore, firms were registered locally but share ownership was closely controlled in an inner circle of former partners, their families, and close business contacts.

However, by the 1880s there was intense pressure for additional finance to fund service diversification and the increasing capital intensity of farming. In addition, the movement of the wool market to Australasia would require agents to make further fixed capital investments. The local companies realised they were at a disadvantage against British corporations such as AMLF and NZLMA who could borrow more easily and cheaply. Therefore, from the 1880s local firms increasingly resorted to being registered in London as well as locally, a move facilitated by the matching company legislation. This gave them access to wider sources of finance than were available in the emerging capital markets of Australasia. The sale of debenture stock against the security of the large, uncalled portion of the company's closely controlled equity enabled them to raise additional finance but retain the benefits of being a private company, benefits which were extended in the 1890s by judicial and legislative recognition of this corporate form.[28]

Not all agents were initially attracted by incorporation even in its private form. Russell Ritchie & Company, who were acquired by NMA, bemoaned these 'impersonal and all-pervading institutions' but, nevertheless, conceded, 'they do business so cheaply'.[29] In 1884 Dalgety had been one of the largest agent incorporations with a subscribed capital of (stg)£4 million.[30] The partners of Dalgety had extensively debated the merits of incorporation in the early 1880s. Most of them, including the senior figures of Doxat and Blackwood, supported immediate incorporation, citing the advantages of raising greater finance more cheaply and avoiding the risk of capital withdrawal by a partner. Incorporation would also take some of the work pressure off the partners by facilitating a reorganisation of the structure of management. Fundamentally, it would allow the firm to lend more extensively and complete the diversification of its pastoral services by establishing a wool selling business in Australia in competition with the likes of Goldsbrough Mort and Elders.[31]

Frederick Dalgety, however, strongly opposed incorporation and had 'always set his face dead against anything that savoured in the least of financing'. The other partners pressured him to change his mind and talked of selling out of the business. Dalgety was criticised for his lack of hands-on experience: '[if he] took the management into his own hands . . . he would I think be disposed to alter his views'.[32] Dalgety was out-voted by the other partners in 1883 in a decision that was critical for the future of the firm in entering the expanding local wool market. As we shall see, Dalgety's emerged as the leading agent firm over the next couple of decades and maintained that position for half a century.

In the course of the twentieth century companies like Dalgety, Elders, and Goldsbrough Mort realised the need to reduce the high debt ratios which had left them precariously placed in the financial crisis of the 1890s. They turned increasingly to the expanding local equity market to finance their continued expansion. While this led to loss of control for founding families, it put the companies in a stronger position against smaller firms like Donald Reid, who persisted as private companies, and the producer cooperatives who were constrained by the requirement that their shareholders be farmers. In addition, it broadened their access to

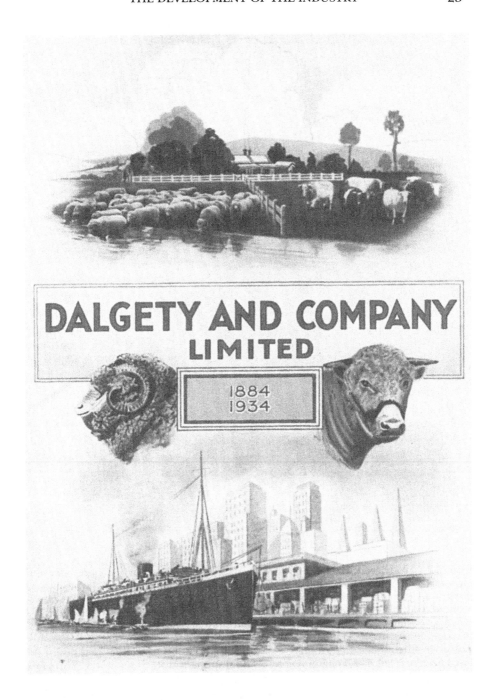

Plate 2.1 Dalgety and Company Fiftieth Anniversary of Incorporation, 1884–1934. Dalgety and most of the leading firms in the industry incorporated in the 1880s. By its fiftieth anniversary celebrations in 1934 Dalgety could boast about its success which had helped to make it one of the largest companies in Australia and New Zealand. (Dalgety and Company Limited, Jubilee souvenir booklet, 1934.)

Plate 2.2   Frederick Dalgety, 1817–1894. Dalgety arrived in Australia aged sixteen. He was a close contemporary of Thomas Elder and equally influential in business circles. His finance and provisions services to gold diggers helped generate a fortune during the Victorian gold rushes before he subsequently established his pastoral business in Australia, New Zealand and Britain. His belief in personal management and ownership, however, made him a strong opponent of incorporation in the 1880s, although he was overridden by a new generation of entrepreneurs led by Managing Director, Edmund Doxat. (Dalgety and Company Limited, Jubilee souvenir booklet, 1934.)

professional managers, made them more accountable to the stock market, and removed the potential conflict of interest associated with farmer managers.[33]

LEADERSHIP AND CONCENTRATION

The continued expansion of the pastoral sector enhanced the opportunities for the scale and scope economies discussed above and, helped by incorporation, produced some very large agent firms by the 1880s. They soon dominated the industry and were among the largest businesses in Australia. In addition, the cathartic impact of the prolonged economic, financial, and climatic crisis of the 1890s was to clear out many smaller and weaker firms. Whether measured by company assets, wool handling, numbers of branches, or volume of loans, the industry in each country was dominated by about five firms and this continued to be the case until the major reorganisation of the early 1960s.

By the 1890s the leading five pastoral agents brokered nearly half of the wool sold in Australasia and maintained a fairly constant share (around 48–55 per cent) until the 1960s. Indeed, these leading agents are sometimes referred to as 'the woolbrokers'. The two- and four-firm concentration levels (that is, the combined market share of the leading two or four firms) remained fairly stable at 25–33 and 42–48 per cent respectively. These represent high concentration levels for the period.[34] There were thirty-two firms in Australia and thirty-three in New Zealand selling wool locally by 1925–26, and thus the leading 15 per cent of firms accounted for around 50 per cent of the market.[35] The composition of the leading group of five firms was quite volatile at first but settled down after about 1910 into quite stable oligopolistic structures with the five positions being shared between Dalgety, Goldsbrough Mort, Elders, NZLMA, AMLF, and Winchcombe Carson in Australia. Prior to 1910 Harrison Jones & Devlin featured in the top five but gradually lost ground. Australasian Mortgage & Agency Company and John Bridge were also periodically in the top five until AMLF in 1904 and Farmers & Graziers in 1919 bought them respectively. In New Zealand, Dalgety, NZLMA, Wright Stephenson, NMA, Murray Roberts, Levin, and Pyne Gould

Table 2.1 Firm concentration levels in woolbroking

Year	Australia			New Zealand		
	2-firm	4-firm	5-firm	2-firm	4-firm	5-firm
1891–1900	0.30	0.48	0.55			
1901–10	0.27	0.44	0.51	0.33	0.46	0.51
1911–20	0.28	0.43	0.49	0.29	0.42	0.48
1921–30	0.27	0.45	0.52	0.28	0.44	0.50
1931–40	0.26	0.43	0.51	0.30	0.46	0.52
1941–50	0.25	0.42	0.50	0.28	0.43	0.49
1951–60	0.27	0.47	0.54	0.30	0.48	0.53
1961–70	0.45	0.60	0.65	0.42	0.59	0.64
1971–80	0.46	0.57	0.62	0.48	0.64	0.70

Note: Market fraction held by leading firms. Ten-year averages.
Sources: Based on data from *DAWR, AIBR* and NZWBA.

Plate 2.3 Sir Thomas Elder, 1816–1897. From a Scottish mercantile background, Elder was one of the pioneer figures in the Australian stock and station agent industry. He was also an inland explorer, a horse-breeder, was responsible for the introduction of the camel to Australia, and renowned for his educational and philanthropic donations including a gift of £20 000 in 1874 towards the endowment and building of Adelaide University. (*Australian Pastoralists Review*, 15 March 1897.)

Guinness led the industry. Williams & Kettle were briefly fifth during World War One but failed to match the subsequent expansion of the other firms. Overall, Dalgety was the leading woolbroker, in Australasia and globally, for much of the twentieth century (see Table 2.1).[36]

In spite of the apparent leadership sclerosis there were changes in market share among the leading firms, each of which was acutely aware of its relative position and pursued strategies to protect or improve its standing (see Table 2.2 and Figure 2.1). In Australia, Dalgety became the market leader in terms of wool brokered in 1903 and maintained that position until 1959 with a market share of 14 to 18 per cent. However, Dalgety had been gradually losing ground over several decades prior to 1959, which they attributed to the 'activities of cooperative concerns, the breaking up of large estates, and the go-getting methods of one or two opposition companies'.[37] This remark was particularly aimed at Elders which had been barely among the top ten firms in the 1890s but improved its position throughout the next sixty years to become the market leader in 1959, with a market share that rose from 3 to 16 per cent.[38] Goldsbrough Mort had been the leading woolbroker in the 1890s, as the pioneer in moving the market to Australia, but slipped rapidly in the following two decades to fall out of the top five at the end of World War One before recovering to second or third. Its volatile market share fluctuated from 31 per cent down to 5 and up to 12 per cent. NZLMA's position declined gradually from second in the 1890s to fourth by the 1960s and its market share from 15 to 7 per cent.[39] AMLF was a late entrant to local wool auctions but reached third in the 1920s and then fell back after World War Two to sixth. Winchcombe Carson frequently led the Sydney auctions but rarely rose above fourth or fifth nationally. The only other serious competitor was the Farmers and Graziers Cooperative which came to prominence between the wars as part of the resurgence of the cooperative movement, to reach sixth or seventh position. Goldsbrough Mort, as well as Dalgety, was aware of the seriousness of their challenge noting that it was doubtful that 'the Company fully appreciate the formidable position and competition that we have to contend with as regard the Co-operatives Companies now so strongly represented in Sydney'.[40]

Table 2.2 Market share of Australian woolbrokers (%)

Year	Dalgety	NZLMA	ES	GM	AMLF	WC	DNZL	Elders
1889	7.5	16.6	5.2	31.1				
1892	8.2	15.0	3.8	20.3				
1893	10.2	14.9	3.4	20.4				
1894	10.6	14.3	3.8	15.6				
1895	9.9	11.9	3.6	18.0				
1896	9.2	10.6	4.3	15.5				
1897	9.5	12.0	3.6	15.2				
1898	9.6	11.7	2.7	15.1				
1900	15.1	11.5	4.5	13.0				
1902	12.4	11.1	3.5	12.6		7.4		
1903	12.6	10.9	4.1	10.6		7.6		
1904	12.7	10.7	3.8	11.6		7.8		
1905	13.7	10.9	3.8	11.5	4.9	7.3		
1906	15.2	11.4	4.0	11.2	5.6	7.5		
1907	17.0	11.5	4.1	9.9	6.4	6.9		
1908	17.3	12.0	4.8	8.4	5.9	7.4		
1909	16.9	11.7	4.6	8.6	5.6	7.9		
1910	18.8	11.7	4.5	8.1	6.1	6.7		
1911	18.7	11.6	4.7	8.3	6.1	6.2		
1912	17.9	11.5	4.4	8.2	6.3	5.9		
1913	18.4	10.4	5.2	7.5	6.0	5.9		
1914	18.5	10.7	4.4	7.4	7.2	6.0		
1915	17.9	10.5	3.4	7.5	6.9	5.9		
1916	17.6	9.9	4.0	7.0	7.4	8.3		
1917	17.8	9.9	5.4	6.4	7.6	6.5		
1918	18.7	9.5	7.2	5.6	7.6	6.4		
1919	18.3	9.4	7.3	5.5	7.9	6.9		
1920	18.1	9.0	7.7	5.2	7.1	6.8		
1921	16.0	9.2	7.1	5.3	6.8	7.9		
1922	16.4	9.9	6.9	5.5	9.9	7.5		
1923	16.1	10.9	6.4	8.7	9.9	8.3		
1924	16.4	10.4	7.7	7.5	9.9	7.9		

Table 2.2 Market share of Australian woolbrokers (%) (*cont.*)

Year	Dalgety	NZLMA	ES	GM	AMLF	WC	DNZL	Elders
1925	15.7	10.4	7.1	10.8	9.7	7.6		
1926	15.9	10.0	6.4	11.5	9.6	6.9		
1927	15.0	9.6	6.4	11.8	9.8	7.8		
1928	15.2	9.1	7.3	11.9	9.1	7.4		
1929	15.1	9.2	6.3	11.4	8.9	7.3		
1930	15.7	9.2	6.0	11.1	8.8	7.2		
1931	15.9	8.9	5.9	10.9	8.9	7.6		
1932	16.0	8.8	5.9	10.4	9.2	8.0		
1933	15.7	8.2	6.1	11.0	9.2	8.4		
1934	15.6	8.0	6.5	10.5	8.8	8.1		
1935	16.1	7.9	6.6	10.6	8.3	7.8		
1936	15.5	8.2	6.8	10.1	7.9	7.6		
1937	15.1	8.6	5.6	10.4	8.0	8.2		
1938	15.3	8.1	7.6	10.4	7.8	7.7		
1939	15.2	8.4	8.2	10.8	7.7	7.1		
1940	15.3	7.9	7.6	10.7	7.9	7.1		
1941	15.0	7.8	7.6	11.0	7.6	6.9		
1942	14.6	7.9	7.4	10.7	7.3	6.9		
1943	14.9	8.1	8.4	11.2	7.1	6.8		
1944	14.6	7.8	8.6	11.0	7.3	7.1		
1945	14.3	8.1	8.4	11.6	6.7	7.2		
1946	14.2	8.8	7.8	10.3	6.9	8.1		
1947	14.6	8.2	8.9	10.9	6.9	7.2		
1948	14.6	8.2	10.1	10.9	6.9	7.0		
1949	14.3	8.1	10.1	10.8	6.7	7.3		
1950	14.3	8.9	10.5	10.9	7.2	7.7		
1951	14.2	8.4	11.0	11.4	7.2	7.4		
1952	14.4	7.7	12.5	11.8	6.8	6.9		
1953	14.6	7.8	11.9	11.7	6.8	7.4		
1954	14.4	7.7	11.5	11.6	7.1	7.8		
1955	14.6	7.7	11.5	11.8	7.0	7.5		
1956	14.6	7.4	12.1	12.0	6.9	7.2		
1957	14.8	7.9	11.4	11.8	7.2	7.3		
1958	14.6	7.6	12.4	12.0	6.9	7.0		
1959	14.4	7.7	16.1	12.0	6.9	7.1		
1960	14.4	8.1	15.6	11.7	7.1	7.2		
1961	14.2	8.2	16.0	11.8	7.1	7.0		
1962	14.3	7.7	16.5	12.2	6.9	6.9		
1963					7.4	7.4	21.7	28.0
1964					7.5	7.5	21.6	27.0
1965					7.4	7.5	21.2	26.5
1966					6.7	6.3	20.5	28.0
1967					6.5	6.2	20.1	27.9
1968					6.7	6.7	19.8	27.8
1969					6.5	6.5	19.5	28.2
1970					6.3	6.1	19.2	28.9
1971					5.9	5.9	18.8	28.7
1972					5.6	5.6	17.8	33.1
1973					5.8	5.7	16.7	32.6
1974					5.5	5.3	16.5	32.1
1975					5.8	5.3	13.8	31.4
1976					5.6	5.5	13.0	31.9
1977					5.7	6.0	12.9	30.5
1978					5.9	5.7	12.1	29.3
1979					3.7	5.4	11.5	29.4
1980					3.9		15.7	30.2
1981					3.4		14.1	31.7

Sources: Based on data from *DAWR* and *AIBR*.

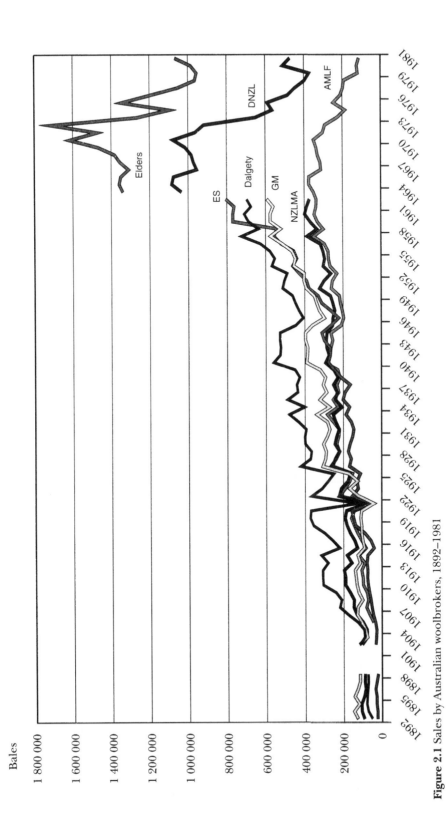

Figure 2.1 Sales by Australian woolbrokers, 1892–1981

Source: See Table 2.2.

In New Zealand, Dalgety have also led the way and with a larger and more dominant, but also more volatile, share (14 to 24 per cent) than in Australia. Its nearest competitor for most of the period to the 1960s was NZLMA averaging 9 to 14 per cent of wool sales. Although slipping back to third from 1945, NZLMA maintained a stronger relative position than in Australia. Wright Stephenson was a success story, rising from sixth at the beginning of the century to third by World War Two and subsequently to second, increasing its share in the process from 4–6 to 12–15 per cent to erode Dalgety's dominance. By contrast, Murray Roberts slipped while NMA maintained a fairly stable fourth place. Levin have hovered around the bottom of the group while Pyne Gould Guinness gained ground with the merger of the three constituent firms in 1919 but that advantage was soon eroded. The only other serious competitor was the New Zealand Farmers Cooperative Association which, like Farmers and Graziers in Australia, came to prominence between the wars to stand in fifth position in 1921 (see Table 2.3 and Figure 2.2).

Table 2.3 Market share of New Zealand woolbrokers (%)

Year	Dalgety	NZLMA	WS	NMA	MR	PGG	DNZL	WNMA
1906	17.2	14.0	5.2	6.9	4.3	6.0		
1910	23.8	11.1	5.4	6.7	3.7	5.6		
1911	23.2	11.0	6.3	7.4	3.5	6.1		
1914	21.9	10.0	6.2	8.6	5.5	5.9		
1916	22.1	9.7	4.8	6.3	9.2	4.4		
1917	18.0	12.6	5.2	5.3	7.2	3.5		
1918	17.1	11.6	4.6	5.3	6.4	3.6		
1919	14.6	10.2	4.2	5.2	5.1	3.2		
1920	13.6	8.9	4.4	5.1	4.9	5.8		
1921	15.7	7.0	5.3	8.5	4.2	10.6		
1922	17.8	9.2	8.1	6.1	6.1	6.9		
1923	17.9	9.0	6.7	5.8	5.8	6.3		
1924	17.6	9.7	7.0	5.7	6.2	6.2		
1925	18.2	9.4	7.9	5.9	5.9	5.7		
1926	19.2	9.1	8.5	6.3	6.0	5.7		
1927	19.1	9.9	9.0	6.4	6.2	5.7		
1928	19.5	10.4	9.1	6.4	6.3	5.7		
1929	19.1	10.9	9.1	6.7	6.1	5.5		
1930	19.8	11.2	8.8	7.8	5.6	5.7		
1931	19.9	11.4	10.0	8.3	5.2	6.4		
1932	19.9	12.2	8.7	8.2	5.1	6.3		
1933	20.0	11.7	8.9	7.3	5.1	5.5		
1934	19.5	11.9	9.1	6.3	5.4	4.7		
1935	19.4	11.3	8.6	7.5	6.1	6.1		
1936	18.6	11.8	8.9	6.1	5.4	5.0		
1937	18.2	12.3	8.2	6.5	5.5	6.2		
1938	18.1	12.0	8.3	6.7	5.3	5.9		
1939	17.7	11.5	8.1	6.8	5.9	6.1		
1940	16.9	10.6	7.7	6.6	5.1	5.0		
1941	16.7	10.4	7.5	6.4	4.9	4.8		
1942	16.8	10.4	7.5	6.3	5.1	4.5		
1943	16.7	10.0	7.7	6.2	5.1	4.5		

Table 2.3 Market share of New Zealand woolbrokers (%) (*cont.*)

Year	Dalgety	NZLMA	WS	NMA	MR	PGG	DNZL	WNMA
1944	16.8	9.9	6.7	6.3	4.7	4.4		
1945	16.8	9.7	10.7	6.4	4.6	4.6		
1946	16.8	10.0	11.2	6.5	4.3	4.4		
1947	17.0	9.8	11.5	6.6	4.9	5.0		
1948	17.2	9.8	11.6	7.2	4.9	5.1		
1949	17.1	9.7	12.0	7.6	4.5	5.2		
1950	16.7	9.9	12.1	7.2	4.5	5.0		
1951	17.6	10.2	12.4	7.8	4.0	5.7		
1952	16.4	10.1	12.1	7.0	4.3	5.0		
1953	16.7	10.3	13.3	7.2	4.0	4.8		
1954	16.4	10.2	13.6	7.2	3.9	5.3		
1955	16.3	10.2	14.1	7.7	4.0	5.2		
1956	16.3	10.2	14.7	8.4	3.8	5.2		
1963			16.8	10.3	3.2	5.1	25.6	
1964			16.7	10.2	3.1	5.1	25.0	
1965			16.8	10.0	1.6	4.8	25.2	
1966			16.4	11.6	1.7	5.0	25.0	
1967			16.9	11.6	1.8	4.9	24.2	
1968			17.3	11.1	1.8	5.0	24.7	
1969			17.1	11.6	1.7	5.4	24.7	
1970			16.9	20.4		5.1	24.6	
1971			16.5	21.6		5.5	24.3	
1972			16.8	20.6		5.6	24.2	
1973						5.7	24.7	35.9
1974						5.3	24.1	34.5
1975						6.0	24.1	35.2
1976						6.5	17.4	25.7
1977						6.7	15.1	26.2
1978						6.4	14.8	26.4
1979						6.3	14.8	26.8
1980						6.5	15.3	27.8

Sources: Based on data from *DAWR*, NZWBA, Statistical Handbook, New Zealand Wool Board.

The wool auctions were predominantly in the hands of these market leaders but they relied on a network of smaller localised agents and contacts to forward wool and represent them outside the major centres. As competition intensified and returns declined in many years of the twentieth century, the leaders increasingly acquired smaller, and then larger, firms and imposed their own corporate practices and provided their own more extensive resources. Thus, alternative measures of size and concentration are desirable. The rising dominance of the leading firms is indicated by the numbers of branches operated: together, the big five of Dalgety, Goldsbrough Mort, Elders, NZLMA, and AMLF accounted for 13 to 18 per cent of branches before World War Two, rising to as high as 37 per cent in 1954 (see Table 2.4).[41] Dalgety had the largest number of branches until 1954 when the resurgent Goldsbrough Mort surpassed it.

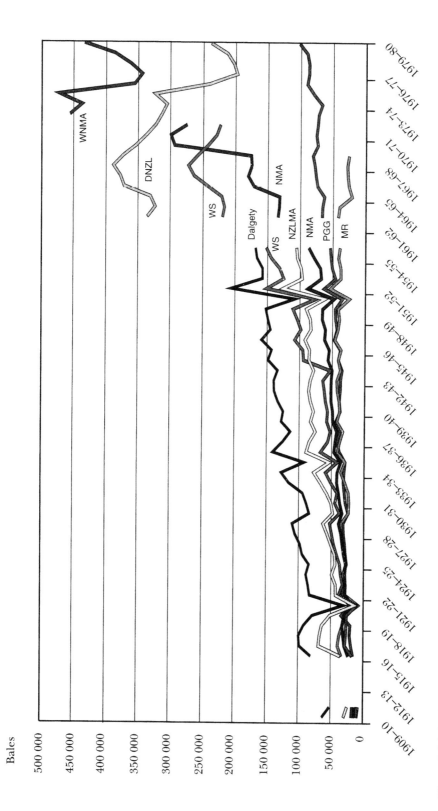

Figure 2.2 Sales by New Zealand woolbrokers, 1909–1980

Source: See Table 2.3.

Plate 2.4 Goldsbrough's wool stores, Melbourne, 1911. The 'rural entrepreneurs' also invested heavily in city and port-based facilities to support their wool auction and consignment activities. (By permission of the National Library of Australia.)

Elders branch numbers grew rapidly in the 1950s and had surpassed Goldsbrough Mort by the time of their merger. The loss of ground of NZLMA and AMLF is reflected in their slower branch expansion. Evidence of branch numbers in New Zealand is more sporadic but suggests a similar pattern of increased domination.

Table 2.4 Australian branches of stock and station agents

Year	Branch locations	Total branches	Big 5 share
1907	27	68	17.7
1915	57	165	15.8
1923	103	258	13.6
1931	96	246	18.7
1943	106	242	25.6
1954	362	1041	37.2
1963	413	1422	31.2

Note: Refers to Elders, Dalgety, GM, NZLMA and AMLF.
Source: APR.

Plate 2.5 Principal Australian branches and sub-branches of Dalgety, 1934. In the twentieth century agents expanded into, and pioneered, new areas of settlement. In addition, they located themselves more closely to existing farming communities in order to provide a wider range of rural services. (Dalgety and Company Limited, Jubilee souvenir booklet, 1934.)

Data in chapter 5 indicates the important role of the same group of companies, along with one or two livestock specialists, in the organisation of livestock auctions. Information on rural lending in chapter 4 confirms Dalgety's market leadership for much of the twentieth century, together with Goldsbrough Mort's volatility, Elder's ascendancy, and NZLMA and AMLF's slippage. In New Zealand, Wright Stephenson's growth relative to NMA is again highlighted.

Measurement of assets is less useful as an indicator of concentration since data does not exist for all firms in the industry, but it permits comparison of large-scale enterprise across the economy. In 1910 the pastoral agents dominated big business in Australia, with Dalgety as the largest company and NZLMA (fourth), AMLF (sixth), Australian Estates (seventh), Goldsbrough Mort (eighth), and Elders (tenth), all in the top ten of companies. In all, there were twelve pastoral agents in the leading one hundred companies in Australia, which made it the most heavily represented sector. By 1930 the sectoral diversification of the Australian

Plate 2.6 Principal New Zealand branches and sub-branches of Dalgety, 1934. Dalgety and New Zealand Loan and Mercantile Agency expanded across both Australia and New Zealand. (Dalgety and Company Limited, Jubilee souvenir booklet, 1934.)

Plate 2.7   New Zealand Loan and Mercantile Agency, Melbourne Wool and Grain Warehouses, 1889. Grandiose company buildings, even in the case of warehouses, symbolised the power and influence of the leading firms. (*Melbourne Stock and Station Journal*, 3 April 1889, supplement.)

economy was reflected in the reduced rankings of the pastoral companies. None the less, they still constituted the leading sector with eleven inclusions in the top one hundred: Dalgety was second, Goldsbrough Mort seventh, NZLMA eighth, Elders tenth, and AMLF sixteenth. The process of relative decline continued up to 1952 but also reflected relative movements among the agents, with Dalgety remaining the leader at sixth, Elders gaining ground to ninth, NZLMA dropping to sixteenth, Goldsbrough Mort to twenty-second, and AMLF to twenty-seventh.

The list of the top one hundred firms also periodically includes a number of medium-sized pastoral agents including Westralian Farmers, Younghusband, Farmers and Graziers, Harrison Jones & Devlin, Bagot Shakes & Lewis, and Australasian Mortgage & Agency, many of whom were gradually acquired by the market leaders.[42] Australian Estates, although not one of the dominant brokers, is amongst the corporate leaders because of its assets in the form of pastoral properties and sugar mills. Winchcombe Carson ranked highly as a broker because of its strength in the Sydney wool market but its lesser role as a mortgage lender placed it much lower amongst the leading Australian corporations ranked by assets (see Table 2.5).

Table 2.5 Pastoral agents in top one hundred Australian companies

Company	1910	1930	1952	1964
Dalgety	1	2	6	
NZLMA	4	8	16	
AMLF	6	16	27	73
AE	7	21	33	49
GM	8	7	22	
ES	10	10	9	
AMA	47			
QIL	54			
BSL	76			
SALM	78			
HJD	79			
WC	85	82	74	
SAFC		63		
F & G		65		
Westralian Farmers		73		
Bennett & Fisher		86		
Younghusband			89	
DNZL				6
Elders				14

Source: Ville and Merrett, 'Development'.

There is no similar study of New Zealand big business from which the standing of the leading pastoral agent companies can be measured. However, Dalgety and NZLMA were among the largest firms in Australia and therefore most certainly would have been corporate leaders in the smaller economy across the Tasman.[43] Calculating the assets of the two leading New Zealand-only firms reveals that they were significantly smaller than their Australian-only counterparts. In 1910 NMA would have come twenty-sixth and Wright Stephenson below fiftieth in the list of the top one hundred non-financial Australian firms.[44] In 1930 NMA would have been forty-first and Wright Stephenson thirty-eighth, confirming the relative improvement in Wright Stephenson's standing. In both years Elders and Goldsbrough Mort were at least two or three times larger than either Wright Stephenson or NMA.[45]

NATIONAL GROWTH

The additional resources resulting from incorporation and selling company properties enabled firms to extend their geographical reach. During the financial crisis of the mid-1890s many firms suffered severe losses. Goldsbrough Mort and NZLMA, for example, suspended their operations in June and July 1893 respectively. Continued losses were due in part to adverse environmental conditions, notably the Australian drought, but were made worse by strategies that had locked up much of their capital in a few large and illiquid long-term loans. The shocks of the 1890s alerted firms to the need for changes in policy, essentially of the need to spread themselves across more clients and a broader geographical area. As well as risk spreading,[46] this policy recognised the changing nature of farming, particularly the subdivision of properties into larger numbers of farming enterprises. James Kidd, Sydney manager of AMLF, advocated this change of policy as early as 1899, noting: 'the splitting of big estates, and the increasing difficulty of obtaining large sound accounts has for some time been pointing to the desirability of cultivating the smaller connection . . . men who graze . . . say 5000 [sheep] upon their own freehold . . . some of them no doubt combining small farming operations'.[47] The associated expansion of mixed farming units also encouraged agents to turn to a wider range of farming products, as did technological changes associated with refrigeration and dairying, which particularly benefited the cooperatives.

The geographical expansion of farming after 1900, particularly in Queensland, Western Australia, and the north island of New Zealand, was an additional factor behind their extended reach. Each firm closely monitored the spatial spread of farming and recognised the prime-mover advantages from getting in early to win the loyalty of pioneer farmers and help others get established. In 1898 AMLF were considering establishing a branch in Brisbane in recognition of the 'rapid expansion of the pastoral industry' there.[48] In 1903 Elders noted that their Western Australian operations were unprofitable but in the future the company would 'reap the benefit of having got in early'.[49] In 1938 Winchcombe Carson believed that Tara in southern Queensland would expand rapidly over the next few years following the eradication of prickly pear and proposed strengthening their representation by setting up a branch.[50]

Agents also turned increasingly to targeting 'free clients' who required no long-term finance. This was consistent with their strategy to 'extend the commercial, and contract the loan and investment, business'. Thus, as competition intensified among agents to attract financially unencumbered clients they increased the range and quality of non-financial services such as the sale of farming and general household products.[51] Targeting the free clients was therefore consistent with the changing strategies of agents since it focused on a broad range of services provided through a national network of branches.

These new strategies of client and geographical expansion required large well-resourced national organisations with an expanding network of branches. A more extensive network would cover new production locations, and a more intensive one serve closer settlement and compete more vigorously for free clients. While the cost of investing in a national network was provided in part by shifting resources from individual loans, the extent of this policy was constrained by the fact that smaller farmers frequently required finance to continue.[52] In addition, more farmers in a fixed area of farming land raised the company's costs even without further branch expansion. Finally, agents would operate at a loss for some time in new areas because of the set-up costs, remoteness, and limited customer base.

Firms were alive, therefore, to ways of achieving scale economies from supplying more clients and a wider geographic area. More clients brought more sales of goods and services by the agents which were directly related to the number of farming families such as household needs and some types of farming machinery. A wider geographic area provided for more goods and services directly related to the area under production such as livestock, dips, and fertilisers.

Developments in transport, communications, and office technology facilitated increased geographical reach and heightened the scope and scale economies available to firms. The coming of a national rail system in the final decades of the nineteenth century and the development of the automobile industry at the beginning of the twentieth increased the ability of agents to develop a more extensive and intensive range of clients. Dalgety's arrival in Western Australia in 1889, for example, coincided with the extension there of the Great Southern Railway.[53] Improved transport enabled agents to visit their growing number of clients regularly, canvass for new customers, and assess the prospects for expansion in particular areas. When AMLF's Australian manager, Falconer, toured Queensland in 1898 to investigate whether the company should expand in to the colony he travelled by train, coach, and private buggy.[54]

Unlike the railway, car ownership involved a substantial investment for the firm and some degree of personal risk for its officers. However, it was a flexible asset that could be used for many agency purposes and for the larger firms provided economies of scale through savings on train and other fares. It was also more versatile in its journey deployment than rail, reaching many remote farms and, by saving time, increased the productivity of branch managers. The leading agent firms were thus amongst the earliest owners of car fleets in Australia and New Zealand. Wright Stephenson, for example, had a fleet of De Dion cars by 1907.[55] In 1910 Winchcombe Carson were using motor vehicles as their main form of short haul transport, supplementing them with horse and buggy during the busy wool season.[56] In 1912 W. Robson, a traveller with Pitt, Son & Badgery in the Maitland region, suggested that provision of a car would substantially increase his competitive edge over local rivals.[57]

Improvements in office technology helped firms handle larger numbers of clients effectively. Duplicators, typewriters, telephones, adding machines, and vertical filing systems were key innovations occurring at the turn of the century.[58] They helped firms standardise and process information held about large numbers of customers and to communicate with them more easily. The telephone, like the motor car, was viewed as a competitive weapon by the firms. Winchcombe Carson would phone some of their free (financially unencumbered) clients to obtain their wool despite the high cost of phone calls, and noted that the Queensland Primary Producers 'pay special attention to this service, and concentrate on other brokers' free clients'.[59] Because of the expense of telegrams and the need for security codes, telegrams were rarely sent to clients and only used to discuss the more important accounts.

The larger, well-resourced agents realised they could use their extended reach as a competitive tool. Targeting free clients helped to deflect the influence of the cooperatives that provided these farmers with rebates rather than finance.[60] Increased rural branching took business away from local agents and wool dealers to whom they paid wool-forwarding commissions. The new policy was also targeted against the banks who had fewer additional services to offer and would incur greater lending risks with smaller, less well-known clients. As Elders noted in 1915: 'the cutting up of stations has virtually brought their [banks'] influence to an unimportant point'.[61]

The geographical extension of the agent industry can be demonstrated in various ways. The Australian States that held major wool auctions expanded from Victoria, New South Wales, and South Australia in the 1870s to include Queensland by the 1890s, and Tasmania and Western Australia in the following decade. New Zealand wool was being sold in the seven provinces of Auckland, Hawke's Bay, East Coast, Wellington, Canterbury, Otago, and Southland by 1906. The early spread of pastoral agent services across the major States and provinces, however, antedated the growth of local wool auctions since most wool was consigned to London for sale in the later nineteenth century. Thus, in 1888 Dalgety was assessing whether to have a branch in Western Australia 'where our interests are now so considerable'.[62] By 1900 the company had at least four branches in the State, eight years before Western Australia became a wool-selling centre.[63]

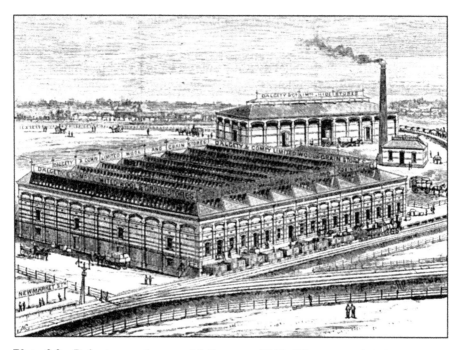

Plate 2.8   Dalgety, warehouses, Melbourne, 1889. The pastoral industry drew heavily on different transport services for the movement of produce, materials and equipment. Company stores were therefore located at the apex of transport facilities, at port cities and contiguous to road and rail networks, in order to minimise trans-shipment costs. (*Melbourne Stock and Station Journal*, 4 January 1889.)

Under the astute leadership of E. T. Doxat, Dalgety was one of the prime movers in national expansion (see Table 2.6).[64] The firm sold wool in two Australian States in 1892 but by 1909 was in all five mainland wool States. Goldsbrough Mort's expansion occurred later in the mid-1920s. A notable feature of Elders' experience has been its belated geographical expansion. Until 1918 it sold only in South Australia at which time it moved into Western Australia but did not sell in a third State, Victoria, until 1938. NZLMA, confirming its relative slippage, sold in three States as early as 1892 but never improved on this. AMLF and Winchcombe Carson made only modest geographical expansion, the former remaining equivocal about expansion into Western Australia and Queensland on a number of occasions.[65] None of the major companies organised auctions in or branched into Tasmania for very long, which constituted only a few per cent of national output, relying instead on connections with local agents. Dalgety had a branch there between 1869 and 1875 and periodically considered returning, but as late as 1960 concluded there was little to gain in terms of market share or cost economies from acquiring the main local agent.[66] Agent operations in the Northern Territory have mostly occurred in recent postwar decades. When Dalgety–NZLMA were developing plans for the Territory in 1962 they were conscious that primary producers were unaccustomed to dealing with agents and 'some time must elapse before they are fully appreciative of the advantages to be gained'.[67]

Dalgety also proved to be the most expansive company in New Zealand, selling in five provinces in 1906 but in nine by 1917. NZLMA was the early leader with auctions in seven provinces by 1906 but expanded only marginally thereafter. Wright Stephenson's success story is reflected in its expansion from two to five provinces, NMA remained largely stable, and Murray Roberts contracted somewhat. Membership of regional stock and station agent associations and woolbrokers associations gives an alternative measure of geographical spread. Sensitive to its own progress relative to the other firms and the extent of their representation in regional and

Table 2.6 Regional spread of Australian woolbrokers

Year	Dalgety	GM	ES	NZLMA	AMLF	WC	F & G	DNZL	Elders
1892	2	2	1	3					
1900	3	2	1	2					
1910	5	2	1	3	2	1			
1920	5	2	2	3	3	2			
1930	5	5	2	3	3	2	2		
1940	5	5	3	3	3	2	2		
1950	5	5	3	3	3	2	2		
1960	5	5	5	3	3	2	2		
1970					3	2	2	5	5
1980					2		2	3	5

Notes: Number of colonies/States in which company sold wool.
Source: DAWR.

national industry bodies, NZLMA kept a record of the membership of these associations. Thus, by 1956 Dalgety was most widely represented throughout New Zealand in twenty-two associations, followed by NZLMA with twenty, Wright Stephenson with fourteen, NMA with ten, Murray Roberts with nine, and Pyne Gould Guinness with six.

One of the key geographical developments in New Zealand was the expansion northwards of the leading agents, particularly Murray Roberts, Wright Stephenson, and NMA, who all began in Dunedin. Wright Stephenson and NMA initially expanded their branch networks within Otago, then moved up through the south island before establishing a presence in the north island at Wellington, Auckland, and Hawke's Bay by 1914. The head offices of these agents also shifted northwards from Dunedin to Wellington or Auckland, reflecting the changing geographical balance of economic activity and farming output. In 1919 Wright Stephenson decided on Wellington as 'a more convenient place to centre our accounts than Dunedin'.[68] When NMA finally moved north in 1970 it noted the closer proximity to financial, commercial, and government contacts in Wellington.[69] In addition, Auckland and Wellington were more centrally located and their harbours could more easily handle large ocean-going steamships. By contrast, Williams & Kettle and Pyne Gould Guinness moved little beyond their original regions of Hawke's Bay and Canterbury respectively, although they branched intensively in those areas (see Table 2.7).

The more intensive growth of agent firms is reflected in their rural branching. Before 1900 they confined their representation to the major regional centres. Even market leader, Dalgety, restricted representation to Sydney, Newcastle, Perth, Rockhampton, Brisbane, Townsville, and Adelaide in 1897. Thereafter, total numbers of branches in Australia rose rapidly from under 100 to over 1000 in the first half of the twentieth century and a rising share was accounted for by the leading five firms. This is also reflected in the growing number of locations of agent branches around Australia, rising from twenty-seven to 106 during 1907–43

Table 2.7 Regional spread of New Zealand woolbrokers

Year	Dalgety	NZLMA	WS	NMA	MR	PGG	Levin	DNZL	WNMA
1906	5	7	2	3	2	1	1		
1910	7	7	2	3	2	1	1		
1920	9	9	4	3	3	1	3		
1930	8	8	3	3	3	1	1		
1940	9	9	4	3	3	1	3		
1950	6	6	4	3	2	1	1		
1962			7	3	2	1	1	7	
1970			7	7		1		7	
1980						1		4	5

Notes: Number of provinces in which company sold wool.
Source: DAWR.

(Table 2.4). Their location also became more widely distributed among the States.[70]

While the secular expansion of clientele and geography over the course of the first half of the twentieth century is evident, during the sustained economic downturn of the interwar period firms sought to cut their costs by reducing fixed investments, which included halting the expansion of branches and closing some down. The estimated number of branches in Australia shows a fall from 258 to 242 between 1923 and 1943. The same policies were adopted in New Zealand where the number of wool-selling centres had been thirteen in 1920 but by 1931 had reduced to eight by merging small local centres.

After World War Two the boom conditions in the industry encouraged firms to extend their reach much further. Most firms maintained the same number of wool-selling centres, except the expansive Elders and Wright Stephenson. The expansion is more noticeable in numbers of branches and their locations. Total locations of branches for all agents grew in Australia between 1943 and 1963 from 106 to 413, while total branches rose from 242 to 1422 (see Table 2.4). Elders also developed an extensive branch network in Queensland and New South Wales in the 1950s.[71] Similar to their belated entry into wool auctioning, AMLF was slow to develop a national network of branches, operating from only a handful of offices as late as 1945 but then expanding rapidly through the eastern States to forty branches and sub-branches by 1952 and seventy-two by 1962.[72]

INTERNATIONAL ACTIVITIES

The leading agents developed some multinational interests but these were quite limited beyond Australasia. The companies that originated in London, such as AMLF, NMA, and NZLMA, conducted most of their business outside Britain, although each had a London office that was involved in chartering and trading activities. The subsequent formation of London offices by Australasian companies, such as Elders in 1891 and Wright Stephenson in 1906, suggests significant benefits accrued. While these functions might have been conducted by an overseas agent, Dalgety, which also had a London office from a very early stage (1854), drew attention to the trust and incentive benefits derived from internalising activities in both countries within the firm. In a classic statement, Dalgety noted it would:

> enable them to take up business avoided by houses purely English or colonial, for the reason of one not obtaining a direct profit from it ... and ... the means of avoiding business which might produce a commission to one and a loss to the other – besides the confidence inspired in men well known to each other and banded together for a common interest must naturally lead to a more successful issue than where they are exposed to contending interests, as is the case between correspondents at so great a distance acting as mere agents.[73]

The option of internalisation was only available to the larger agent companies whose volume of activity was sufficient to justify the additional fixed capital investment.[74]

Dalgety and NZLMA also operated in both Australia and New Zealand. Their activities were much more common than complementary although the differences in climate provided some opportunity for risk spreading. NZLMA's 1903 earnings in New Zealand, for example, helped offset its shortfalls from the drought in Australia.[75] New Zealand agents, Wright Stephenson, were also based in Australia from 1938 but rather than marketing farm produce concentrated on areas less well covered there, especially seed dressing and bloodstock sales.[76] AMLF's initial establishment of an office in New Zealand at Dunedin, however, lasted only five years.[77] Elders moved across the Tasman in 1984 with its acquisition of Allied Farmers Cooperative.

Dalgety, NZLMA, and AMLF experimented with operations in East Africa and South America, the similarity of development in primary industries suggesting the opportunity to employ their skills, resources, and expertise. Most of these experiments proved unfruitful. AMLF established an office in Argentina in 1913 but within a few years had incurred significant losses due to unstable financial conditions, poor port facilities, infrequent shipping movements, and government interference in the form of price maintenance schemes.[78] Dalgety and NZLMA were planning similar investments when World War One intervened.[79] Instead, Dalgety (Kenya and Tanganyika) and NZLMA (South Africa) bought out former agents in the 1920s but by the following decade were also suffering losses.[80] The relatively minor importance of operations beyond Australasia can be gleaned from Dalgety's woolbroking profits in 1952 which were apportioned 64 per cent to Australia, 22 per cent to New Zealand, 8 per cent to East Africa, and 6 per cent to London.

Different climatic conditions, infrastructural problems, and the need for diversification into unfamiliar commodities such as coffee and sisal crops may have accounted for a lack of foreign success. In addition, as discussed in chapter 6, private sales and wool dealing by intermediaries were more common overseas and at odds with the local strategies of centralised broking.[81] Australasian pastoral output continued to grow rapidly and therefore maintaining this geographic and product specialisation appeared sensible. Indeed, foreign investment was most common when the local market was performing poorly, especially in the interwar years, suggesting it was a crisis management option rather than a long-term strategy.

MERGERS AND ACQUISITIONS

In developing into national organisations the pastoral agent companies could choose between a variety of paths: internal growth, or acquisition of, or contractual arrangements with, smaller local firms. There was no dominant choice of mode at first although over time internal growth or acquisition gradually replaced interfirm contracting.

In the case of interfirm contracting, a large national firm came to an agreement with a local agent who would represent its interests in the area. The local agent influenced growers to sell their wool at the larger company's auctions, supplied information about the creditworthiness of local farmers, and conducted other business on its behalf, such as sales of livestock, farm materials, and equipment. This mode of expansion brought a number of benefits. The larger firm could extend its reach without much additional investment and benefited from the established local knowledge and image of the smaller firm, while the latter could improve its local competitiveness by access to the superior resources of the larger agent.

However, these relationships broke down periodically. The cause might be a disagreement or a change in strategy by either firm, the larger seeking to establish its own branch in the area or the smaller preferring to be independent or taking up the offer of another firm. As the leading firms expanded, many of their costs were overheads connected to a national and regional structure, and in such cases they judged that the cost of establishing a branch was more than offset by not paying rebates and commissions to the smaller firm. The process was cumulative, as firms expanded the marginal cost of another branch fell, particularly in terms of experience in assessing its viability, stocking it, and possessing a pool of staff from within the firm. Extension of the dominant firm also enabled it to exert greater control over the branch manager and his workforce and ensure that local policies and practices were consistent with those of the company as a whole.[82] Finally, increasing the profile of the leading firms was becoming more important as they competed locally across a wide range of services. AMLF was aware that agency representation limited its exposure in Queensland before World War Two:

> the first thing you notice when you come into a town is their big sign-boards . . . they all had plenty of advertisements . . . in all my long trip I did not see one sign of the AML & F Co . . . He [AMLF agent] had no sign up . . . and his office is poked away in the corner of this town.[83]

The larger company sometimes addressed these problems by taking an equity share in the other firm and subsequently expanding it to full ownership if greater control over policy was needed. Thus, two-stage acquisitions were quite common, especially in New Zealand where the leading firms were smaller than their Australian counterparts and the capital market developed later.

Sometimes the dominant firm was under pressure to acquire the local agent, particularly where a succession crisis in a small family firm or a downturn in the pastoral sector made it difficult for it to continue in business. Goldsbrough Mort acquired Stuckey's in 1938 because the owner's son was not considered suitable for the stock and station agent business.[84] The larger agent would therefore have to buy the business or risk losing that friendly connection to another national firm. During the interwar downturn, in particular, the large agents often received offers from smaller firms which were in desperate straits and were seeking to sell their business.[85]

Mergers and acquisitions also occurred amongst firms which had not previously cooperated with each other and where the smaller firm was not necessarily known to the bigger one. The motives for such mergers included functional and geographic expansion and the acquisition of valuable goodwill. Some of the larger firms became highly skilled in selecting takeover targets. Dalgety kept a document outlining some of the key considerations when assessing a takeover target, the considerations included an indication of how to measure net asset value per share. Elders had its own merger team whose job it was to arrange and effect acquisitions, and it even developed a verb, 'Elderise', to describe its action.[86] In some cases, firms were assisted by a third party who would contact them indicating the opportunity for a friendly, or even hostile, takeover and providing information about the smaller firm in the hope of receiving a commission. H. E. Hallett, owner of a lime crushing works at Devonport, approached Dalgety in 1960 about acquiring the leading Tasmanian woolbroker, A. G. Webster. Had the acquisition proceeded Hallett wished to receive 1 per cent commission.[87]

The Australian firms, Elders and Goldsbrough Mort, were both acquisitive. In the 1920s Goldsbrough Mort increased its share of wool sold from 5 to 11 per cent, its relative standing from seventh to second, and its sale locations from two to five States by a series of important company acquisitions. The most significant of these were Harrison Jones & Devlin (1922), based in New South Wales, which had been one of the leading agent firms before World War One, and Bagot Shakes & Lewis (1924), one of the principal South Australian firms. The 1937 acquisition of Pearson Rowe introduced Goldsbrough Mort to stock selling in Victoria.[88] After 1945 Goldsbrough Mort concentrated more on acquisitions in Queensland.

Elders began its geographical acquisitiveness somewhat later, moving into western Victoria by acquiring Hague's of Geelong in 1937. After World War Two it acquired a number of important firms, particularly Commonwealth Wool and Produce (1955) and Moreheads (1956), which facilitated the firm's expansion into New South Wales and Queensland and enabled it to raise its share of wool sales from 8 to 16 per cent between 1945 and 1960 and its position from third to first. The acquisition of local firms also helped Elders to expand through Western Australia in the postwar period against strong competition.

New Zealand firms were involved in merger activity for similar reasons. When Wright Stephenson acquired Abraham and Williams in 1922 it enabled the company to increase its share of national wool sales from 5 to 8 per cent. Most of its subsequent growth, however, was by internal expansion not acquisition.[89] In the postwar period NMA have used the acquisition tool to improve its market share and representation on the north island, acquiring well-established regional firms such as Alfred Buckland of Auckland in 1957 and Levins of Wellington in 1964.

Acquisition in preference to internal growth enabled more rapid expansion by acquiring an existing business, including its staff and premises, rather than taking the time to develop new outlets. The firm could expand into new areas or rationalise its existing resources if the acquired firm had been a competitor. The acquisition of an existing pool of clients was reflected in the relatively high value placed on goodwill. Looking at two acquisitions by Elders, goodwill accounted for £78 000 of £165 000 (47 per cent) of the purchase price of De Garis and £76 000 of £127 000 (60 per cent) for Hague.[90]

Given its valuable but somewhat intangible nature, however, disputes over goodwill were one of the main reasons for breakdowns in merger negotiations. Goldsbrough Mort, for example, would have acquired De Garis ten years earlier in 1937 but for a failure in negotiations over the valuation of goodwill.[91] Sustaining that initial advantage from the acquired goodwill whilst also integrating the new firm into the existing company organisation was a major challenge. When NMA purchased J. G. Ward in 1960 it decided to run Ward as a separate subsidiary for the first few years to minimise client loss, although in the longer term it believed full integration would yield the benefits of control, drive, and central direction.[92] Another solution was to employ the former owners in order to maintain the local personal connection and ensure they did not set up a rival firm. However, when Goldsbrough Mort hired two managers from Henry Wills, acquired in 1926, they found them, 'a positive menace . . . deplorable lack of accuracy in submitting financial statements'.[93] The other obstacle to the De Garis and several other takeover bids was the value placed on indebted accounts. This was a large portion of the assets of most agents and its real value was clouded in uncertainty for anyone outside the firm. While the acquiring firm found it difficult to maintain the goodwill value, it was easier to enhance the worth of debtor accounts through the more effective financial management of the leading corporations, a point readily acknowledged by Goldsbrough Mort during their acquisition of Pearson Rowe.[94]

Although it assessed takeover targets and acquired several smaller agencies, Dalgety generally opted for internal growth in both countries. This reflected its larger resources, earlier pioneering advance into new areas, and preference for a closely controlled strategy. The firm was also critical of its Australian competitors for expansionist policies undertaken in prosperous times that might prove less sound following a downturn in the industry. However, this may have been more a case of wishful thinking as Dalgety's leadership was being gradually eroded by these firms, especially Elders.

The interwar challenge from the leading cooperatives was based on both internal growth and acquisition. The Farmers' and Graziers' Cooperative acquired John Bridge & Company in 1919, Weaver & Perry in 1923, and by the mid-1920s was one of the largest wool and stockbrokers in New

South Wales. Similar strategies were pursued by the Queensland Primary Producers' Cooperative Association to acquire woolbroking and stock selling activities. Cooperatives also extended their reach by mergers with other cooperatives.[95] Finally, some cooperatives grew by internal branching. The Westralian Farmers' Cooperative established seventy branches in its first four years and organised a Federal wholesale cooperative in 1918 with branches in Victoria, New South Wales, Western Australia, Queensland, and South Australia.[96] In 1944 Elders was particularly concerned about Westralian Farmers whom it viewed as a 'serious obstacle' to its postwar expansion plans in Western Australia; unlike most cooperatives Westralian Farmers was well-resourced and efficiently run by motivated managers.[97] Elders' assessment proved correct, the renamed Wesfarmers acquired Dalgety in 1993 and was its major rival in the 1990s.

PRODUCT AND MARKET DIVERSIFICATION

The large national firms that grew up in the first half of the twentieth century, therefore, targeted the 'man on the land' with a full range of farming services. However, as the relative importance of the farming sector declined with the maturing of manufacturing, especially in Australia, and the challenges from substitute fibres and products emerged, agents began to consider new products and markets. The interwar cost-price squeeze and the postwar increase in government intervention also suggested the need for changes in strategy. The desire for a broader strategy in line with macro-economic change was expressed by Dalgety's Australian General Manager in 1958 in hoping that, in future, 'the investor wishing to participate in the growth of Australia and New Zealand would automatically turn to Dalgety's shares'.[98]

Already during the interwar years some firms recognised the secular as well as cyclical changes taking place. Moves to diversify into related products therefore reflected concern at the short-term downturn and the longer-term prospects for farming. More positively, they saw opportunities for economies of scope in marketing due to their ready-made farmer clientele and the use of the branch network. Agents had often supplied specific items of merchandise before 1914, especially where farmers were distant from retail stores or the agent could buy in bulk. In the interwar period, though, a broad and regular range of merchandise sales to farmers became an important and self-conscious part of company activities. Merchandise sales helped to cover branch overhead costs and reduced the seasonal and cyclical fluctuations.[99] Another successful area of diversification was into travel agency which built on their existing links with shipping companies and their experience in handling the travel arrangements for their own personnel and farming clients moving between Australian, New Zealand and London offices. Elders also held local agencies for Imperial Airways and Australian Airways.[100]

A more controversial form of product diversification was into the motor trade. Scope economies from farming demand for tractors and cars, and the firm's experience and investments in operating its own fleet, complemented by the absence of powerful local automobile firms, suggested this was a promising choice for diversification. By the late 1920s Wright Stephenson had secured the New Zealand franchise for General Motors and an agency for Renault, and had its own workshops, showrooms and garages. Agents' close knowledge of the trading and financial standing of their farmer clients meant they were also in a position to provide finance for motor vehicles and other consumer durable purchases. However, diversifying into a luxury, capital intensive, and complex product such as motor vehicles was a risky strategy, as Dalgety found when it belatedly received imports of American vehicles at the onset of the 1921 slump. The motor department incurred large losses and was closed down a few years later leaving the Melbourne manager to bemoan that 'there is too much underhand . . . trickery . . . with the motor trade for firms of high repute to touch without considerable risk'.[101] The real problem was Dalgety's ignorance of the industry. Goldsbrough Mort was more circumspect believing that diversification into a new and unfamiliar industry was too risky during an economic downturn.[102]

The movement towards diversification can be measured through figures on company earnings and profits. In 1919 Dalgety regarded merchandise as one of the key future areas for the company. In that year it accounted for 8 per cent of Victorian earnings, rising to 14 per cent in 1929 and 17 per cent by 1956. By contrast, Dalgety's early abortive move into motor vehicles yielded 16 per cent in 1919 but had been abandoned by 1929.[103] By 1929 Goldsbrough Mort conducted merchandise activities across its national organisation and its share of earnings had also reached 17 per cent by 1958.[104] In New Zealand, NZLMA moved into merchandise activities more extensively: by 1935 it accounted for 35 per cent of earnings, rising to 44 per cent by 1946 and in the process surpassing wool and livestock.[105]

The return to farming prosperity wrought by World War Two and the good harvests of the early postwar years delayed further diversification as pastoral services continued to dominate corporate profits.[106] However, by the late 1950s the resumed decline of the farming sector, adverse movements in the terms of trade, and greater government intervention in traditional agency functions called for more radical solutions. The firms began to broaden their product range and markets much more extensively into areas in which they had no existing knowledge nor did they have a strong client base. Thus, firms moved into a wide range of manufacturing and services including engineering, property, construction, home appliances, wineries, brewing, hardware, sheet metal, and international trading.[107] This bolder approach was enunciated in discussions at a conference of Dalgety managers in 1961 where it was noted that: 'the best diversification is not always something aligned with what you are already doing'.[108] This postwar strategy was consistent with the advance of conglomeration overseas, especially in the United States.[109] Significantly, senior managers of agent companies travelled overseas to the United States and Britain to discuss diversification with company executives.[110]

However, some Dalgety managers were more circumspect, noting that related diversification was preferable and that in the past the company had performed poorly in areas beyond its pastoral expertise.[111] This bifurcation of views was reflected in the fact that while Dalgety became highly diversified, to include in its activities property, construction, mining, and wineries, it also developed activities which made use of its core pastoral expertise, including meat and dairy products, refrigeration, animal breeding, seed production, and farm ownership and management. Likewise, Elders combined its broadening diversification with pastoral vertical integration through the scouring and purchase of wool.[112] Thus, both dominant firms began to move away from their special role of serving farmers as intermediaries.

A further break with the past was to sell their broader range of consumer products beyond farming communities. This required changes in the nature of their trading business. As long as they continued to supply the needs of their long-standing farmer clients most merchandise business could be conducted on a commission basis with the agent importing and distributing according to orders. Once the range of customers broadened the firms could not rely solely on orders and had to trade on their own account.[113] In addition, rather than act as importers, distributors, and wholesalers, agents began to acquire local manufacturers as a defensive move against manufacturers integrating forwards into wholesaling and distribution, and expanding retail stores like Myer buying directly from manufacturers.[114]

By the 1960s, therefore, the companies had moved far beyond their original activities. They had chosen to diversify by function (trading and processing rather than commission), by market (beyond their farmer clientele), and by product (from the simple consumables and hardware items of the prewar period to complex sealed technology). This created enormous organisational challenges for the companies (see chapter 8).

RATIONALISATION, AMALGAMATION, AND REBIRTH

Dalgety's equivocation regarding diversification reflected a deeper uncertainty in the industry about its future direction. By the 1960s the leading firms recognised that competition in the pastoral agent industry had become severe, that the farmer was being 'over-serviced', and overall, that they were trying to do too many things. A senior London officer of Dalgety's expressed the point succinctly in a report of his visit to Australia and New Zealand in 1961: 'It is abundantly clear, as previous visitors to Australia and New Zealand have noted, the stock and station agents . . . are in such strong competition with one another that clients are being seriously (and expensively) over-serviced'.[115]

More than half a century of geographic, corporate, market, and product expansion had gone too far. As a result the agents' costs were too high and their expertise overextended. Reducing the cost of their core pastoral services to facilitate diversification, however, proved difficult. While firms had embraced postwar phases of technological change, automation provided only limited opportunities for cost cutting in an industry based around individual service and know-how.[116] The synergies of financial, wool, and livestock services made it difficult to cut back anywhere without risking a significant loss of income. Environmental factors worsened their problems, notably rising corporate taxes and a high domestic cost structure resulting from protection and centralised wage fixing.

Thus, earnings rates were falling and rationalisation of the industry became imperative.[117] Whilst in the interwar cyclical crisis firms had co-operated with each other and bought out many of the smaller and medium-sized enterprises, the longer term structural problems facing the industry required more drastic action. Therefore, the big four firms in Australia, Elders and Goldsbrough Mort, and Dalgety and NZLMA, merged to create two dominant firms in 1962–63. Dalgety and NZLMA sought to reduce costs and capital outlays.[118] They viewed similarities in their strategies and structures as important in choosing each other: both were British-registered overseas trading corporations, each was represented in the same localities but neither owned stations nor produced wool, sheep, or cattle.[119] Similar factors motivated the merger of Elders and Goldsbrough Mort, particularly the reduction in the number of branches and the costs of central administration. By 1963 Elders had 221 branches in Australia and Goldsbrough Mort 192, of these 121 shared identical locations.[120]

The two-firm share of wool brokerage which had been a fairly constant 25 to 30 per cent for seventy years jumped overnight to around 50 per cent and halted the relative decline of the leading agents in the top one hundred Australian firms. It also kept concentration levels in the industry higher than the average for manufacturing.[121] In the case of Dalgety–NZLMA, however, this reversal of fortunes was temporary, their share of woolbroking collapsing from 20–22 to 11–13 per cent by the late 1970s while Elders rose from 26–28 to 29–31 per cent. In many respects this post-merger trend reflected the progress of the constituent firms prior to 1962. NZLMA had been in long-term decline, Dalgety had abandoned its pioneering leadership over the previous few decades, while Elders and Goldsbrough Mort continued their postwar expansion acquiring Victorian agent Younghusband in 1971.[122] AMLF, the fifth firm, dropped sharply in relative national standing from twenty-seventh to seventy-third in 1952–64. It merged with two of the leading and oldest Victorian agents, Dennys Lascelles and Strachan, in 1978 but its market share continued to diminish falling below 4 per cent by the end of the 1970s and was itself acquired by Elders in 1982. Dalgety boosted its standing by acquiring several major competitors, including Farmers Grazcos and Bennett Farmers, both in 1983. As a result, by 1983 Elders (51 per cent) and Dalgety–NZLMA (31 per cent) brokered over four-fifths of wool sold in Australia.[123]

In New Zealand the simultaneous merger of Dalgety and NZLMA was also part of a broad cost-cutting rationalisation among the major firms of the industry, with NMA acquiring Murray Roberts and Stronach Morris in 1963 and Levin the following year. Wright Stephenson was also highly acquisitive, achieving eleven major takeovers in the 1960s before merging with NMA in 1972 to form Challenge Corporation (renamed in 1975). The final trigger for the merger was discussions between agents and farmers in 1970–71 at which the farmers rejected a proposed increase in agent charges and asked them to investigate ways of reducing costs.[124] As a result, the two-firm market share leapt to 61 per cent in 1973.

Merger activity involving pastoral agent firms had become increasingly tied up with the conglomeration movement in the 1970s and 1980s. Many firms were either absorbed into conglomerate empires or took evasive action. Australian Estates was taken over by Colonial Sugar Refining in 1975 reflecting their common interests in sugar but in 1981 its pastoral agency business was purchased by AMLF. Ron Brierley's Industrial Equity Limited acquired Pitt, Son & Badgery in 1971 but sold it to Elders five years later while his attempt to buy Dennys Lascelles drove it into the 1978 merger with AMLF. The following year Winchcombe Carson sold its pastoral activities to Dalgety in defence against Brierley. In 1981 Elders became part of a major conglomerate, Elders IXL, when it merged with Henry Jones IXL, its Chief Executive, John Elliott, announcing that pastoralism would be 'our key business', and set about acquiring most of the remaining companies.[125] However, by 1984 this conglomerate had five main divisions of pastoralism, international trading, finance, resources, and brewing.[126] The establishment of the Fletcher Challenge conglomerate in 1981 resulted from the merger of Challenge with Fletcher Holdings; the new company's main activities besides pastoral agency were motor trading, merchanting, engineering, machinery, finance, fish processing, and property.[127] In 1983 Dalgety was acquired by Crown which in turn was absorbed into Fletcher Challenge in 1986. Thus, by the mid-1980s the leading figures of the stock and station agent industry had become largely subsumed in giant conglomerate enterprises. However, contestability has, none the less, been maintained by local stock and station agents merging with one another, drawing on their close client contacts, and the preference of some farmers for private or local selling.[128]

In the 1990s the industry re-established some of its identity with the reversion from broad conglomeration and government involvement, and began to evolve in multiple directions. In 1993 Wrightson was floated off by Fletcher Challenge, and Elders by Foster's. Wrightson extended its primary industry services to include horticulture and forestry. Elders, supported by its new parent Futuris, ran counter to the industry's modern history by extensive backward vertical integration into farm production and forwards into processing. Dalgety, under the influence of its Wesfarmers owners, followed the long-term path of pastoral service while giving particular attention to new marketing methods. The contrasting perceptions of the industry's future were starkly illustrated in 1995 in a fundamental exchange of views. Dalgety noted: 'we have never been in the game of being in competition with our customers. We are not farmers, we are service providers. We don't have the skills to manage properties and we want to remain focussed'. Elders retorted: 'to stand still as a five per cent stock and station agent industry, we are going nowhere. It's a sunset industry'.[129] It remains to be seen which of these strategies proves to be the more successful.

CONCLUSION

This chapter has provided the background and dynamics from which to launch into more detailed discussions of key issues in the industry's development and the nature of its contribution to the expansion of rural Australasia. It has sketched the emergence of pastoral specialists, the diversification of their services within the industry, corporate expansion, extended geographic reach, and finally product diversification across sectors, culminating in an industry largely dominated by a few large, diverse conglomerates. In each case, prime-mover advantages appear to have been gained by large powerful enterprises. In the first half of the twentieth century, Dalgety achieved leadership from its innovative service diversification and geographic growth while the postwar expansionism of Elders, Goldsbrough Mort, and Wright Stephenson, regarded as risky by Dalgety, led them to catch up with, and in some cases surpass, Dalgety. In chapter 3 the focus is on the cohesive role of agents in forming a network of close relations between the key players in the pastoral industry. The following four chapters then look at the major services provided by the agents: finance, marketing, and business advice and advocacy. This is followed by an analysis of the changing organisational structure of the agent companies in the light of their shifting strategies. An assessment of the nature of interfirm relations within the industry then follows. The conclusion seeks to summarise the extent and effectiveness of the role played by the agents in the economic development of rural Australia and New Zealand.

CHAPTER THREE

The Farming Community Network

Networks are an alternative mode of conducting business to that of market transactions or operating within the hierarchy of a large corporation. Some writers have viewed them as a hybrid form of organisation that is unstable and ephemeral.[1] Recently, however, researchers have begun to investigate networks more closely and seen in them more enduring and beneficial features.[2] Literature reviews of networks indicate that no clear patterns of development exist and that there is a need for more historical studies.[3]

Networks were a key feature of the Australasian pastoral industry where streams of trade, information, and financial services were provided to farmers by pastoral agents, banks, shipping companies, agricultural equipment manufacturers, and other groups. In most cases the stock and station agent was the focal point in a network which brought the farmer into contact with this wide range of service providers. Agent firms recognised very early that regular transactions with network members generated trust, reputational effects, and mutual information exchange that were vital for the successful provision of pastoral services. This chapter examines the nature and structure of farming networks, how they changed over time, and their significance for agent and farmer.

NETWORK FORMS OF ORGANISATION

A network is a cooperative group, a cluster, or web of individuals or firms organised into a tight or loose federation. Each party is dependent on the other for resources, and cooperation brings gains for both parties.[4] Networks describe relational contracts that emphasise bonds of trust, reciprocity, and obligation. Network members are drawn together by common and complementary interests (such as the same information, labour, capital, materials, distribution, marketing) and propinquity, which may include bonds of trade, finance, geography, religion, culture, politics, or kinship. Alvesson & Lindkvist usefully distinguish three network types.[5] 'Economic cooperative' networks focus on economic relations and are a means of providing greater economic returns to participants. 'Social integrative' networks influence group behaviour, integrity, and satisfy a need to belong; thus they operate on a socioemotional basis. 'Blood kinship' networks are based on the strength of family ties and represent the polar opposite to economic spot exchange.

Bonds of trust, the establishment of reputation, and the evolution of 'traditions' to govern behaviour are necessary aspects of network relations.[6] In an atmosphere of trust, information is exchanged freely, providing network partners with a 'thicker', more complete, amount of information than that obtained in a market, and which is 'freer' than that obtained through a hierarchy where members may protect themselves from opportunism. Reputation commits members to the network relation in that their track record ultimately determines the success of ongoing economic exchange. Emphasis on the long-term nature of contractual relations means that members are less likely to gain from opportunistic behaviour that severely inhibits future exchange. The sanctions of breaking a tradition are more severe than breaking a bureaucratic rule or a market contract, as the direct utility cost to the recalcitrant in the form of private or public admonishment pervades all aspects of social and economic existence.

The network form of organisation provides particular advantages to firms that foster intangible assets such as knowledge or human capital. It permits the sharing of diffused and uncodified information, and provides an environment conducive to feedback processes important in technological change. In these types of firms networks may allow a reduction in transaction costs without incurring higher administrative or bureaucratic costs. Scale and scope economies may also be achieved by smaller firms. Networks may also be adopted to reduce uncertainty, to provide fast access to reliable information permitting firms to respond to changing economic circumstances, and to accommodate a variety of entrepreneurial visions or product niches.[7]

The above survey helps to understand what general circumstances give rise to networks and an indication of some of their principal benefits. Work by Casson is suggestive of how networks develop and change over time, an approach that is valuable to historically based studies. Networks may cover a range of different forms of economic activity including production, trade, finance, and research. Casson shows how a network based on trade can evolve into a more widely embracing trade and financial network, as technology-driven expansions in scale cause individually financed small production units to be supplanted by joint financing of a single large unit; the independent financiers are thus brought together. His second insight is that as networks grow and become more complex intermediation by a well-placed and highly competent member can reduce communication costs and engineer higher levels of trust. The leader is presented as personal and consultative because of the wide dispersion of types of expertise and the need for coordination.[8]

NETWORKS IN THE AUSTRALASIAN PASTORAL INDUSTRY: SOME STYLISED MODELS

As described in chapter 1, the Australasian farmer suffered from domestic and international isolation which made him remote from the markets he sought to supply and from the sources of finance and raw materials he required. Not only would the individual small farmer be unable to supply these services himself but establishing contact with and coordinating specialist shipowners, suppliers, and financiers would be a difficult task, requiring many transactions and filled with uncertainties. Similarly, since neither buyers nor sellers of services can have a buffer of inventory stocks, a regularised and flexible transacting environment was vital.[9] In an industry characterised by rapid technical and commercial change, remote farmers would find difficulties keeping abreast of the latest developments and knowing whether suppliers were receiving honest and objective information. Equally, it was difficult for farmers to prove their creditworthiness to service providers such as lenders. Each side of this industry interface, therefore, encountered uncertainty through ignorance of individual or community-wide conditions on the other side.

Remoteness also took on an intangible form; farmers, many of whom were new to the industry and all of whom lacked experience of Australasian conditions, faced an industry going through rapid growth and development. They required not only access to pastoral services but an understanding of how they should best be applied to their own unique circumstances in terms of such factors as the farm size, its location, geology, technology, and product mix. Acquiring this expertise or tacit knowledge is one of the most difficult but important criteria for establishing a competitive advantage, and yet it is rarely captured through a simple market transaction since it is effectively a zero-priced good. The variety of individual circumstances and their change over time in this rapidly moving industry also required a transactional flexibility rarely embodied in a single organisation.

At the core of the intra-industry structure, therefore, stood a specialist intermediary, the agent, who was well known and connected to all groups. He served as a conduit for the flow of financial, commercial, and technical services that connected farmers to other stages of the production process. The regularisation and reciprocity of intra-industry relations, by promoting trust and emphasising reputation, distinguished these transactions as being of the network kind and allowed for the full mutual benefits to be derived including fewer transactions, less opportunism, and a broad exchange of information and expertise. Agents, as we shall see, sought to make long-term commitments to individuals and the industry as the best way of maximising the returns for themselves and the sector. The network structure, by fostering loyalty among groups in the industry, enabled each to plan ahead. This was especially important for agents with growing volumes of fixed capital assets.

Figure 3.1 demonstrates the agent's role as mediating network leader in the principal information, finance, and trade flows. Agents intermediated

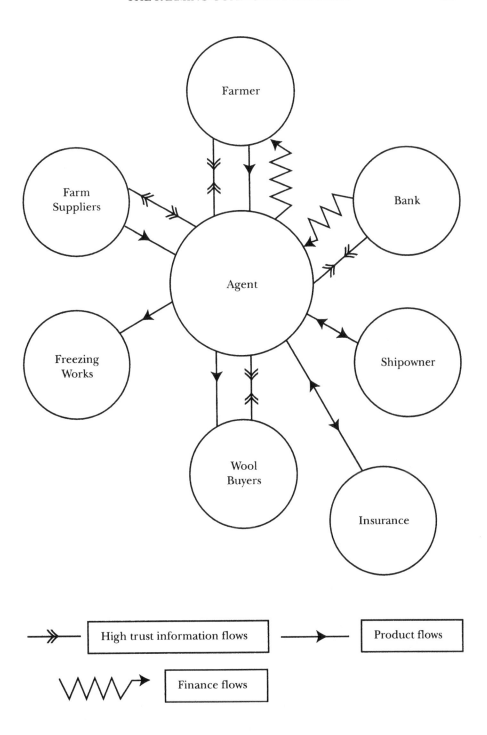

Figure 3.1 Service flows in agent-led pastoral network

trade flows from farmers to shipowners, insurers, wool buyers, and freezing companies. In the reverse direction they intermediated trade flows from agricultural suppliers to farmers and finance flows from banks to farmers. Information flows were intermediated in either or both directions particularly between farmers, on the one hand, and wool buyers and agricultural suppliers on the other.[10]

While the nature of the transactions may have been conducive to the development of networks, they can only come about where bonds between the different groups promote cooperative behaviour. The following sections show aspects of all three of Alvesson & Lindkvist's bonding instruments – economic, social and kinship – existed to differing degrees over time. Indeed, it appears from this study that one of the merits of the network is its flexibility to change in nature with evolving conditions while still fulfilling the basic cooperative ideal.

The dynamic nature of the development of pastoral networks can be seen from the four transactional maps (Figures 3.2, 3.3, 3.5, 3.6) showing their evolution from about 1860 to the eve of World War Two. The pastoral industry is represented as a whole as a network, with each functional group (farmer, agent, banker, and so forth) as a node with networking style activity occurring between nodes. Edges connecting nodes have been categorised according to their relations – economic cooperative (■), social integrative (●), or kinship (*). An edge may indicate more than one style of relationship. The simple network of 1860 centred around a single intermediary and evolved from a small cohesive settler society. This changed over time to a more complex diagram embodying different intermediaries (agents, cooperatives, government bodies) who learned how to foster network relationships, and the emergence of national players relying mostly on economic cooperation to sustain the network.

PHASE 1: RISE OF THE MONOCENTRIC NETWORK

In the mid-nineteenth century the pastoral industry was evolving around a monocentric network, diagrammatically akin to a hub with spokes, whereby many functional groups were drawn into the network by dint of their close relationship with the agents. A common characteristic of the pioneer stock and station agents was their embedment in local colonial society, closely connected with many groups, which helped promote trust, reputation, and traditions vital for successful networks. In Dunedin, Donald Reid formed an agency in 1878 by which time he had been a successful local farmer and politician in North Taieri. His son-in-law, Thomas Fergus, who joined the partnership, was a director of several Dunedin companies, and was well known in Central Otago where he had been an engineer, railway contractor, and politician. NMA originated in the business of Dunedin entrepreneur, George Gray Russell. Wright Stephenson held interlocking directorates with other local businesses such as the Dunedin Savings Bank and featured prominent farmers and breeders amongst its leading figures.[11] The Stronach and Morris families had been local farmers and landowners who boasted that 'the members of our firm have all been brought up in Dunedin and are well known to all classes of the community'.[12] At least two directors of Winchcombe Carson were farmers. Conversely, members of agent firms sometimes turned to farming.[13] Thus social and kinship links connected agents to the local farming community (see Figure 3.2).

Local embedment helped agents understand the significance of social structure for the farming business and to be familiar with many farming families. This is confirmed by their detailed comments and notes about farming families, including character assessments. Wright Stephenson noted of Robert Meek of Fairfax that: 'while he is a particularly straight-forward, decent man himself I don't think he gets any assistance from his family . . . they are rather a drain on him'. Contrariwise, Duncan Kerr of Titiroa: 'is a lazy, useless creature but his wife and family are I think good workers'.[14] In recently settled areas with poor external communications and small migrant populations, social and familial cohesion was common. This often involved large extended families working in the local pastoral industry. Wright Stephenson noted of a farmer in 1906: 'he is a member of the large Beck family who are nearly all good men and most of whom deal with us'. The same report also noted that many MacDonalds had a farm around Invercargill.[15] As late as the interwar period AMLF noted the importance of family connections and geographical closeness in farming communities.[16] In 1932 when assessing two indebted clients, Elders noted that their brother owned three stations and sold his wool with the company, 'blood is thicker than water . . . Harry Lewis may . . . view . . . our refusal to assist his brothers [as] an unfriendly attitude'.[17]

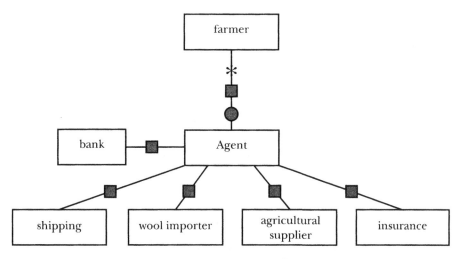

Key: economic cooperative (■), social integrative (●), kinship (✳)

Figure 3.2 Transaction map, *c.* 1860s

This social structure encouraged networking investments by agents: by developing a close and continuous relationship with one farmer the probability of gaining the business of others was increased. This was especially the case where they gained an influential local figure as a client and supporter. Thus, Elders noted: 'securing Mr Campbell as a client will strengthen our position in the district as he has a large following . . . prominent position among Western Australian station owners'.[18] In addition, there were returns to loyal and honest behaviour on both sides of the network, the agent risked losing many clients by falling out with one, while each farmer in the family might suffer if one of their number crossed an agent. Confined space had the additional benefit of increasing the amount and accuracy of information available to each group about other groups. This mitigated dishonesty and ensured that where monitoring was necessary its costs were low. Dalgety had noted in 1887: 'in the colonies it seems to me everyone knows his neighbour's business', while Dennys Lascelles observed the significance of 'wagging tongues' seven years later.[19] This indirect or discreet version of monitoring also avoided farmer resentment of being 'watched'.

Agent firms built on these environmental bonds and their local connections by engineering additional local flavour to build high levels of trust. They hired employees from the vicinity and decentralised responsibility to their country branches which were the principal conduits between the firm's head office, normally in an urban commercial centre, and its rural clients. Reids, for example, employed several former pastoralist clients as branch managers, while its agents working on commission included a publican, bailiff, and bank manager.[20] NMA adopted similar policies, including amongst its appointments the son of the local mayor at Gore.[21] Dalgety was also conscious of employing someone 'whose position also socially admits of his talking to our clients not only in . . . business . . . but on equal and friendly terms'.[22] AMLF emphasised the importance of its managers being 'greatly respected' by their local clients and having much 'influence in, and knowledge of, the districts'.[23] Finally, Elders, like most firms, gave its local managers expense accounts: 'to maintain a strong standing in the community'.[24]

Local social and economic connections were clearly important in winning and retaining customers. When making appointments to its Local Board of Advice in 1904 AMLF recognised this in choosing Walter Watt, manager of a local wool business, and member of the Boards of the Union Bank and the Perpetual Trustees Company. This was also a strategic move to head off Dalgety from acquiring Watt's connection. However, use of 'names' was not always sensible; AMLF appointed the Honourable A. H. Whittingham as its Brisbane local adviser, his name being 'the best advertisement we could have'. AMLF also admitted that this had lost it the business of another figure and that it had not 'been able to make much use of his [Whittingham's] services'.[25]

Branch managers were the main client contact point, and the office was centrally located in the main street adjacent to the hotel, community centre and shops.[26] Firms reinforced ties through social and business visits to individual farms and by receiving farmers in their home.[27] On farm visits they used the opportunity to be introduced to friends and neighbours as prospective clients.[28] The importance of this direct contact was noted by William Turner of Hepburn Leonard, who noted: 'there really ought to be someone in the office during the time I am away . . . as people say they can never find me'.[29] In order to minimise such problems firms used 'travellers' to keep in contact with more remotely located clients. The traveller was normally a local person who knew the area and had established local contacts. The value of such contacts was made apparent by Pitt, Son & Badgery in 1918 when they replaced a deceased traveller with his wife.[30]

Branch managers were involved with local social and sporting activities, and organised agricultural shows, exhibitions, and competitions. They also did a lot of business in the local public house.[31] The branch manager's wife provided moral and social reinforcement to her husband's local standing.[32] The firm's auctioneer had a face and voice known to many, and possessed the commanding personality necessary for the occupation.[33] Social integration and kinship were reinforced by economic cooperation as agents extended their services and branching, drawing them into close, long-term, and regular trading with farmers that reinforced the elements of trust and reputation.[34] Agents also sustained their focal position in local networks by assuming some responsibility for community-wide matters, including acting as a legal and political advocate and spokesman, and providing finance for infrastructural improvements such as road, railway, and port development.

Agents were additionally the focal point for the extended functional and geographical connections of the network beyond the locality, linking the farmer to different industries and to the regional urban commercial centre. Being outside the local community, these were economic rather than social or kinship relationships. Some of the early Victorian agents were led by individuals well connected with the Melbourne business community. David Elder, of NZLMA, was referred to in 1880 as 'a gentleman well and favourably known, in financial circles in Melbourne'.[35] Large national or international firms in banking, wool buying, shipping, insurance, and farming supplies viewed the agents as the vital conduit into the local pastoral network through an economic cooperative relationship. English sheep dip manufacturer, Morris Little & Son, regarded AMLF's 'considerable influence' as vital in winning market share from competitors.[36] Pastoral agents also acted as local commission agents for shipping and insurance companies within the broader local trading community, emphasising the repeated and two-way dealings of the relationship. Product flows in both directions occurred as agents arranged wool shipments and received local handling business from shipping companies.[37] Agents additionally played an important go-between role in the development and testing of new products, passing on feedback from the farmer to the agricultural supplier. A similar informational role was played with wool buyers who reported market conditions.

Agents conducted their own financial transactions with the banks as well as intermediating on behalf of farmers. Banks also networked directly with farmers through personal accounts, although the relationship was rarely of a close socially integrative nature. The reason for this lay in the broader geographical and sectoral interests of the banks, features that were later to loosen the agent–farmer bond (see below).[38] The economic cooperative relationship of bank and farmer was limited by infrequent transactions. From about the 1870s, however, several banks fostered closer relationships with farmers by imitating the networking features of the agent through 'localisation' and offering a wider range of pastoral services. The subsequent shift of the wool market from London back to Australasia served to undermine the networking influence of the banks with farmers (see chapter 6).

From the 1880s agents faced competition from freezing companies which, as specialist and localised enterprises, might develop close relations with the farming communities. The response of the agents was to interpose themselves between the farmer and freezing company especially through the provision of credit for farmers and the extraction of a commission from the companies (see Figure 3.3). Given their accumulated experience, contacts, and access to bank finance, agents were well placed to sustain their pivotal role. Alternatively, agents directly competed by establishing their own freezing works or resorted to cooperative strategies with the freezing companies, which included interlocking directorates or equity strategies by acquiring a shareholding in a freezing company. Agents

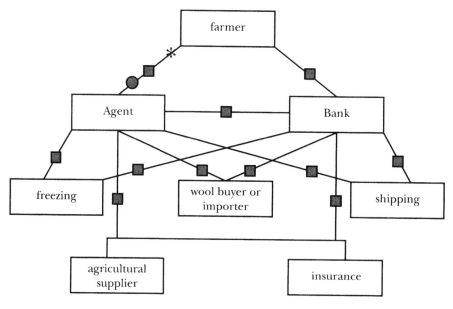

Key: economic cooperative (■), social integrative (●), kinship (✳)

Figure 3.3 Transaction map, c. 1880s

had also to contend with cooperative freezing works and dairy factories formed by farmers (see below).

By a more focused study at the local level of the southerly New Zealand province of Otago and its port city of Dunedin, the social structure and the firms involved in specific pastoral networks can be identified. The Central Otago gold rush from 1863 accelerated economic progress in the province and particularly stimulated agricultural output to supply the rapidly expanding population. While gold speculation was believed to have created 'deep-rooted distrust' in the local trading community, the wool staple attracted 'excellent constituents'.[39] The region was dominated by Scottish emigrants, many of whom were known to each other and retained strong links to their country of origin.

There is extensive information for the network involving NMA. NMA transacted its banking business with National Bank of New Zealand, much of its shipping with Union Steamship, its insurance with National Insurance, its agricultural equipment with Reid & Gray, and its refrigeration with Longburn Freezing works (see Figure 3.4).[40] Personal business links drew these firms together. NMA's General Manager in the late nineteenth and early twentieth centuries, G. R. Ritchie, was chairman of Union Steamship and National Insurance, and also sat on the Boards of several other closely linked local companies. NMA's chief accountant and secretary were also involved in similar interlocking directorates. Conversely, James Mills, chairman of Union Steamship, sat on the Board of NMA. These firms had contiguous head offices in Water Street, Dunedin, and, indeed, exchanged premises on several occasions. In smaller centres, office sharing was common, National Insurance and NMA, for example, using the same offices at Timaru.[41] Sharing of travellers with insurers or agricultural suppliers was also not unknown.[42] The links with Longburn and Reid & Gray were reinforced with equity investments. Correspondence confirms such business behaviour, NMA writing to Union Steamship: 'you know you can rely upon us always working in with you to our mutual advantage'.[43] Likewise, NMA looked to the National Bank to influence customers to send its pastoral business to NMA in the same way as Bank of New Zealand and Bank of New South Wales did for their friendly agents.[44] Some connections were formed in the English business community rather than locally, and generated valuable reciprocal information flows.[45] In the development of frozen meat shipments from Dunedin to London beginning in 1882, a key figure was William Soltau Davidson, whose links with NMA's circle were critical in bringing together the various parties to the project.

These high levels of connection within the network helped agents to coordinate policies and arbitrate disagreements. In this way network loyalty could be maintained, NMA stressing the maxim, 'never to change business relationships unless compelled to do so', aware of all the benefits of long-term transacting in terms of trust and reputation.[46] None the less, the networks sometimes came under pressure. The pastoral agent's closest connection and first loyalty was to the farmer as the source of most of his income and most extensive trading, financial, and informational transactions. If the agency

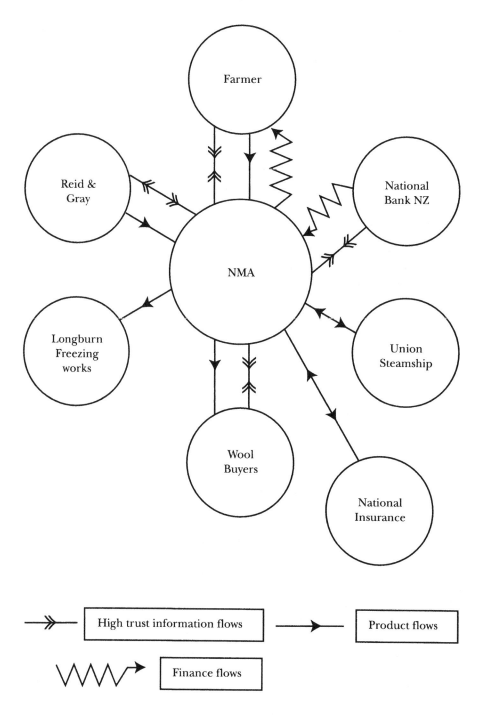

Figure 3.4 Otago agent-led pastoral network by the 1880s
Sources: NMA papers, various.

was not satisfied with the shipping terms being offered by the network company it might look to another firm from outside the network, even though it risked losing long-term benefits and agency commissions. For example, NMA fostered competition in the shipment of frozen meat in the 1880s between Shaw Savill Albion and White Star to try and prevent either company gaining a monopoly of this valuable new trade.[47]

The origins of competency-based leadership of pastoral networks are thus quite clear: many agents were experienced entrepreneurs, had good local connections, cooperated on key issues with other firms, and, by providing a widening range of financial and trading services, quickly developed sectoral expertise. The growing size and complexity of the networks emphasised the need for a coordinating leader.

PHASE 2: THE POLYCENTRIC NETWORK

From the early twentieth century the bonds of the agent-led pastoral network began to weaken. While the agents continued to play an important role in the local economy, the kinship, then social, elements of propinquity were reduced in favour of an economic cooperative relationship.[48] As described in chapter 2, the larger agents expanded their geographical coverage and acquired many smaller local firms. As a result, employees and managers were moved between locations with which they had no kinship ties. Dalgety were later to lament, 'we never leave anyone in one place long enough to build up a personal connection' and therefore found it needed to provide a higher ratio of finance to get business than did local firms.[49] Moreover, expansion was achieved through additional equity, which extended the weighting of ownership outside the locality. Thus, social disengagement weakened the bonds of trust and reputation.[50]

The large dominant firms competed strongly with each other and possessed the resources and expertise to develop specific policies designed to win clients from other firms. These included offering discriminating terms, particularly on loans, to attract 'good' clients and to offload bad ones (see chapter 4). By discriminating between clients in closely-knit communities the agents were aware of the potential disruption to social and family relations this might cause and the damage to their own pivotal role. That they chose to pursue this approach suggests there were good returns to be gained. The accumulated experience, or corporate capability, of the large enduring firms enabled them to develop new strategies and to recognise long-term changes in social structures. They could also employ staff who were not influenced by local sentiment nor distracted by their own farming commitments. At the same time, the shift of emphasis towards more trading services in place of long-term loans meant farmers were better placed to move between agents periodically. Dalgety complained of the need to go canvassing because of 'the "floating" clientele, who flit from broker to broker; they are unstable in their support owing no loyalty to any particular firm'.[51]

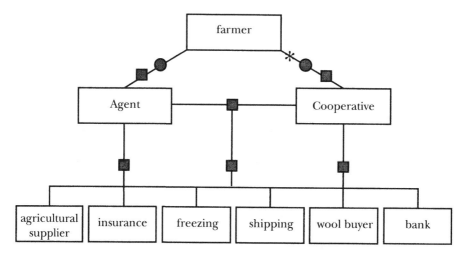

Key: economic cooperative (▪), social integrative (●), kinship (✳)

Figure 3.5 Transaction map, *c.* 1900s

These changes reduced the local networking influence of the firms as direct contact with farmers, whom they had come to know well over many years, declined. Their relations with other network members were changing in a similar way. Informal agreements were gradually being replaced by specific contracts setting out clearly the terms of doing business.[52] Taken together these various factors caused the agents to lose their unique leadership role in the network.

The farmers' cooperatives began to compete with agents as the focal point of pastoral networks (see Figure 3.5). Their competitiveness was especially based on their ability to replace the agent firms as small locally networked intermediaries with strong social and kinship ties. Otago Farmers Cooperative, established in 1895, was typical of many cooperatives. Its local branches through the province were the 'eyes and ears' of the firm and its local managers were preferably married, 'for social reasons and because of the great assistance possible'.[53] The value of close links with farmers is indicated by the fact that from one farmer a branch 'gathered an immense amount of information'.[54]

While the cooperative imitated many of the features of the nineteenth-century stock and station agent, its relationship with its clients was equity based as it was owned and controlled by local farmer shareholders and therefore responsibility for it fell on the local rural community.[55] The greater community accountability which this implied can be indicated by the foreclosure of the problem account of the Stewart brothers and the resignation of their father from Otago Farmers' Board, which contrasts to Stronach Morris where large-scale and long-term support of an indebted relation brought the firm close to bankruptcy.[56] The powerful monitoring which also resulted can be seen when Otago Farmers instructed its solicitor to search a particular will since it had 'heard' that an indebted client may have been a beneficiary.[57]

Change in network structures depended on produce types. By 1900 cooperatives were well established in the Australasian dairy industry, leading to a reorganisation of production in that sector and contributing to an 'economic transformation' in New Zealand.[58] Closer settlement and the growth of the factory system in the dairy industry encouraged a co-operative spirit in such areas as the Waikato (New Zealand) and Illawarra (New South Wales). However, cooperative networking was less popular amongst sheep and grain farmers, with a few outstanding exceptions (for example, the Farmers' and Graziers' Cooperative Co. in New South Wales).

The smallness of most cooperatives and their limited access to national and international networks, especially in their early years, meant that stock and station agents often still connected the farmer to other functional groups. Thus, in an increasingly competitive industry with agents drawing on national and international sources of finance, information, and entrepreneurship, strong emphasis on the local network could put cooperatives at a competitive disadvantage. Poor quality entrepreneurship helps explain Otago Farmers' problems throughout the 1920s and the heavy write-down of its shares in the following decade. In response, it sought to be tied increasingly to the world of the larger national agency firms, cooperating with them in local auctions and commission rates, and exchanging information about clients. Employees moved between agents and cooperatives: John Grindley, for example, worked for Donald Reid before joining Otago Farmers.[59] Reid maintained its local identity more clearly than did larger agents, which made for a closer relationship with Otago Farmers. In 1933 when firms were attempting to reduce their costs in the middle of a crisis Otago Farmers and Reid agreed 'to confer at any time, and exchange lists of . . . debts'.[60] Continued cooperation eventually led to the merger of the two firms in 1974.

The prolonged interwar depression drove the farmer and agent further apart. It revealed the hopeless state of accounts that had been supported previously to maintain intergenerational links or to avoid the reverberated backlash from foreclosing. Agents continued to support most clients, although this was as much to protect their own exposed asset position with the banks as being driven by a strong sense of social loyalty. The decrease in the number of country branches and reduction in their social investments were also caused by the need to lower costs, as one Winchcombe Carson manager noted in 1930:

> We are endeavouring to curtail the expense of entertaining. It is impossible to completely disregard the custom of the . . . country districts where we are continually meeting woolgrowers at hotels, clubs, races, shows and carnivals . . . [However] a great deal of the last three will be eliminated over the next year or two. Mr Clarke is a complete teetotaller and myself virtually . . . we have a natural disinclination to this method of assisting business.[61]

Clearly, Winchcombe Carson had also stopped employing socially integrative staff as well!

Cooperatives also turned increasingly to 'economic cooperative' means to attract clients. They enhanced their regional and national networks which helped them compete in a wider range of services. The development of transportation, marketing, and selling services by cooperatives, especially after World War One, helped to create a polycentric trade-financial network. The Farmers' and Graziers' Cooperative (New South Wales) moved into insurance and stock selling, while the Westralian Farmers' Cooperative (Western Australia) expanded its branch network in an attempt to supply finance and other pastoral services to farmers.[62]

An increasingly complex web of intermediaries also included government agencies, a legacy of wartime reorganisation and the subsequent downturn. They provided mechanisms that encouraged further cooperative activity amongst farmers. The emergence of government marketing boards in Australia and New Zealand was partly a legacy of World War One and the experience of the bulk purchasing agreements of the Imperial Government Supplies Department. Marketing boards were first given legislative support in New Zealand in 1922 when the government enacted the Meat Export Control Act. A year later the New Zealand dairy industry received similar powers under the Dairy Produce Export Control Act, and other experiments in state marketing were tried in the fruit, honey, kauri gum, wheat and flour, poultry, and tobacco industries. The operation of these producer boards was left to the individual industry. Most boards aimed to ensure that farmers received the highest returns possible on the British market by minimising transportation and marketing costs, undertaking advertising, and better timing the arrival of produce to coincide with high prices.[63] In some areas the boards facilitated trade and financial networks in the pastoral sector; in others they took control of functions previously undertaken by stock and station agents and cooperatives (for example, in exporting meat and dairy produce). Thus, for farmers supplying the export market the establishment of a state monopoly (often located in capital cities) caused the social-integrative bonds of earlier networks dominated by agents and cooperatives to atrophy.

The establishment of marketing boards was followed by State and national government involvement in the provision of other services, especially bridging finance. Several Australian States enacted legislation in the 1920s that included provision for cooperative credit. Queensland experimented with the Primary Producers' Co-operative Association Acts 1923–26, and the New South Wales government registered cooperatives under the Cooperative, Community Settlement and Credit Act 1922. In New Zealand, the Rural Intermediate Credit Act in 1927 provided administrative and financial backing for local cooperative credit associations which were locally based organisations providing a limited liability structure to farmers. By 1930 there were more than thirty operating in the north island of New Zealand. Economic considerations and community spirit were at the heart of several associations. As a contemporary noted:

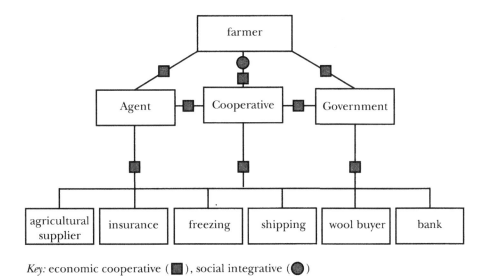

Key: economic cooperative (■), social integrative (●)

Figure 3.6 Transaction map, c. 1920s

many substantial farmers 'who were not likely to require loans themselves, have nevertheless joined the associations in order to ensure their formation and to see that they receive a good start. By doing so they are playing their part in fostering the co-operative spirit among the farming community along the lines provided for'.[64]

The associations provided bridging finance in competition with stock and station agents and testify to the complexity of the trade-financial network by the late 1930s.

Federal and State governments also entered the network as providers of agricultural research. Of particular importance were State departments of agriculture, the Council for Scientific and Industrial Research, and Massey Agricultural College.

PHASE 3: THE DECLINE OF PASTORAL NETWORKS

After World War Two the notion of a pastoral network seemed less tenable. Firms became much larger again as mergers substantially raised concentration rates and absorbed smaller and medium-sized enterprises, including many cooperatives. In addition, their diversification of products and markets moved the focus of agent firms away from the pastoral industry and their traditional client base. These two trends culminated and coalesced when the leading agent firms became absorbed into broadly diversified conglomerates in the 1970s and 1980s. This mitigated their perceived competency and the trust and loyalty generated by firms which had solely served farmers.[65]

On the other side of the network, the 'man on the land' was increasingly being replaced by large agri-businesses. The pastoralist was no longer closely linked with individual local communities. The pastoralist's need for inter-mediary services was much reduced and, where needed, would be chosen on the basis of competitive spot exchanges rather than through the devel-opment of long-term relationships. The agri-businesses had their own internalised sources of finance, information, and sectoral and business expertise, the types of zero-priced services that had traditionally encouraged farmers to tie themselves into long-term relationships with specific agents.

Loss of network members, such as shipping and insurance companies, lessened the need for a coordinator. Expanded levels of commercial activity caused many companies in these sectors to set up their own branches. Dalgety noted that such 'ideas are current' and, despite claiming that 'owners' interests are best served by agents who have the confidence of the business community and . . . the public', soon faced this competi-tion.[66] In turn, agents wanted more freedom to choose between service providers rather than be tied into long-term partnerships. In 1955 Dalgety's chairman noted that the company had once had a common chairman with one of the banks which put them under some pressure to deal with that bank, and concluded that he would not want 'to be put in that position'.[67]

In the rural economic crisis of the 1990s farmers sometimes sought help from an alternative source, the 'rural counsellor'.[68] Often working from home as an individual consultant, and based in the local farming commu-nity, the counsellor retraces many of the networked experiences of the agents and cooperatives. Relying heavily on a car, a telephone, and a persuasive personality, rural counsellors travel between farms providing a range of business, farming, legal, and social advice. Two specific roles cited by one female counsellor are acting as a buffer between farmers and bankers, and helping to patch up marriages. The counsellors' role is specifically concerned with crisis management and they do not provide the trading services of earlier intermediaries.

CONCLUSION

The pioneering stock and station agents, therefore, stood at the middle of a network in the nineteenth-century pastoral industry, connecting farmers with a wide range of service providers. Networking relationships emerged out of the endemic social and geographic closeness of settler societies. Recognising the synergies for themselves and farmers from providing a diverse set of services, agents fostered further propinquity and joint inter-ests within farming communities through social, sporting, and trading relationships. The network thus enabled agents and farmers to respond rapidly and effectively to economic change by providing an intensive ex-change of commercial and technical information and business expertise. As a well-placed and competent leader, the agent also mitigated communication and coordination costs in an expanding and geographically diverse network. This was achieved by reducing the number of bilateral transactions between different groups and lessening uncertainty through the auspices of an honest broker, the agent. Opportunist behaviour was mitigated through the risk of social alienation and the loss of zero-priced goods, such as tacit knowledge, acquired in long-term relationships based on trust and reputation. Finally, it gave farmers access to scale economies through the agents while the agents derived scope economies from the range of services they were able to provide as part of the long-term and broadly based trading relationship.

In the early twentieth century cooperatives began to displace the large nationally oriented firms with their own form of local social networking. Agents concentrated on economic networking at a national and international level, recognising the returns from access to broader resources and strategies. At the same time, they were conscious of the changing nature of settler society, now less isolated, uncertain, and locally cohesive. Alternative sources of information were available to the farmer, different functional groups were better known, and contracts and economic reputation were used to control behaviour. By the 1930s cooperatives also began to realise that local connections were insufficient to compete with the leading agent firms. In addition, the moral suasion associated with local social networks, while averting opportunism, also provided scope for free-riders and cross-subsidy between good and bad farmers, a state of affairs which ultimately neither the agent firms nor the farming community would accept. Since World War Two it would be difficult to characterise most relationships in the pastoral industry as of the networking type, particularly with the diversification of agent firms and the growth of agri-business.

The following chapters look at the main types of service provided by the agents – financial, trading and informational – and show how the existence of network relationships supported and shaped their provision. While it is not uncommon to find networks based on trading or financing or informational relationships, the agents provided a combined trade-finance-information network which served as a powerful organisational form, fostering the rapid expansion of Australasian farm production and export.

CHAPTER FOUR

Financial Services

Finance provider was one of the key roles of the stock and station agent. Farmers needed short-term support for seasonal outgoings and longer-term developmental support for equipment, livestock, and property. Agents competed with and complemented other finance providers, particularly banks and private mortgagees. Their close connections with the farming community, and specialist expertise, ideally placed them to ration credit between borrowers and mediate on behalf of other lenders. Over time agents developed sophisticated contract design strategies to attract and maintain the best risks. While some of the early British companies made good profits from lending, increasing competition led agents to offer finance at zero economic profit in order to secure valuable wool-handling commissions. Agent loyalty to their borrowers carried many farmers through the cyclical depressions and thus minimised lost commissions, legal complexities, and network disloyalty as a result of foreclosure.

DEMAND FOR FINANCE

There were four main sources of demand for pastoral finance. Short-term seasonal finance covered the time lag between incurring seasonal costs such as shearing, transport, insurance, and sale presentation. The farmer drew against his agent who would cover his working costs and debit him for transport and marketing costs incurred on his behalf. When the wool had been sold the agent would deduct his commission and the seasonal finance and credit the farmer with the balance. Since inland and overseas transport was slow and unreliable and most Australasian wool was being sold in London by the middle of the nineteenth century, demand for this form of finance was initially substantial and extended over at least six months. Steam shipping, railways, improved roads, and the relocation of the wool market back to Australasia by the early twentieth century, however, shortened the period of seasonal finance considerably although finance for inputs sourced outside the sector grew.

Seasonal short-term finance became cyclical medium-term if low wool prices, droughts or poor harvests meant that sales revenue was insufficient to cover the farmer's expenses and any loan repayments with his agent. In such circumstances the farmer would rely on his agent to accept his debits until the following year's sales. Extended depressions and droughts, particularly in the 1890s, early 1920s and 1930s, late 1960s, and early 1980s were times when farmers looked for crisis support over several successive years.

Farmers sought longer-term advances to establish, extend, and modernise their business. Farming became more capital intensive in the later nineteenth century as permanent stations replaced nomadic herding. The introduction of water bores, plant, paddocking, and fencing placed financial demands on the farmer. The movement inland away from the most fertile regions and the development of an active market in stations by the 1880s also increased the demand for finance. In addition, there was a strong trend towards purchase of the freehold on the land as a result of legislation passed in the 1860s and 1870s. Land policies towards the end of the nineteenth century gave a fillip to finance-hungry small-scale farmers through the sub-division of large estates. The provision of land for returning soldiers initiated further cohorts of small and needy farmers. Greater mechanisation, especially since 1945, increased the capital intensity of farming.

Farming communities required finance to develop public goods whose non-excludability and high costs discouraged individual expenditure. These included local infrastructure such as road and rail links and port improvements. It also involved the provision of venture capital to initiate development projects for the pastoral industry, such as scientific breeding, new crop experimentation, or the development of dairy factories.

Some of their needs were financed by farmers from current expenditure through the use of underemployed farm labour and by investing profits and savings. The extent of self-finance is impossible to calculate precisely. Given the rapid expansion of the industry, its high capital needs, and the limited savings of small farmers, reliance on external funding would appear to have been substantial. Butlin's estimate that by 1874 only one-third of capital formation could have been financed by farmers gives some indication of the demand for support.[1] AMLF's historian, Bailey, states unequivocally that 'many pastoralists owe their very existence to financial assistance extended by the pastoral companies'.[2] It was difficult for contemporaries to measure the level of lending since some loans were made informally, farmers preferring to avoid mortgage registration, even if this meant higher interest rates, in order to keep their indebtedness out of the public and trading eye.[3] Anthony Trollope, though, was in no doubt about the importance of external finance:

> The business of squatting would be very restricted, country life in Australia very different from what it is, the amount of wool produced for the benefit of the world wofully [sic] diminished, and the extension of enterprise over new lands altogether checked, if no capital were to be invested in the pursuit of squatting except that owned by the squatters themselves.[4]

Legislative developments designed to support the expansion of the pastoral sector facilitated the growth of borrowing. The Lien on Wool and Livestock Act passed in New South Wales in 1843 and the Wool and Oil Securities Act in New Zealand in 1858 enabled pastoralists to borrow by giving security in the form of a preferable lien on an ensuing wool clip or by mortgaging livestock. Reliance on external support, while undoubtedly highly cyclical, declined over the last half of the twentieth century with extensive land development mostly completed, fewer new entrants, and the growth of agri-businesses.[5] Net indebtedness of the farming sector fell to below 10 per cent of farm capital by the 1970s and 1980s.[6]

COMPARATIVE FINANCE PROVISION

The main lenders to farmers were the agents, banks, government, and private mortgagees (including trust funds). Estimates of market share are difficult to make, particularly as bank finance to farmers is difficult to separate from their lending to other sectors until recent times. Personal financiers are even more difficult to trace. While banks generally lent more to the rural sector, in sheep farming agents held a similar, sometimes larger, share of the finance market.[7] In turn, this meant a lower agent share of rural lending in Australia compared with New Zealand, due to the former's larger non-pastoral crop production. None the less, there are good reasons for believing that the pastoral agents played a key role in finance particularly in terms of their constancy, the breadth of projects they supported, and the great care taken in their lending decisions.

Bank finance was initially constrained by conservative attitudes inherited from British banking principles towards lending on rural real estate. The 1830s had witnessed the beginning of a major banking expansion with the formation of British banks in Australia.[8] While banks could acquire land or property in settlement of a debt, they were generally barred from lending on this security. This problem was gradually overcome by a little legal ingenuity, particularly in the creation of equitable mortgages and the amendment of bank charters in the third quarter of the nineteenth century.[9] By the 1870s many banks had entered into pastoral finance although their lending volumes and ratios were 'reasonably conservative'.[10]

In the twentieth century the banks had a sizeable share of the rural market although their lending was intermittent and of a low priority, reflecting their broad spread of financial interests across the economy.[11] In 1908 and 1913 bank lending to Australian farmers was cut back sharply. On the first occasion they diverted funds into State government securities at tax concessional rates while agent lending to farmers rose sharply in response to high demand. In 1913 AMLF noted a preference of the banks for their 'commercial customers whose business in exchange and discounts is more liquid and profitable'.[12] By the interwar period the banks were keenly aware of the limited collateral business from pastoral lending due to the agents' control of the expanding Australasian wool auctions. AMLF noted that the banks 'made reference to the fact that they lend without getting collateral wool and stock commission . . . our lending . . . was more profitable'.[13] However, the frequent preference of agents to limit their long-term advances and the negotiation of shared wool commissions provided opportunities for the banks. As evidence of market share, 53 per cent of livestock mortgages in Adelaide in 1934 were held by agents, compared with 26 per cent by the banks, and 10 per cent by private mortgagees.[14]

Government financial support for farmers was also intermittent although it tended to come in times of need. The State Advances Corporation provided crisis finance for New Zealand farmers between the wars. Knowledge of the rural credit market was yet more limited than with the banks and therefore funding through, or in cooperation with, agents and banks was a common strategy. As described in chapter 3 the Rural Intermediate Credit Act encouraged New Zealand farmers to form local cooperative credit associations. The New Zealand government financed the land and livestock to put returning servicemen on the land after World War Two, leaving the agents to provide working expenses and seasonal support.[15]

In the decade after World War Two, with the banks facing demands from industrial expansion and government monetary policies, agents again increased their share and volume of rural finance substantially. By the mid-1950s bank support had increased once more by which time the two groups had similar market shares in New Zealand but the banks lent more in Australia.[16] Agent diversification in recent decades may have contributed to increased volatility in their lending patterns. In the more interventionist postwar years governments have provided special rural financial assistance and established arms-length financial institutions, including the Commonwealth Development Bank in Australia and the Rural Banking and Finance Corporation in New Zealand. However, such institutions still draw on industry specialists for advice and to channel lending.[17] In the financially deregulated environment since the late 1980s both institutions have converted into commercial enterprises and farmers have sought alternative capital markets, including equity finance and property trusts.[18] An increasingly congested rural finance market is revealed in a mid-1990s study that identified eight sources of support in New South Wales.[19]

The implications of intermittent and low-priority bank lending require investigation. Bank knowledge and expertise of the sector was thereby lessened, making banks reluctant to deal directly with pastoralists.[20] It has put additional pressure on the agents to help farmers at times when their own specialisation in the sector has exposed them to similar economic vicissitudes. In spite of the postwar decline of farming networks, agent financial support to Australian farmers rose by 40 per cent between 1965 and 1970 during one of the worst droughts faced by the industry.[21] Banker indifference has not gone unnoticed among farmers who have been less keen to borrow from banks in the light of this uncertainty and the realisation that they would gain few of the informational and trust benefits that are generated by a long-term relationship with the pastoral agent.[22] Thus, the banks' policy of 'exit' may be contrasted with the 'loyalty' and 'voice' approach of the agents. The agents exploited this perception as a competitive advantage wherever possible; in 1937 Goldsbrough Mort hoped to win several accounts from the banks: 'these people knowing our reputation in the past for carrying clients through difficulty . . . and [our] knowledge as to the best way of handling difficult accounts during the depression'.[23] None the less, the periodic entry of the banks into pastoral lending, and the ever-constant threat of their doing so, has helped to make it a contested competitive market. Thus, when agents were considering raising interest rates in 1920 the threat of being undercut by the banks persuaded them against this course of action.[24]

Bank circumspection was perhaps justified. Pastoral lending is characterised by large and fluctuating risk levels both between individuals and over time. As seen in chapter 1, pastoralism is a highly volatile industry with substantial variations in performance. Until recent times, most farmers operated on a small scale; they had few resources to fall back on and farming assets were highly illiquid, so defaulting on loans cost agents dearly not only in money which was lost or tied up, but also in time expended resolving problem accounts.

The nature of credit markets added to the risks for lenders. Finance markets differ from normal commodity markets where the price mechanism enables sellers to find appropriate buyers. However, the price of borrowing (rate of interest) is a poor signalling device in finance markets and may attract undesirable borrowers; the contract is incomplete until the loan is fully repaid and therefore may attract opportunists. Indeed, rationing demand through higher interest rates may cause adverse selection in attracting those prepared to take high risks and discouraging the low-risk customers which the lender wants in order to maximise his rate of return. To avoid this problem and allocate, or ration, credit to preferred borrowers, the lender must have extensive information about them in order to judge whether they are a good risk.[25] The close link between lending volumes and company profits together with big discrepancies in the return to capital employed with different customers meant good risk assessment was vitally important.

In the Australasian pastoral sector of the nineteenth and early twentieth centuries there were particular problems in acquiring accurate information cheaply. Most Australian farmers were geographically isolated in a large country with poor transport. While New Zealand is smaller, its geology and geography also made communication very difficult. Many farmers were new settlers about whom little was known. The convict origins of Australia and its bushranging reputation made the shortfall of personal information a particular problem. Even where individuals could be traced back to Britain they often had no previous record in farming. Given the small size of most farming enterprises, the relatively high cost of acquiring information might not have justified the expected returns on the loan.

Agents, through their close network links and extensive trading with farmers, were better placed than many banks to have access to extensive and accurate information on individual and community-wide conditions in the pastoral sector. Contemporary writers were aware of this advantage, one observing: 'knowing the character of its country, the carrying capacity, the available supply of water, and the probable waterfall during the year, they are in a position to appraise its value, if anything, more closely and accurately than the banks'.[26] The trust and reputation engendered by networks also mitigated the risk of opportunism by borrowers and encouraged them to make a full and honest disclosure of relevant information that could not be observed by the lender. Information costs were cheaper for agents because they were defrayed across a number of income-generating activities with the farmer, and their specialisation in pastoralism provided them with the expertise to interpret information effectively.

Some banks responded to agent lending by broadening their range of pastoral services but faced severe competition from the experienced agents. Most have shied away from specialisation in the sector although the agricultural banks in Queensland and Tasmania, the Rural Industries Bank of Western Australia, and rural departments of some of the savings banks have established a niche.[27] The agents appear to have been quite happy to work with these institutions and other mortgagees such as the Scottish Widows Fund which, in most cases, enabled the burden of long-term lending to be spread without competing for wool commissions. Sometimes a bank has held ownership of an agent firm, most famously NZLMA by the Bank of New Zealand. This enabled NZLMA to use the Bank's branches for its own agencies and to receive direct applications for pastoral loans. The relationship appears to have been an uneasy one; in 1879 the Board of NZLMA made the unsubstantiated statement that it was at a disadvantage in the pastoral finance market because of 'the continued close association of the Bank and the Company . . . the separation in management and premises should as soon as possible be made complete'.[28] Unless the Bank had acquired an undesirable reputation amongst its farming clients, the most likely explanation of this view was the desire to develop closer and more specialist ties with the pastoral sector. This disassociation was completed with the NZLMA's reconstruction in 1893. While formal associations of this kind were uncommon for most of the twentieth century, in 1998, as part of their radical break with traditional practices within the industry, Elders announced a joint venture with Bendigo Bank to provide rural banking services.[29]

The more common cooperative strategy was for the banks to lend to farmers indirectly through the financial intermediation of agents. Close relationships between particular banks and agents in local networks gave the former access to the pastoral finance market (see chapter 3). This was a popular strategy among all of the major banks since it brought them the benefits of lending to the expanding pastoral sector without the informational disabilities. Additionally, it enabled them to rely on the agent's balance sheet and liquidity for repayment. While it was most common for the agent to hold the mortgage over the property and therefore effectively relend the bank's money, agents could also act as the farmer's financial advocate when loans were provided directly by the bank. Agents were also well placed to offer their services as financial guarantors. NZLMA, for instance, acted as guarantor for the personal accounts of some farmers with the Bank of New Zealand, National Bank of New Zealand, and the Bank of Australasia in return for a 1 per cent commission and retaining a mortgage security.[30]

Agents played a similar intermediary role for lending to farmers from other sources, particularly from private mortgagees and trustee companies. In 1890, for example, Victorian agents Hepburn & Leonard mediated in the lending of the funds of a marriage settlement in connection with the purchase of 950 acres in Kangaroo Valley.[31] Dennys Lascelles was asked by Perpetual Executors Trustees Association to act as an intermediary in relation to their loans to farmers since 'your local knowledge of the security & the people place you in a better position to judge'.[32] The same firm also intermediated lending from London trading house Brooks & Company, while Elders intermediated a loan from one of their farmer clients to another.[33] The risk that agents would support undeserving cases to get more business existed but was lessened by the fact that their reputation would be lessened and with it their opportunity to mediate future loans and gain the ensuing trading commissions. In addition, agents would risk being embroiled in costly foreclosure proceedings against the farmer.

THE DEVELOPMENT OF AGENT LENDING

Various estimates of long-term agent lending have been made but the large number of firms and differences in reporting procedures limits their accuracy. Figure 4.1 indicates the long-term trend splicing three series which draw on the lending policies of some of the leading agents, mostly in Australia.[34] The figure concentrates on data taken from the leading seven firms in Australia and New Zealand: notably Dalgety, Elders, Goldsbrough Mort, AMLF, NZLMA, NMA, and Wright Stephenson. In contrast to woolbroking it is impossible to separate Australian and New Zealand business in most cases. The market share of the leaders is not easy to calculate but intermittent evidence suggests it was similar to that for wool and livestock services. This is to be expected given the practice of providing finance and receiving commissions in return. Moreover, agents had a clear idea of the ratio between lending and commission values. However, the ideal mix of loans and commissions was not always achieved and agents also handled wool from financially unencumbered farmers.[35] None the less, by calculating the share of wool handled by the leading seven Australasian companies the assessment can be used as a multiple to estimate total lending by agents. For example, the leading seven firms lent A$70 million between them and had a 48.8 per cent share of the wool-broking market in 1939 which factors to total lending from all agents of A$144 million.

Figure 4.2 reveals heavy short- and medium-term fluctuations in lending by the major companies. Elders loan volumes, for example, increased by

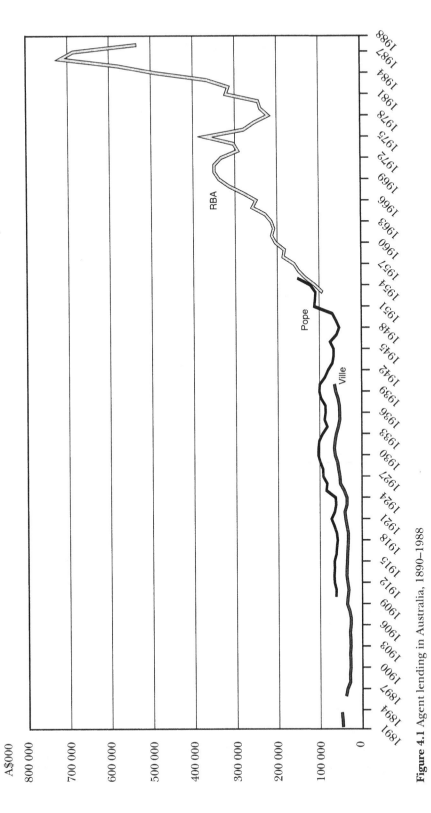

Figure 4.1 Agent lending in Australia, 1890–1988

Sources: Pope – based on data in D. Pope, 'Private finance'; RBA – based on data in *AIBR* and Reserve Bank of Australia data; Ville – see note 34, this chapter.

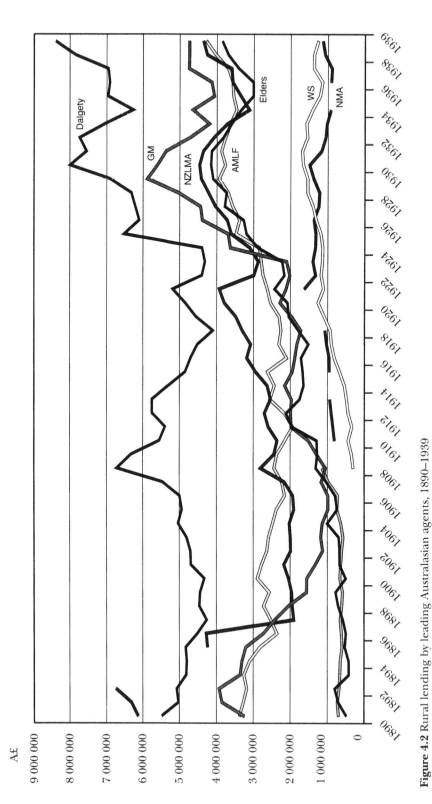

Figure 4.2 Rural lending by leading Australasian agents, 1890–1939

Source: Based on data in *AIBR* and *JID*.

46 per cent in 1904 at the end of the long drought as farmers, particularly severely hit in South Australia, had built up large deficits and, in addition, needed support for restocking. The smaller fluctuations of New Zealand-only agents confirms 'the comparative immunity enjoyed by agriculturists and run-holders in New Zealand from the financial difficulties which have borne so heavily upon Australian enterprise'.[36] When the interwar crisis reached its nadir in the late 1920s and early 1930s indebtedness to agents rose steeply (see Figure 4.3). The risks to which agents exposed themselves by such support can be indicated by the financial reconstructions of the 1890s. The rising ratio of loans to total assets, and the inverse relationship of lending volumes to profits in the interwar years reveal the firms' continued exposure to volatility in the industry in which they specialised (see Table 4.1).[37]

Learning from previous downturns, the larger enduring firms developed improved strategies for assessing risk, managing problem accounts, and structuring their assets and liabilities (see below), and considered smaller and less experienced firms to be using 'loose method[s] of financing'.[38] They also built up reserves and contingency accounts, a strategy which in more recent times has endured criticism for being too conservative compared with financial management in other industries.[39] Many began to follow this course at the beginning of the twentieth century and by the mid-1920s all of the leading companies showed large reserves on their balance sheets of around 20 per cent of total liabilities. In a typical move Goldsbrough Mort decided in 1933 to transfer £420 000 from their reserves to a contingency account to help struggling clients with interest payment moratoriums.[40]

Initially, there was some specialisation in finance provision, with the English companies concentrating on mortgages, and the local firms on shorter-term funding for livestock purchases and seasonal outgoings. With the subsequent service diversification strategies and the increased resources available from incorporation most agents considered all forms of lending, except for the smaller cooperatives and private local firms. The financial crisis of the 1890s, when many agents were burdened with illiquid assets from long-term loans, encouraged a movement towards more short-term funding and the entry of other lenders into the rural mortgage industry.[41] The subsequent history of the industry is littered with policy shifts on long-term lending, grasping it as a competitive tool to 'buy' wool clients in a boom but bemoaning 'hard core', 'stale' mortgage accounts

Table 4.1 Lending ratios: loans as a share of assets, 1910–1930 (%)

	Dalgety	**Elders**	**GM**	**NZLMA**	**AMLF**
1910	69	64	55	54	45
1930	74	73	81	70	79

Sources: Based on data in *AIBR* and *JID*.

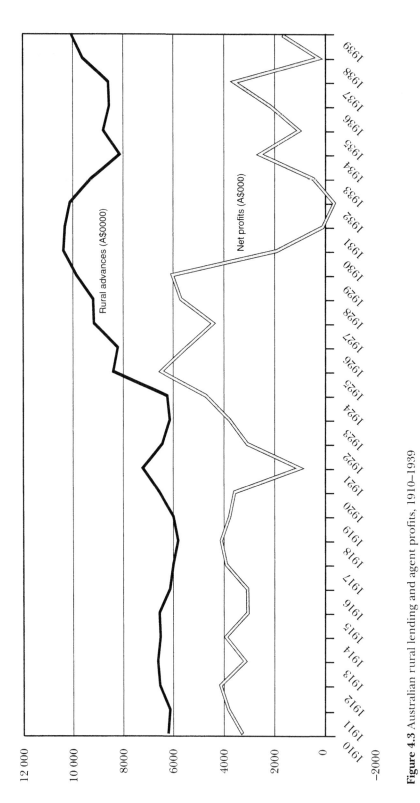

Figure 4.3 Australian rural lending and agent profits, 1910–1939

Sources: Pope 'Private finance', p. 251.

that could not be reduced or liquidated in downturns. In the 1960s New Zealand agents considered amending their constitutions to provide only short-term finance and asserted that other financial institutions should take responsibility for long-term pastoral finance. However, by the late 1970s their advances rose sharply again. Agents continue to equivocate over long-term pastoral lending.[42]

Agents initially concentrated their lending on several large farmers, AMLF's two largest borrowers in the 1860s accounted for 30 per cent of its lending volume. While this minimised administration costs it concentrated risks on a few key accounts. The growth of the small farmer and the financial crisis of the 1890s shifted policy to spreading debt more widely. In 1892/93 the Elders Board discussed 'our gigantic losses . . . our large foolish advances' and confessed that it had to learn to avoid large accounts.[43] AMLF decided in 1898 to avoid large squatting accounts.[44] Years later Dalgety acknowledged with pride that support for small farmers ran through its history although its Managing Director and General Manager disagreed on whether the firm had been quick enough in supporting smaller clients when it first moved into Western Australia.[45]

Pastoral agents were active in providing venture capital for new farming developments, particularly where trading commissions were likely to result, and in the financing of public goods since the fortunes of the agents and the farming communities were closely tied. This might involve either loan finance or investment by agents. Wright Stephenson financed a farmer's expansion into a flax-milling plant: 'the quantity of hemp they are now putting through their account will be a valuable one to us'.[46] NMA was one of several New Zealand agents that financed dairy factories. In 1882 it established a factory at Edendale in order to attract farmers into the area; the building was intended to serve as a combined factory, experiment station, and dairy school. Pitt, Son & Badgery contributed to the building of a wire bridge 'to facilitate the travelling of stock to the railway yards at Narrabri'. NZLMA supported a rail link between Rakaia and Ashburton which passed through important agricultural areas. In 1905 Murray Roberts financed G. M. Harvey on longer terms than normal: 'in order to introduce Marshall's threshing machine & traction engine into the Rangitikei District.'[47]

The breadth of financial support for industry-related initiatives is illustrated by Dalgety's support for the establishment of the Veterinary Science Faculty at the University of Melbourne in 1959. The tradition of such support is reflected in the scepticism of the Managing Director in London who observed: 'the Australian idea of automatic participation by companies . . . in such projects seems to be carried rather far' but conceded 'the need for contributing can only be seen against an Australian background'.[48] The difference between British and Australian views on this matter reflects the later economic development of Australia and therefore the absence of necessary infrastructural investment which the agents helped to fill.

However, when agents diversified lending too far beyond their specialist knowledge and expertise in the pastoral sector they often met with failure. Part of the difficulties faced by NZLMA in its early years was the breadth of activity covered by some of its loans.[49] Murray Roberts faced serious problems when it began to diversify its loan portfolio in the early 1890s into overseas trading. In 1890 it took on the account of Goodwin & DeLisle, traders in the South Sea Islands, noting: 'we have the utmost confidence in both these men'. By 1894 this account's indebtedness had grown to £6773 and Murray Roberts was intent on running it down. Two years later the account was noted as the 'most unsatisfactory in our books'.[50]

THE FINANCIAL STRUCTURE OF AGENTS

Firms drew on both debt and equity to fund their lending. Debentures, bank overdrafts, and customer credit balances were the main sources of debt. The structure of their liabilities affected their lending policies and varied between types of agent and over time. This discussion is focused by concentrating on data from three firms: NZLMA, Murray Roberts, and Otago Farmers.[51]

London companies which began as pastoral financiers, such as NZLMA and AMLF, were highly geared with high debt to equity ratios. Equity was, initially, quite small and used to acquire limited physical assets. The unpaid capital, which was a large proportion of subscribed capital, was used as loan security to sell debentures in London. In 1880, for example, debentures provided NZLMA with £2.6 million of funds, compared with £0.48 million from shorter-term sources. Long-dated funds enabled NZLMA to concentrate its lending on rural mortgages: the company lent £2.58 million on mortgages and £0.59 million in produce loans. After the company's collapse in 1893 and four subsequent reconstructions by 1912, it began to reduce substantially its holdings of debentures and replaced them with equity in paid-up shares to finance its national expansion of branches, a practice followed by the other companies.[52] Learning lessons from its collapse, its lending portfolio also became more diverse, concentrating more on current account overdrafts and less on long-term loans. In the course of the interwar period its lending and borrowing structure diversified further, including more extensive use of client deposits (see Figure 4.4).

Agencies which began as private firms had quite different financial structures relying initially on partner equity, bank support, and farmer creditors. At the end of the financial year 1890 (30 June) Murray Roberts had an overdraft with the Bank of Australasia of £32 808 and sundry creditors of £20 215. This was set against loans, mostly on livestock and current account, of £64 999. In addition, consignment advances of £83 717 for that year were covered by a temporary expansion of the bank overdraft. Through much of the 1880s and 1890s a pro-cyclical relationship existed between the needs of Murray Roberts' debtors and its reliance on bank support. By 1908, however, by building up its client base, Murray Roberts

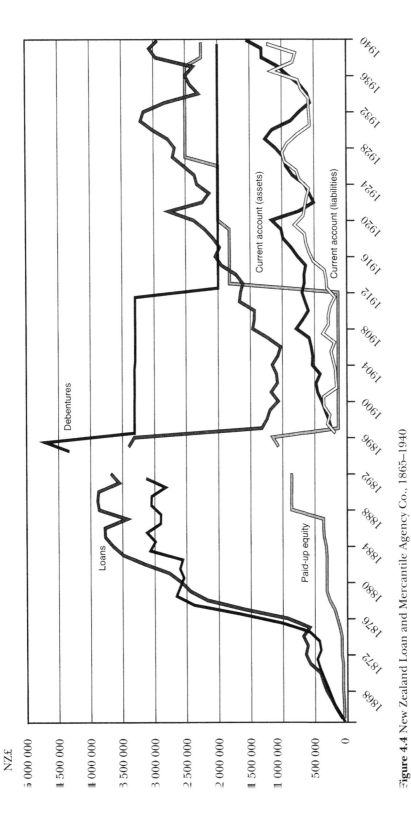

Figure 4.4 New Zealand Loan and Mercantile Agency Co., 1865–1940

Source: annual reports.

Notes: Debentures (includes 'fixed deposits' before 1875); Loans (includes 'investments' before 1875). Company restructured in 1893. No annual reports issued 1893–94.

NZ£

5 000 000
4 500 000
4 000 000
3 500 000
3 000 000
2 500 000
2 000 000
1 500 000
1 000 000
500 000
0

1868 1872 1876 1880 1884 1888 1892 1896 1900 1904 1908 1912 1916 1920 1924 1928 1932 1936 1940

Debentures

Loans

Paid-up equity

Current account (assets)

Current account (liabilities)

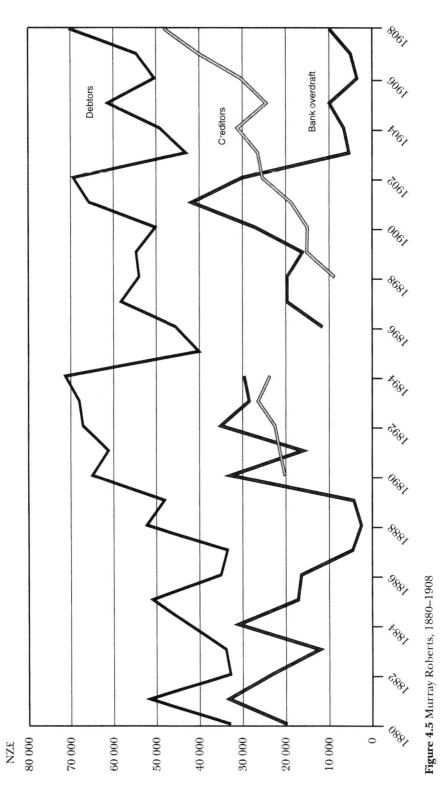

Figure 4.5 Murray Roberts, 1880–1908

Source: Murray Roberts 0575, reports and accounts.

had been able to reduce its reliance on its bank overdraft through expanding its customer credit balances (see Figure 4.5). The advantage in this shift of debt was that the bank charged 5 per cent while Murray Roberts paid 3.5 per cent to creditors. Another important advantage was enunciated by Wright Stephenson: 'if farmers with spare cash deposit it with us my experience is that they bring their business here also'.[53]

Cooperatives were somewhat different again, relying heavily on support from farmer members and avoiding long-term lending. In 1905 Otago Farmers' main sources of finance were fixed deposits of £10 706, current accounts of £9982, and an overdraft with the Bank of Australasia of £12 260. The firm regularly negotiated an annual and seasonal overdraft limit with the bank that was closely tied to the value of the unpaid capital and secured against this and the real assets of the firm. Most of its loans were concentrated on short-term produce and livestock advances. In the years of pastoral expansion before and during World War One, Otago Farmers was also able to reduce its reliance on bank support by attracting more clients' deposits. The interwar slump in primary produce prices, however, led Otago Farmers to lean more heavily on the Bank of New Zealand as its supply of funds from a now impoverished farming community fell sharply in the early 1920s. Equity had also been increased substantially in the 1920s but the firm struggled to keep its head above water, writing its £1 ordinary shares down to only 3s 4d in 1936 (see Figure 4.6).

These different financial structures had important implications for their lending policies. Heavy reliance on debenture issues removed the threat of short-term recall of loans and interference by a powerful lender. It also meant that where current rates of interest were rising the company benefited from its lower borrowing rates to undercut other financiers, as was the case for much of the 1870s and 1880s. Conversely, where short-term rates were falling, the company faced severe pressures and the prospect of borrowing at higher than prevailing loan rates. Distance as well as time could also create mismatches.[54] In 1874 the Colonial Board of NZLMA requested extra funding in order not to lose business to other lenders. Two years later, however, extensive funds were arriving from London so that the Board 'does not see its way to profitably absorb capital at the rate indicated . . . measures should be taken to check the inflow of debenture capital'.[55] By January 1879 the company was again short of funds and advising loan applicants to reapply several months later. In the 1860s AMLF was obliged to invest surplus funds in New Zealand and Tasmanian government bonds that were earning rates lower than those the company was paying for the money.[56] The conversion of debenture stock from terminable to perpetual in the 1880s and 1890s removed the risk of the debentures maturing in the middle of a crisis. The fact that Goldsbrough Mort and NZLMA had ratios of terminal to perpetual debentures of 8 and 4 respectively compared with 0.5 and 0.25 for Dalgety and AMLF was a critical factor in their 1893 suspension.[57]

The greater reliance of local firms on bank support and customer deposits avoided such mismatches in capital markets but brought alternative

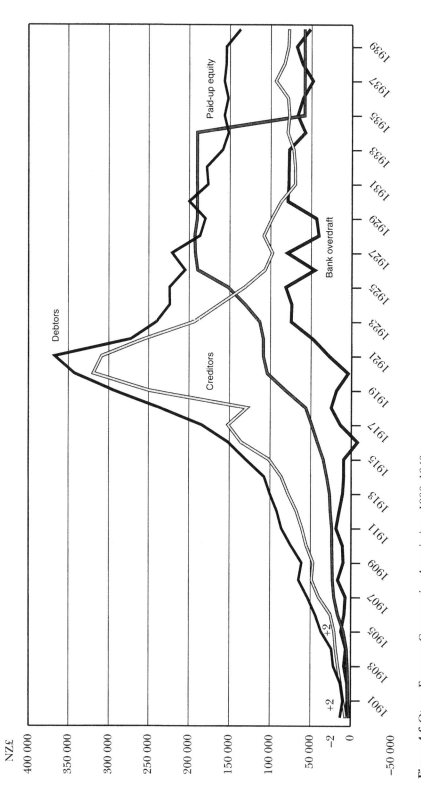

Figure 4.6 Otago Farmers Cooperative Association, 1900–1940

Source: annual reports.

challenges. The inherent risks associated with borrowing short and lending long were appreciated by Australian Estates: 'both the bank overdraft and deposits from customers are liable to be suddenly called . . . whereas advances . . . can only be got in when constituents realise wool and/or stock'.[58] This was a likely problem in either good or bad times since banks had a wide range of borrowers to serve, some of whom it gave preference over farmers. AMLF noted the opportunity to gain some customers from local agents such as Bright and Winchcombe Carson in 1913, who would find their funds squeezed by the banks. Dalgety adopted a predatory attitude towards cooperative customers for the same reason in 1955.[59] Reliance on bank lending also made agents vulnerable to policy intervention which could create tensions between their different lending principles.

Cooperatives, with a heavy reliance on farmer creditors, were susceptible to large short-term calls on debt liabilities. In downturns they suffered from a 'scissor' effect on their assets and liabilities, with reduced deposits and increased demand for accommodation. In 1920–21 Otago Farmers' debtors rose markedly while its creditors began a sharp decline. Time deposits of three to five years were protected in the short term but cash on call fell from £137 000 to £85 000 in 1921–22. As a result Otago Farmers spent the following decade trying to block the decline in credit balances by increasing paid-up capital, offering higher deposit rates, and inducing employees to keep credit balances with the firm. Most cooperatives were small firms with limited equity and making further calls on farmer shareholders in difficult times was impossible. Instead, cooperatives were forced to seek support from the banks who were conscious of the competition for client deposits and might be less than cooperative. Even a large firm like Dalgety noted that the 'psychological aspect of the relationship with our bankers is extremely important'.[60] This may help explain the summary manner in which the Bank of New Zealand dealt with Otago Farmers: in March 1931 the Bank refused to provide the finance for Otago Farmers to pay a dividend to its preference shareholders and in August again pressed for a reduction of the overdraft, 'otherwise I shall have no other option but to hold up payment of the Company's paper'. Two months later the Bank forced the resignation of Otago Farmers' manager and a reduction in the directorate while also refusing to pay due deposits held with Otago Farmers, which obliged the company to renew them at higher rates of interest.[61]

LOAN SCREENING AND CONTRACT DESIGN

The suspensions of 1893, while partly a product of the inappropriate capital structures, also resulted from the agents' inexperience as lenders and adverse environmental changes. Falling wool prices in the late 1880s, combined with plentiful British finance and pastoral expansion on to marginal land in western New South Wales, required the judgement of an

experienced lender. Cain has shown that Goldsbrough Mort failed this test;
its client reporting, inspection, and accounts were all inadequate.[62] The
cathartic experience of 1893 caused a major rethink of lending strategies.
There was a shift to more clients, shorter-term loans, and the building up
of reserves. The following sections analyse the lending strategies developed
by agents after 1893.

Agents were able to gather extensive information about farmers as a
basis for assessing loan applications. Developments in office technology
(mentioned in chapter 2), improved their information acquiring and
handling capabilities. Agents developed standard printed loan proposal
forms to reduce the cost of search and analysis. The establishment of an
Information Department by Pitt, Son & Badgery in 1905 suggests careful
information processing. The records of many agents demonstrate their
detailed client information. In 1906 when the firm went public, a Special
Report on the Invercargill office of Wright Stephenson included a detailed
statement on each of its farming clients for the benefit of its new Board
of Directors.[63] The report, probably no more than a synopsis of its records,
is testimony to the extensive information acquired. It details the personality and health of the farmer, marital status and dependants, experience
and degree of success in farming, other working activities, any transactions
with competing agents, and the character of the farm including the
condition of the properties, the countryside, and the stock. In addition,
financial statements contained evidence of the current and capital
accounts of the farmer, including current and permissible levels of credit.

Board minutes demonstrate the extensive senior management input
into assessing loan applications, discussing and sifting through detailed
information for each customer.[64] In screening a loan application companies analysed a range of criteria relating to the borrower and his farm.
These included the personal circumstances, motivation, social standing,
financial position, and business acumen and experience of the applicant.
The location, condition, and history of the farm were also considered
together with the purpose for which the loan was intended. Since most
farms were family units details of all members were listed. The social and
geographic closeness of settler societies meant the social standing of a
farmer would affect his business in numerous ways. A good reputation
would enable him to rely on support from other farmers in the exchange
of advice, information, and farming equipment, and he might additionally influence wool business towards the lender.[65] A strong financial
position reduced the risk of agent losses in the case of default and might
be indicative of business acumen and experience. The agent looked closely
at the state of the farm, whether it was well maintained, free of major
infestations, appropriately stocked, and located in an area with a suitable
climate and geology and where good returns had been achieved by others.
Again this told him much about the farmer's motivation and judgement.
The agent would also need to be convinced that the loan was for an
appropriate purpose, especially as most loans were provided for the
collateral benefit of trading commissions.

Many farmers borrowed repeatedly from a particular agent which made screening easier. A farmer who had survived a previous downturn in the industry was regarded as a particularly good risk. First-time borrowing was more difficult to assess but the agent would probably still be familiar with the area, even the property, and used his skills at interpreting the farming and financial information offered. He might also send a traveller to visit the applicant or consult with local contacts, including other clients, to seek social information and a character assessment. For example, in March 1905 Pitt, Son & Badgery traveller, Taylor, recommended that the company make an advance to a sheep farmer named Potter who 'is thoroughly honest – has a splendid property – is perfectly solvent – has known him for a number of years – has no hesitation in recommending that the advance be made'.[66]

Such warm recommendations were not always accepted at face value by the Board which might request further information or simply reject the application. Where the search costs for an individual account began to rise, in smaller cases it might prove not to be worth even a stock and station agent pursuing. Alternatively, the firm could offer a short-term wool lien as a soft or low risk introduction to a new client from which to build up an opinion. Where additional costs particularly related to acquiring further personal and financial information, it might be a signal of significant riskiness. Reputable clients were generally easier to identify and had an incentive to be straight, while higher risk clients might seek to send out confusing signals.

Two additional considerations in assessing loan applications were the prospects for the industry and the current state of the agent firm itself. In prosperous periods when firms were awash with money and optimism prevailed, many proposals were supported. Firms struggled to keep up with the opportunities for new business and spent little time analysing individual applications. In 1909 Goldsbrough Mort accepted most applications.[67] Branch managers were given greater latitude which sometimes led to excess lending and directives from the Board to be more discriminating. Failure to understand the extent of foreclosure costs meant that indiscriminate boom-time policies could build up latent problems, the seriousness of which only become apparent in a downturn. Agents took a much more cautious approach to lending during downturns with their own financial position made fragile by rising client debts. This meant that each pound of new loans was more significant and justified greater expenditure in reaching a decision. In 1893 AMLF emphasised safety as its prime consideration and had refused all new loan applications in the previous year to concentrate on supporting its existing clients. However, faced with a similar crisis two decades later, and learning from previous experience, the company acknowledged that new business was still important so long as it yielded sufficient contingent returns from produce handling.[68]

Having screened out applicants it considered too risky, and assigned the remainder into one of several risk 'pools', agents offered a standard contract according to the risk category. The key items in the contract were the rate of interest, the collateral required, the term of the loan, and the volume of produce business to be handled by the agent. The rates of interest varied according to prevailing conditions in financial markets. The term of the loan was normally three to five years for advances against property, one or two years for livestock, and up to six months for seasonal outgoings. Since the main aim of most loans was to secure the produce handling business, contracts often included a stipulation that the farmer would consign his produce for sale through the lending agent. Firms had a reasonably clear ratio between the amount lent and the anticipated volume of wool business, the details of which were sometimes stipulated in the contract.[69]

With the decline of agent networks, screening processes became less effective because of reduced observation. This particularly applied to the personal and social information that affected behavioural patterns. The enduring and larger firms, however, learned how to use contract negotiation and design as an additional means of reducing their exposure to risk. They did this by varying the standard contract terms with the intention of eliciting unobserved information and a particular response from the borrower in terms of his aptitude to take risks and work harder. Thus, the agent might suggest relatively high rates of interest to all applicants. The lower risk clients, however, would want to negotiate a reduced rate or reject the offer, viewing it as likely to reduce the returns of a project expected to be successful. Both agent and client also knew that other firms might make a better offer to such clients. Clients who accepted the higher rate marked themselves as more prone to take risks and the higher rate served as an insurance premium for the agent against the greater probability of failure.[70] Willingness to accept inferior terms also suggested that the farmer had few alternative offers, thereby giving the agent insight into the risk assessments of other firms.

The growing practice of taking security on a loan also provided for greater contractual variation. In the early years of the industry most firms relied on a 'moral security', doubtless a product of the social and kinship webs of local networks. Indeed, NMA noted: 'if we attempted to ask for a proper legal security it generally resulted in the client paying us off'.[71] In the early decades of the twentieth century agents began taking security on most loans, which provided them with a stronger guarantee as they became more distant from local communities. In addition, it prevented farmers playing firms off against each other: 'competitors will not interfere with clients when they can see they are secured to another firm, and again clients cannot get credit from anyone else if it is known they are secured'.[72]

Security was often in the form of a mortgage over the item being acquired with the loan but also included life insurance policies, personal guarantees, or other tangible assets belonging to the borrower. Loans were normally made up to a maximum of about 75 per cent of the value of this security.[73] The lower risk clients were sometimes required to provide more collateral, the intuition being that this would induce greater effort from them to reduce the high personal losses that would result from failure. The higher risk applicant, though, would be offered more generous collateral terms which, by increasing his financial stake in success, would mitigate risky behaviour. Goldsbrough Mort understood this behaviour when it noted in 1894: 'where an owner has but little margin there is some temptation for him to speculate by trying experiments, by overstocking or gambling with seasons with the hope of strengthening his position by making a big hit and as he has nothing to lose if a smash should occur we will be the sufferers'.[74] In a similar fashion, shortening the loan period for low-risk clients induced harder work and lengthening among higher risks discouraged chancy behaviour.

MONITORING AND ENFORCEMENT

Effective screening and contract design increased the likelihood of successful completion of the loan, but problems still emerged with individual clients and the more general impact on risk from community-wide changes. Problem accounts cost agents dearly through internal discussion, increased monitoring, contract amendments, and capital write-offs.[75] Careful monitoring enabled problems to be addressed and palliative measures adopted at an early stage. Routine monitoring included annual report forms and six-monthly inspections.[76] Where problems were revealed companies could inform the farmer of their concerns and work with them to develop new budgets and modify expenditure patterns.

The example of an Elders client, J. E. Pick, testifies the impact an agent could have on the operations and success of a family farm. In 1934 Elders expressed concern at the heavy expenditures of Pick's five sons, two daughters, and especially his wife, 'who dominates him'. In 1941 it noted the success of its policy of installing a bookkeeper, 'who runs the station accounts and stores. In the past the storeroom was apparently open to everybody; now, even Mrs Pick has to sign for all stores and rations'. Elders considered the account now on a businesslike footing and also observed the change in interpersonal dynamics:

> [Pick is] a much happier man now that he has the reins in his own hands, and it is typical of the position that in spite of the protests from Mrs Pick he has arranged his shearing date to clash with the Port Augusta annual race meeting, presumably with a definite purpose of making it impossible for him and his wife to attend . . . to save his private pocket quite a lot.[77]

An alternative was to modify the terms of the contract. 'Should we not stir him up?' Dennys Lascelles pondered of one client who had paid no loan interest for a year.[78] This presented a dilemma to the agent, however, who on the one hand might want to send a warning to the farmer through stricter conditions but did not want to elicit a negative response leading to less effort, more risky strategies, or desperate measures. It was alleged of George Whyte of Glenledi that he 'is feathering his nest with a view to walking off the property', while Hugh McMaster of Gladstone was suspected of having sold many of the sheep over which Murray Roberts held mortgage security.[79] An increase in rates might be used to drive the farmer to another agent although such strategies were relatively transparent: 'several people have approached me with regard to our taking over their accounts from other firms . . . an indication that our rivals are embracing the favourable opportunity of "squeezing" those accounts which they consider undesirable'.[80] Where a farmer had loans with several agents some restructuring of poor accounts was inevitable and probably desirable. If the farmer had a long-term advance with one agent against the property's purchase and a shorter loan with another against restocking, the latter might raise its rate or limit accommodation to force the client on to the first lender who was also likely to have better security.[81] However, such action was constrained since the suspicion of such behaviour could lead the first mortgagee, with the superior collateral, to foreclose.

Contractual flexibility was also necessary to retain good clients against the competitive intrusions of other agents. In 1910 Australian Estates introduced a lower 5 per cent interest rate since 'competitors have offered to take business on the terms named in which event valuable business will be lost'.[82] In 1899 General Manager Niall had persuaded the board of Goldsbrough Mort to move away from a uniform rate in response to similar policies by other agents.[83]

The moral suasion of the local network could also be used to pressure a farmer to improve his performance, since the knowledge that he was in trouble could have significant negative connotations, sending warning signals through a closely knit rural community. The agent was also under pressure to behave fairly, especially if it was unclear how far the defaulter's problems were due to mismanagement or cyclical fluctuations caused by random events such as a drought. Over-zealous action might cause damage to his local reputation and lose him good client farmers. Nevertheless, agents recognised that 'going soft' on a known opportunist would send out a dangerous message to other potential poor performers and might alienate good clients.

It was in downturns that accounts most often ran into trouble and foreclosure became unavoidable. Network pressures were again a significant restraint and agents sometimes used the subterfuge of pressuring another creditor to instigate proceedings.[84] However, there were also good financial reasons why agents were hesitant to foreclose. Proceedings could be costly especially where a solicitor was required.[85] Foreclosure and sale also meant lost trading commissions. Therefore it might be better to support a defaulting farmer in the knowledge that foreclosure could still be exercised in the future. Wright Stephenson noted: 'always carry the man with you. Forced sales against the clients must do our business harm'.[86] Dennys Lascelles emphasised the financial and legal drawbacks of foreclosure: 'we won't gain anything by having the property in our hands except incurring unnecessary expense & should we sell could give a perfect title, we could also sue him at any time either for the whole or if we sold

BACKCOUNTRY SQUATTER, A.D. 1892.

Plate 4.1   The burdens of the backcountry squatter, 1892. The farmer already faced a plethora of financial, climatic and political concerns in 1892 on the eve of the worst economic, financial and natural crisis of the nineteenth century. (*Australasian Pastoralists Review*, 15 August 1892, supplement.)

for the balance due'.[87] Realisation of capital losses was a serious risk for agents whose own weakening financial status put at risk the support of banks and farmer creditors. Taking over the farm left the agent firm with additional and loss-making responsibilities. Since cyclical downturns were a key feature of agriculture many agents sought to bring their struggling clients through to better times and used this argument to maintain support among their own creditors. As Wright Stephenson noted, 'time and care will work out most if not all our accounts'.[88]

The fact that exit costs rose to such high levels during downturns had a major impact on contractual policies for existing clients. Many farmers became discouraged and the risk of opportunism increased. If the farmer's business was essentially sound, agents were sympathetic to modified loan terms through an extension of the repayment period, lower rates or a temporary cessation of repayments. The correspondence of Dennys Lascelles indicates the company's willingness to postpone loan repayments during the rural Depression of the mid-1890s. In 1897 it delayed further payment of two-thirds of a sum of interest already overdue by station holder Murdoch Buchanan after he provided details of recent progress and referees able to vouch for his past achievements in farming.[89]

Bailey has argued that foreclosure rates were lower in the 1930s than in previous downturns because of the accumulated experience of firms in handling crises.[90] During the interwar period, with the dominant firms well established and social networks waning, discriminating policies were used to maximise economic returns for the agents. In the 1930s Goldsbrough Mort, Dalgety, and AMLF moved from a two-pool categorisation of high or low risk to a three-tier system of hopeless, hopeful (reasonably safe) and sound. Discriminating against the weak accounts at this time could worsen problems of effort and honesty and was unlikely to offload the farmer on to other lenders who would be adopting conservative lending policies. Firms also distinguished drought accounts as reflecting conditions beyond the control of industrious farmers and worthy of preferential treatment.[91] A modified form of discrimination was developed with the weak accounts, when foreclosure was ruled out, being charged the lowest rates of interest or none at all. In 1932 Goldsbrough Mort had a list of clients who were receiving relief by a rate reduction or a partial debt write-off.[92] 40 per cent of Dalgety's New South Wales clients did not meet all their financial commitments to the firm in 1931. By giving some encouragement to these accounts it was hoped that the goodwill and financial leeway would encourage economy and industriousness by the farmer and enable the business to be kept in a good condition.[93]

Firms were less clear about their Depression policies towards hopeful and sound accounts. Dalgety in 1931 suspended all interest payments on hopeless accounts, required partial payment by hopeful, and full payment by sound but remained sensitive to the injustice: 'at a time when thoroughly deserving clients require every assistance, the company's funds should be in the hands of undeserving clients'.[94] In fact, Dalgety may have been less altruistic and more concerned not to lose good clients if word got back to them. As AMLF noted: 'the relationship between many of our clients, and a number of them residing on properties adjoining . . . makes . . . differentiating in the interest rates . . . a somewhat dangerous one'.[95] However, the atrophying of local social networks together with the incentive for beneficiaries of the differential system to remain quiet, probably overrode such concerns. AMLF and Goldsbrough Mort discriminated their interest rates in favour of the best and worst accounts leaving the hopeful ones to pay the full amount and noting, 'we are not prepared to lose business we value on a question of rate'.[96] The error of calling up good accounts for the sake of liquidity in a slump was also recognised, retrospectively, by NZLMA.[97]

Agents thus accepted the need to make major concessions to struggling clients and in most cases attempted to persuade other creditors, most of whom had no trading business to protect, to do likewise rather than take the action of foreclosing.[98] Agents spent much time during downturns acting as a farmer's advocate in negotiations with mortgagees. They put forward the compelling argument that no one would benefit from fore-closure. Since an agent was often one of the creditors this gave them greater leverage in debt negotiations, persuading banks and other mortgagees to face up to inevitable interest suspensions and debt write-offs. In 1893 Goldsbrough Mort, under enormous financial pressure, wrote to the Bank of New South Wales pleading forbearance with farmers: 'we are straining every nerve to keep our customers going and insisting on station expenses being cut down to a minimum'.[99] NMA was also heavily involved in this role in 1933, arguing with creditors that forbearance would be rewarded with rising land values in due course, that it was closely monitoring the farmer, and had resolved with him previous mistakes.[100]

LENDING MARGINS AND PROFITABILITY

While agents had an informational advantage over banks as pastoral lenders, their often heavy reliance on the latter for funds made it difficult to relend at a competitive rate of interest. To make a profit they would have had to relend to farmers at 1 to 1.5 per cent higher than the rates at which they borrowed the money in order to cover the administrative costs of the loan. To compete, therefore, the agents concentrated on collecting com-missions from produce handling and used loans as a way of tying farmers to consign with them. In most cases, therefore, they accepted a loss on their loans. This point is stressed repeatedly by the firms. Pitt, Son & Badgery and Goldsbrough Mort both borrowed from the Bank of New South Wales at margins insufficient to cover the cost of relending. UMA, in com-paring its borrowing and lending rates, noted: 'the difference of interest is not enough to pay for the risk . . . [but] we are always prepared to take up business at current rates of interest . . . it is not so much the interest on the advance but the wool selling business which goes with it which is prof-itable'.[101] Information from agents suggests they may have been relending bank money at 1 per cent higher. Dalgety's Managing Director, M. D. Hunter, in a detailed assessment of the firm's pastoral lending in 1960, suggested that allowance must also be taken of the incidence of interest suspensions and capital write-offs that could raise the break-even differ-ential to an average of 3.25 per cent.[102]

Agents added their income from wool and other commissions to the interest accruing on the loan to calculate an overall rate of earnings on the capital directly employed for each client. Details from a cohort of twenty-five clients of Australian Estates for the mid-1920s illustrates how this worked. Virtually all of them were charged interest of 7 per cent on their advances. On top of this the company earned commissions aggregating to a further 3.8 per cent of the capital employed (wool 2.9, livestock 0.6, produce 0.13, and insurance 0.12). Assuming that the company paid 1 per cent less for the funds than it received, the net rate of return on capital was 4.8 per cent. The total rate of return on capital varied significantly between these clients from a probable loss-making 7 per cent to a highly profitable 31 per cent, confirming the importance of careful risk selection.[103]

An alternative way of looking at the question is to see the loss on a loan absorbed by the agent as a subsidy to venture capital for farmers, which was recovered as they developed their business through the payment of handling commissions. If all went to plan the agent's loss on the loan decreased as the capital was reduced and the commissions increased with the development of the client's business, reaffirming the importance of long-term relations. These arguments lend weight to Butlin's intuition that the system of lending 'gave the pastoral industry a critical advantage over other expanding industries . . . assured supplies of funds at considerably lower rates of interest'. He estimated that advance rates in pastoralism were 3 per cent lower than the other major sectors in the 1860s, 2 per cent in the 1870s and 1.75 in the 1880s.[104]

Hunter's pessimistic assessment of these practices suggests Australian Estates was making no profit from its lending and commission business. The interwar years were bad ones for the industry and Hunter recognised that negative lending margins had been widening during the twentieth century and, like other aspects of agent business, had reached a critical stage by the end of the postwar boom. The interest rate differential from borrowing in London was narrowing and by 1930 was no longer profitable.[105] Client deposits were cheaper but risky and competed with the banks, while shareholder funds were becoming more costly due to rising corporate taxes.[106] Dalgety's reignited a debate over the merits of long-term lending which had been raging intermittently in the company for over a century. Reminding his Australasian managers that wool business could be obtained either by financing secured accounts or offering outstanding service to free clients, Hunter accused them of favouring the former too strongly and noted that secured accounts were not so secure because 'a sense of obligation tends to magnify any grievance'.[107] The Australian managers denied unduly favouring secured accounts and pointed out that the rising level of financial support was unavoidable because of seasonal cycles and the withdrawal of bank lending. They also retorted that finance was still the most potent factor in winning new business although service was important in retaining them, and that free clients took a great deal of looking after! Goldsbrough Mort was in a similar reflective crisis noting that its need was to raise additional finance simply to defend its market position, and rehearsed the options for acquiring such funds.[108] As in other areas of their operations, therefore, concentration on a single, volatile industry brought high risks, strong competition, and regular policy swings as each managerial generation repeated the experiments and debates of its forerunner.

CONCLUSION

This chapter has traced the development of agent lending and shown that agents rarely made an economic profit from it but engaged in the practice for the collateral benefits of the ensuing wool and stock handling commissions. This enabled competitive interest rates to be offered. The problem of rationing credit to small firms about whom little was known was overcome by a mixture of agent expertise and low-cost information acquired in the course of various service activities. Networking features helped mitigate opportunism in loan contracts and when these systems declined in the twentieth century agents learned how to use contract negotiation to elicit unobserved information and behaviour, and discriminating terms to overcome problems in completing the contract term.

The widely held perception that agents were loyal to their clients during the many severe cyclical downturns at significant risk to themselves is upheld. This loyalty was partly driven by network obligations in early colonial settlement but had more to do with financial imperatives as the firms did not wish to lose the trade of farmers. Lenders are often criticised for financing those clients most likely to repay the full loan rather than those with the best overall prospects.[109] However, the pastoral agents are largely free of this charge since their lending decisions were based on a broader consideration of the prospects of the farmer's business due to the ongoing trading relationship between the two parties. In this sense, therefore, the agents probably filled the role of social accountants quite effectively, sending out mostly accurate signals about the business acumen and performance of individual farmers. This important developmental role is also reflected in their provision of infrastructure and support of new initiatives.

CHAPTER FIVE

Marketing Services: Livestock, Land, and Produce

The marketing of land, livestock, wool, and other produce was a central part of the business of pastoral agents. Marketing services, especially the sale of wool, was their main source of income, justifying the provision of loss-making financial and information services. It involved undertaking or arranging a series of linked activities including transport, storage, insurance, classification, display, and sale. Isolation and the industrious demands of farming made it difficult for farmers to find a good market without assistance. In this and the following chapter it is argued that agents filled this need by using their network influence, financial, informational, and organisational capabilities to find much better markets for farmers than the local and private transactions made by the earliest pioneers.

MARKETING THE FARM

Marketing was a difficult task for all but the largest farming enterprises. The long distances and poor communications made the costs of individual marketing prohibitive. Wool and refrigerated foods were especially difficult to sell since buyers were less common locally and more specialised in their needs than were consumers of fresh food produce. Effective selling also required farmers to have a close understanding and up-to-date knowledge of movements in volatile markets, something difficult to achieve from isolated homesteads.

Agents were well placed to relieve the farmer of marketing functions, which they did in three ways. They used their resources to undertake many marketing tasks, yielding scale economies and developing specialist expertise in the process. Second, for more specialised tasks, they used their size, market power, and friendly network connections to negotiate improved terms, for example, for freight rates, insurance premiums, and overseas selling charges. Finally, their access to a wide range of market knowledge and accumulated expertise provided them with strong powers of judgement which they used in deciding how, where and when to sell the farmer's produce and additionally advised him about future production and marketing. As one contemporary noted in the 1880s: 'the opinions of such houses are often very valuable as to which way the market is likely to go'.[1]

While the network originally provided some reassurance that the agent would market his goods in the farmer's best interests, other aspects of the transaction reinforced this belief. The payment of a percentage commission on the sale price encouraged agents to secure the highest price for their produce rather than choose the cheapest or most convenient method of sale. Significantly, marketing commissions were their main source of agent earnings and profit. After several decades of postwar diversification this remained the case: in 1958, 76 per cent of Goldsbrough Mort's earnings in Melbourne came from livestock (24 per cent) and wool (52 per cent) commissions.[2] Agent-lending on the transaction reinforced their vested interest. Finally, by acting solely as brokers and consignors and not dealing this promoted fair and objective treatment.

Generally, firms became involved in handling both wool and livestock, recognising that production and marketing synergies linked these activities. Since sheep constitute a form of capital stock for wool production, changes in the price of the latter will affect demand for the former. Thus, a rise in wool prices will stimulate the demand for sheep.[3] This impact can be disproportionate since a small increase in the demand for wool will require a farmer to purchase new sheep to meet this extra demand as well as the normal replacement of sheep lost through natural causes.[4] Clients who regularly sold their clip through a particular agent were most likely to turn to the agent for help in the periodic purchasing or selling of livestock in response to wool market fluctuations, particularly where such sales were undertaken in response to anticipated changes in the market advised by the agent. This causality works best for the purchase of store stock for wool and fat stock for the meat market, rather than bloodstock for breeding.[5] Bloodstock is more strongly influenced by longer-term changes in the conditions of supply and demand, such as the increased popularity of long wool fibres for worsted clothing or the development of refrigeration techniques for the overseas sale of meat.

Dalgety emphasised the reverse causality that 'wool business follows stock business' and that livestock auctions were 'a necessary adjunct to a prosperous wool business'.[6] While wool auctions were held in the major ports and cities, livestock auctions were more localised in rural communities. This provided closer contact between farmers and agents as Dalgety noted in 1943: livestock is the 'first line of contact between the client and Company . . . through that department our old wool associations are preserved and new wool business secured'.[7] In 1954 the decline of Levins' wool business was attributed by part-owners, NMA, to its absence from livestock auctions.[8] In addition, the purchase of valuable livestock through an agent generated trust in the honesty and knowledge of that agent. Thus, the contact and reputation initiated in the sale of the capital asset was important in generating a subsequent long-term income flow for the agent from handling the product of that asset.

Marketing synergies extended to property sales. As a more illiquid asset than livestock, the demand for land and property responded to severe or sustained changes in the price of farming products. By arranging the sale of a property to a farmer the agent would again use that initial connection to obtain longer-term trading relations, especially where he was familiar with the farm and could offer advice and assess its prospects. The sale of previously unfarmed land could also provide long-term opportunities. It was recognised as a way of attracting a large share of new settlers in Western Australia to the firm together with gaining good publicity and kudos.[9]

The ability of agents to influence the marketing decisions of individual farmers depended on their segmentation into different types of customer. Financially encumbered ('tied') clients with mortgages were normally expected to transact their wool and livestock business with the lending agent. Others sought only short-term seasonal accommodation but would be heavily influenced by the lender who would expect to handle the sale and use the proceeds to clear the debt. Instead, it was the 'free clients' who were particularly targeted by the marketing strategies discussed above.[10] An example of their importance can be seen by Winchcombe Carson's estimate that 19 per cent of its wool commissions at Longreach came from free clients. Since losses were often incurred on loans the free clients were effectively cross-subsidising the tied, and therefore firms were prepared to incur extra costs on some livestock trading to attract free clients.[11] Because free clients could choose between agents they had a higher price elasticity of demand for their services. This had become a potent issue by the early twentieth century as network loyalties between farmer and client weakened and periodic brokerage rate wars were fought over this group.[12]

Scope economies existed in the joint provision of these marketing services through use of the same information and expertise, negotiating with the same network partners, dealing with the same farmers, and finally through the use of similar selling techniques. Land, livestock, and produce could be sold either by auction or through private contract. Agents were strong advocates of centralised selling through the auction system in preference to private contracts. Centralised selling produced lower total costs above a certain level of sales by introducing fixed, or set up, costs that reduced the variable cost of each transaction. These fixed costs included the wool stores, auction rooms, publicity, and specialised handlers such as woolclassers. Auctions increased competition and choice by bringing together more sellers and buyers and enabled prices to reflect more accurately the variety and quality of products.[13] Inspection was facilitated and expert advice on hand. It also kept farmers in close contact with current prices and market demand and attracted attention from the media. The main advantage of a private sale was quicker realisation if an auction was not imminent but it involved agents in time-consuming personal visits and correspondence with the buyer and seller.

LIVESTOCK

Functions of Livestock Marketing

Agents particularly sold sheep and lambs together with good numbers of cattle and pigs.[14] The main marketing functions included providing a suitable saleyard, publicity, livestock handling (including negotiating transport, insurance, and paddocking), conducting the sale, and arranging for payment including deduction of their commission.[15] Agents also offered their expert advice on related matters such as when to trade livestock in response to changes in produce markets, or as a means to ensure optimum stocking and debt levels.[16] Although they provided general advice on the condition of livestock, they did not undertake the range of classing tasks that were a common feature of the wool sales. This would have involved extensive inspections at short notice, and farmers attending the auction could form their own judgements.[17] For more expensive bloodstock the selling breeders mitigated the contractual uncertainty, as Elders noted: '[they] are different to ordinary stock sellers . . . in their case everything depends on reputation'. Moreover, if there were any subsequent disputes between buyer and seller, it enabled the agent to act as an objective mediator rather than be a party to the dispute.[18] This most often occurred where an animal died shortly afterwards or was subsequently revealed as having been pregnant.[19]

The Development of Livestock Auctions

While agents sold livestock both privately and at auction, the latter appears to have become more popular over time, bearing out its competitive advantage.[20] Although livestock sales were more volatile and grew less rapidly than those for wool, their expansion enabled auctions to be held regularly, often monthly, at many sites, and to be specialised by animal type and use (store, stud and fat). Extensive statistical data is not available for wool auctions but periodic figures bear out these conclusions. Figures recorded by Elders for Adelaide between 1913 and 1952 indicate that in spite of the depressed interwar market and highly volatile movements in stock sales the secular trend was sharply upwards: 1939 total animal sales were 71 per cent higher than those for 1918. Sales took a further leap upwards during World War Two, reaching double their 1913 level in 1944, before falling back sharply in the late 1940s and early 1950s.[21]

In Adelaide private sales constituted around 30 per cent. Although the agent knew many potential buyers and sellers who could be contacted for a private sale, it was still likely to be a more costly transaction than through the auction so long as a good crowd of buyers and sellers could be attracted. Transactional uncertainties arose from private sales where the farmer gave instructions to more than one agent or additionally placed a newspaper advertisement. With poor communications this could create confusion over double sales and disputes regarding commissions. Hepburn Leonard warned against these practices as early as 1864, noting it was

Table 5.1 Adelaide livestock sales, 1913–1952

Year	Total	Growth index	Elders (%)	GM (%)	Dalgety (%)	Bennett Fisher (%)
1913	826 186	100	27	25	11	10
1914	834 691	101	30	19	10	13
1915	640 647	78	33	19	16	13
1916	553 977	67	26	18	14	18
1917	775 279	94	25	26	9	16
1918	744 959	90	34	19	9	14
1919	1 003 387	121	34	19	12	13
1920	1 072 598	130	29	16	10	19
1921	999 728	121	30	17	11	19
1922	1 115 641	135	25	20	11	19
1923	897 154	109	28	20	11	18
1924	825 644	100	26	22	11	19
1925	954 545	116	27	23	9	19
1926	1 016 540	123	26	22	10	18
1927	1 080 132	131	26	22	10	18
1928	1 103 538	134	27	21	10	16
1929	1 037 715	126	25	22	9	18
1930	1 026 764	124	25	24	11	17
1931	1 092 210	132	26	22	14	17
1932	1 015 108	123	24	22	12	19
1933	1 234 760	149	26	22	11	18
1934	1 233 617	149	28	23	10	17
1935	1 236 247	150	26	24	9	18
1936	1 319 946	160	24	21	9	18
1937	1 210 944	147	25	22	10	20
1938	1 292 330	156	27	23	10	18
1939	1 272 590	154	26	23	10	18
1940	1 342 545	162	27	21	10	16
1941	1 325 696	160	24	22	10	18
1942	1 380 548	167	22	21	12	19
1943	1 369 607	166	26	15	11	19
1944	1 659 159	201	25	20	11	18
1945	1 148 871	139	26	18	9	18
1946	1 042 337	126	25	21	9	18
1947	1 037 680	126	27	21	8	17
1948	1 202 025	145	25	21	9	18
1949	1 332 282	161	25	21	8	18
1950	1 243 928	151	25	21	9	19
1951	1 036 113	125	25	20	10	19
1952	1 262 378	153	24	23	9	16

Notes: Figures for GM, 1913–24 are BSL before its acquisition.
Source: Elders N102/252, Adelaide stock numbers.

unwise to handle sheep that were also being advertised in the newspaper, adding: 'should two agents sell on the same day endless confusion and litigation would arise'.[22] Private sales were more common and less of a relative cost disadvantage when a farmer was seeking a specific breed or where local conditions, such as drought, necessitated purchase from another area.

The expansion of livestock auctions was led by the larger stock and station agents. In one case the combined share of Dalgety, Elders, and Goldsbrough Mort in 1939 was in excess of 90 per cent.[23] In the more extensive Adelaide figures we can see that in most years there were eight to ten selling agents. Elders, confirming its South Australian domination, was the leading seller in each year averaging between a quarter and a half of all sales. Combined with Dalgety and Goldsbrough Mort the three firms accounted for a market share of 50 to 70 per cent. By combining the figures for Adelaide stock and wool sales it can be seen that the same agents dominated both types of auction.[24] While there were one or two small local agents represented only at the stock sales, all the main woolbrokers also sold livestock, confirming the notion that marketing synergies existed.[25] Therefore, it would not be surprising to see a similar pattern of regional expansion from State to State in livestock selling to that identified for wool auctions (see chapters 2 and 6). The belated development of livestock auctions in Western Australia, as for wool, is suggested by comments about the poor quality of livestock unimproved by the influence of a competitive market and the specialist advice from agents that accompanied it. Elders noted in 1903: 'very little attention has been paid to breeding and a more mongrel class of sheep or cattle would be hard to imagine'.[26]

While their broad pattern of expansion across Australasia may have been similar, wool auctions were centralised at major port cities, while livestock auctions were numerously spread across the main pastoral localities. Their decentralised proliferation can be seen from the experience of Elders who in 1913 participated in livestock auctions in Adelaide and a further sixteen towns across South Australia.[27] Thus, there were more livestock saleyards in South Australia than wool auctions in the whole country. The greater transportation costs of animals compared with wool, the direct participation of farmers as buyers and sellers, and the fact that most transactions were between locals explain their proliferation. The potentially high fixed costs of having many auction sites were mitigated by joint saleyard ownership or leasing between firms.[28] In 1910 the saleyard at Broken Hill was jointly owned by Elders, Bagot Shakes & Lewis, and Dalgety. It appears generally that the larger firms were more often involved in ownership.[29]

Taming Market Volatility

The volatile demand for livestock due to its capital good nature led to strong vicissitudes in the livestock market with some severe falls in prices and profitability. In 1893 UMA referred to 'the great depression in the market for sheep and cattle – sales being extremely difficult and prices at a very low point'.[30] The subsequent drought made matters far worse within a few years. In 1907 livestock values were again low because of the impact of the American financial crisis and a further drought.[31] Likewise, between the wars agents referred to the low prices and depressed state of the livestock market in a number of years.[32] Unlike most other forms of capital assets, however, livestock is reproducible which means that the total volume of such investment can expand rapidly without this being clearly signalled through the marketplace. In addition, both buyers and sellers of livestock are mostly farmers, which will accentuate shifts in the market as they are influenced by the same sentiments. Thus, when wool prices are low there will be few buyers of sheep and an increase in the number of farmers trying to sell, some of them in quite desperate straits and trying to realise on these assets, thus creating a 'scissors' or double effect. Similarly, when wool prices are good there will be many livestock buyers but few sellers.[33] Since most auction transactions occurred amongst buyers and sellers from the vicinity, any localised shocks would be felt intensely. Finally, where the influence on the livestock market comes from within the farming sector the impact will be most severe.

The conjoining of a number of these factors explains the severe downturn in the livestock market in the 1890s. In particular, the financial crisis led to pressure on farmers to reduce their debts by selling some of their livestock, while the prolonged drought in eastern Australia forced many farmers to try and sell animals because of the high cost of maintaining them, particularly with fodder prices rising.[34] The building up of their livestock numbers over several decades by many farmers exacerbated the problems, a practice encouraged by buoyant demand from new settlers and the fact that reproduction was a simple way of increasing relatively liquid capital assets.[35]

Stock and station agents played an important role in the recovery from the 1890s and in the search for longer-term solutions to market volatility. Their broad-ranging and long-term interests in farming enabled them to give good and objective advice that was not orientated towards particular lending or trading interests. Although they often advised selling in the early part of a drought, more severe policies followed. In the 1890s they advised farmers to kill livestock even though the agents might have had a financial interest in it and would lose the opportunity of a sale. In a prescient and sagacious statement in 1895 Goldsbrough Mort's colonial adviser, Horsfall, argued that it was in the best interests of pastoralists to cull:

> As there seems a probability of a prolonged drought over the greater portion of NS Wales . . . owners and managers . . . in the affected areas should . . . kill [sheep] before being shorn . . . the expense of shearing is avoided and more is secured . . . at the same time the runs are being relieved of stock unprofitable to feed in time when both grass and water are valuable.[36]

As well as saving on shearing and fodder costs, this cathartic shakeout enabled periodic readjustment against the tendency of farmers to overstock cumulatively.

Sheep were also allowed to die during droughts as a form of natural selection. In 1897 UMA was optimistic about agreeing stock reductions because most of the losses were of old and weak animals, and lambing rates among the survivors had been good.[37] The survivors' higher fecundity levels and survival ability also meant such animals would yield improved relative prices as the quality premium rose during difficult periods.[38] The knowledge that these strategies mitigated some of the worst effects and positioned farmers well to take advantage of opportunities to sell or breed with good livestock at the end of the drought made agents more inclined to continue with financial support. In addition, they used this knowledge to advocate continued support of farmers by other creditors (see chapter 4).

As the drought drew to a close agents adjusted their advice, recommending the purchase of livestock. Frequently, this involved further financial support which stretched the resources of agents who had made little or no profits themselves. Judging whether the drought had finished was difficult in itself, pre-emptive policies could end in disaster if it continued, while waiting too long left farmers paying high prices to restock. These were the challenges facing agents in 1902 when the long drought drew to a close. By 1903 livestock prices had risen beyond the level of affordability of many farmers for whom natural increase was the only option.[39]

The experience of disasters like the 1890s led agents and farmers to seek more permanent ways of mitigating the impact of drought on livestock. Transhumance, the movement of livestock for grazing purposes, was a possible palliative solution but droughts tended to cover quite large areas making the cost and availability of transport a barrier.[40] However, the development of fodder areas to build up supplies in times of plenty was more widely broached.[41] On the farm, agents encouraged better stock management techniques including smaller paddocks to reduce stock movement and distances to water supply, improved fodder storage, and the development of water bores. Mixed farming reduced exposure to livestock crises and encouraged fodder production on the farm. The two major long-term solutions to the problem of volatility in livestock markets arose from the 1890s crisis: they were the development of improved breeding and alternative livestock products.

Livestock Breeding and Products

The drought illustrated the survival abilities and higher relative values of better livestock. Improved breeding also provided a way of increasing yields without overstocking. As a result livestock auctions increasingly featured stud stock. By 1895 Elders was conducting an annual stud ram sale and noted that these were becoming more popular each year as farmers began to recognise the importance of flock improvement.[42] Although the market in stud stock would never match that for store or fat stock there was sufficient need for specialised knowledge and handling for several firms to develop a particular interest in it and to foster the bloodstock business. This development was particularly important in New Zealand where Wright Stephenson became the dominant company handling bloodstock. By the

Plate 5.1 Glentanner Station, Canterbury, New Zealand. Set in the foothills of the Southern Alps, this station exemplifies the remoteness of New Zealand sheep farmers from their markets, financial backers and equipment suppliers. (By permission of the National Library of Australia.)

1920s it was importing and exporting agents for pedigree stock, and was sending specialists overseas to observe and to display New Zealand breeds in international shows.[43]

As attention focused on breeding improvements greater thought went to widening the types of animal breed particularly where it diversified the products they yielded. While farmers had learned that boiling down to produce tallow and the canning of meat helped to combat an oversupply of sheep, these alternative products were limited by the value and size of their market.[44] The major breakthrough in alternative products came as a result of the introduction of refrigeration in the 1880s. Thus, dual-function sheep became more highly valued because of their flexibility to changing product markets. Crossbreds such as the Polwarth and Corriedale, with their ability to produce both wool and meat, expanded rapidly during the 1890s drought, their share of the Australian sheep population jumping from 32 to 52 per cent in 1895–1904.[45] However, there were many uncertainties at first. The wool was coarser and crossbreds were better suited to some climates than others, particularly the wetter, cooler conditions of Victoria and New Zealand where they resisted footrot better than merinos. The agents gauged emerging views on crossbreds through their clients. Goldsbrough Mort, for example, wrote to its farmers in 1895 asking their opinion on the popularity and suitability of these breeds in their area.[46]

The success of the dual-purpose sheep in countering the uncertainty and slowdown of livestock markets was celebrated by agents. Elders noted in 1908 that 'the outlet of sheep suitable for freezing may save the value of store sheep'. Goldsbrough Mort believed fat stock had put new life into the livestock auction system.[47] Winchcombe Carson, however, offered a word of caution: 'the man who breeds for crossbred wool, abandons the class of staple which can be grown nowhere to such perfection as in Australia, in favour of a commoner grade which is being produced in immense quantities in various other parts of the world'.[48] Such assessment was valuable in helping the further development and refinement of new breeds such as 'comebacks', which involved breeding back towards merinos while retaining the dual function. In fact, while the expansion of crossbreds was inevitable in light of the benefits, the long-term trend maintained the merino as the largest single group of sheep in Australia.[49]

Charges and Costs

These changes in livestock selling provided farmers with regular, localised, and specialised auctions. The impact on the profitability of the agents may have been less positive. In chapter 6 there is a detailed discussion of the cost-price squeeze suffered by the agents in their main income-generating activity of wool selling. Less is known about livestock sales but the problem of falling profit rates seems to be relevant here. Earlier in the chapter it was shown that some livestock sales made little profit and were used to attract more wool clips. In 1932 the NZLAAA claimed that livestock prices were no higher than in the late nineteenth century but the cost of service provision had risen by 200 per cent.[50] Falling commission rates also afflicted livestock sales.[51] Rates varied somewhat between auctions but appear to have been about 4 to 5 per cent in the late nineteenth century but subsequently fell to around 2.5 to 3.75 per cent with increased competition, especially from cooperatives. For example, Otago Farmers forced down commission rates in Otago to 2.5 per cent by the early twentieth century.[52] Agents also found themselves periodically at loggerheads with banks, who demanded a share of the commission where the seller was financed by a bank. However, the localisation of sales mitigated the problem of local dealers attempting to mediate in sales, a problem that plagued wool auctions.

It is not entirely clear what were the sources of the increased selling costs. Most likely they were the fixed or overhead costs incurred as agents increased the number of saleyards in which they had an equity interest. The segmentation of the market into stud, store, and fat stock may have increased costs by breaking down some scale economies.[53] It also threatened to raise transaction costs as agents found themselves dealing with new and relatively unfamiliar groups of butchers, freezing works, and animal breeders in contrast to the farmers with whom they already dealt extensively. When the interwar slump hit the industry the agents sought to minimise their overheads through greater resort to joint saleyard ownership or

Plate 5.2 A stock and station agent's country office. The local office was the first, and often the only, connection for farmers with the wider world of business and international pastoral markets. (Dalgety and Company Limited, Jubilee souvenir booklet, 1934.)

Plate 5.3 A country saleyard. Local livestock auctions brought agents into closer contact with their farming clients and helped them to win more wool clips. (Dalgety and Company Limited, Jubilee souvenir booklet, 1934.)

leasing; by World War Two NZLMA solely owned only one and jointly owned three saleyards of thirteen in the Waikato region, the rest being leased.[54] However, while companies were good at sharing infrastructural costs, over-competition still occurred. At one Dunedin livestock sale in 1930 'there were half a dozen auctioneers, a great number of agents; one cow was put up for auction but not sold'.[55] New Zealand firms then experimented with the formation of a joint venture company to organise auctions. The Associated Livestock Auctioneering Company was formed in 1931 and expected to achieve a 30 to 40 per cent reduction in overheads. However, the operation still lost money and was closed in the following year.[56]

Prices recovered in the postwar period and thus deflected attention from some of these problems. However, a further collapse of livestock prices in the 1990s facilitated the introduction of computer-assisted

Plate 5.4 Livestock auctions in town and country. Refrigeration stimulated metropolitan fat stock markets in addition to the traditional rural store stock auctions. (*Elder's Directors' Report*, 30 June 1957.)

livestock marketing. Exploiting the flexibility of information technology has wrought a fundamental change in favour of remote livestock sales and perhaps, more than ever, traders will rely on the advice and reliability of selling agents.

LAND

The role of agents in the sale of land and property included publicity, advice, conducting the auction, and providing or arranging finance for the buyer. For private sales, negotiation over price and other conditions was an important part of their work. Since there were fewer benefits from localisation and buyers might be distant from the property, private sales were comparatively more important than in wool and livestock disposals.

Thomas Mort was one of the pioneers of station auctions in about 1848, and he was followed by other agents as a market in rural land and property developed among the second generation of settlers after the land grants.[57] The increasing resort to rural lending and the development of land tenure laws also stimulated the market. Land sales commission, however, was never a consistently large part of the income and operations of agents. Not all agents conducted land sales but rather introduced buyers and sellers to a land-selling agent through their network of contacts and with whom they shared the commission. A critical part of that role was offering advice and staking their reputation since often the buyer was remote in terms of distance and knowledge. Franklyn noted that the agents offered advice to migrants from Britain and the credibility of a large agent firm provided 'a certain guarantee against deception being practised'.[58]

The type of advice proffered particularly related to when to buy or sell and what sort of property would be appropriate. Elders, for example, recommended a client sell his property in February rather than December because more money would be around after shearing and harvesting, and the banks would be more favourably disposed to lend with seasonal debt levels in the sector falling.[59] Wright Stephenson advised clients that it was preferable to pay more for a well-established farm than to spend plenty of time and money bringing a cheaper property into working order with the risk and uncertainty which that also entailed. Such advice, they suggested, was informed by the experience of several decades in the industry.[60]

The development of new areas of settlement and new groups of settlers provided opportunities for agents to offer their property services. Goldsbrough Mort, Elders, and Dalgety competed with each other to extend land settlement and rural production in Western Australia from the late nineteenth century. Dennys Lascelles played an active role in the development of agriculture in the Mallee in the 1890s, using its network contacts such as shipping lines to publicise land sales on board ship and in British newspapers.[61] Agents were also actively concerned with bringing small farmers on to the land with the subdivisions of the late nineteenth century and in helping returning soldiers establish themselves. Involvement in land sales additionally occurred when agents foreclosed on indebted clients. While agents tried wherever possible to avoid forced sales, none the less the numbers of such sales rose sharply during economic downturns such as that in the 1890s, with agents trying to judge whether it was better to incur a loss or wait for improved times though run the risk of seeing the loss increase.

PRODUCE, FARM EQUIPMENT, AND HOUSEHOLD REQUIREMENTS

The conduct of wool marketing by the pastoral agents is closely analysed in chapter 6. Although wool was the predominant commodity, the agents handled a variety of other farm products. The development of refrigeration and the expansion of dual-function crossbred livestock fostered the growth of frozen meat exports. Agents were actively involved in consignment to the European market. Refrigerated products required greater preparation in Australasia than did wool, including slaughtering, processing, freezing, and packing. Agents were closely involved in these activities either through investments in freezing works or by negotiating with freezing companies for which they received a draft fee.

Agents helped to pioneer dairy production but gradually made up their mind to avoid these accounts, local managers frequently being warned of their riskiness.[62] Instead, dairying was largely handled by the cooperatives. In 1900, 42 per cent of New Zealand dairy factories were organised as cooperatives, a figure that had risen to 90 per cent by 1925.[63] There are several explanations. The expense and complexity of the technologies required significant additional investments in know-how and finance. In spite of this, the inconsistency surrounding the more complex perishable goods remained substantial. It was noted that 'so much depends in dealing with butter as to the way in which it is prepared and the condition in which it arrives here'.[64] There was thus significant scope for opportunism by farmers in submitting their products to the dairy factory. Dairying was carried on by large numbers of small farmers working in close proximity to each other. As one contemporary noted, contact 'with fellow-farmers resulting in the recognition and expression of common interests is . . . encouraged when farmers cart their milk to the factory daily; . . . the fact that all farmers are similarly affected by the manufacturing policy provides a very definite urge to common action'.[65] Such conditions therefore suited the high levels of mutuality embodied in the cooperative, especially as the industry was expanding at a time when the local social networking of the pastoral agents was in decline.

Australian firms experimented with marketing wheat but their experiences were generally negative. Winchcombe Carson terminated its wheat marketing in 1911 and AMLF two years later because it was making a loss.[66] The sensitivity of the wheat crop to even short droughts made it a highly risky business for agents to handle at a time when they were still recovering from the fallout of the 1890s financial and climatic crises. Dalgety and NZLMA had similar results from trying to build up a wheat business between the wars. Floods had also presented problems, NZLMA noting the dangers of financing a wheat farmer 'whose crop can be destroyed in one night'.[67] Instead, wheat farmers sold much of their grain in private transactions, either directly to millers or to merchants before the establishment of the Australian Wheat Board in 1939. Merchants were regarded with suspicion by growers since they dealt in the crop, unlike agents, and were perceived as acting more in the interests of powerful foreign buyers than of the farmer. By the 1920s wheat farmers favoured government-controlled marketing.[68]

Farm equipment and materials were also handled by agents. In the case of farm equipment this was normally on a commission basis as an intermediary. With smaller items that were in more regular demand, such as fertilisers, seeds, fencing, and small tools, agents more commonly bought stocks of these goods for resale to the farmer. The strong competition from bulk-buying cooperatives and the relatively small markets in some of these goods meant that several of the larger agents specialised in their provision, buying larger volumes to gain economies of scale and reselling wholesale to other agents. In New Zealand, NMA was the dominant handler of jute goods such as woolsacks.[69] In the nineteenth century agents normally acted as the local handlers for imported equipment and materials. However, increasingly they supported its substitution by local production as being more convenient and reliable, sometimes backing this up with investment in a local manufacturer. In 1907 Elders decided that local superphosphate production reduced the risk of loss or damage in transit and farmers could obtain it at shorter notice. As a result Elders invested in the Wallaroo Phosphate Company. NMA took a similar view on local equipment, noting the saving in time and transport costs and its greater suitability to local farming conditions.[70]

Most agents stocked a wide range of general household items which they resold to farmers. Stocklists of agents included hardware, food, clothing, alcohol, and cigars. They were not always keen to provide these general goods and services which were hardly part of their core business, but the need to serve their farming market effectively was vital to secure valuable wool commissions. NMA noted in 1916: 'in some districts . . . we are forced into it by our competitors'.[71] The remoteness of many farms meant that obtaining these items was costly and therefore an agent who could provide a convenient household service was at a competitive advantage. Some even delivered goods to their more valued customers. The stock and station agent clearly was the first line of contact with the outside world for the farmer and his family.

By extending into household items, therefore, the agent was attempting to provide a one-stop service for all of the needs of the farmer and his family. Thus, 'if we could supply the man on the land with all his requirements . . . we would strengthen our chance of retaining his wool

Wool! Use more Grow more

PRICE REDUCTIONS
OF
MEGGITT'S SHEEP NUTS AND
LINSEED MEAL

To assist the Pastoralist and the Dairyman in these lean times, Meggitt Limited, manufacturers of the original pure Linseed Sheep Nuts and Linseed Meal, have substantially reduced their prices.

Now is the
time to feed
Meggitt's

Sold through all Stock and
Station Houses

MEGGITT'S
LINSEED SHEEP NUTS
MLM
MEGGITT Lᵗᵈ
ADELAIDE

ELDER, SMITH & CO., LIMITED.
Sole Selling Agents.

Plate 5.5 Elders' advertising material for supplementary sheep feed, 1930. Agents acted as a conduit and critical filter for new farming products. (*Adelaide Stock and Station Journal*, 23 July 1930.)

and stock business'.[72] Where this policy eventually broke down was when it became a full-blown strategy of unrelated diversification in an age of increasingly sophisticated and specialised consumer and industrial technology which over-extended the expertise of the pastoral agent (see chapter 2).

CONCLUSION

Agents played a central role in making a market in rural produce, live-stock, land, farming materials, and more general requirements of the homestead family. They used their external network influence to nego-tiate with other service providers (such as transport and insurance), their internal corporate competencies to undertake other tasks (such as publicity, selling, and payment), and their expertise to advise on when and where to buy or sell. The larger emerging firms tended to internalise more of these marketing functions and the smaller agents drew more extensively on network partners. Farmers benefited from the scale economies of having these tasks performed collectively by an agent, the latter also yielded scope economies across the bundle of goods marketed. Amongst those scope economies were synergies resulting from the realisation that the more services an agent provided the greater was his opportunity to secure valuable wool commissions. As we shall see in the following chapter this locked agents into an inflexible cost structure; removing any of the pieces would seriously obscure the view. Most marketing was undertaken on commission except for smallgoods where it made sense for the agent to hold stocks. Auctions were more common in livestock than land sales. However, the auction system reached its apogee in the marketing of wool.

CHAPTER SIX

Marketing Services: Wool Consignment and Brokerage

The stock and station agents brought Australian and New Zealand wool to the dominant nineteenth-century market in London. In the course of the late nineteenth and early twentieth century they played a leading role in relocating the market to Australasia which brought many immediate benefits to the growers, and, in the decades that followed, introduced various improvements to the system of wool marketing. These improvements required additional costs which, when combined with falling relative produce prices and intense competition, created a severe squeeze on profitability in the industry eventually forcing the merger movement of the 1960s and 1970s to rationalise costs, and subsequent experiments in price regulation and joint selling.

FUNCTIONS OF WOOL MARKETING

As we saw in chapter 5 the agents' role in marketing involved the provision of services, negotiating with other service providers, and furnishing expert advice. The better the deal they could obtain for their clients the greater was the likelihood that they would maintain their business in future years and perhaps extend it as word got around. Moreover, as they extended their wool handling this increased the economies of scale and further strengthened their negotiating power with shipowners and other groups.[1]

Agents handled wool clips either as consignors to foreign markets or as local selling brokers. As consignors they received the wool from the farmer, graded it, insured it, arranged for transportation to the port of shipment, temporary storage there if required, its overseas shipment, and receipt by the foreign selling broker. After the sale the agent received payment and credited the farmer with his net receipts after deducting the consignment commission, handling charges incurred, and any agreed debt repayments. Consignors might also arrange for the wool to be scoured prior to shipment, although falling freight rates in the later nineteenth century and buyer preferences eroded this activity.[2]

As local selling broker the agent directly undertook more extensive handling processes. These began at the woolshed with the initial separation out of wool in each fleece into uniform quality by the company's sorter.[3] It was then pressed into bales, branded, weighed, and dispatched to the agent's wool store. Here the wool was classed into uniform lots and carefully displayed so that it could be inspected by buyers prior to the sale. Agents took responsibility for printing and distributing catalogues as well as organising the sale itself.

OVERSEAS CONSIGNMENT

The early sales of Australasian wool occurred in a disorganised and speculative fashion. Sales were often completed by private contract in country towns or on the road into Sydney or Melbourne. Graziers were anxious for an early sale to finance their shearing expenditures. Merchants and shopkeepers bought speculatively, shipping the wool to England for resale. Some of the larger runholders arranged for direct shipment for sale in London.[4] Finally, general colonial merchants, dealing in a range of products, would sometimes arrange consignment to England. Thus, by 1818 Australian wool was being sold in London as a minor addition to European sales; by 1835 there were specific auctions for Australian wool. In the 1840s about 50 per cent of the clip was sold locally to colonial buyers and then resold in England, 10 to 20 per cent was shipped directly by larger growers, and the remaining 30 to 40 per cent was consigned to England by general colonial merchants.[5]

By mid-century many graziers looked to ship their wool to London for sale. The fact that London was the premier wool market, that Australasian wool was given greater prominence by separate auctions, and had developed an improving reputation for quality merino promised good realisation values. By the 1860s around 80 per cent of Australian wool was consigned for sale in England, mostly through stock and station agents.[6] Somewhat less is known about the New Zealand wool industry where most of the clip was also being consigned for sale in England by the later nineteenth century, some directly by large growers but mostly through agents.[7]

Movement to the London market was made possible by the provision of seasonal finance and international marketing functions. In contrast to the colonial buyers, the agents intermediated consignment in return for a commission. Table 6.1 lists the principal consignors for selected years between 1878 and 1913. Dalgety was the largest consignor from Australia, and NZLMA from New Zealand. AMLF, UMA, and NMA also played an important role. The market share of the leading agents varied between about 30 and 40 per cent, but this increases if one includes smaller agents who consigned, sometimes with the assistance of importing houses and colonial merchants. Their share was probably larger before the 1870s when

Plate 6.1   A shearing shed. The agent's involvement with the wool trade occurred at every stage starting with the removal of fleece from the sheep's back. Advice on new shearing methods and initial sorting practices was provided. (Dalgety and Company Limited, Jubilee souvenir booklet, 1934.)

the leading banks became significant consignors, including the Colonial Bank of Australasia by 1868 and the Bank of New South Wales by 1869.[8] The share of wool consignments made by those banks most committed to wool handling averaged about 10 per cent until the end of the century when it rose to almost 30 per cent.

The role of the agents in effecting wool consignment to London is easily illustrated. Of particular importance was the shipment function. Overseas shipping companies were large, powerful organisations and their operations were highly technical and involved substantial risk. The agents decided when and how to ship wool. By the late nineteenth century shippers could choose between sailing vessels and steamers, the latter being quicker but more expensive. This required a careful assessment of short-term trends in the market based on the latest information received by agents from their London office. In 1889 Dennys Lascelles recommended sail because steam rates were too high to justify the additional speed, although in 1897 UMA supported steam so shipments would arrive in time for the January sale in London at which a shortage of wool was anticipated.[9] When the market was low and expected to rise only slowly sailing vessels provided a cheaper form of transport and acted as a floating warehouse. Shippers also had to choose between liner companies which provided regular high quality services or tramps whose older irregular vessels came at a lower cost.[10]

Table 6.1 Principal London wool consignors of Australasian wool

Year	Dalgety	NZLMA	AMLF	NMA	UMA/AE	GM	ES	SM	NZAL	RA
1878	51 753	65 223	51 031		14 949			34 434	10 562	15 852
1879	65 368	83 972	58 897	16 730	16 730	12 983			9 682	17 135
1880	68 802	71 251	63 729	10 383		8 634			10 073	
1881	71 820	75 904	85 044	13 543		19 188			10 170	
1882	83 524	72 087	81 597	12 969		13 522			10 527	
1883	87 030	72 721	66 711	16 119		17 146			10 507	
1884	88 184	76 186	80 775	16 596		19 819			11 113	
1885	85 251	82 131	48 018	16 944		25 328			11 533	
1886	88 070	85 923	76 076	18 198		28 154			10 771	
1887	97 094	90 291	66 246	20 297	45 218	25 251			11 216	
1888	100 147	94 805	84 161	16 092	49 905	30 473	27 640	73 818	11 454	27 865
1889	95 230	93 118	77 912	12 473	46 005	25 157	28 896	69 282	11 509	30 461
1890	93 216	96 170	92 279	12 947	51 379	13 865	20 713	75 485	13 403	33 318
1891	118 584	124 661	92 738	17 652	52 914	38 789	30 595	97 005	15 508	24 159
1892	119 031	114 865	88 111	16 954	56 969	39 419	35 604		14 988	
1901	113 361	72 933	99 345	27 077	36 461		33 968	70 930	14 477	
1908	124 130	71 016	46 233				23 022	55 382	24 353	
1909	77 993	47 544	33 914				26 379	34 677	28 372	
1910	67 311	42 911	29 115	20 140	20 402		18 283	38 003	30 379	
1913	60 535	33 187	29 450	12 256	16 637		22 433	50 446	31 732	

Table 6.1 Principal London wool consignors of Australasian wool (cont.)

Year	SAI	BNZMA	Morrison	Brooks	BA'sia	BNSW	CBC	UBA	BNZ	Banks total	Banks (%)	Total
1878			15 870	16 214		7 305	14 178					826 357
1879	2 293		14 542	19 600	8 560	16 758	18 610			72 647	9	863 817
1880	3 447				7 806	15 414	19 298			59 758	7	931 889
1881	5 349				12 320	17 033	22 587			73 834	8	999 731
1882	3 372	5 558			16 568	16 301	18 362	737		80 451	8	990 792
1883	7 230	5 946			21 812	24 225	17 621	1 053		103 142	10	1 084 355
1884	7 236	6 814			25 042	20 919	18 366	1 769		111 318	10	1 027 723
1885	6 072	7 074			16 327	19 250	14 743	1 032		91 611	9	1 139 842
1886	7 025	7 438			25 951	22 716	22 841	8 258		121 932	11	1 116 538
1887	8 918	6 690			28 274	21 902	17 901	13 368		120 286	11	1 245 433
1888	9 425			29 593	30 100	29 827	22 019	17 202		142 457	11	1 238 679
1889	8 842			28 599	27 729	33 988	18 951	25 403		154 528	12	
1890	9 321			33 266	26 848	36 293	18 690	28 993	2 828	169 939		
1891				35 901	30 878	45 251	29 050	42 488				
1892	17 023				43 262	59 201	37 338	48 087	5 824	261 056	18	1 488 146
1901	4 777		18 182	32 933	39 010	64 792	43 084	75 760	42 506	316 231	29	1 073 292
1908			26 105		33 387	42 768		50 067	48 800			
1909			26 871		32 639	28 706		52 478	44 594			
1910			31 504		26 272	26 432		45 339	42 442			
1913			34 980		19 912	27 409		43 926	46 924			

Note: Figures are numbers of bales and may include Cape wool equivalent to c. 10 per cent of total.
Sources: Based on data in AIBR and Mortimer Franklyn, A Glance, p. 204. Data not available for private firms in all years.

Plate 6.2   A bullock team transporting wool overland. Early overland transport was slow, arduous, and required constant attention. (Dalgety and
Company Limited, Jubilee souvenir booklet, 1934.)

Choice of ship also depended on the ability of the agent to strike the
best deal, using his influence as an equity investor in, or agent for, the line,
and the market power of the amount of freight he had to offer. In 1905
Elders admitted that it sometimes handled freights not so much for the
commission but because 'it assists us in our general position in . . . shipping
circles to have as much power as possible'.[11] Murray Roberts and Williams
& Kettle used their control of Hawke's Bay pastoral output to pressure
Shaw Savill Albion to reduce its freight rates in the 1880s Depression and
to persuade Tyser to visit the area to provide competition for the other
line.[12] Dennys Lascelles coaxed overseas shipping to call at Geelong as well
as Melbourne; for example, negotiating with Federal Steam Navigation
Company for its vessel *Cornwall* to visit the port in 1897 and take in cargo
on her way to Montevideo and London.[13] Agents were also aware of the
importance of timing in contractual negotiations with shipowners, the longer
they refrained from finalising terms, in the hope of more ships arriving,
the greater the risk of being forced to accept inferior terms in order to get
the cargo out of port promptly.[14]

Effective stowage was vital to minimise delays, to maximise the cargo
carried, and to ensure the safety of the ship and its cargo. Agents took the
lead in the development and use of the hydraulic press to reduce freight
costs and storage space, and also showed an understanding of the relative
stowage characteristics of different forms of produce.[15] They had to juggle

other cost factors in loading, such as whether to use lighters to get the vessel off early, and took a close interest in port infrastructure, campaigning for regular dredging of navigation channels and advising shippers and shipowners of any problems.[16] These two great issues of stowage and navigation coalesced in their ability to advise shipowners whether specific cargo mixes would clear the port in particular ships under prevailing states of tide and harbour repair. This was especially important for some of the smaller ports like Geelong with which shipowners were less familiar and where water depth was often limited.[17]

Agents intermediated shipping disputes, responding to farmers' and buyers' complaints and investigating the matter. In 1895 Dennys Lascelles achieved a fair insurance settlement for shippers following the loss of the vessel *Timaru*. In the same year they also investigated the reasons for the slow passage of the vessel *Port Stephens* which delayed its arrival at an early market.[18] When wool reached the London market, agents provided feedback to growers about standards of wool presentation.

The contractual power of the larger agents could become a cause for concern. Shipowners reminded them of their commitments to both parties: 'it is necessary for you to draw the line between conserving your connection amongst shippers & sacrificing the steamer's interests', remarked Birt & Company in 1900.[19] Smaller local firms like Dennys Lascelles expressed concern at the ability of national agents to control the local freight market, particularly in smaller ports like Geelong.[20]

Plate 6.3 Bales of wool awaiting shipment from Sydney. Road and rail shipment facilitated much more rapid movement of larger wool volumes by the early twentieth century. (By permission of the National Library of Australia.)

THE DEVELOPMENT OF THE AUSTRALASIAN WOOL AUCTION

Local wool selling in Australasia never entirely ceased in the mid-nineteenth century. Colonial textile manufacturers continued to buy locally and some smaller growers still preferred quick realisation to the promise of higher London prices. What is striking, however, is the relocation of the wool market to Australasia from the late nineteenth century. While less than 30 per cent of local wool production was sold in Australia at the beginning of the 1880s, this rose to an average of 53 per cent in the following decade, and continued to rise sharply to 76 per cent in the first decade of the twentieth century and 93 per cent in the second. The relocation of wool sales to New Zealand occurred somewhat later and was less complete; 24 per cent was sold locally in the 1890s, rising in subsequent decades to 37 and 75 per cent respectively, and remaining around this figure by 1939. The relocation occurred earliest amongst merino wool types for which Australia had already acquired a strong reputation on the London market. By 1907, 94 per cent of the Victorian, 86 per cent of the South Australian, and 83 per cent of the New South Wales merino clip was being sold locally (see Table 6.2).[21]

The local auction system centralised earlier colonial sales by private contract. The Australian railway system provided radial connections between the pastoral areas and the nearest major port. In New Zealand coastal shipping services brought produce from the rural areas to the major regional ports. Auctions were organised at the major port cities since most wool was still bound for overseas destinations. There were eight auction centres in each country by the start of the twentieth century. Their number continued to expand in Australia to around fourteen by the 1960s. New Zealand auctions each sold far less wool and therefore growth in centres was limited, except for temporary additional wartime centres (see Table 6.3).

Melbourne dominated the early years of Australian auctions by dint of its gold rush-led expansion in the 1850s and 1860s. By the early 1890s the extension of New South Wales' railways to the Riverina, particularly Wagga Wagga from 1878, together with the expansion of the colony's river system

Table 6.2 Local and overseas wool sales, 1881–1939

Year	Australia			New Zealand		
	Total exports	Local sales	Sales/exports (%)	Total exports	Local sales	Sales/exports (%)
1881	671 063	197 272	29			
1891–1900	1 409 140	742 894	53	383 471	93 137	24
1901–10	1 415 026	1 077 379	76	424 206	158 069	37
1911–20	1 819 031	1 690 445	93	538 232	402 251	75
1921–30	2 235 756	2 098 307	94	640 633	465 997	73
1931–39	2 799 772	2 819 044	101	767 538	602 304	79

Notes: Bales, decennial averages. NZ figures from 1895.
Sources: Based on data from *AIBR* and *DAWR*.

Table 6.3 Wool-selling centres in Australia and New Zealand

Year	Australian centres	Bales per centre	New Zealand centres	Bales per centre
1901–10	8	184 260	8	28 869
1911–20	9	191 133	11	40 458
1921–30	10	207 509	10	46 732
1931–40	11	261 136	9	73 049
1941–50	12	275 897	12	75 643
1951–60	12	340 440	8	121 149
1961–70	14	363 696	8	176 116
1971–80	14	281 582	8	168 056

Notes: Ten year averages.
Sources: Based on data from *DAWR* and NZWBA.

to the Murrumbidgee, helped divert some of the Riverina wool to Sydney. In addition, the sheep population of New South Wales was growing more rapidly than that of Victoria.[22] Thus, by the 1890s Sydney had become the leading wool auction centre. In the twentieth century the stranglehold of these two cities over wool selling gradually receded with the recovery of Adelaide from the severity of the 1890s drought in South Australia and the opening of auctions at Brisbane in 1898–99 and Hobart in 1902–03.[23]

Regular auctions began in Fremantle in 1904. Previous attempts had failed to attract sufficient buyers because of the low volumes and quality of wools offered. In addition, since Western Australian wool had often been shipped via Melbourne and Adelaide to London to pick up lower shipping freight rates and more frequent sailings, most of the early local sales of the colony's wool occurred at these more established markets. It was not until World War One that 1 per cent of wool was sold at Fremantle and this was because of the wartime problems of shipping wool from Western Australia to London.[24] The tradition of overseas consignment continued for a long time and only in the post-World War Two era did Western Australian wool auctions grow substantially, placing the State as the third largest seller by the 1970s. The dispersal of sales amongst the Australian States is shown in Table 6.4. By the 1960s at least 10 per cent of national sales were completed in each of the mainland States, but none held more than a 30 per cent share.

In New Zealand wool auctions took place in Dunedin from the 1860s and Wellington by the 1870s, although the volumes sold were quite small until the 1880s. By the beginning of the twentieth century selling centres were quite broadly spread through the country (see Table 6.5). The main geographical shift was away from the south island towards the north island auctions with the relative decline of Christchurch and Dunedin and expansion of Wellington and Auckland in the first half of the twentieth century. Some recovery in the share of the south island cities has occurred in recent decades.

The local auction system was closely controlled by the leading pastoral agents. Just as the banks were increasing their share of wool consignments

Table 6.4 Regional distribution of Australian wool sales

Year	NSW	%	Vic.	%	SA	%	Qld	%	WA	%	Tas.	%	Total
1893–1900	408 700	52	306 716	39	63 566	8	19 030	2		0			783 740
1901–10	566 786	53	347 742	32	88 305	8	61 108	6	1 213		16 495	2	1 077 379
1911–20	725 906	43	480 826	28	150 935	9	262 407	16	48 266	3	26 929	2	1 690 442
1921–30	895 701	43	532 785	25	197 362	9	327 599	16	111 234	5	33 627	2	2 098 307
1931–40	1 223 199	42	697 066	24	265 309	9	487 299	17	182 434	6	47 681	2	2 902 988
1941–50	1 239 419	37	843 752	25	333 331	10	557 647	17	279 879	8	56 735	2	3 310 762
1951–60	1 455 822	35	1 174 950	28	477 559	11	635 972	15	374 659	9	74 735	2	4 193 697
1961–70	1 498 955	30	1 481 435	30	582 679	12	735 173	15	574 493	12	108 155	2	4 980 890
1971–80	972 332	25	1 206 306	31	505 873	13	401 901	10	689 744	18	115 891	3	3 892 047

Notes: Bales, decennial averages, figures from 1893.
Sources: Based on data in *DAWR*, *AIBR* and Franklyn, p. 202.

Table 6.5 Regional distribution of New Zealand wool sales

Year	Auckland	%	East Coast	%	Hawke's Bay	%	Wellington	%	North Island (%)
1906–10	10 688	5	4 528	2	28 982	15	33 675	17	40
1911–20	34 929	9	41 069	10	76 919	19	129 211	32	70
1921–30	39 357	8	3 687	1	81 918	18	149 457	32	59
1931–40	69 083	11	42 007	7	94 983	15	178 267	29	62
1941–50	117 097	14	29 418	3	135 748	16	218 910	26	59
1951–60	154 415	15	1 729	0	165 815	16	240 153	24	56
1961–70	242 413	17			224 986	16	285 049	20	53
1971–80	178 415	13			251 305	19	227 113	17	49

	Canterbury	%	Otago	%	Southland	%	South Island (%)	Total
1906–10	76 100	39	34 272	17	16 326	8	64	196 594
1911–20	104 178	26	59 469	15	28 654	7	48	402 257
1921–30	99 317	21	66 052	14	25 716	6	41	465 997
1931–40	125 268	20	96 077	16	44 864	7	43	616 136
1941–50	147 541	17	104 704	12	78 287	9	43	854 801
1951–60	201 448	20	131 312	13	112 388	11	44	1 006 274
1961–70	276 771	20	191 755	14	187 958	13	47	1 408 931
1971–80	299 694	22	200 902	15	187 021	14	51	1 344 451

Notes: Bales, decennial averages. Percentages do not always sum to one hundred because more years survive for national than regional totals.
Sources: DAWR.

to London, the agents began to shift their interests to the Australasian markets. The banks never became directly involved in local auctions, which required additional handling services and investments too specialised for their interests. Winning the large sales volumes necessary to justify these expenditures was improbable unless they competed through a wider range of pastoral services. Instead, banks mostly concentrated on working co-operatively with agents in their network and claimed commission rebates where they influenced a clip in the agent's favour.

The pioneers of local selling were private firms. Thomas Mort commenced small weekly auctions in Sydney from 1843 and Richard Goldsbrough was one of its leading pioneers in Melbourne from 1848. Elders had begun selling in Adelaide by 1878. In New Zealand NMA began weekly auctions at Dunedin in 1864 and Wright Stephenson there the following year. Several Wellington agents, including Levins and Bethune & Hunter, conducted regular auctions from 1871.[25] All of these agents were firms of local origin and lacked the strong financial base of the British companies to win market share in the consignment trade to London; they therefore competed by offering earlier realisation through local selling.

As the move to local selling gained pace in the late nineteenth century the other leading agencies were obliged, sometimes reluctantly, to follow suit. Most of the larger companies entered the market in the 1880s including Dalgety, UMA, and NZLMA.[26] Although local selling was designed as a competitive move by Goldsbrough Mort, in 1886 their General Manager welcomed the entrance of Dalgety which he believed would help make Melbourne and Sydney the leading wool markets in the world within about ten years.[27] UMA still strongly supported the London market in 1891, noting: 'London will always be the ultimate market for wool, and only here will the grower benefit by a large competition for his staple'. It is a measure of how quickly events were developing that in the following year UMA looked more seriously at expanding local sales although it ultimately chose to diversify its interests much more broadly than the other firms and never became one of the leading woolbrokers.[28] AMLF did become one of the leading brokers but did not sell locally until 1903, held back by the conservative opposition of their London Board which was conscious of the extent of the company's influence and investment in the consignment system.[29]

The advantages of early entry into local selling can be shown by the fact that in 1889 Goldsbrough Mort sold 142 000 bales in Australia, double its nearest rival, NZLMA. Goldsbrough Mort consigned just 25 000 bales to London making its local sales 85 per cent of its total at a time when the national figure for Australia was less than 40 per cent. However, this prime-mover advantage was soon whittled away; its leading 31 per cent share of the local market fell rapidly to only 13 per cent by 1900 when the firm was surpassed by Dalgety. Goldsbrough Mort, in retrospect, might not have been quite so welcoming of Dalgety's move into the local selling market.

The conjunction of a series of factors explains the relocation of the wool market. Shifts in the patterns of supply and demand meant that a majority of both buyers and sellers viewed the relocation of the market as more convenient and cost-reducing. The expansion of the small grower and the popularity of mixed farming created a class of sellers that was anxious to achieve quicker realisation. Local sales also reduced transaction costs by passing through fewer intermediaries. A common chain for London sales was grower–consignor–shipowner–importer–broker–buyer. Local sales normally meant grower–broker–buyer.[30] Smaller producers were concerned at the delays caused by infrequent but large London sales at which buyers did not have time to inspect many of the smaller lots.[31] Pressure from smaller growers for change did not go unnoticed by agents.[32] AMLF's General Manager, Falconer, noted with resignation in 1898: 'I cannot shut my eyes to the fact that the inclinations of an increasing number of our clients are in the direction of selling locally' and arranged for local sales through Goldsbrough Mort for those clients reluctant to consign to London.[33]

Evidence of comparative costs of sale for growers is quite sparse. Several agents, particularly Goldsbrough Mort and AMLF, debated this issue at the time but their results were coloured by a preference for one or other market.[34] In 1932 the NZWBA made a careful estimate of comparative costs which came down decisively in favour of the local market. While commission charges were broadly similar in the two markets, the relative costs of getting the wool to the market were, perhaps not surprisingly, quite different, 0.35d per bale for local sale and 2.19d in London.[35] Savings on interest for at least three months were additional to this. While these figures were influenced by the desire to discourage growers from being seduced back to London by the banks, the existence of a cost advantage for the local market is hardly open to question. However, until sufficient buyers were attracted into the new market these savings would be offset against the higher prices achieved in London.

Some of the benefits to growers were not initially realised but developed from the experience of local selling, particularly the fact of being more closely connected to the market which gave the grower a greater sense of influence and involvement. This bred responsiveness to changing buyer requirements and competition with other growers that encouraged farmers to concentrate on improving quality and developing a reputation. This heightening of competition is reflected in the comments of Elders in 1907: 'The woolgrower . . . has a chance of seeing his wool on the show floor, and this is often very instructive, and gives him a chance also of comparing his clip with other clips'.[36]

The pattern of demand for wool was also changing significantly. The English woollen industry, the traditional source of demand for Australasian wool, was undergoing significant changes in size and structure in the second half of the nineteenth century. The growth in scale and concentration of worsted manufacturers enabled them to by-pass wool merchants and buy more directly and thus more cheaply.[37] In addition, the severe and extended depression of the British textile industry from about the mid-1870s prompted a search for cheaper sources of supply; at this time wool prices were lower in Australasia than in London.

The English were soon followed by Continental European buyers, particularly from France, Germany, Italy, and the Netherlands, as the textile industries of those nations followed a similar pattern of growth, concentration, and stagnation. Their rising importance is suggested by Barnard's estimate that one-half to two-thirds of Australian sales were destined for Continental Europe and the *APR's* specific calculation for 1897/98 to 1901/02 during which the British share varied between 22 and 42 per cent, the Continental European from 41 to 70 per cent, and that of United States/Canada from 2 to 6 per cent.[38] Wool purchased by Continental buyers at the London market was a lower one-third to a half of disposals. Agents fostered these new markets, emphasising cheapness and quality. Dennys Lascelles sent out wool samples to British Columbia in 1891 and noted: 'If Canadians want wool of good quality . . . they should be able to purchase . . . from here cheaper and better than London'.[39] Finally, by 1901 a significant share of 17 per cent was taken by the expanding Australian textile industry.[40] Thus, by the end of the nineteenth century, geographically dispersed buyers saved time, freight and other handling costs by buying closer to the source of production and shipping directly to the country of consumption. In Table 6.6, using the five efficiency criteria discussed above (transaction costs, realisation speed, grower–buyer contact, sale costs, and market size), local sale is preferable in all but market size.

Improvements in transport and communications encouraged Australasian selling. Although more efficient sailing vessels and the adoption of steam increased the speed and reduced the cost of shipping to London, they did not aid that market since most wool production was destined for overseas whether sold locally or not. Instead, those who bought in Australia and New Zealand could now get their wool to the manufacturer much more quickly, thus mitigating one of the comparative disadvantages of local selling. Perhaps more important than improved shipping was the laying of the ocean cables which enabled foreign buyers in Australasia to keep in close and regular contact with their principals and the state of the London market.

In the early years of the twentieth century the relative merits of the alternative markets were still being worked out and growers chose between London and Australasia according to the prevailing state of prices. Arbitraging activity occurred as speculators bought in Australia and resold in London.[41] The price differentials were thus a source of flexible choice for genuine buyers. As the *AIBR* explained in 1908: 'when high prices rule preference is given to local selling in order to obtain a quick realisation, but when they are low, and the demand is sluggish, shipment for realisation in London is often preferred'.[42] Thus, volumes sold locally or in London fluctuated quite violently in response to changing prices.[43] Since the wool auctions were located at the major port cities, decisions of whether to ship or sell could be taken at a late stage, indeed the wool could

Table 6.6 Alternative marketing strategies

Point of sale	Transaction costs	Realisation speed	Market size	Market contact	Sale costs	Total
Farm	0	1	0	1	1	3
ANZ auction	1	1	1	1	1	5
London auction	0	0	1	0	0	1

Notes: Scores are 1 for a positive facet and 0 for a negative and are based on the discussion in the text. Thus the highest score represents the preferred strategy.

even be offered locally and, if a sufficient price was not reached, be shipped to London. For Western Australian growers a triple choice existed between the small local auctions, shipment to Melbourne auctions, and sale in London.[44]

Pastoral agents were alert to the opportunity for lower financing costs and greater marketing control relative to the banks and London brokers. Other benefits soon flowed. Firms could offer farmers dual choice between the two markets; their knowledge and expertise meant they were well placed to advise farmers where to sell.[45] Scope economies existed between the two markets in terms of knowledge, handling skills, and fixed assets such as wool stores and warehouses although these changes also required additional investments and learning a good deal more about organising a wool sale.

Overseas consignment was never entirely halted by the agents. They remained alive to the importance of offering the dual option and in years of particularly low prices, sale in London was still considered an option by some growers.[46] In 1961 Dalgety identified three types of grower who still shipped to London: those who had always sold there; those located in a distant outpost far away from the major auctions; and those who believed they could get a quicker sale in London at certain times of the year, given the seasonal differences.[47] Elders was also alert to the continued existence of small British buyers unable to purchase wool in Australasia and await its delivery four to five months later or those who wanted a supply of a specific type of wool at short notice.[48] Firms also believed it would be impolitic to abandon London since many buyers were from Britain.[49] Even-handedness buttressed attempts by the banks and London houses to relocate the market and helped the agents to retain valuable shipping agencies because of their control of freights of unsold wool.[50]

While conditions and policies were similar in the two Australasian nations, differences of scale and product help explain the slower relocation of the market to New Zealand. Nearly four times as much wool was produced in Australia as New Zealand in the 1890s. Thus, it was much more difficult for New Zealand agents to risk fragmenting the market by setting up local sales that would take a long time to attain the minimum scale necessary to cover the additional fixed costs involved. The problem of insufficient scale was magnified by the geographically diverse nature of wool production in New Zealand and the absence of cheap and effective railway systems to foster market concentration.

Rather than the relocation of the market to New Zealand being belated, it might be considered premature. The Australian auctions handled 50 per cent of sales by the mid-1890s out of a total volume of 1.5 million bales; New Zealand reached the same local share immediately before World War One from an aggregate of 0.5 million bales. The problem was exacerbated by lower concentration levels between the local points of sale. While New South Wales and Victoria provided a dominant 90 per cent local market share in the early years of auctions in the 1890s, helping to achieve scale economies, the leading two New Zealand provinces jointly handled less than 60 per cent before World War One. This marked difference in market concentration is reflected in the selling of more than six times as many bales per centre in Australia (see Table 6.3) in the early years of local auctions. The 'lack of one great centre' was seen by the *AIBR* in 1899 as explaining why New Zealand auctions had been 'comparatively a failure' at a time when they were growing rapidly in Australia. However, its prediction that New Zealand wool was likely to find its way to the Sydney or Melbourne sales in the future proved to be incorrect.[51]

The lack of scale economies that afflicted the early development of New Zealand auctions can be illustrated by reference to the same problem somewhat later in Western Australia. In 1933 Goldsbrough Mort compared earnings and costs at its selling centres at Sydney, Melbourne, Adelaide, and Perth. The company found that Sydney, with the highest turnover (136 106 bales), had the lowest cost of 7s 7d per bale while Perth, with the lowest volume (19 265), had the highest cost of 15s 5d. Perth was the only centre making a loss but was persisted with because of the expectation of growth and the desire to maintain the advantages of being an early entrant.[52] Significantly, the turnover at Perth was much closer to the average volume handled by agents in New Zealand than in the other Australian centres.

Product differences were also significant in the graduated rates of transition to local selling. It was noted earlier that local selling in Australia was most prominent in the sale of merino wools since it was here that the quality reputation of Australian wool was most established. New Zealand, being stronger in dual-product crossbreds, was less of an attraction at first for overseas buyers.

IMPROVING THE AUCTION SYSTEM

In the first two or three decades of the twentieth century the Australasian auction matured as volumes and types of wool handled expanded, the price converged with that in London, emphasising the benefits of lower costs, and fewer bales were resold there as the number of speculators declined.[53] Thus, selling locally became the norm for most growers who would only consider London in an exceptionally poor year. With their primary focus on the local auction, the agents concentrated on improving its efficiency in order to make it more profitable and attractive to growers.

One of the earliest innovations was the introduction of joint selling by the various brokers in a central salesroom at each of the main centres. By 1887 in Dunedin and 1892 in Melbourne, Geelong, and Sydney, wool sales were organised in a central salesroom.[54] This reduced the sale costs for individual brokers by sharing overheads at a time when they were serving both markets, and their desire to invest locally was constrained by uncertainty about the future market. Centralised sales also bolstered the number of buyers and sellers in the early years of thin volumes. The brokers drew lots to decide the selling order at the first auction of the year. From this a system of rotation for the rest of the selling season could be mapped. The amount to be sold by each broker at each sale was also agreed.

From this environment of closer interaction between larger numbers of buyers, sellers, and brokers flowed many benefits. Competition was heightened between and within each group of stakeholders, which helped to improve the quality of wool offered and the manner in which it was presented. It also fostered cooperative behaviour to standardise selling procedures in a set of written rules, thereby minimising disputes and misunderstandings. Future planning and improvements to the organisation of sales were also facilitated.

Planning and cooperation were vital if the Australasian sales were not to be overwhelmed by the rapidly expanding volume of wool being offered for sale. In place of the insufficient scale of individual company auctions before the 1890s, centralisation and the expansion of wool volumes in the early decades of the twentieth century meant that some auctions were becoming too large to operate efficiently. Farmers complained of delayed realisation, particularly smaller farmers whose lots were again sometimes overlooked in the rush to inspect and bid for the larger disposals, and warehouses became overloaded with wool waiting to be sold. However, additional sales risked clashing with those held in other regions.

The cooperative structure evolved to address such problems. From local cooperation sprang national coordination to draw up a roster of sales throughout each country for the whole selling season. This enabled more effective organisation of regular wool sales, with an auction in a different centre every four or five days and about one sale per month in each of the larger centres. Thus, buyers could move between different sales and plan their schedule in advance. It also enabled sales to be more effectively coordinated with the amount of wool that was being shorn at different places during various times of the year. Brokers could also plan more accurately in advance when wool should be transported to the various selling centres to minimise storage congestion.[55] Further downstream, shipowners could make use of these rosters in organising their sailing schedules.

With the continued expansion of output, extension of the selling season was an additional solution to the problem of congestion. It had the added benefits of mitigating seasonal fluctuations in handling capacity and discouraging farmers from selling privately or in London between auctions.[56] The precise timing of this change is difficult to measure but it appears to have occurred earlier in New Zealand than Australia despite the smaller volumes handled there. A roster for New Zealand in 1922–23 shows that wool auctions were being held for much of the year, though the size and number of sales was reduced in April to July because many foreign buyers left the country during these months.[57] Australian agents also discussed extending the auction season, although as late as 1955 Dalgety was uncertain as to whether to stay at ten months or extend the season to the full year. While generally favouring a longer season to minimise the competition from London and avoid a gap, Dalgety noted that an off-season break was helpful to undertake repairs to stores, and leave wool experts free to go out canvassing.[58]

Brokers also responded to the problem of auction size by changes in practices. They began to combine into single-sale lots the clips of small growers where the wool was of the same grade, in processes known as inter-lotting and binning. This created a larger sale lot and reduced inspection costs.[59] The practice appears to have been introduced in Sydney in 1924 but spread rapidly. Inspection by sampling wherein buyers assessed only a limited proportion of the clip also reduced costs. Grouping and sampling practices were also common in New Zealand by the early 1930s but were not believed to be part of the London auction system. These improvements to presentation were backed up by well presented and brightly lit ware-houses, the gradual development of quality symbols, and advice to farmers on shed preparation of their wool.[60]

For sampling to be effective buyers had to know that brokers would pro-vide uniform samples, and therefore the trust and reputational considerations associated with large agency firms came to the fore. Such trust was aided by the large firms gaining reputations as effective wool-classers, a skilled function which became of increasing importance when they took over local wool selling. A good classer had to be highly knowl-edgeable about the different properties of wool, which included length of staple, its strength, appearance, condition, spinning quality, and yield. In addition, it was necessary to be well informed about the locality from which the wool came, the season, and the health of the sheep. Such requirements were particularly well-suited to a member of a firm possessing extensive sectoral expertise and local knowledge.

The demands of woolclassing increased during the twentieth century with the expanding numbers of sheep breeds. By World War Two there were in excess of 1500 wool types and sub-types.[61] This heightened the value of the woolclasser since divisions into more precise distinctions of quality made the job of the buyer easier in securing appropriate wool types for different forms of textile manufacture. Agents also used this expertise to provide advice to farmers on the shed preparation of wool. This was all a far cry from the mid-nineteenth century when Dalgety's bemoaned the shortage of local woolclassers able to improve the presentation of Australian wool and who 'really understand the relative values of wool'.[62]

As local selling brokers, the agents continued to show the same com-mitment to handling technologies which they had as nineteenth-century

Plate 6.4 Classing wool at Dalgety's store. Woolclassing developed as a highly specialised skill permitting an increasing number of wool types and qualities to be distinguished. (Alexander Turnbull Library, National Library of New Zealand, Te Puna Mātauranga o Aotearoa.)

consignors. Close attention was paid to technical developments in Australasia and overseas. Much care was taken, for example, to keep up to date with the latest mechanical handling methods, denser dumping, and unitisation.[63]

CHARGES, COSTS, AND PRICES

The wool auction system has had many supporters. The Empire Wool Conference of 1931 and the Wool Enquiry Committee of 1932 in Australia both came out firmly in favour of auctions, as have economists such as Gruen and agricultural specialists like Munz.[64] The auction system was seen as providing lower cost trading for large numbers of buyers and sellers in a sophisticated market whose high quality classing enabled prices to reflect accurately the many wool varieties and provide uniformity within each purchase.

The auction was compared favourably in each of these respects with sale by private contract, which was more prominent in Argentina, Uruguay, Canada, and the United States. In particular the American system, wherein wool merchants bought from growers and resold to manufacturers, was criticised by the Australasian agents as providing limited woolclassing and encouraging attempts to control the market. Where auctions did occur, the Boston merchants were said to 'have done their best to strangle' them and this was contrasted with the honest broker role of the Australasian agents.[65] A similar pattern of control occurred in Canada where the textile merchants of Toronto exercised strong control.[66] Australasian agents also compared standards of wool and its grading in Western Australia unfavourably with the standards of the east coast as a result of belated and infrequent auctions.[67]

In spite of these many advantages, the auction system was becoming less profitable for its central organiser, the pastoral agent. It had become, perhaps, a victim of its own success as excessive competition among agents and the falling relative value of wool created a serious cost-price squeeze for the firms. This was a point emphasised repeatedly during the merger movement of the 1960s and 1970s.[68] As early as 1939 Dalgety was concerned enough to state: 'the cost of service brokers give clients is out of all proportion to earnings from the sale of wool'.[69] Whilst in 1922 firms had considered asking for higher commissions on private wool sales because of the extra cost involved, by 1960 they believed private sales might be cheaper.[70] Table 6.6 shows that private sales were a more serious competitive threat than the London market.

Plate 6.5 Buyers inspecting wool at the warehouse of Winchcombe Carson in Sydney. Buyers for large British, European, American and Japanese woollen manufacturers were attracted to the burgeoning auctions in Australia and New Zealand. (By permission of the National Library of Australia.)

The relocation of the market to Australasia and the taking over of the selling function by the leading agents required them to invest extensively in fixed capital.[71] Although they already had wool warehouses, they now required more modern showrooms and wool stores in which auction wool could be carefully classed and displayed to favourable effect. In 1903, for example, Elders noted that it was spending £8000 updating its wool facilities which 'would make the Company's showfloors equal to anything in Australia'.[72] Salerooms were a further requirement at each selling centre. The purchasing of expensive urban and quayside land in Australia's burgeoning port cities emphasised the increase in costs. It was also noted that 'labour costs have made the auction system, with all the handling involved, including the practice of show floors etc, so expensive'.[73] The permanent employment of increasing numbers of skilled, well-paid officers such as woolclassers and auctioneers meant that much of the salary bill was effectively a fixed cost. The growing importance of small growers fragmented many handling processes, as did the differentiation and grading of wool into greater numbers of types.[74]

These additional costs came on top of the acquisition of larger numbers of branches as firms shifted to closer service contact with farmers. While the relative move away from mortgage finance had been intended to reduce the commitment to tying up money long-term, its replacement by increased property investment by the company created an alternative form of illiquidity. Large fixed costs made it difficult for agents to cut back during short-term fluctuations in demand. While seasonal fluctuations had been minimised by introducing all-year sales, annual volatility was more difficult to eliminate. During a record wool season in 1938 Elders found itself with insufficient space in its store and thus 10 000 bales remained outside, the firm noting with concern: 'if our clients were in a position to know the conditions under which their wool is being held it would certainly be detrimental to our future business'.[75] In the light of these comments, it is clear firms planned capacity for the better years and endured underutilisation in other years.[76] That fixed assets, both human and physical, were mostly only of value to the woolbroking industry ('asset specificity') also made it difficult for the firm to dispose of or lease them out periodically.

In the long run, fixed costs might be reduced by natural wastage in response to a secular reduction in demand, but this was not easy. Since wool commissions were the main source of income, firms were reluctant to make cuts in this department. Yet synergies linked their various activities: finance, livestock sales, technical advice, and the sale of farming and household necessities were all vital supports in the bid to win extra wool commissions, especially from the large numbers of free clients.[77] Since the local branch was the main point of contact with farmers there was little saving from vertical cuts of a particular activity spread around all of the branches. The alternative was to reduce the number of branches. This was done during the interwar downturn by expanding the coverage of the remaining branches. However, in the postwar revival, with wool volumes rising once more, under-representation at the branch level would damage

a firm's ability to gain or retain market share. The firms were also aware
that the strong networking amongst farmers meant that losses tended to
be cumulative on each other as word got around about reduced service
or poor treatment by particular agents.[78]

While battling amongst themselves, the national brokers also encountered competition from smaller regional firms chipping away at market
share in particular localities. This was achieved by arranging private sales
and small country auctions including 'selling in the shed'.[79] Smaller firms
lacked the expertise of the large nationals but had close local connections
that they exploited by hiring local personalities, often farmers themselves,
on a commission basis to gain more wool clients. In many ways this imitated
the policies of the market leaders in their pioneering days of the nineteenth century.[80] Private selling and commission-based canvassing both
required fewer fixed costs. Brokers expressed concern at the rise of private
selling and country sales in the 1930s which increased the amount of
canvassing they had to do to protect their market share. This trend was
encouraged by the direct buying practices of several major European
buyers.[81] In the 1950s and 1960s private selling was growing rapidly in both
countries, thus the share of wool sales handled by the national auction system
in New Zealand fell from 90 to 84 per cent between 1952/53 and 1965/66.[82]
Private and country buying was becoming more systematic and well organised. In 1952 a company was formed, Sheep and Wool New Zealand Ltd, with
the purpose of conducting private sales. Improved coordination of private
sales, bringing together buyers and sellers at lower cost, would be a serious
competitor to the auction.[83] In the 1990s country selling by small 'tin
shedders' continued to concern the major brokers in both countries and
was backed up by government encouragement, such as the Growers Alternative Selling System organised by the New Zealand Wool Board.[84]

As we saw earlier, the number of wool selling centres in New Zealand
was quite large from the outset and changed little for most of the twentieth century. This explains why the most serious competition probably
came from private selling. However, in Australia, where centres were more
widely dispersed and handled much larger volumes of wool, the greatest
threat to the national brokers came from establishing new auction centres.
Agent hostility to new centres was reflected in their prosaic language:
Goldsbrough Mort, 'so hate the idea', Elders claimed, 'nothing would do
so much harm to the wool trade', and Dalgety believed such moves to be
'suicidal'.[85] The firms recognised the scale economies from centralised
auctions and pointed out that wool was a special article that required highly
trained personnel to handle. They felt, if anything, there should be fewer
points of sale. Additional centres meant more investments in property,
skilled staff, and time and expenses moving existing staff and buyers
between extra locations. The firms claimed, with some legitimacy, that
although selling benefited from the economies of centralisation, extensive
branch networks confirmed their service to a widely dispersed farming
community. They pointed out that they arranged for the movement of
produce to the point of sale and also continued to consign wools directly

Plate 6.6 An Australian liner discharging wool at the South-West India Dock, London. Whether auctioned in Australasia or Britain, most wool was destined for overseas markets. (By permission of the National Library of Australia.)

to the London market, 'which should prove that we look at our business from a broad point of view and are not wedded to centralisation'.[86] They were also concerned that additional centres outside the control of the NCWSB would make it more difficult to continue the high level of co-operation and organisation of the auction system.

Additional centres would also make it more difficult for the leading brokers to impose their control over the wool trade and act against private sales and similar competition.[87] Smaller agents were aware that more points of sale meant lower costs for farmers getting their produce, and perhaps themselves, to the market and saw this as a valid manner of gaining market share. While the existing infrastructure was limited at some of the proposed regional sites, land was generally cheaper. The attitude of the buyers is more difficult to gauge. While favouring competition among brokers, decentralisation would impact on the volume of wool available, the quality of classing, and the time travelling between selling points. Brokers also took heed of the views of State and Federal politicians. In 1947, for example, the Federal Labor government suggested the opening of seven new selling centres. The Liberals were also keen to see competition among brokers: a young Malcolm Fraser (later to be Prime Minister) informed them of his support for wool selling at Portland.[88]

The expanding number of selling centres prevented agents offsetting rising costs with scale economies. The average number of bales sold per centre increased through the twentieth century (see Table 6.3) but not as quickly as it would have done if additional centres had not been added.

Of particular importance was the opening of a centre at Newcastle in 1930, which was initiated by the New England North and North-West Producers Co. Ltd. Pitt Son & Badgery also contemplated selling there but did not do so for a decade. In 1940 selling began at Goulburn under the aegis of two local agents. The addition of Albany in 1958, however, was an initiative of the leading brokers as part of the belated development of local selling in Western Australia under pressure from Westralian Farmers Coop. The much-disputed question of wool selling at Portland was resolved in 1964 when Portland Woolbrokers began business there drawing on facilities used for wool disposal during World War Two. Accepting the inevitable, Dalgety's was already planning to buy land in the area in 1961 and began wool selling there in 1965, together with Elders.[89]

Agents also endured the activities of intermediaries, such as local 'dealers', who interposed themselves between grower and broker in return for a share of the commission. Local stock and station agents, banks, and other wool growers also made claims to have 'influenced' clips in favour of a broker who was obliged to share the commission or risk losing that business in the following year if the influence proved to be genuine. Goldsbrough Mort estimated that up to 9 per cent of its wool came through other growers in the interwar period. Groups of farmers sought subterfuges to claim rebates by forming into associations as forwarding agents. In 1918 the WWBA rejected a claim for commission rebates from the Marlborough Coast Settlers Association, 'it being an association of farmers handling their own wool'.[90]

While most of the time the agents and banks worked cooperatively to channel wool clips to the auctions, periodic disagreements occurred over the extent of commission rebates. When the New Zealand agents attempted to halt the payment of rebate commissions to the banks in 1931, alleging that the clips would still come their way and the banks made no special effort beyond serving as lenders, the banks encouraged their indebted clients to ship to London with them. The following year the decision was reversed after the Wellington agents reported losing 8000 bales to the London sales.[91] Clearly, the threat of leakages from the Australasian auction system still existed and the banks were a powerful institutional force to implement this. The threat re-emerged in 1958 with reports that the Committee of London Wool Selling Brokers, which controlled the London wool market after World War Two, was planning to form a company to canvass for business in Australia and New Zealand.

Intermittent price wars and rate fixing meant that commission rates fluctuated, in itself a concern for firms whose turnover was already highly volatile. In the 1860s a charge of 2.5 per cent for consignment plus 1 per cent for London-selling brokerage making a gross charge of 3.5 per cent, was common. This was reduced to 2.5 to 3 per cent gross in the 1870s, probably in response to competition from the banks, and appears to have fallen further by the turn of the century, maybe in response to the growth of local selling. By the early 1950s, 2 per cent was commonly charged for consignment to London and 1 per cent for its sale. The Committee of

London Wool Brokers' battle with the agents in the late 1950s forced down the gross rate to 2 per cent of which the consigning agents received 1 per cent. The agent's share was forced lower to 0.75 per cent by 1961, which was clearly unprofitable.

Local-selling brokerage generally varied between about 2 and 2.5 per cent, falling to about 1.5 per cent during price wars such as in the 1930s, and rising to about 3 per cent during brokers' agreements, such as in the 1890s.[92] Rates were staggered into volume bands reflecting the scale economies in handling larger clips, and there were some regional differences probably due to variations in handling costs. Thus, in 1931 Sydney had band rates of 2.5, 1.5 and 1.25 per cent, while those in Perth were 3, 2 and 1.5 per cent.[93] There were also lower per-bale charges to cover insurance, transport, advertising, repacking, and related activities.[94]

There appears little evidence of a secular increase in charges to reflect the rising level of costs. The crisis was made more acute by a long-term relative decline of the wool prices, on which commissions were calculated, in relation to the domestic price index. The sector endured sustained low prices for most of the interwar period. A recovery in wool prices after World War Two was shortlived with the terms of trade moving strongly against the sector in the 1950s.[95] Thus, not only did the volume of inputs required to provide wool handling services increase, but so did their average cost relative to wool prices. One of the key reasons for this was that growers and agents were paying artificially high prices for wages and machinery as a result of high levels of protectionism and the accompanying policy of central wage fixing, while relying on unprotected world markets to determine wool prices.

Brokers were also sensitive to the impact of the growing market for artificial fibres. In the 1920s rayon and artificial silk were viewed as serious competitors and by the 1950s the use of non-cellulosic fibres (nylon, terylene, orlon) was expanding rapidly. The share of man-made fibres in world consumption of apparel fibres rose from 16 to 22 per cent between 1952 and 1958.[96] This threat to market share, moreover, was most probable in years of high wool prices. This threatened the intertemporal cross-subsidies which were critical in farming, with good years cancelling out bad ones. The competitive properties of artificial fibres therefore included price and output stability.

CONTROLLING THE MARKET

In addition to the diversification discussed in chapter 2, firms tackled the cost-price squeeze through greater collective control over the wool market. These divided into measures designed to mitigate leakages to the central auction system and efforts to regulate the market.

Agents sought to seal leakages to the auction system through their relations with the various parties involved. Brokers lobbied farmers to enter into exclusive dealing arrangements through the use of discriminating terms. In 1920 the NZWBA accepted that there were times when farmers preferred to sell privately but sought to have those sales conducted by the farmer's normal woolbroker rather than a direct sale or through a local agent.[97] How NZWBA sought to enforce this is not clear though presumably it was through discriminating prices. In 1934 the Australian agents considered asking farmers to sign agreements not to sell wool outside the established system at the new auction centre at Newcastle or in the country. If they failed to do so, they would be excluded from special conditions regarding payment, delivery, discount and storage.[98] Agents also considered discouraging private sales by the introduction of higher handling commissions.[99] It is not clear how successful or enduring these proposals were. They were made at the height of the interwar slump, and the intensity of competition and the fact that the proposals were rarely mentioned suggests they were soon dropped.

An alternative approach was to reach agreement with outside competitors. It was seen earlier that attempts to exclude banks from rebates were unsuccessful. Agents also targeted local businesses that were mostly not concerned with the wool trade but might collude with growers to obtain commission rebates.[100] The NZWBA drew up a list of bona fide influencing agents whom it defined as working solely as agents and being reliant on wool commissions.[101] The need for regular amendments to this list and disputes with local agents suggest the system was not working. The monitoring costs of maintaining such a list were high, and disagreements among brokers occurred when several were revealed as providing finance to local agents and dealers.[102] In their relations with medium-sized regional agents such as Pitt, Son & Badgery, who were seeking new selling centres, the brokers proposed market-sharing agreements. This particularly applied to the opening of Newcastle which was feared as a serious competitor for mid-State farming regions between Sydney and Newcastle. Goldsbrough Mort proposed specifying wool selling volumes by these firms at Newcastle and offering its own existing clients freight rebates to cover the implied saving if they had sent their wool to Newcastle rather than Sydney.[103] The proposal had too many drawbacks, not least that there was insufficient incentive to attract firms like Pitt, Son & Badgery and that the freight subsidy nullified many of the benefits for the larger broking firms. Restricting new entrants like the Portland Woolbrokers from participation in industry associations was also considered but the benefits were quite limited and would give the impression of restrictive practices to groups like graziers, farmers, and politicians.[104]

One further attempt to mitigate leakages from the broker-controlled auction system involved changes to the organisation of the auction itself. Agents were concerned that direct private buying and the activities of dealers were particularly prevalent with free growers producing high quality wools. Therefore, changes in the order of sale were introduced, particularly at Sydney, to favour free sellers of high quality wool. Until then wool had been sold in order of arrival. A zoning system gave preference to wools arriving from designated 'burr-free' areas in order to avoid delays in selling high quality wools.[105]

Market regulation measures have been mostly concerned with bolstering or stabilising prices through controlling output. Since commission is a percentage of wool prices these policies benefit agents and have the support of farmers.[106] That agents fostered a well-organised and ordered market is reflected in the many developments discussed above. In addition, they (individually or collectively) intervened from time to time in the free operation of the auction, delaying the marketing of some clips in the hope of prices rising. This applied only to growers whose finances were sound enough to bear the risk of the market falling further.[107] Evidence of this surfaces as early as 1907, and in 1909 Elders noted that brokers were not obliged to take the conditions of sale literally; if prices were low there was no commitment to sell to the highest bidder.[108] This was no more than stating the need for a reserve price at an auction. It was more noticeable during the interwar period; in 1930, for example, the season was extended and a controlled release of wool on to the market took place.[109]

However, the agents regarded such measures as temporary and ad hoc in nature, used to steady the market and remove minor distortions. Their sustaining view was opposition to significant and ongoing interference with the mechanism of the auction. They had invested heavily in developing the auction system and argued strongly for its unfettered retention. The possible impact of regulation on competing geographical and product markets was cited; whether this might trigger an exodus of buyers back to London or to other wool producing countries. One of the perceived benefits of reducing price fluctuations was to compete with the greater stability of man-made fibres but such a move would also deny wool some of its competitive edge in years of good production. Allowing prices to fluctuate had advantages through its role as a signalling device, forcing agents and farmers to search for efficiency improvements, as had occurred during the interwar slump. If greater price certainty was desirable this could be done through the marketplace; although brokers were initially opposed to futures markets when they were proposed in the 1930s, by the 1960s their value as an alternative price-smoothing mechanism was beginning to be appreciated.[110]

Agents were again sensitive to the strategic implications of their action. As Elders noted: 'collective selling is likely to lead to collective buying'.[111] If buyers were aware that wool stocks were being held back they might reduce their current purchases, knowing that the stocks would have to be released on to the market later. Thus, prices might be driven down rather than up.[112] While the agents might be considered a more coherent group, better able to collude than a variety of buyers from different countries, there were several powerful individual buyers and buyers associations. The problem of 'pies', whereby buyers collectively agree not to bid against each other, was observed as a factor depressing wool prices at Goulburn.[113] Agents were equally conscious that market regulation might incur the wrath of governments if they viewed it as a trade restraint. Even more worryingly, they might approve of it and take over the regulatory process!

In the exceptional circumstances of the two world wars wool marketing was closely regulated. Through the Imperial Wool Purchase the British government committed itself to buying the whole clip of both countries at a single fixed price. The agents undertook their normal handling procedures. In place of the auction, however, they appraised each lot against a table of limits to value it in relation to the unit price so as to achieve a fair distribution of the payments from the British government.[114] During both wars the system appears to have worked quite smoothly. The generosity of the price, together with the expertise and reputation of the agents, ensured the wool was carefully handled and disagreements over revenue distribution minimised. Price fixing also removed a source of uncertainty.

However, the uncertainty was simply shifted to the postwar period. Agents had played an important role alongside the Australasian governments in arguing successfully for a high price: in 1916 it was set at 15.5d per pound, being 55 per cent above the 1913–14 prices.[115] The price was undoubtedly a generous one, agents modestly noting it as 'satisfactory'.[116] In effect, the British government and taxpayer provided a generous subsidy to guarantee their exclusive use of the wool. High prices encouraged farmers to increase output which the British government was committed to buying, without knowing whether it would be needed. This led to the creation of large stocks of unused wool after each war. The threat to postwar wool sales was mitigated by the controlled release of wool on to the market and the further generosity of the British government. After World War One the British Australian Wool Realisation Association was given the task of disposing of the surplus wool; after World War Two it was left in the hands of the Joint Disposals Organisation. The agents were closely involved in the activities of these organisations, Dalgety and Goldsbrough Mort having representatives in BAWRA, and the firms offering advice about movements in prices and demand.[117]

In spite of the large profits and close involvement with centralised wool selling during and after the two world wars, agents remained strong supporters of the auction system and canvassed extensively with growers and the government for its postwar re-establishment.[118] They had much closer control of this system than in wartime, where responsibilities were shared with government agencies whom the agents regarded as inexperienced and unknowledgeable.[119] Moreover, wartime conditions were considered exceptional and the generosity of the British government important. The postwar collapse of the market was only narrowly avoided and it still engendered enormous uncertainty over prices and demand, together with logjams of stocks on the farm and at the woolstore until the surplus had been sold.[120] Ironically, price and output stability were seen as the main benefits of regulation by its advocates.

While the auction system was revived after World War Two it was tempered with various experiments in price stability. The New Zealand government introduced a minimum or reserve floor price scheme once the wartime arrangements had ended as a buffer against downward price movements. The New Zealand Wool Commission was to buy up wool once it threatened to fall below the reserve price and sell it in years when the price rose above a particular level. The reserve price was not invoked until 1958 but then a large stockpile had accumulated by the time of the scheme's abolition a decade later.[121] Modified price control schemes were introduced under the aegis of the New Zealand Wool Marketing Corporation (from 1971) and the New Zealand Wool Board (from 1977) with the same result: large stockpiles of unsold wool.[122]

Australian agents were opposed to a report of the Australian Wool Board in 1966 recommending a similar scheme. Drawing on their wartime experiences, they pointed to the difficulties of trying to estimate the price of an heterogeneous commodity especially one estimated by a statutory body.[123] The introduction of an Australian reserve price scheme in 1970 under the administration of the Australian Wool Council, and extended under the Australian Wool Corporation in 1974, proved no more successful than in New Zealand.[124] The minimum reserve price proved to be too high and led to overproduction. The experience suggested that to leave price setting to a farmer-dominated organisation was no more successful, as was evidenced by the rise in the floor price by 71 per cent in the two years after this responsibility was ceded to the Australian Wool Corporation in 1987. The floor price was forced down in 1990 but this came too late to avoid a huge stockpile of 4.7 million bales and industry debts of A\$2.8 billion which cast a long shadow over the industry in the 1990s.[125]

INNOVATION AND DEREGULATION

While the regulatory schemes occurred in a postwar culture of increased government intervention, deregulation was a stronger feature of the 1990s.[126] The reserve price schemes were abolished in both countries in 1991. The New Zealand Wool Board began to take a more hands-off and market-oriented approach in general, a change which was codified in a 1997 Act that changed the Board's powers from direction to persuasion. This approach also led to a complete selling off of the wool stockpile by 1996. At the time of writing, the most recent report on the Australian wool industry recommended the abolition of most statutory authorities except for the creation of Australian Wool Services Ltd as a listed company with scaled-down responsibility for innovation and promotion. The report's opposition to centralised price control is unequivocal: 'Under no circumstances whatsoever should any form of RPS [reserve price scheme] ever be reintroduced in Australia'.[127] Finally, a cultural shift from collective reliance to greater individual responsibility among farmers is also advocated.

The control of the agents over wool marketing receded during the postwar intervention, but they are now playing an active role in the changing environment of individual responsibility and market forces, seeking new and innovative solutions to the present problems. These have included promoting, and persuading the farming community to consider, alternative forms of individual price risk management through hedging in futures markets and forward contracts. Agents have sought modernisation of the auction system through electronic selling. A consequent reduction in sales centres from nine to just three at Sydney, Melbourne, and Fremantle would save substantial expenditure but faces opposition from growers in regional centres. Ironically, this centralisation strategy, which was instituted in New Zealand in 1984 with one centre for each island, was originally pursued by Australian agents in the early post-World War Two years but faced political opposition. In the 1990s it was supported by statutory authorities, particularly the Australian Wool Exchange.

Elders and Dalgety now control about 60 per cent of Australian sales and have also sought closer working relations. Efforts at joint ventures have historically achieved little because of the strong competitive instincts of the agents and their determination to remain independent, a topic considered in more detail in chapter 9. Forms of joint activity had been widely discussed during the interwar slump, including a proposal for joint wool warehousing in the major centres. Goldsbrough Mort opposed this as promising limited savings when set against the capital costs of construction and the high fire insurance and other risks if the clip were to be stored on a single site. AMLF opposed it because of the loss of company identity.[128] In 1997 Dalgety and Elders proposed a joint venture company, Global Wool, for wool handling and marketing, which it was claimed would reduce handling costs by 20 per cent. In spite of this strong incentive the project failed almost immediately due to 'commercial and institutional barriers'. An alternative proposal in 1998 involved only wool handling, would not have interfered in the relationship between individual agent and farmer, and could have been run separately from the two companies, all of which suggests competition and independence continue to be potent forces in the pastoral agent industry.[129]

CONCLUSION

The stock and station agents played an important role in getting farmers' wool to the dominant London market in the nineteenth century, conducting some handling services themselves, and using network influence and market power over other service providers. The international reputation gained by Australasian wool and the expertise developed by agents were important prerequisites for the relocation of the market to Australasia from the late nineteenth century. The leading agents dominated the development of the local auction which brought a host of benefits to both buyers and growers, including lower transaction and transport costs, greater choice, improved classing and selection, and closer connections to the market and source of production. As the volumes that were being handled expanded, agents introduced various innovations to avoid congestion and delays, including all-year sales, national rosters, sampling, and interlotting. The Australasian auction was compared favourably with the London market and forms of private selling.

However, the local auction imposed a cost-price squeeze on agents.

Adverse movements in the terms of trade, together with strong competition, limited the growth of commissions, the leading income source for the firms. Costs rose as agents fought harder for market share by offering additional inducements and services. The high proportion of fixed costs and synergies between their various pastoral services made it very difficult to reduce costs in the short or long term. The ultimate solution was merger and diversification. The farmers clearly benefited from the additional services and lack of increase in commissions although falling relative wool prices were a concern. Attempts at centralised price control have proved futile in an industry of high volatility. Since 1990s there has been a return to the ethos of individual farmer responsibility with the advice and role of the agents likely to be enhanced once more but in a rapidly changing environment of remote and centralised markets. It remains to be seen whether a return to market remoteness will discourage farmer innovation, and if centralisation will reverse regional and rural economic development. More than half a century earlier Elders had been emphatic about the impact of the auction system for South Australia: 'wool selling by various firms . . . through bringing men from all parts of the world, had been a great advertising asset . . . had lifted the State out of provincialism, and in its reaction had greatly added to South Australian trade'.[130]

CHAPTER SEVEN

Information, Advisory, and Advocacy Services

In order to be successful farmers required access to a wide range of information on commercial, technical, legal, and political issues. The rapid secular growth of the industry combined with its highly volatile nature meant keeping abreast of the latest developments was critical. The simultaneous fragmentation of farming units but increased technical sophistication of the industry in the second half of the nineteenth century spurred the demand for such knowledge. This covered subjects as diverse as the progress of foreign nations, new agricultural machinery and materials, property improvement, pastoral accounting, general station management, and new statutes or case law affecting the industry.

Arguably, the greatest problem for the inexperienced, industrious yet isolated farmer was the scarcity of information and the high cost of acquiring it. The limited contribution of governments or industry groups, especially in the nineteenth century, restricted access to information as a quasi-public good. Nor was it easy to buy and sell information. This chapter discusses the role of the agent in furnishing farmers with a wide range of relevant information. Simply passing on information was not always sufficient. The farmer needed someone with the expertise to sift, sort, and interpret information as an adviser and someone with the connections to create feedback loops to those experimenting with new techniques and equipment. Information, if effectively marshalled and selected, can also serve a powerful justifying role. Agents used information as tools of advocacy for the farming community.

THE INFORMATION PROBLEM

Stigler has shown that information is a scarce good and therefore there is a cost involved in its acquisition. Diminishing returns occur in searching for information and therefore the entrepreneur must decide how much to acquire before making a decision.[1] While Stigler was predominantly concerned with price information, there are search costs in acquiring a diversity of types of information of value to an enterprise. Acquiring knowledge of efficient administrative techniques, for example, has been a major concern of modern corporations.

The price mechanism was an ineffective means of rationing credit among farmers (see chapter 4). Acquiring information through the marketplace can also be problematic and lead to uncleared markets. Arrow drew attention to this through the so-called 'paradox of information': 'its value for the purchaser is not known until he has the information, but then he has in effect acquired it without costs'.[2] Developing the issue, Williamson observed that the paradox of information explains why it is difficult to buy or sell information by a simple contract especially where the knowledge is diffusely distributed, poorly defined, and the recipients have little understanding of it.[3] These three features were often characteristic of information flows in the Australasian pastoral industry. Information was diffusely distributed among many groups connected to the industry; scientific and technical developments were often weakly understood by farmers; legal and general business issues required definition and interpretation within the context of the industry.

Where information was more easily understood it took on some of the features of a public good, particularly non-excludability. Weak patent laws and poor property rights created a problem of free-riding and thus little incentive existed for individual farmers to invest in agricultural research. That the returns to research were mostly yielded only in the long run and were highly unpredictable acted as further discouragement.[4] Cooperative information channels to solve free-riding did exist in the nineteenth century, particularly farmer-led local agricultural and pastoral societies, and government-sponsored agricultural colleges and experimental farms. However, the colleges and experimental farms were targeted mostly at arable farming and the societies often suffered from local isolation and inadequate resources that limited their ability to experiment and to publish their findings. In addition, both sources concentrated on farming science and technology rather than business management and commercial decision-making.[5]

With the limited opportunities for acquiring information in a simple market transaction or through public good access, alternative methods had to be found. Two important considerations were that information needs in the industry were frequently reciprocal, and information was zero-priced since it had no sale value that could be pre-determined. This meant that both farmers and agents would benefit from the exchange of information and this could appropriately feature as part of a contractual package that included priced transactions such as brokerage and merchandise sales. The direct and immediate benefits from trading information with other services were additional knowledge for the farmer and a means of attracting priced services for the agent. Firms were well aware of the value of information as a competitive tool, Dalgety complaining in 1940 that one of its largest clients had begun sending some of their wool to Australian Estates since that company was 'rendering him special service in making recommendations regarding bettering his pastures'.[6]

The maximum benefits were only realised in an ongoing relationship between the two when the transfer of information became purposeful rather than an unintended spillover of a trading contract. Repeating the transaction enhanced the usefulness of the information service in maintaining the loyalty of farmers who knew the information previously acquired was valuable. Farmers, on the other hand, knew that the agents would provide additional information each time to keep their attention and this might be of a nature increasingly inaccessible to farmers. Whilst the finance contract tied the farmer for months or years at a time, no such bonds existed with information services. The long-term information relationship resulted from the realisation that full and honest exchange of information was most likely in highly recurrent transacting. Over time the information became more valuable to both sides: agents could use accumulated information about clients to assess loan applications and the like, while the farmer realised that a closer understanding of his business by the agent meant information would be accompanied by its enhanced by-products, advice and advocacy. Thus, as each side invested more in the relationship over the course of time, mutual self-interest came to the fore.

Information flows must be seen within the context of the networked relationship, which provides a thicker and freer exchange of information than market or hierarchical forms of trading. The information is thicker or more complete than in a single transaction and it is freer where honesty is paramount and opportunism attenuated by the bonds of the network. Indeed, trust is critical in the trading of information where much rests upon it and the asymmetries on either side can be immense. If the information proves not to be accurate or impartial both sides stand to incur substantial and permanent losses. Since the agents earned commissions on farming products sold to farmers it was vital that they did not offer advice that conflicted with the farmers' interests. In 1926, for example, AMLF was offered the local agency of Little's sheep dip but rejected it because many of its clients were happy with the competitive product, Cooper's, and 'should a grower find that Little's dip does not give him good results, he would be apt to blame the Company [AMLF] and the loss of his wool consignments might result'.[7]

As a result of their pivotal position in the farming network, agents were involved in complex trading relationships with many groups that yielded extensive information. Using their expertise and effective information processing capabilities, they could distil and generalise information acquired from multiple sources into useful knowledge which was preferable to much larger numbers of bi-lateral transactions, such as between individual farmers and shipowners, which were less likely to reveal extensive and typical information. Indeed, the realisation that agents were centrally placed and could act as information conduits encouraged the other party to reveal information in the hope of receiving feedback benefits. Even when the social and kinship aspects of the agent's network declined in the twentieth century, the mutual economic relationship discussed above continued to act as a strong incentive to information sharing.

Although information services were provided at zero price they were not costless and therefore were undertaken at an economic loss. Much of the information processing could be integrated within the agents' existing structure of operations and therefore benefited from scope economies. However, the creation of specialist research departments created extra costs, as did additional distribution channels. It took two typists three weeks to send out Winchcombe Carson's *Review* in 1918.[8] However, similar to the provision of loss-making loans, the firms judged the collateral benefits of attracting and maintaining wool business sufficient to justify the additional expense. The demand for information services increased during economic downturns at a time when agents were desperately trying to bring down their costs and eliminate any apparently superfluous or unprofitable business. Dalgety's noted the need to eliminate 'unnecessary services which are so often rendered free to clients'. However, even in hard times, it was reluctant to axe services for fear of losing customers to other firms.[9]

INFORMATION ACQUISITION

Agents were well placed to acquire their knowledge from a wide variety of sources, individual and institutional, verbal and written. Most obviously, they drew on their own resources and experience. The larger agent companies with an office in London had direct access to extensive and reliable commercial information. As early as 1848 Dalgety's correspondence between London and Australia was full of detailed analysis about the social and political crisis affecting Europe and its likely economic impact. The enduring large companies also drew on their corporate memory. Dalgety distinguished the global nature of the 1876 crisis from previous ones in 1847, 1854, 1857 and 1866: 'former panics & crises have been more or less confined to certain trades & countries or to certain financial institutions'.[10] By the end of the century frequent and regular correspondence moved between the British and Australasian offices of the leading firms. In the case of AMLF this consisted of more than four letters a week by 1897.

This was supplemented by telegrams for vital and up-to-date commercial information. Cost and security limited their more extended use, while misunderstandings and misinformation were more common than by letter due to incorrect translation or transcription. After World War One NMA decided that their importance in information gathering should be increased: 'regardless of cost . . . send a weekly message advising the market price of different principal items'. By World War Two, however, NMA had still not mastered this form of communication; an incorrect telegram in 1940 read: 'good raids lately will assist winter feed'. Wartime activity, including German bombing during the Battle of Britain in that year, may have boosted Australasian farming even though 'rains' was the intended word![11]

Organisational improvements were achieved by the larger firms (see chapter 8). While the needs of some of Australasia's largest companies were different in many ways from those of small farming units, some business management principles could be usefully adapted by farmers. Thus, for example, NMA included farm accounting, budgeting, and taxation among its services to farmers.[12]

Firms also undertook quite extensive scientific and technical experiments. Australian Estates was one of the leading firms in this respect. The firm was distinguished from other agents by the number of stations it continued to own. While its lack of functional specialisation may have weakened its competitive edge in some respects, its stations could be used as laboratories.[13] The company established a dynamic research culture where members kept up to date and discussed the latest findings. For example, it considered the problem of jute and hemp getting mixed in with wool in 1907. In 1911 it responded to the problem of worm nodules in beef exports reported in the Melbourne *Argus* and sent a memorandum to the Federal Minister for Customs.[14] In 1933 the company formalised its work by establishing a research department. Staffed by Veterinary and Agricultural Science graduates it had 'the object of helping in the application of science to the pastoral industry'.[15] On a more modest level in 1957 Dalgety established a Soil Testing Laboratory designed to establish whether soil deficiencies and livestock ailments were related. NMA appointed a scientific officer in 1928 and was also one of many companies who employed engineers for guidance on new farm machinery.[16]

Direct and regular contact with different functional groups within the network helped keep agents up to date with a wide range of relevant developments, particularly commercial information and new farming equipment and techniques. This was particularly important for smaller firms that lacked the resources to hire engineers and scientific officers. Agents who lacked a London office had regular contact with overseas correspondent firms. Dennys Lascelles' correspondence with Robert Brooks & Company of Cornhill, London, dealt in detail with the current and future prospects of the pastoral industry:

> People on this side are quite alive to the increased quantity to be expected from your side, and should trade not improve, this must affect prices when the clip begins to arrive . . . things are very hard in Germany, and there are large unhealed sores in the trading community in France . . . the near future of the wool trade is more than unusually open to the influence of outside matters.[17]

During the 1893 commercial crisis, Brooks observed: 'the entire destruction on the side of credit of all things Australian' but by 1905 Brooks was able to report: 'the manufacturing districts are generally favourable and we look forward to a good trade for some time'.[18] Technical information was also received from foreign manufacturers of agricultural equipment although some agents sent employees overseas to observe personally the complex operation of new machinery.

Firms supported external teaching and research. Financial support was provided for the Veterinary Science Faculty at the University of Melbourne (see chapter 4) and favourable comments were noted of Massey Agricultural College: 'Students can learn woolclassing and all manner of things connected with farming'.[19] Employees were encouraged to participate in professional groups, and publish their results. G. Colman of Australian Estates reported favourably on research into the cross-breeding of Zebu bulls and Shorthorn cows to a meeting of the Council for Scientific and Industrial Research (CSIR) in 1935 suggesting that this produced animals that were more disease resistant, ate more grass varieties, and needed less feed to grow at the same rate.[20] More unusually, S. William of Goldsbrough Mort pioneered placing rugs over shorn sheep which, *Pastoral Review* claimed, produced cleaner, better quality wool, and a better condition of sheep.[21] Firms cooperated with government-sponsored work, New Zealand agents supplying the Department of Agriculture with wool for experimentation in 1927 and proffering their opinions on the spinning quality, clean yield, and estimated price of different types.[22]

Farmers were a source of information as well as recipients. Agents sent out circulars particularly to their 'tied' clients in recognition that their loss-making loans were effectively being cross-subsidised by the company and its free clients.[23] More extensive feedback from long-established clients was common. In 1892 Dennys Lascelles received a detailed letter from one of its clients explaining the benefits of growing lucerne which had enabled him to fatten at least four sheep per acre.[24] In 1929 when Goldsbrough Mort were studying publications on pasture improvement a Wimmera client told them that the use of superphosphate over a series of years had increased his carrying capacity from 0.75 to two sheep per acre.[25] Agents also used farmers for organising trials of new ideas and equipment.

Firms drew heavily on published sources for information. These included specialised scientific publications read by veterinary and agricultural scientists within the larger firms. They were supplemented by newspapers and other regular publications which were scanned for additional commercial information and also legal and political developments. An extant scrapbook of newspaper cuttings kept by Wright Stephenson during 1936 to 1954 indicates its awareness of some key commercial issues. Articles included the impact of the land tax, mortgage debts and the provision of relief from liabilities, wages and farm prices, freight rates, export prices, the trade outlook, and the economic condition of the rural industries.

INFORMATION DISSEMINATION

Information was disseminated to farmers through various contact points. Personal contact occurred between farmer and branch manager at the country office, while travellers and inspectors conveyed information and advice during visits to the farm. Firms increasingly resorted to the use of telephones in the early twentieth century as the cost of calls began to fall, the extent of the network broadened, and the number of clients increased. Specific sections and departments of the firms made direct contact with farmers on scientific and technical questions. Australian Estates' research department dealt individually with farmer enquiries, 'tender[ing] their advice free of charge'. Dalgety's charged customers a small fee for the company's soil-testing laboratory but reported that it was 'creating widespread interest'.[26] Social occasions and agricultural shows also provided a meeting point appropriate for information exchange. Levins acted as importing agent for a wide range of agricultural machinery and organised events such as sheep shearing competitions to publicise new developments.[27]

Written communication was widely used for a more formal and permanent transfer of information, especially when the issues were too complex or detailed to be dealt with orally. Improving office technology facilitated this mechanism, especially the adoption of typewriters. The increasing use of written communication perhaps also reflected the increased technical complexity of farming from the end of the nineteenth century and the reduced emphasis agents placed on personal contact. With further developments in printing and duplication, firms introduced standardised letters, leaflets, magazines, booklets, and manuals for farmers. This yielded immense economies of scale in information transfer for expanding national firms in supplying standardised information and advice to large numbers of clients simultaneously. In 1897 Goldsbrough Mort published a guide entitled *A Practical Treatise on Wool and Sheep Breeding, Edible Scrubs, The Economical Use of Tank Water, Station Book-Keeping*. As the title suggests it covered a wide range of topics in simple language, with illustrations and explanations. For example, it reminded farmers of the importance of undertaking an annual financial analysis and advocated double-entry bookkeeping.

More common, though, were regular broadsheets and periodicals designed to keep the farmer up-to-date and in regular contact with the agent. As early as 1882 Reid began to publish *Farmers' Circular and Weekly Report*. This free weekly leaflet had a circulation of around 1000 and carried articles on such topics as mechanisation, crossbred sheep, growing winter feed, and topdressing with lime.[28] More extensive was Wright Stephenson's monthly journal *Farm Economy*. Significantly, this initiative began in 1922 in the middle of a serious farming depression when the demand for information and advice was at a peak. Its first editorial noted: 'In the hope of spreading sound and reliable information upon various points connected with farming, we have initiated this monthly newspaper to circulate gratuitously amongst our clients.' The journal was a goldmine of information for farmers and encouraged them to contribute articles as part of a process of information exchange and discussion. In the earliest issues there was advice on calculating annual profit and loss accounts and on the employment of cost accounting to test the use of such items as manures and stock feeds.[29]

Another highly successful company publication has been *Dalgety's*

Annual Wool Review, which contains extensive information and statistics of the wool trade and has been used widely in the current study. It has also played an active part in bringing new publications to the attention of farmers.[30] Australian Estates' research department published regular bulletins, 'full of valuable practical instruction and advice'.[31] Sometimes local branches initiated their own circular for a specific reason. For example, Winchcombe Carson's Longreach branch started a weekly circular in 1920, which it sent out to most farmers in the area. Clearly, the circular was valued by farmers since the company received many appreciative letters, and when it tried to cut costs during the Depression in 1930 by reducing its circulation objections were raised.[32] Industry-wide publications included the *Stock and Station Journal*, the *Wool and Stock Journal*, and the *Australasian Pastoralists Review*.

The contents of brochures and magazines from other functional groups in the network were assessed and, if appropriate, passed on to clients or summarised in the company magazine. Agricultural suppliers realised that providing written information could also be a way of selling their products and turned to agents for assistance. Thus, in August 1929 NZLMA received a manufacturer's leaflet explaining the value of a nitrogen culture which they could supply. In September 1929 G. Holford, a representative of ICI, sent NZLMA a copy of a booklet, *Grassland – Its Treatment and Management*, asking for a list of farmers who might be interested in a copy.[33] The publication was more than a simple product leaflet and included information on the use of sulphate of ammonia for grass seed, ensilage, and hay production, but ICI hoped that it would increase its sales. The agents had to use their expertise and corporate resources to interpret and assess the information they received before deciding in what form, if any, it should be disseminated. This included filtering out inappropriate information sources for the farmer, particularly as the volume of available information expanded rapidly from the late nineteenth century. In 1893 the Melbourne-based publishers of the *Australasian Pastoralists Review* approached Dunedin agents, Stronach Morris, to try and persuade Otago farmers to subscribe. The agents replied that the journal mostly dealt with Australian matters and would be of limited interest to Otago farmers.[34]

Agents stood between the providers of technical and scientific knowledge on the one hand and the practical users of it on the other. Their ability to connect theorists and practitioners was noticed by the *Pastoral Review*:

> there is a gap between the practical man and the scientist which it is thought should be more adequately bridged by spreading information from one to the other. The company's [Australian Estates] research department . . . is in touch with both the scientist and the practical working of sheep and cattle properties . . . interpreting to the practical man new knowledge as it becomes known to the scientist.[35]

As well as simplifying complex scientific developments in a manner that could be understood and applied by farmers, agents coordinated with the scientific community in relation to problems experienced by farmers, consulting with the CSIR or Department of Agriculture if the firm could not find the solution.

The role of the agents as acquirers and disseminators of information was frequently a reiterative process with regular feedback mechanisms. This was particularly the case in trialling new products. William Dawson of Fortrose reported to NZLMA that he had been very satisfied with the 'Farmer's Favorite' drill purchased from the company: 'the drill gave every satisfaction. I found the draught very light. The manure and seed distributors worked smoothly & did excellent work'.[36] The agent continued the circular flow back to the farmer, for instance in overcoming faulty use of a product. Thus, in 1904, Edwin Harrison, a sales representative for sheep dip manufacturers, MacDougall Brothers, noted in a letter to NZLMA:

> I find people in this district very careless in regard to using sheep dips . . . they don't take into consideration the far too short baths . . . many of them have to keep the sheep sufficiently long in to allow to get thoroughly saturated, and . . . they don't seem to understand there is any difference between hard and soft water . . . where water is hard . . . more dip must be allowed.[37]

Agents could also serve as disseminators of information and advice unconnected to the pastoral industry but of significance to the personal well-being of a farmer and therefore the prosperity of his business. This included a range of legal and social advice that was often not available from other sources, either because such services did not exist or the farmer was remote from them. A striking example occurred in 1898 when Abraham Cuffe wrote to Dennys Lascelles: 'in all probability I will be compeld by January next to go both to the Insolvent and the Divorce Courts'. He noted that he was 50 miles (80 km) from the nearest source of legal advice. The firm replied, presumably after consulting its solicitor, with appropriate advice.[38]

SOME KEY DEVELOPMENTS

A focus on three major farming issues – refrigeration, rabbit infestation, and shearing technology – illustrates the role played by the agents.[39] Refrigeration provided greater production flexibility for farmers, rabbit eradication would remove a major source of uncertainty, and mechanical shearing achieved labour savings.

The role of agents in providing finance and network connections to aid the development of refrigeration has been mentioned in previous chapters. The firms also played an important role in providing information and convincing farmers of its value. John Cooke, while working for NZLMA, was a leading figure in the adoption of refrigeration in New Zealand in the early 1880s. A decade later, as Manager of AMLF, he worked hard to persuade Australian farmers to follow the same path.[40] He drew attention to its positive impact in New Zealand where livestock had been almost unsaleable in the early 1880s but a decade later commonly fetched two or three times the price in New South Wales or Victoria. Besides opening up a much larger international market for meat and dairy products, Cooke observed the operational flexibility which refrigeration provided for Australian pastoralists who could turn to these forms of production when wool markets were depressed.

Cooke emphasised that agents, possessed of superior resources and information, were best placed to initiate this new development. He noted the 'indisposition and inability of pastoralists to attack this great question vigorously and intelligently . . . had the frozen meat trade of New Zealand been initiated by growers rather than their business agents the trade would not have assumed its present proportions, nor would it have reached such a profitable stage'.[41] Using his experience acquired in New Zealand, Cooke advised on the establishment of freezing works and improved shipping facilities. Dennys Lascelles was also closely involved with spreading information about refrigeration in Victoria and in 1894 was in close discussion with NMA about plans to establish a large chilling and freezing enterprise. The two firms discussed issues such as the need for a large national enterprise to avoid clashes and competition, the desirability of having farmer shareholders, and the need for up-country chilling works closely connected to slaughterhouses and supporting a centralised freezing and storage facility at the point of overseas shipment.[42]

Agents also acted as the farmer's advocate in helping to break down shipping monopolies in this new trade, P & O having initially granted a monopoly of frozen meat space in its steamers to Nelson Brothers. Cooke was concerned that limited space and high freight rates would discourage farmers from supporting refrigeration and indicated that the agents were willing to use their 'powerful lever in the form of wool shipments' to break any such monopoly.[43] He went on to use emotive language that was designed to emphasise where the agent's first loyalty lay: 'nothing will ever induce me to sacrifice the producer by joining a league that regards him [farmer] in the light of a lemon to be squeezed to the utmost possible extent'.[44]

In 1874 four pairs of imported rabbits were released in Victoria and within five years there had been an 'inordinate increase of rabbits . . . eating everything before them'.[45] Agents regularly reported on the extent of the problem in different regions and sought various solutions. Australian Estates experimented initially with rabbit containment methods on their properties, particularly by using wire netting to enclose stations. The company reported in 1893 that the methods developed on its farms were now being used by many of its clients as a result of the company's efforts to disseminate the practice. Other agents also encouraged farmers to enclose and provided finance for what could be a significant additional investment; AMLF noted in the same year that it did not 'stint the supply of funds for this specific purpose'.[46]

When the attack on rabbits turned towards chemical poisons the agents intermediated by arranging for clients to trial products and report back

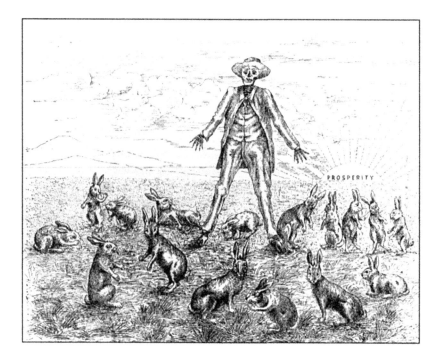

Plate 7.1   'The strongest union in Australia.' This cartoon depicts the twin issues for farmers of rabbit infestation and union strength among shearers, 1892. Although the *Australasian Pastoralists Review* was a focus for concern about labour troubles, the massed ranks of the rabbit were a far more serious threat to the farmer. (*Australasian Pastoralists Review*, 14 May 1892.)

the results to them; they in turn contacted the suppliers. In December 1896 Pitt, Son & Badgery sent a client, J. Higgins, a supply of 'Patent Phosphorised Annihilator' to deal with a rabbit problem. The next stage was biological warfare to infect the rabbit population with diseases, preferably infectious ones. In 1906 Australian Estates donated £500 towards the establishment of a Bacteriological Institute in New South Wales with the aim of finding ways of exterminating the rabbit population. On another occasion, Dalgety organised a meeting of the leading London-based agents which led to the company hiring Dr Danysz of the Pasteur Institute to conduct experiments on Broughton Island. The experiment established ways of killing rabbits by germ warfare in their natural habitat but without initiating an epidemic.[47] The agents have continued to play a prominent part in the long-term battle with the rabbit.

On a happier note, agents pioneered the development of improved shearing methods. Australian Estates experimented with the use of contract shearers on its own farms and decided that they were 'a better and quieter lot than those that go travelling about'.[48] Elders advised of the importance of timing in shearing, if too early the weight would be light, if too late the condition would deteriorate. In 1907 Elders went on to organise trials of damp detectors which would enable farmers to see if the wool was dry before commencing shearing.[49]

Agents led the way in the introduction of mechanical shearing equipment. As early as 1887, 'an exhibition was given at the Melbourne wool stores of Goldsbrough Mort . . . in the presence of leading pastoralists and wool notabilities . . . demonstrated that sheepshearing by machinery was not only practicable, but was a vast improvement on the old hand methods'.[50] In spite of this 'vast improvement' it took many years of experimentation and improvement to convince most farmers of the new shearing methods. In April 1897 Australian Estates was busy experimenting with different shearing machines on its properties. By 1903 few farms possessed a shearing machine but Australian Estates already owned as many as eight.[51] In New Zealand, Levins pioneered the sale of shearing machines. Levins acted as the local agent for the Wolseley Shearing Machine Company and publicised the machine's merits among the farming community. At the 1902 Hawke's Bay agricultural show the company organised a demonstration stand and the relative novelty of a shearing competition to emphasise the benefits of the new machine. In 1909 one of Levin's employees, Alexander Hutchinson, designed an improved shearing machine and in the following years cooperated with manufacturers, Listers, in its development.[52]

THE FARMER'S ADVOCATE

Agents served as advocates, representing farmers collectively or individually in relations with third parties. They provided references for farmers and station managers seeking new employment and served as estate trustees. In 1892 Stronach Morris provided a favourable reference for Robert MacGregor, recommending him for the position of station manager on a Canterbury farm.[53] They acted as the farmer's advocate in response to native title claims. Murray Roberts reported in 1888: 'during the last year we have had to fight two petitions from some of the native owners, but which have now been satisfactorily disposed of'. By 1906 the same firm was still helping farmers to get land titles through the Native Land Court in New Zealand.[54] Part of the agents' finance-related services was to act as the farmer's advocate in negotiations with mortgagees, particularly in seeking rescheduled loans in difficult times (see chapter 4).

Agents used their size, expertise, and connections to act as influential spokespersons in local, national and international debate. Their size and influence meant that they could more easily absorb the high costs of lobbying and were often well represented in business and commercial associations. Marcel Conran of Dennys Lascelles served as President of the Geelong Chamber of Commerce in the 1890s and used this position to pursue local matters of concern to pastoralists, such as rail freights, postal facilities, telephone and telegraph charges. Political representation was frequent: from AMLF Sir James McBain was a member of the Victorian

Legislative Assembly and then Council, and Arthur Stanley became Governor of Victoria. Such influential figures made strong representations when prospective legislation, such as land laws, affected the interests of farmers.

Many agents backed this up with financial contributions to sympathetic political parties and interest groups. Winchcombe Carson donated £5 to the Land Owners Defence Committee in 1911, a lobby group formed to watch the progress of the Federal land tax, then gave £25 to the Liberal Association of New South Wales in 1916 and £50 to the Nationalist Country Party Campaign Fund in 1929.[55] Opportunities often arose to gain a return on these political investments. UMA records show how one of its executives was able to take advantage of travelling in the same ship as the Queensland Treasurer to enter into discussions about proposed land legislation.[56] Industry associations were also participants in national debate. In 1933 the NZLAAA established a committee to publicise and advise on the problems of the dairying and cereal-growing industries.

The rising political influence of the agents can be particularly dated from the late nineteenth century when the growing size of the leading firms coincided with the waning influence of the graziers' own representation due to changes in electoral divisions and the break-up of the large rural estates.[57] Early evidence of agent influence can be seen in securing the passage of the 1889 Land Act in New South Wales and the formation in 1886 of the Commercial, Pastoral, and Agricultural Association of New South Wales as an industry pressure group.[58]

Their influence was tested to the full during World War One when farming operations were thrown into uncertainty. In his study of the political economy of the Australian wool industry, Tsokhas notes the wartime vulnerability of an exporting nation with a small shipping fleet. That very generous purchase terms were extracted from the British government owed much to 'the ability of woolgrowers and brokers . . . to organise themselves into a government-led coalition'.[59] In the postwar crisis of large wool surpluses, brokers mediated between the Australian government and woolgrowers in bringing BAWRA to an end. Additionally, their superior knowledge of wool markets and production along with their gently persuasive negotiating style with the British is contrasted with Prime Minister Hughes' aggressive but less convincing approach.[60] Similarly, in New Zealand the NZWBA pressured Prime Minister Massey to avoid flooding the wool market with sales of wartime surpluses.[61]

As in other services, the agents' capabilities were highly specific to farming. When they strayed more generally into the nature of national and international politics and society their views and advice were often naive and undiplomatic. Elders, for example, observed in 1938: 'in Mr Chamberlain the Empire has a man of strength, courage, and patience who will do his utmost to prevent any widespread conflagration'.[62] The jingoism and hostility to *fin de siècle* Parisian lifestyles by NMA's New Zealand manager in the 1890s would have created a diplomatic incident if they had been made public.[63]

CONCLUSION

The information paradox means that information is often difficult to trade in the marketplace. Free-riding and limited resources discouraged individual and even cooperative research by farmers. The remoteness and inexperience of Australasian farmers working in a rapidly changing sector made accurate and up-to-date information essential but difficult to obtain. The solution to these problems came through agent intermediation. Their internal resources and broad contacts made them vital information receptacles. The ongoing relationship between farmer and agent overcame the problem of buying and selling information; instead it was an externality of other transactions between them, incidental at first but increasingly preconceived as the relationship developed. Nor did they worry about free-riding when some developments became widely known to other farmers since their broad interests were tied in closely with the progress of the sector as a whole.

The agents' expertise enabled them to interpret and translate the more complex information in a manner suitable for practical farmers. The building of trust between the two and the vested interests of agents provided for higher value advice to flow in the wake of information transfers. In effect, these unpriced information services rewarded farmers as a loyalty rebate. Finally, the size and influence of agent firms enabled them to use their information and expertise as a powerful advocate for the farming sector. Agents were never the sole suppliers of useful information to farmers, and in the twentieth century pluralism increased particularly as a result of the increased role of government in providing public good access. However, the agents retain an important role as intermediators and translators in the flow of large volumes of complex information.

CHAPTER EIGHT

Organisational Structures and Administrative Practices

Chapter 2 outlined the growth and changing strategies of the leading pastoral agent companies as they came to dominate their industry and become among Australia's largest corporations through strategies of spatial and product development. However, institutional growth is generally accompanied by coordination difficulties such as rising administration costs, slow decision-making procedures, and employee opportunism. Therefore, as firms develop they look for improved ways of structuring their activities to avoid such organisational inefficiencies. This chapter examines the evolution of sophisticated patterns of organisation developed by the companies, the forces to which they responded in making these changes, and the effectiveness of their solutions. Organisational development is most commonly associated with changes in hierarchical structure. There are many other aspects to the question of organisation building that deal with how the structure actually operates. These include the internal systems of communication and reporting between tiers, the standardisation of procedures, the system of accounting, and the fostering of human resources.

THE MOTIVES FOR ORGANISATIONAL DEVELOPMENT

As firms grow, managerial diseconomies of scale can occur as key decision-makers become overburdened with routine work and are therefore unable to develop effective long-term planning. The work of Penrose and of Chandler demonstrates that this barrier to firm growth is not insurmountable.[1] Chandler showed how expanding American firms in the second half of the nineteenth century overcame this constraint by introducing more systematic and efficient organisations. By designing integrative hierarchies of specialist managers routine functions could be performed more systematically leaving key decision-makers sufficient time to develop strategies critical to the long-term performance of the company.

Chandler summarised the causality with his epithet, 'strategy determines structure', and went on to show that different forms of strategy required distinctive organisational responses.[2] The growth by vertical integration of many American firms in the late nineteenth century led to the creation of functionally specialised departments such as marketing, research or production, which yielded economies of scale in administration and helped create a company with a centralised management structure. Diversification in the early twentieth century led American firms to divide their activities into a set of regional or product divisions. This multi-divisional form decentralised operational management, above which a general office determined overall strategy. An alternative approach is for firms to separate their diverse operations into different companies under a holding company structure where more strategic decision-making is delegated to the individual subsidiary.

A second and related consequence of the growth of the firm is that principal–agent problems intensify as employees and junior managers become more distant from the owners and senior managers, and information asymmetries between the two groups increase.[3] Firms there-fore seek to redesign their organisational structure to mitigate the risk of opportunism. Better reporting procedures and regularised channels of communication, for example, enable more effective monitoring of em-ployees. Decentralising groups into distinct profit or cost centres enables more targeted monitoring and provides greater performance incentives.

Thirdly, external changes also influence the process of design. Improve-ments in communications technology, for example, provide firms with new ways of structuring their activities which improve information flows for monitoring and policy development.[4] On the other hand, an economic downturn or intensified competition may force firms to rethink the shape of the organisation in a way that reduces their costs.

The pastoral agencies were influenced by each of these factors. The rapid growth of the firms occurred in distinct phases of strategy which heavily influenced their overall structure. Mitigating opportunism was an important question for geographically distended firms. External influences included major changes in transport and communications technology, the impact of the economic crises of the 1890s and 1930s, and the postwar cost-price squeeze. Firms were strongly aware of these influences on the shape of their organisation; Dalgety's noted in 1959: 'organisation is of increasing importance as the company grows'.[5] Tensions and inconsisten-cies between motivating factors were revealed in periodic changes and swings in policy. Pressure to reduce administrative costs in a downturn can weaken the benefits of organisational growth especially where this leads to additional workloads, cuts in training programs, and the merging of different sections. Similarly, decentralisation, by separating out different products or areas, encourages competition and promotes monitoring, yet centralisation is more likely to yield economies of scale.

PATTERNS OF HIERARCHICAL DESIGN

Many of the earliest pastoral agent businesses of the mid-nineteenth century were small private firms with simple structures. They were located at only one or a few sites, particularly Sydney and Melbourne, with several owner managers, skilled in the particular specialism of the firm such as livestock, produce, or finance, and making most of the decisions. Travellers and rural agents, often working on contracts and commissions, were the firm's link with the local farming community. Where the firm was based on multiple sites in Australasia there was little coordination between each site, which operated at arm's length. As Wright Stephenson was to note later: 'each branch had its separate balance sheets, and dealt with the other branches . . . as if it were a separate business'.[6] Indeed, several firms, including Dalgety and Murray Roberts, were owned and operated through a series of local partnership agreements consisting of a core of partners together with several different local partners in each area.

Organisational charts have been constructed using extant personnel records, correspondence, and accounts. Some company charts also survive. Structures were regularly modified and no two firms were identical in organisation, therefore stylised charts represent common patterns at different periods.

Somewhat more complex structures were required by those companies which were owned and managed from London, such as NZLMA and AMLF. Their need to exercise control over remote Australasian operations required a London Board of Directors together with colonial management. Initially, there was a minimalist senior management structure in Australia and New Zealand. Branch managers were key appointments of people who were often well known to members of the London Board. They worked to close contractual instructions laid down by the company and often reported directly to the London Board. Branch managers were commonly supported by a Local Board of Advice although their powers appear to have been limited to a periodic consultative role rather than being a regular part of the management hierarchy.[7] A Colonial Superintendent or Inspector was a periodic visitor from Britain, reporting directly to the London Board on Australasian operations (see Figure 8.1). However, NZLMA, which was organised as an offshoot of the Bank of New Zealand, was managed in the colonies from the outset by a Local Board of influential local financiers and entrepreneurs associated with the bank. This predated the general shift southwards of management responsibilities by other companies and may have mitigated the policy conflicts between London and Australia which plagued AMLF.[8]

Service Departments

Service diversification by agents from about the 1880s was examined in chapter 2. These services complemented one another in attracting clients and yielding scope economies but required additional and somewhat

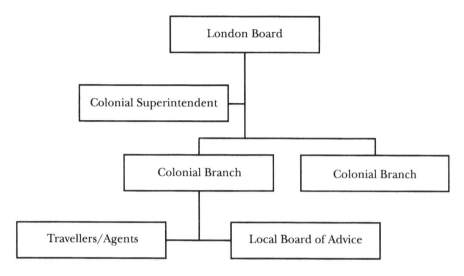

Figure 8.1 Organisational design, 1871: remote control

different skills. Organising livestock sales required a knowledge base about animals distinct from dealing with insurance and shipping firms in the overseas consignment of wool. Therefore, as the firms continued to grow, there were economies of scale to be earned from splitting up the different services into separate departments, and yet some form of centralised coordination between them was necessary to ensure complementary behaviour for the good of the firm.

The result was to organise each of the main branch offices into a set of departments by pastoral service activity, most commonly one each for wool, other produce, and livestock. They were sometimes subdivided into sections, thus livestock might have store, stud, and fat stock sections. Each department had its own manager expert in this area.[9] Additional departments supported branch level functions such as farm inspection, accounts, and correspondence (see Figure 8.2). Since lending tied up a large portion of the companies' resources, often for long periods of time, these decisions were taken by senior management. Therefore, in most firms the branch manager directly controlled lending services and for some decisions required the Board's authority. In assessing a loan application and monitoring its subsequent progress, however, he relied heavily on specialist information and expert opinions offered by departmental managers.

Strengthening Colonial Management

Concern with rising levels of long-term farmer loans in the late nineteenth century, culminating in the crisis of the 1890s, heavily influenced the organisation of companies. The London firms, in particular, sought to strengthen their colonial management hierarchy to monitor managers more closely and rein in the level of advances. The improvements in long distance

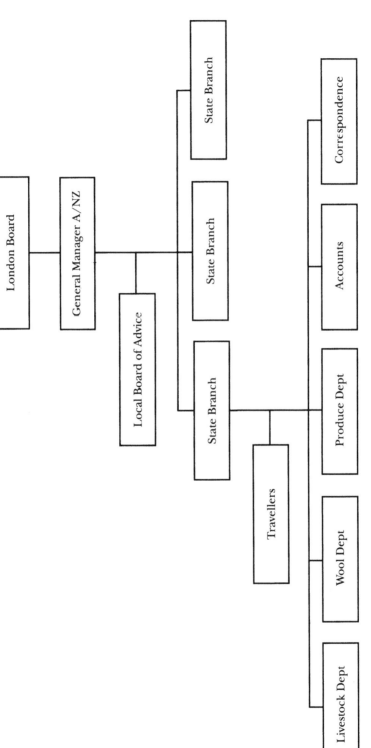

Figure 8.2 Organisational design, 1901: departmentalisation and centralisation

communications also fostered a shift of responsibilities towards colonial-based management; Dalgety noted in 1882: 'the gradual change in business thro' steam & telegrams which may throw the business far more ... on colonial partners'.[10] A decade later Dalgety instituted a major restructuring of its colonial management.[11] The improvements in communications meant that rather than rely on carefully selected branch managers, occasionally monitored by a visitor from England, it was possible to delegate ongoing responsibility to a permanent and expanding Australasian management team with whom regular contact could be maintained.

The shift of the wool market back to the colonies similarly affected the locus of executive responsibility. Organising local sales required additional responsibilities, functions, and local knowledge. The late entry of AMLF into the local wool market resulted from the London Board's fear that it would undermine their own executive authority. Finally, with the maturation of the sector, the accumulation of specialised knowledge and contacts, and heightened competition, the pastoral agents went through a similar life-cycle to other British free-standing companies, a point clearly recognised by Doxat of Dalgety in 1887: '[men] on the spot are better judges than a number of men around a table in Lombard Street'.[12]

Initially, firms responded to those challenges by making the position of Colonial Superintendent more permanent and locally domiciled. His basic reporting powers were substantially strengthened with the conversion of the position into General Manager.[13] He was to be the highest authority in colonial management, responsible for seeing through the Board's policy and making recommendations to the Board. In particular, he would arrange regular inspection of all branches and control the appointment and working conditions of company officers in Australasia.[14] NMA's New Zealand General Manager, J. M. Ritchie, recognised the enhancement of his role and the appointment of a second in command in 1900: 'I shall not be expected to be concerned with daily details to the same extent as hitherto: but rather with supervision and advice'.[15]

Centralisation

Local as well as London firms realised the need for greater coordination and monitoring of branch lending through a strengthening of higher management. The incorporation of many of the largest local private firms from the 1880s created an additional centripetal tendency by ending the multiple partnerships system and obliging firms to think about the implications of a unitary ownership structure. On its incorporation in 1906 Wright Stephenson decided to switch to a centralised form of administration. An informative policy statement drew attention to perceived disadvantages of the prevailing decentralisation which had also been practised by its rivals in New Zealand including Dalgety, Murray Roberts, and NMA. These disadvantages were the loss of economies of scale especially in buying power, the weakening of market strength especially in freight negotiations, the lack of uniformity in working methods, the time wasted disputing commissions shared between branches, and the poor inter-branch relations that resulted. The new system introduced by Wright Stephenson centralised many operations at its Dunedin Head Office including accounts, purchases, and exporting, although the other branches maintained core activities in livestock and land sales, and wool sales.[16]

Country Branches

The expansion of rural branches was a key aspect of company growth in the twentieth century (see chapter 2). This added an additional layer to their organisation, what Chandler entitled 'field units'.[17] The firms clearly saw their expanding network of branches as a competitive tool serving as a feeder to the State branch in the provision of wool and livestock business. Dalgety later referred to, 'the country organisation [as] the backbone of our business . . . without it, we would be akin to a tree trying to live without its roots'.[18] As such it was also a useful counterbalance to the centralisation of senior management. As the company expanded, the country branches were organised into a hierarchy of regional branches, sub-branches, and agencies (see Figure 8.3).

Regional Divisions and Decentralisation

Rapid geographical expansion of the firms made it difficult to maintain the centralising tendencies. Country branch expansion increased the difficulties of local management as AMLF noted: 'it is very difficult indeed to obtain really capable men and to control them so far out in the country'.[19] AMLF's solution, initially at least, was to maintain the system of travellers and non-company agents but most others saw continued expansion of the branch system as preferable in most locations for the reasons mentioned above. Control problems were heightened by the development of multiple tiers of branches. Dalgety later distinguished five hierarchical tiers of branches or other local representation.[20] Administrative complexity was increased by the addition of extra departments at the main State branches reflecting heightened activity in shipping and insurance agencies, and vehicle and general merchandise sales to farmers.

In response the firms decentralised their activities into a series of regional divisions based on their main state branches. The idea was to push daily routine administration and management back to the regions rather than overburden the senior managers in Australasia. The change was more discreet than the opening of country branches and therefore its timing more difficult to specify, but most probably it was occurring in the 1930s and 1940s. The decentralised structure, however, was quite different from that of the nineteenth century. Each main branch, or division, had its own local management team, headed by the State Manager and the State Board (or management committee), which presided over its centralised service departments and its geographically dispersed country branches. Another difference was that all firms now had central coordination based locally in Australasia.

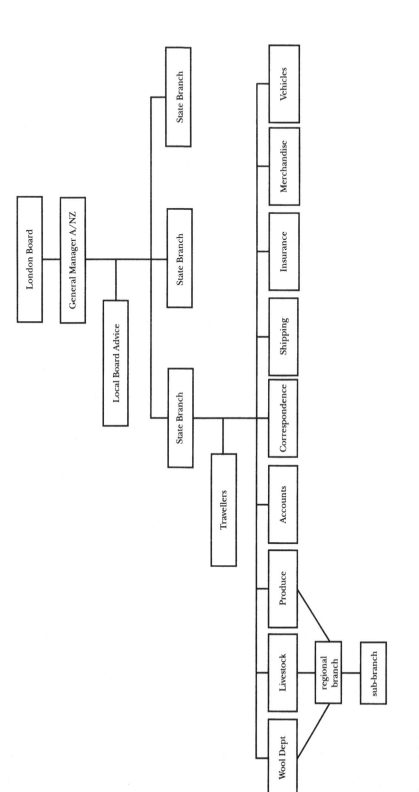

Figure 8.3 Organisational design, 1931: regional divisionalisation and decentralisation

A second influence on regional divisionalisation was the extended
interwar crisis. In this atmosphere, and coming so soon after multi-
directional growth, the agents were keen to establish which parts of the
organisation were underperforming. Dividing the firm into distinct and
separate groups made it much easier to compare relative performances.
The companies began to generate financial accounts for the different
main branch networks. This also encouraged internal competition
between the regional divisions. In this sense the companies had gone full
circle since the nineteenth century, Elders noting: 'firms who have offices
in both states [Victoria and New South Wales] treat each other virtually
as opponents'.[21]

Regional rather than product divisions have been viewed as incomplete
forms of managerial decentralisation.[22] Each division shares similar
competencies and therefore, since none is unique, full delegation of
responsibility is not deemed necessary. However, in the case of pastoral
agents almost all non-strategic tasks were decentralised to the major State
divisions.[23] This most likely derives from the historical independence of
individual States and the difficulties of central coordination of administrative operations over very long distances. Some firms went further down
the path of decentralisation than others. Dalgety, for example, supplied
its State branches with capital and left them to employ it while the head
office of NZLMA kept a closer control over its use. Dalgety judged their
main branches by the return on company capital while NZLMA assessed
them more closely, looking at all sources of capital.[24]

General Office

By the 1940s, therefore, pastoral agencies were beginning to look akin to
the multidivisional company. What they lacked was a top level general
office which made broader strategic decisions. The General Manager
normally operated head office with only a small staff and concentrated on
national coordination and monitoring functions more than policy development. Before 1939 Goldsbrough Mort's head office staff consisted of no
more than the General Manager, an accountant, tax officer, and a few
clerks, indicating the largely non-executive nature of its role.[25] The largest
State branch served as the Australasian head office and its strategic tasks
and personnel overlapped with State-wide routines and responsibilities.
Elders had created a head office at Adelaide in 1920 but its early years were
mostly filled with the daily affairs of the South Australian business.

In 1944 Goldsbrough Mort, under the impressive leadership of its
new General Manager, W. E. M. Campbell, enlarged the policy-making
group at head office. In 1946 Elders South Australian office was admin-
istratively separated from the Adelaide head office of the company. This
move does not appear to have worked successfully since in 1953 the firm
created an Internal Board of Management for South Australia comparable
to that for other States. The reason for this was that head office staff were
'too much tied to State detail to be able to give the proper thought,

analysis, consideration and time to all the Inter-State accounts and statistics, the sole purpose of which is to make H/O review and control on an overall company basis'. This carefully considered proposal was seen as central to future strategy; it 'will make possible a more efficient and smooth working control of the Company as a whole' – and would remove some of the 'enormous risks . . . which have involved us in huge losses'. Finally, in 1957 Elders ended the continuing overlap of personnel between head and State offices and provided for a further delineation of functions between the two groups.[26]

The British-controlled firms had strategic decision makers in the form of their London Board. However, these distant, non-executive Boards were considered increasingly inappropriate for the highly competitive Australasian stock and station agent industry. In 1939 the New Zealand management of NZLMA on several occasions bemoaned the inability of its London Board to appreciate the finer points of the local industry.[27] Moreover, it was generally felt that these organisational shortcomings had hindered a more effective response to the severe crisis of the 1930s.

By 1947 NZLMA had shifted strategy away from London: 'whatever we did in the old days, we now leave the running of our New Zealand business to our New Zealand executive'.[28] The local head office now controlled internal finance and directed most areas of policy. However, it may have been the case that they did not support the geographical shift with sufficient additional local staff to foster new strategies in addition to coordination responsibilities. The General Manager noted that all his 'working hours are required for the successful control of the Company's New Zealand business'.[29] Dalgety was also aware of the importance of not overburdening the General Manager when it appointed an executive assistant in 1959. This left the General Manager with more time to deal 'without interruption to the major problems that arise from time to time'.[30] None the less, this suggests an emphasis on short-term problem-solving rather than long-term planning.

The correspondence of NMA's General Manager, G. R. Ritchie, through the interwar period suggests someone with a strong grasp of the industry but whose time was taken up with policy implementation rather than development.[31] He received support from a very limited staff. NMA also developed a powerful local head office after the war. One of the key changes occurred in 1951 when the New Zealand General Manager also became a director of the company and two years later changed his title to Managing Director to reflect this combination of executive and directorial functions. In the following years he substantially expanded the size of the local head office in Dunedin to include by 1968 an assistant general manager, chief farming officer, chief accountant, administrative officer, pastoral officer, publicity officer, wool officer, merchandise officer, and data processing officer. In 1969 the company's head office was transferred from London to New Zealand confirming this shift of executive authority.[32] The Chairman and General Manager had extensively discussed the relative merits of London or Dunedin control of the company in 1944. The fear of possible nationalisation in New Zealand and the status associated with a London head office persuaded them against a shift at that time but both believed that it would occur in due course with the continued expansion of New Zealand.[33]

Subsidiaries and Service Divisions

A further major restructure of the firms began in the interwar period and continued after 1945 in response to extensive and unrelated diversification strategies into new products, markets, and functions (see chapter 2). Coordination with their traditional pastoral service functions and market was minimal and the skills of these new activities quite different (see Figure 8.4). This posed a major dilemma for the firms which had structured successive layers of their organisation to reflect the changing developments of the pastoral industry. As Dalgety's noted in 1957: 'trading on our own account requires . . . possibly even a different organisation'.[34] A second problem came as firms attempted to diversify their markets towards the population growth of the towns and cities whilst their branch structure was focused on rural communities.

Initially, the firms simply created additional departments within the division dealing with new product lines individually or under the umbrella of 'merchandise' with individual product sections. However, they encountered problems handling goods and processes with which they were unfamiliar; the failure of vehicle departments was examined in chapter 2. Dalgety's lack of expertise in handling consumer goods was confirmed in comments by Electrolux: 'Although your officers may possess high qualifications in office management . . . the technical aspect associated with sealed unit merchandise . . . could not be fully appreciated'.[35] In New Zealand, NZLMA failed to secure an agency to sell Benelux washing machines because of its inexperience and lack of showroom and service facilities.[36] The problem was accentuated by continuing to regard pastoralism as its core and concentrating its most talented workers in these departments.

In response, Elders experimented with alternative forms of organisational design. In particular, it added an additional tier to their State-level bureaucracy. Recognising that sales was a quite distinct function from most of the firm's other activities Elders established a sales manager in the merchandise department with his own sections or departments covering accounts, records/statistics, ordering/distribution, and five travellers each with their own regional territory.[37] In effect, this was superimposing a product division on to a geographic division. While such multiple divisionalisation is an acceptable structure it did not work well here.[38] The product division did not fit easily with the rest of the company. It duplicated in an uncoordinated fashion several existing functions at different levels, including those of accountants and travellers.

The solution to this dysfunctional hybrid was found in more extensive decentralisation. Subsidiarisation avoided complicating further the

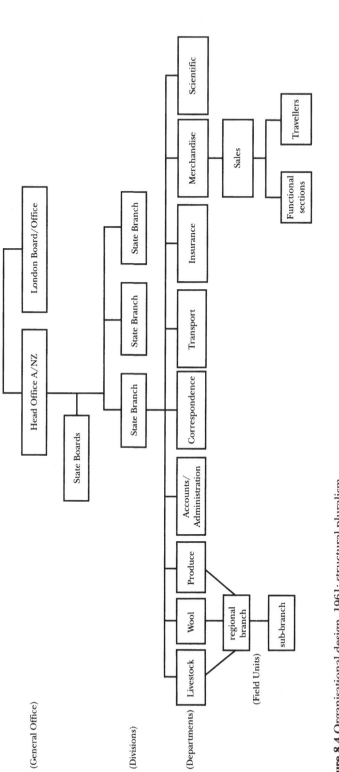

Figure 8.4 Organisational design, 1961: structural pluralism

(General Office)

Head Office A/NZ

London Board/Office

State Boards

(Divisions)

State Branch

State Branch

State Branch

(Departments)

Livestock

Wool

Produce

Accounts/Administration

Correspondence

Transport

Insurance

Merchandise

Scientific

(Field Units)

regional branch

sub-branch

Sales

Functional sections

Travellers

organisational structure and removed the organisational pluralism created by merchandise divisions. Additionally, it helped protect firms from claims that they were abandoning the rural community. Dalgety's separated its merchandising into Dalgety Trading Company in 1961 and thus the remaining 'operations engaged in now all bear a relationship one to another'. The trading company was a wholly owned subsidiary registered in Australia but controlled by its London Board.[39] NZLMA adopted a similar policy by using its subsidiary in New Zealand, Gollin and Company, to handle the products most diverse from its core pastoral activities such as soft goods, tin plate, and carpets. Elders, which had experimented with subsidiaries much earlier in its history,[40] also restructured along broad product lines. When Wright Stephenson and NMA merged in 1972 they created a parent holding company (Challenge) with a series of sectoral subsidiaries including 'Wrightson–NMA Rural Limited'.

Within these pastoral agent subsidiaries further organisational development has occurred. Vast improvements in transport and communications have mitigated regional control problems and enabled firms to restructure nationally into service divisions. For example, Wrightson is organised into a series of service divisions including Wrightson Wool, Wrightson Livestock, and Wrightson Research.[41] National service divisions yield greater scale economies than former regional geographic ones, and complement rather than replicate each other to extend scope economies. At the local level Dalgety has experimented with franchising branches which represents a further decentralisation of management and has enabled the company to pursue a capital minimisation strategy.[42]

PATTERNS OF OPERATIONAL DESIGN

A carefully designed hierarchical structure facilitates innovations in the routine administration. It establishes chains of command and communication between and within the different tiers of authority which lead to the development of reporting procedures. A second consequence lies in the extension of company rules and standardised methods. A rationally designed organisation also facilitates management accountancy practices. Finally, the accurate specification of individual and group duties and functions in such organisations encourages investment in human resources. These features helped the firms to respond to the organisational challenges. Better communication and reporting counters agency problems and improves the information available to policy-makers. Procedure standardisation saves times on routine management. Management accountancy provides both planning and control information. Human capital investment improves decision-making and routine task performance at all levels, and facilitates a sense of identity and loyalty to the company, and the development of skills specific to it.

Many of these elements of operational innovation are captured by the term 'systematic management' that Joanne Yates has applied to the experience of American firms from the late nineteenth century.[43] She argues that managerial efficiency increased as rational and impersonal systems replaced personal and idiosyncratic management. The benefits are perceived in terms of improved efficiency and control. The innovativeness of the Australasian pastoral agents in a system that was more rational than impersonal is shown below. The awareness of the importance of such changes is illustrated by the comments of Pitt, Son & Badgery in 1918 that it was seeking to hire a manager with a 'thorough knowledge of systematic organisation'.[44]

The work of Mintzberg can also be a guide in examining the operational development of agents. He distinguishes several types of operational evolution. The 'machine bureaucracy' is a tightly controlled organisation with formal rules and procedures directed by a strategic core over a relatively deskilled workforce. The 'professional bureaucracy', by contrast, describes the exercise of externally acquired complex skills by a relatively autonomous labour force working closely with their clients.[45] While agent firms evolved into more closely controlled and formal organisations with improved reporting practices and standardised procedures, its employees remained highly skilled and relatively self-contained, drawing on their training to diagnose farmers' needs and implement a preferred solution.

Communication Channels and Reporting Practices

The explicit mapping of the company organisation clarified chains of command and communication. It also enabled employees to see their position in the company more clearly and understand their specific role and relationship to other officers, which was of increasing importance as the size and complexity of the company increased. It fostered accurate task allocation and the development of specialised functions. This clarification of responsibilities mattered at all levels. AMLF's Australian General Manager in 1918 argued that there should not be dual local control by himself and the Local Board of Advice, 'so that I could not shelter myself behind any advice that might be tendered to me by the local boards'.[46] This was recognised in the 'advise only' role of such boards. Such clarification facilitated the development of well-organised reporting systems, as did the improvements in communications technology discussed in chapter 2. Indeed, it was the effectiveness of internal reporting systems that made the companies such important information receptacles for the pastoral industry.

Yates identifies the emergence of three-way reporting systems: downwards for rules, procedures, and instructions; upwards for data and other information required in strategic policy and monitoring; and laterally to coordinate decisions and actions.[47] Upward reporting became quite extensive among the companies from their early years. The London-controlled companies were anxious to receive regular reports about the state of farming in Australia and New Zealand. Periodic visits by the company's inspector or superintendent were the means of reporting on the operations of individual branches. The crisis of the 1890s enhanced the demand for more regular upward reporting, which the development of new steam-shipping services helped to make possible. At the same time, the centralisation of colonial management funnelled branch reporting through the General Manager. By the turn of the century AMLF's Australian General Manager was sending weekly written reports back to London that consisted of standard subject headings such as climatic conditions, recent wool sales, and the volume of loans.

As the local organisational structure of firms expanded in the twentieth century so too did their reporting procedures. Service departments reported to their main branch manager. The country branches also reported directly to the main branch manager although there existed some doubt as to whether this should go through the manager in the wool or livestock departments with whom much of their business was done. While initially concerned with monitoring distant employees, upward reporting became increasingly motivated by efficiency needs. Regular and standardised reporting procedures between each tier meant more effective meetings and decision-making at each level. Thus, meetings of State Boards increasingly consisted of receiving the reports from lower levels, particularly the service departments and country branches, which summarised recent developments and made recommendations. This made for efficient handling of the increasing volumes of information generated. Upward reporting generated valuable information for the expanding head offices to employ in strategic decision-making.

Downward reporting was less detailed and regular. Most often it conveyed general information, remarking perhaps on prices or volumes at recent London wool sales. Alternatively, extremely specific instructions were directed at the failings of an individual or group, such as the increase in loans from a branch. Crises, particularly the growth of client indebtedness, increased the detail, and degree of imperativeness, of downward instructions. Companies also recognised that visits by inspectors and accountants could be a two-way process, not only to gather information but to advise local managers about policy changes, clarify procedures, clear up any areas of uncertainty or extreme complexity, and perhaps even inculcate a sense of corporate cohesion and culture. Goldsbrough Mort was using inspectors for these dual purposes by the interwar period and noted that visits by the inspector to Western Australia and South Australia would help bring those offices 'into line with our methods'.[48] With the strengthening of general or head offices after World War Two, downward reporting became a more extensive means of enforcing new, proactive strategies.

Lateral reporting developed slowly. Most channels of communication in the firms were vertical and most units on the same hierarchical level tended to operate in relative isolation from one another as characteristic of a professional bureaucracy. That firms were slow to recognise the benefits of sharing ideas and experiences among lateral groups may have been a source of weakness, particularly in light of the synergies between different services and points of comparison and contrast between different regions. Lessons were learned slowly and mistakes repeated in different parts of the same organisation because communications often took circuitous vertical routes and missed many horizontal connections. Dalgety's was one of the pioneers of interwar managers' conferences, which brought together the heads of the different State organisations. NMA organised managers' conferences every six months by 1920 and noted the benefits both in terms of the firm communicating its new strategies to all sections simultaneously and the lateral interaction and sharing of experiences by regional managers.[49] Dalgety's conferences demonstrate three-way communications since managers were also invited to comment critically on policy initiatives.

Standardisation of Procedures and Rules

The standardisation of procedures and the creation of general rules is an important part of the development of rational systems. Standard practices and rules can easily be transferred from one individual to another thus giving greater continuity to institutional practices. In addition, by routinising procedures, uncertainties and mistakes are lessened. Standardising a procedure also provides a basis for classifying the salary, skills, and level of appointment connected with it, for training someone into the position, which in turn provides for flexible movements of employees within the firm including a career ladder.[50] As we shall see below these requirements fitted closely with the increasing attention of the firm to the fostering of human capital skills.

The larger firms introduced standard practice manuals specific to the needs of the industry. This enabled them to classify periodic decisions in a manner that was easily accessible and designed to promote the generic aims discussed above. The other firms may have used one of the more general administrative publications available. By 1959 Elders had introduced a series of standard practice manuals. Employees were left with no doubts about the intention behind the manual and its limitations: 'This manual is not intended as a substitute for thought, judgement and decision, but as an aid in expediting the routine work'.[51] Elders developed a manual for each department. Each manual included some common observations on the organisation of the company, the nature of its operations, its accounting practices, and the extent of its country branches. The relationship of each of these to the department in question is then identified so that users understand not only the company as a whole but how their area fits into it. The remainder of the manual deals with the functions and positions of the department. Recognising the constantly evolving nature of procedures, the volumes are loose-leafed allowing for easy updating.

Management Accounting

Pastoral agents kept extensive accounts from the outset. The provision of loans and other services necessitated substantial financial records for each customer. Consolidated branch accounts were then submitted upwards as part of the reporting procedures of the organisation. Until after World War One the companies mostly concentrated on financial accounting. In other words, the accounts were balanced out and checked by an auditor for their accuracy and any suggestion of malfeasance by company officers. This could be a long process which by World War One led many firms to conduct a continuous audit throughout the year that was undertaken by a former or current employee who was familiar with the particular features of the industry.[52]

In so far as any analysis of the accounts was undertaken before 1914 it mostly consisted of generalised comparisons between successive years. Goldsbrough Mort, for example, drew comparisons at the company and State level from about 1909. Short-term fluctuations were largely attributed to economic and climatic cycles over which the companies had no control and therefore they simply reported these trends. Comparisons between firms were rarely made, probably because disclosure requirements were limited and firms perceived few benefits from committing resources to such an exercise. Observations about the actions of their competitors were mostly qualitative and based on general observation rather than quantitative analysis.

The failure of these accounting systems to control employee opportunism let alone guide policy was clear. One of many examples of employee opportunism concerned the large losses facing the Christchurch branch of NMA by 1924. The company's General Manager noted that 'over and over again during the past two years he deliberately misled us in his correspondence'. The auditor also failed to pick up the problem.[53]

During the interwar period accounting began to be used more extensively by the firms as a tool of company strategy. The prolonged crisis for the primary industries and the consequent loss of commissions and increased debt burden encountered by the agents necessitated cost cutting. This was difficult to undertake for many reasons, particularly since the organisations had expanded substantially over the previous two decades and significant synergies existed between the different parts. Thus, firms had little idea of where economies should be made. The interwar period also witnessed the beginnings of product diversification by the firms that took them beyond the confines of the pastoral industry and raised internal debate about the wisdom of this change of direction. The adoption of a relatively new and capital-intensive technology in the form of cars and tractors raised additional questions about costs and effectiveness that could not be addressed easily through existing financial accounting practices.

Each of these developments – crisis, diversification, and new technology – therefore increased the pressure for more extensive analysis of company accounts as a tool of policy.[54] The evolving structural features of the firms and the industry also made them probable users of management accounting practices. Larger and more organisationally complex businesses have a high propensity to use management accounting to control and evaluate different parts of the organisation. This is particularly the case where decentralised management systems are used in multidivisional corporations. The competitive structure of the industry can also have a bearing; where industrial concentration is high and firms are no longer price-takers, they are more likely to use their accounting systems to facilitate rent-seeking activity.[55] Management accounting practices are normally driven by two motives, performance evaluation and planning. The former was more important between the wars while the latter grew in importance after 1945.

The trend towards decentralisation by regional divisions made it easier to separate the performance of different parts of the company. Firms began to construct single-page tables comparing the results of their different State divisions over several years. The identification of a below average performance then led to a more concentrated investigation of that branch. While circumstances varied somewhat between different States, the increasing diversification into products that were not geologically sensitive and the implementation of standard company-wide reporting methods meant direct comparisons were mostly valid.

Comparing the performance of different departments within the same State branch was more difficult, given the different types of activity and the synergies that operated between them.[56] Companies experimented with a variety of forms of cost and revenue splitting between departments in an attempt to foster valid comparisons, but with few lasting results. Instead, comparing cognate departments across the different States was a more valid policy and enabled firms to target their investigative resources more accurately. Firms began to construct annual matrices showing the profits of the State offices disaggregated by individual departments. Using company-wide cost and revenue splitting, this enabled more targeted interstate comparisons to be made between departments. In the case of Goldsbrough Mort this included comparisons of overtime costs, telephone charges, and even tea money.[57] Some of these measures, for example, motor vehicle costs per mile, were not specific to a particular service or area and therefore could be used as comparators throughout the company including between departments in a single branch.[58]

The value of such comparisons can be illustrated by their use in 1938 to identify that the average car costs of the Adelaide branch of Goldsbrough Mort were significantly higher than for other States. This revelation enabled the firm to focus its investigation. As a result, it discovered that the Adelaide manager had a personal preference for purchasing British rather than American cars. Since British cars were smaller he arranged for them to be fitted with a larger chassis with a broad rear to accommodate '3 sturdily built farmers . . . in the back seat'. This awkward customisation led to higher maintenance and repair costs and also meant higher depreciation because the unattractive car had a low resale value.[59]

Performance measures were developed comparing a measurement of turnover with a particular input; for example, wool store wages per bale of wool. This approach was used to monitor and evaluate the performance

of travellers since direct observation of them was intermittent. Winchcombe Carson compared the average cost per bale gained by each traveller.
An incentive was attached by paying a bonus to the traveller with the lowest
cost. The company realised the complexity of the work, that some areas
were more expensive to cover than others and some clients easier to
influence, so it backed this up with more detailed comparisons of each of
its items of expenditure and made qualitative observations.[60]

In addition to cross-sectional comparisons between different parts of the
company, longitudinal information was increasingly utilised. Departments
were asked to track and then explain historical trends. Since wool
remained the principal source of income in the 1930s Goldsbrough Mort
asked each State to submit a list of wool clients and the baleage of each
for the current and previous year and to provide an explanation for
declines and lost customers. Such approaches helped to identify weak spots
in the organisation and put the onus on executives to monitor and analyse
their own performance.[61]

The idea of using company data to change attitudes and rectify
problems rather than simply identify them was an approach that gained
increasing popularity with the firms after 1945. The employment of specialist management accountants in the 1950s together with the increased
responsibility given to expanded head offices to develop company strategies encouraged more extensive use of these practices. Under head office
direction, branches and departments undertook greater analysis of their
own performance particularly through charting and graphing changes
over time. Forward planning as well as analysis of historical patterns was
encouraged through the development of an annual budgeting or
targeting system. Before World War Two the firms mostly used budgeting
for occasional and specific purposes where a particular issue was being
examined. In the 1950s budgeting became common practice among the
larger agents.

By 1955 Goldsbrough Mort had developed annual budgeting for each
main department in each State. Significant variations between the
budgeted levels of expenditure and actual results were an early indication
of problems. The introduction of moving annual totals helped to monitor
these variations on a monthly basis. The company believed that these techniques helped it to improve its performance in the highly competitive
environment at the end of the 1950s.[62] Dalgety's encouraged management
accounting practices in the 1950s although it was somewhat disappointed
at the initial outcome, noting in 1959 that most managers 'had a quite wrong
conception of budgets, their preparation and use'.[63] Managers' conferences
in the 1960s were used to help eliminate misconceptions regarding
accounting practices and to foster staff training. Elders believed that competition in the industry would be much more intense after 1945 and used its
greatly extended general office to develop long-term planning.[64] This
strategy included analysing the large amounts of data that it had collected
on its own organisation and drawing comparisons with the other major
firms. Modern budgeting and costing processes were also introduced.

Budgeting procedures were slower to develop at the local branches where managers, as the first point of contact with most farmers, tended to be trained more in farming techniques than office management. Dalgety bemoaned: 'the problem of control at small sub-branches and country branches is common throughout the company's organisation in Australia and New Zealand'.[65] Instead of getting country branch managers directly involved in budgeting practices, Dalgety encouraged departmental managers at the State office to liaise more closely with local managers. As an alternative control system, incentives to branches were pitched in a manner designed to try and elicit honesty and hard work, such as a good share of the commission on produce business they influenced to the main selling centre.[66]

Human Resource Management

The numbers employed in the pastoral agent industry were relatively small. However, the employees' responsibilities and skills were extensive, making effective human resource management vital. In the 1930s Goldsbrough Mort was one of the largest non-financial companies in Australia but had fewer than 1000 employees; BHP, not much larger in assets, employed around 10 000. This meant that the average Goldsbrough Mort employee was responsible for ten times as many assets.[67] The development of human capital skills was vital in an industry characterised by the provision of a wide range of services to a regular and closely connected clientele. As Dalgety noted, 95 per cent of its activity was service and thus the quality of staff was of great importance.[68] NZLMA put it more passionately: 'it depends on a large number of individuals offering first class advice . . . often tiring physical and mental help'.[69] The precise skills required shifted over time with the changing strategies and structures of the industry and its leading firms. In the early years of the industry when social and kinship links with the farming community were vital, firms sought individuals who were well known, connected locally and possessed a wide knowledge of farming matters.[70] This contrasted with the major banks which had already developed internal labour markets by the 1880s and moved employees between branches and regions for training purposes.[71] The decline of social and kinship links with the farming community in the twentieth century and the growth in firm size and complexity in turn caused a shift towards employees who were well-versed in general office skills and had a knowledge of the company's particular ways of doing business. As main branches were divided into a series of functionally specialised departments from the end of the nineteenth century, the pastoral knowledge required of many of its employees narrowed, although the skill base and the judgement powers remained of a high order.

Attitudes changed slowly. About 1902 Elders was criticised, admittedly by a former company accountant, for preferring outdoor types who lacked good administrative and accounting skills and whose only office was under their hat. A pocket compendium produced by the company in 1931 emphasised that staff should be all-rounders who understood the farmer's business; significantly there was no mention of office skills.[72] In a similar vein, when appointing a manager to its main Brisbane branch in 1898, AMLF believed that a knowledge of pastoral matters was more important than a commercial and administrative training. So far as office skills were required, these were to be vested in a particular individual, the accountant.[73]

While country branch managers remained quite closely connected to the local farming community there was a growing need for officers in State branches and at head office who were trained in broader management and administrative skills and picked up their pastoral knowledge by working in the different departments. The comments of the Elders accountant reflected the tension between these different groups of officers and, in some cases, there was an uneasy relationship between the country branch manager and the departmental head at the State office. Branch managers belatedly improved their administrative skills in response to the growing complexity and diversity of their business and pressure from head office to conform to company procedures.

The rapid expansion of the industry created further challenges for labour management. Goldsbrough Mort's total employment rose from 107 in 1915 to 1281 by 1949. This was achieved in spite of the severe impact of the two world wars on employment levels. NMA claimed in 1917: 'there is a considerable feeling throughout New Zealand that the country is sending too many men'. Each employee lost from this industry was more seriously felt than in many other sectors but this did not lead to exemptions for the industry. By 1918 NMA staff enrolled on war service had reached 114 of whom 20 had been killed. An indication of the significance of this number can be indicated by reference to the company's total employment of 220 in 1924.[74]

Things were no better in World War Two: 48 per cent of Elders staff enlisted at the outbreak of war and Goldsbrough Mort had 41 per cent of its staff in the armed services by 1942.[75] Elders observed: 'This heavy drain of trained officers is now being very acutely felt . . . although it has been possible to make some replacements . . . by the engagement of juniors and women, it is becoming increasingly difficult to keep the organisation functioning'. The greatest concern was with managerial vacancies, at least three branches having no manager or trained staff replacement.[76] The firm was also conscious of the ageing nature of its wartime senior management who were all in their fifties and sixties.[77]

Given the importance attached to good employees, hiring for lifetime was regarded as desirable from early in the industry's development and was consistent with close and long-term client relations. However, the limited resources of the early firms and the cyclical volatility of the industry initially favoured more simple and reactive policies. Thus, attracting experienced staff from other companies through higher salaries occurred as early as the 1880s but was regarded, at least before World War Two, as 'unneighbourly' and retarded internal promotion schemes which the firms were keen to encourage.[78] Alternatively, highly valued staff were maintained through generous packages which could include a share of wool commissions.[79] Employees from acquired firms were often kept on although this was not without problems (see chapter 2).

After World War Two, faced with a further period of labour shortage and equipped with strategic-thinking head offices, firms turned to modern human resource management policies, replacing the reactive, 'fire-fighting' personnel management. This involved high-level planning to develop internal labour markets, in-house training, organisational cultures, and performance appraisal. The firms were among the pioneers of human resource management in advance of its more common adoption since the 1970s. The fact that other pioneers were largely multinationals, including General Motors-Holden, Ford and ICI, suggest the agents may have drawn on their overseas connections.[80]

Evidence of these new policies is not hard to find. Dalgety referred in 1947 to the continued postwar skill shortages and suggested a longer-term solution through more determined recruitment of good candidates early in their career, and internal training to accelerate them into senior management positions.[81] The leading firms had developed their own ways of doing business, 'Elderising' as Elders called it, into which young recruits could be coached. By the 1950s the companies were lobbying in schools and universities and finding ways of making employment in the industry appear attractive. Dalgety was impressed with the manner in which Elders showed new recruits around the wool stores and stock yards and then placed them in a specific department. By contrast, Dalgety admitted that its practice had been to put new recruits in the mailroom with the result that many resigned within the first three months.[82] More usefully, Dalgety published a pamphlet in 1960 entitled 'A Career with Dalgety' emphasising the benefits of lifetime employment with the company.[83]

Company training of employees became an important issue once the idea of lifetime employment was developed. This requirement was re-inforced by the growing mix of skills and the emerging organisational structure. Thus, training enabled employees to develop a particular skill base associated generally with administration and specifically with farming matters although, as discussed earlier, this training rarely extended to the sale of complex manufactures into which the company had begun to diversify. Training helped employees to understand the manner in which the organisation operated and the specific way of performing some tasks. Individuals could also be trained for particular positions that were now more clearly delineated within the organisation. The benefits of a well-trained workforce include the ability to perform routines more efficiently and to exercise strategic judgements more authoritatively. Dalgety had expressed concern at the amount of management time expended on routine matters, 'rather than doing something more likely to further the Company's business' and clearly viewed human capital enhancement, as well as organisational design, as a way of strengthening the firm's strategic capabilities.[84]

Training took a variety of forms. Personnel officers were sought to super-vise and implement many of these policies. However, in the 1950s there were few personnel officers to be recruited which often meant sending existing 'staff officers', who simply administered some basic staffing records, on external courses to learn about personnel policies. As a result, continual staff training was introduced for employees especially in the systems and procedures of the firm. More adequate personnel records were kept and performance appraisal was introduced. The personnel officers, generally appointed in each State, were also expected to show human understanding and sympathy towards valued employees and to develop their sense of identity with an expanding, and potentially impersonal, firm.[85]

Particular attention was given to training 'high flyers' for future posi-tions in senior management. They were moved around the company to gain specific experience of particular activities and regions.[86] In 1958 Dalgety introduced a study group of selected younger officers who attended a series of lectures on the history of the company, its chain of command, and business management. Some employees were sent to lectures or courses at the University of Melbourne, Henley on Thames, and the Australian Institute of Management during the formative years of management education in Australia.[87] Elders was also a pioneer, helping to fund the establishment of the Australian Administrative College in 1955 and subsequently sending promising young staff there. NMA even sent some officers for work experience in closely linked firms, such as on the farming properties of the NZAL, 'to learn the stock side of the business'.[88]

The firms were less enlightened when it came to the employment of women. In spite of the importance of additional female workers during World War Two, the companies had limited views about their long-term capabilities, noting that women should be encouraged to fill 'positions which are not . . . stepping stones to more important work'.[89]

With training went retaining. Having invested in their employees the firms sought to capture the full benefits by retaining their services. While the training and personnel policies discussed above helped foster long-term employment, additional measures mitigated staff losses to other firms in the industry, particularly during periods of labour shortages. These measures included a system of internal promotion and pension schemes. Retention was also consistent with their idea of working for the firm as a career. Elders emphasised that employment for the company should be regarded as a career and include attractions such as job security, bonuses, pensions, and death benefits.[90] These benefits also helped to foster a positive corporate culture within the firms, encouraging employees to be loyal, honest, hard-working, and 'keen and energetic' in their dealings with clients. In-house publications were additionally used to foster these consen-sual attitudes.[91]

Internal promotion schemes encouraged employees to remain with the firm. Accelerated training was targeted at those individuals who, it was hoped, would proceed rapidly through the ranks of the company. This was encouraged by emphasising that promotion was based on ability not seniority or age. Firms also began to circulate information of vacancies throughout the company to encourage movement between different parts of the organisation rather than the tradition of filling positions from within a single branch. This provided a wider internal labour market from which to choose and a greater number and variety of opportunities for ambitious employees. The timing of the introduction of such policies is not always easy to measure. Dalgety, for example, flagged the introduction of these policies from the late 1950s.

Companies, however, were aware that their most talented employees, in whom they had invested training, might still choose a wider employment market by applying for jobs with other firms. Moreover, the increasingly generic skills being acquired by employees made them suitable for employment outside the industry in related service occupations. Attractive salary packages, including commissions, could be offered but they were expensive and could still be countered by other firms. Therefore, firms introduced loyalty schemes, particularly superannuation and long-service leave which, by delaying significant income flows for many years, provided a strong incentive to remain with the firm. They were also a powerful force for encouraging honest behaviour in large, distended, impersonal organisations by raising substantially the opportunity cost of being caught cheating. Firms had previously used fidelity bonds but pension funds provided a much stronger and positive incentive to loyal and industrious behaviour.[92]

Firms recognised the value of pensions in 'keeping members of the staff with the company, and getting the best out of them'.[93] Although several of the larger banks had pension schemes before 1890 there was a stronger movement towards their adoption between 1906–14 across a number of sectors.[94] Among pastoral agents, Elders and Wright Stephenson had each begun a pension scheme as early as 1913 and most other large firms followed their example between the wars. As with many of the innovations the small and medium-sized firms followed suit later.[95] The schemes were non-portable in order to emphasise loyalty to the firm and were directed at those employees whom they were most keen to retain, notably high-achieving male staff that had been with the firm a good many years. Most of the leading companies continued to pay the superannuation contributions of former employees on military duty and even topped up their salaries to company rates, thereby ensuring those that survived would return to their employment.[96] Long-service schemes generally came later but were designed to achieve the same mix of loyalty and commitment. Dalgety introduced a long-service scheme in 1957 before it became a statutory requirement in all States.[97] Large bonuses of as much as 10 per cent of annual salaries were paid in good years and were seen as another incentive for employee effort. They additionally helped to tie fluctuations in the salary bill with the vicissitudes in the profitability of the industry.

The human resources policies discussed in this section imply the development of a meritocratic professional management class in place of appointment by dint of personal connection and ownership. This certainly appears to have been the case with many of the leading agent firms. The appointment of Walter Young as Managing Director of Elders in 1929 began the company's move towards control by professional managers.[98] In some cases the most senior executives remained part of a network of family and friends much longer. The New Zealand General Manager of NMA, for example, was a member of the Ritchie family (from whom the business had been originally bought in the 1860s), through to 1968. While this form of personal management has been criticised by Chandler, such firms had a strong professional management class through the middle and lower ranks of management.[99] Moreover, while personally connected, the Ritchies received high levels of education and business training, and each generation of the family benefited from working and living within an 'entrepreneurial' environment and being groomed for the job.[100]

CONCLUSION

Although most large Australian firms had developed divisionalised structures by the mid-1970s little is known of their earlier organisational growth.[101] This study of the pastoral agents suggests they were aware of the need to modify organisational structure in response to rapidly changing strategies and environmental conditions a century ago. As some of the largest firms in each country they were amongst the first to face the organisational challenges of size. The high levels of concentration in the pastoral agent industry meant that clear-thinking strategies, unimpeded by managerial overload, were vital. Mitigating opportunism was an important issue for firms that were geographically distended across remote parts of Australia and often across the world to London. Finally, these firms worked in an industry notorious for cyclical vicissitudes that challenged the size and complexity of the organisation.

Therefore, although agent firms were outside the rapid-growth new-technology manufacturing industries studied by Chandler they developed many similar design features including centralised departments, decentralised divisions, and strategy-centred head offices. The freeing-up of key entrepreneurs was one of the main benefits of organisational design amongst the pastoralists. A more rational structure also facilitated operational innovations, such as better channels for communication and information dissemination, more effective task allocation, and the standardisation of office procedures thereby mitigating many of the coordination problems associated with professional bureaucracies. On the downside, progressive structural changes were based on the outlook of the pastoral industry and made it difficult for firms to achieve cross-sectoral diversification in response to the changing pattern of postwar industrial development.

CHAPTER NINE

Inter-Organisational Relations: Competition, Cooperation, and Collusion Among Agency Firms

The strong competitive instincts of the agency firms were emphasised in their finance, marketing, and information strategies (chapters 4 to 7) which was accompanied by their building of sophisticated organisational structures (chapter 8). At the same time, however, they recognised the benefits of co-operation with other groups in the pastoral industry with complementary interests through the development of vertical networks which linked them to farmers, shipowners, woolbuyers, and similar groups (chapter 3). Similarly, there were times when agency firms derived mutual benefits from cooperating with one another in horizontal alliances. Agent cooperation was most common where it brought benefits to all stakeholders through lower cost services and the representation of the common interests of agents. Sustaining widespread cooperation over long periods encountered many difficulties, particularly when some firms believed they would be better placed to act alone and where collusive activity required secrecy and high degrees of trust amongst agents.[1] It serves to illustrate, along with their network activities, that agent firms, while fiercely loyal to their own corporate identities and internal organisation, were flexible enough to recognise that firms have permeable boundaries which lead them to share resources with rivals where mutual benefits can be derived.[2]

COOPERATIVE STRATEGIES

Cooperation was most extensive and ongoing where everyone stood to gain from lower costs and improved coordination. Since there was no need for secrecy and the punity of transgressors was uncommon, the costs of co-operation were also minimal. Chapters 5 and 6 showed that firms worked closely together in the provision of a market infrastructure for wool and livestock auctions, which included the development of procedural rules, and the negotiation of sale rosters. The breakdown of such arrangements was infrequent, as Goldsbrough Mort noted: 'it is seldom that unanimity cannot be reached'.[3] Disagreements mostly occurred in the early years of local auction sales, and reflected deeper divisions among the firms involved. In 1891–92, for example, widespread disagreements between Dalgety and Dennys Lascelles in Geelong spilled over into a breakdown over the provision of the central selling room.[4]

Cooperation to promote and defend the interests of the pastoral agent industry was also strong when it was under threat from a particular source or suffering economic hardship. Using the vehicle of national and local associations the agents could negotiate more effectively and cheaply with other peak bodies and major institutions such as governments, banks, woolbuyers, and graziers. Cooperative activity spanned such topics as overseas promotion, government taxes, financial and labour legislation, shipping freight rates, wartime commandeer schemes, and the prompt time between wool sale and shipment. Activities included enquiries into matters of mutual concern and getting a representative on to influential committees and bodies. For example, the leading firms wrote a joint letter to the Victorian Premier in 1931 opposing emergency financial legislation that would treat agents more harshly than banks.[5] Agent associations also looked after specific firms in individual disputes, such as in bankruptcy hearings and debt collection activities.

Firms generally cooperated in the diffusion of new techniques and practices, recognising that farmers periodically moved between different agents and that best practice served everyone's interests. In 1967 New Zealand agents jointly financed the production of a textbook on farm accounting.[6] Cooperation was particularly strong in addressing serious threats to farming that were no respecters of farm or company boundaries. Firms cooperated in efforts to mitigate rabbit infestation (see chapter 7). Cooperation, however, might turn to competition where asymmetrical information provided a competitive advantage. Dalgety's soil testing laboratory was designed to retain its clients and attract new ones although it is doubtful whether this involved passing on knowledge unknown to other agents.

Variations in the geographical or functional bundle of services provided by different firms sometimes encouraged complementary bilateral cooperation. This was notable in the earlier years of the industry before some firms had developed a full and national line of services, and during the interwar crisis when they sought to reduce costs by closing branches or cancelling plans for new woolstores. From 1927 Australian Estates sold the wool of Goldsbrough Mort's local clients in Brisbane in return for Goldsbrough Mort handling Australian Estates' wool in Sydney.[7] Such agreements involved sharing commissions and sometimes personnel exchanges. Complementary behaviour occurred when local agents forwarded wool clips to selling brokers in return for farm finance and shared commissions. Over time, though, such arrangements declined as the larger firms became more acquisitive. Finally, the demand for some services, such as bloodstock, minor produce, and farm supplies, was too small to be serviced by most agents and therefore agents introduced local clients to the supplying firm, or sales were held jointly (see chapter 5).[8]

Other forms of cooperative strategy threatened to conflict with the competitive instincts of the more aggressive and expansionist firms. Sharing of private information about clients occurred where mutual benefits emerged but would be suppressed when firms tried to offload bad risks on to other unsuspecting agents (see chapter 4). Information asymmetries were also used to protect good clients from being bought by other firms offering preferable terms. Ceasefires were necessary when this strategy began to damage many firms; Dalgety, NZLMA, Elders and Golds-brough Mort decided in 1962 that a client farmer was only to change service provider if both firms agreed.[9] In 1965 the New Zealand agents organised a series of meetings to try and work out a common policy on lending operations.[10] Intense merger activity in both countries at the time may have inclined firms towards cooperation.

On occasions, firms cooperated over gaining wool clips, which included limits on advertising, canvassing by travellers, community investments, and the activities of local forwarding agents. In 1912 the Sydney woolbrokers agreed not to send out travellers in search of wool clips before February, while in 1942 five Melbourne firms agreed to withdraw their travellers and three other agents would only call on their existing clients.[11] At some point before 1913 the Sydney firms had pooled their advertising budgets. Although Winchcombe Carson considered it a 'considerable saving', others opposed its continuance because it reduced their profile.[12] In 1930 New Zealand firms limited their expenditure on competition for wool clips by reducing their car fleets and level of canvassing.[13] Agreements also limited community investments designed to raise the local presence of each firm. In 1908 the South Australian firms agreed not to subscribe to anything outside Adelaide, Elders noting with some frustration: 'Previous to this agreement every show, church of every description, every cricket club . . . debating societies and even country branches of the Labor Party used to think there were special claims on us to subscribe'.[14] Limiting their number in a locality, requiring their registration, and more clearly defining their nature achieved periodic constraints on the operations of wool-forwarding agents and dealers.[15]

Several areas of cooperative activity involved secret collusive behaviour because it threatened the position of other groups. Agreements on selling and finance charges for farmers were probably the most frequent forms of collusion. In 1893 the SWBA agreed not to lower commission rates and three years later fixed lending rates.[16] An agreement among Dunedin agents in 1903 was broader in its remit to prohibit commission rate reductions and 'bonus, rebate, or return commissions'. This was a response to the alternative ways firms had found of offering better terms.[17] Compro-mise agreements sought to reduce differences of opinion among firms. Thus, in 1911 the Sydney brokers narrowed the differential of charges for handling leather, Winchcombe Carson and Harrison, Jones & Devlin to

charge 3.5 and Pitt, Son & Badgery 3 per cent compared with previous
rates of 4 and 2.5 per cent respectively.[18] Rate fixing intensified again in
the 1930s in an attempt to halt the rate war initiated by the Commonwealth
Wool and Produce Company in 1934. However, they were unable to resist
the downward pressure on rates, the SWBA, accepting the 20 per cent
reduction in commission levels.[19] Agreement was no closer on livestock
rates: in 1939 Dalgety was in favour of raising rates, De Garis was against,
and Goldsbrough Mort wanted to wait until the following year.[20] Multi-
partite opinions were not conducive to the longevity of agreements!

THE LIMITS OF COOPERATION

The foregoing evidence suggests that, with the exception of coordinating
market infrastructures, diffusing new techniques, and defending the
industry's interests, cooperation was limited in its scope and durability.
Firms frequently reneged on agreements or cancelled their membership
of industry associations in response to the actions of others. In a major
study of trusts in Australia in 1914 Wilkinson drew attention to their
widespread existence throughout the Australian economy, including in
primary industries (sugar, tobacco, coal, flour, bread, fruit, timber, bricks,
and beef), manufacturing (jam, brewing, metals), and services (shipping,
retailing). However, no mention is made of either the wool industry or
stock and station agents.[21]

The sustainability of cooperation depends on the internal cohesiveness
of the agreement among participants, and the external influences or threats
to it. Important influences on cohesion include a coincidence of interests,
the costs of collusion, the degree of trust, and the nature of enforcement
against transgressors. External influences include the barriers to new
entrants, outside competitors, and the reactions of affected parties.

Internal Cohesion

Commitment to cooperation relied on a coincidence of interests. If firms
feared that the loss of individuality and the sharing of privileged information would erode competitive advantages they were less likely to
cooperate. When joint arrangements for the Geelong wool auction
collapsed in 1891–92, Dennys Lascelles, which saw itself as the founder of
the local market, complained that 'for our efforts in the past there was to
be no consideration'.[22] It was more often the larger national firms which
believed that cooperation led to a convergence of competitive advantage.
Goldsbrough Mort felt that through its membership of industry associations it had 'submerged our traditional individuality and elected to fight
from the same level as do the least of our opponents'. Thus, when the
reformation of the SWBA was being contemplated in 1894 Goldsbrough
Mort favoured only broad policy agreements, leaving firms free in the
conduct of their internal business.[23] It recommended in 1896 a two-year

rate war so that some of the excessive numbers of Sydney firms 'who are rapidly establishing themselves under the wings of the Assn' can be "blotted out" and the trade "purified" '.[24]

Younghusband opposed a scheme for the sale of hides and skins because of the erosion of its strong position in that area; the firm noted: 'it is hard to see why we should endanger those interests by coming into a common pool, which reduces business to a level and observes no regard for our individual . . . efforts'.[25] Thus, differences in service bundles, while sometimes encouraging reciprocity, could be an obstacle to multilateral agreements. An attempt to reduce wool sales in 1914 in response to curtailed European demand soon fragmented, as smaller agents perceived that the large firms would benefit more due to residual ownership of pastoral properties.[26] In 1926 Goldsbrough Mort feared reciprocal selling arrangements that brought Australian Estates into close contact with Goldsbrough Mort's customers might lead to attempts to detach some of its more valued clients.[27] Since Australian Estates relied much more on wool from its own stations it would have been less concerned about customer loss to Goldsbrough Mort. For similar reasons a firm thought long and hard before agreeing to let other agents provide additional services that it did not offer to its clients. In some cases, such as mortgage finance and estate sales, it might prefer to work with a non-competitor for wool clips, such as an estate agent.

Differences in geographic location also affected the coincidence of interests. This was especially the case in New Zealand where regional variations in commercial and farming practices created tensions within national organisations. In 1911, and on several subsequent occasions, the WWBA was at loggerheads with other regional associations over the desire to restrict wool commission rebates to banks; since banks were heavily influential in financing and influencing wool clips in the Wellington province, local brokers were reluctant to follow national policy.[28]

The costs of cooperative activity included specifying and negotiating an agreement and monitoring adherence to it. Where secrecy was desirable to avoid detection by affected parties, or by government if it were illegal, these costs would increase.[29] Where the number of participants was large or held divergent views, costs would also rise. Tsokhas has argued that amongst the pastoral agents: 'the costs of collusion were not insignificant' and emphasises the effectiveness with which companies concealed transgressions of agreements, thereby raising the costs of monitoring and renegotiating new agreements.[30] With rising concentration levels, the number of parties to most agreements was comparatively small, and the overhead costs of initiating such agreements were low because of the existing mechanism of industry associations to administer the auction system. Such associations, by their identification with the legitimate organisation of the produce auctions, also mitigated the costs of concealment of collusive agreements. On the other hand, alliances and sub-groups among the co-operating parties increased the transaction costs, which is indicated by the many meetings and extensive correspondence necessary to negotiate and maintain agreements.[31]

High levels of trust make contract negotiation and monitoring easier, thereby mitigating the agreement costs. While trust-inducing networks were mostly formed among functional partners (farmers, agents, shipowners, and bankers), connections also existed between agent firms, especially through personnel movements and friendships. By the early twentieth century as networks became increasingly based on economic behaviour rather than social–kinship connections, honest dealing was vital to build up trust. Evidence suggests that the level of trust in associations was sometimes quite low because of opportunistic behaviour. Goldsbrough Mort's Sydney manager noted with exasperation of the SWBA in 1894: 'We're hindered by this damn association – competitors are secretive but we are honest', adding two years later, 'our rivals are offering advantages to country growers which we as an honest member of our Assn cannot extend', and that rules, such as on advertising, are 'broken in the most barefaced manner'.[32] The breakdown of honest behaviour was most common in periods of economic hardship, as indicated by the examples from the 1890s and 1930s.

Enmity between particular firms, or the development of factionalism, evidently damaged trust. The encouragement of firms to report breaches of agreement helped monitoring procedures but could weaken trust in bilateral relationships.[33] The distrust between Dennys Lascelles and Dalgety at Geelong in 1891, which began with disagreements over freighting arrangements, spread more broadly. So serious was this that it led to a breakdown of the normal consensus on sale organisation. Dennys Lascelles noted: 'There is no doubt that war has been proclaimed – especially or rather distinctly with Dalgety'.[34] There is also evidence of Dalgety repeatedly infringing agreements on not selling wool privately in New Zealand.[35] Wright Stephenson was regarded by some of the regional New Zealand firms as an inveterate opportunist. Accusations against Wright Stephenson included claims that they offered rebates on merchandise, failed to make agreed reductions in the activities of travellers, and provided liquor for wool valuers.[36] By the 1930s other Dunedin-based firms regarded Wright Stephenson as untrustworthy.[37] These accusations confirm that the larger national firms, with greater resources and competitive capabilities, believed they had most to lose from some agreements.

Effective enforcement could generate confidence in the agreement and help to make it work. Enforcement procedures, however, were not very effective; the punity terms were modest, procedures lengthy, and the threat of expulsion self-defeating. The 1915 rules of the WWBA contained no fines for a breach of the conditions, simply the right to expel.[38] The absence of an intermediate sanction meant the association would rarely carry through the ultimate penalty of expulsion until the rules had been repeatedly broken. The NZWBA contained provision for a £50 penalty for breach of the rules and a forfeit of the gain. However, this was a comparatively modest amount and there was no increase in punity for repeated offences except expulsion.[39]

The evidence suggests that associations were reluctant to enforce any penalties. By the 1930s the WWBA had recognised the need for penalties below the level of expulsion. However, by 1950 such penalties had never been used. Far from this implying that an effective deterrent now existed, it appears, for example, that Wright Stephenson twice broke the regulations in 1949–50 but the penalty was waived.[40] Likewise, when the New Zealand Farmers Cooperative broke the NZWBA rules on rebating in 1917 the NZWBA said it viewed such behaviour with alarm but appears to have taken no action. Bonds were also used by associations to enforce loyalty, the NCWSB levying £500, but there is little evidence to suggest that they were ever forfeited.[41] Where action was taken the procedure was lengthy and expensive. The rules of the NZWBA provided for a special meeting to judge cases. Where the breach directly affected another member long adversarial exchanges sometimes resulted. In 1922 the New Zealand Farmers Cooperative was charged with selling privately for a client of Levins. The NZWBA decided initially in favour of Levins but the following year New Zealand Farmers was still in dispute with NZWBA about the decision.[42] Enforcing agreements was particularly difficult where the conflict occurred between different regional associations. In 1916 the WWBA complained to the NZWBA about Dunedin exceeding its agreed wool quota, but no action appears to have been taken.[43] Associations were reluctant to expel because it strengthened the external competition, and expelled firms were often readmitted within a few years.[44]

External Influences

The contestability of the market affected the degree to which cooperative agreements within the stock and station agent industry could be effective. (Market contestability addresses the potential competitive threat from firms outside the industry.) Entry barriers into the industry restricted the admission of new firms which might challenge collusive practices. Most firms were not vertically integrated and associations often stipulated that no dealing in wool or livestock was permitted because of the interest conflict.[45] However, as we have seen, firms undertook a wide variety of synergistic services requiring extensive and interlocking capital investments. In addition, to succeed they had built up goodwill and expertise over many years. These entry barriers increased over time with the growth in minimum scales of efficiency. The same group of firms dominated the industry throughout the twentieth century and gradually absorbed many of the smaller firms (see chapter 2). While attempts to control the wool market faced competition from overseas growers and producers of substitute fibres, farmers could not turn to alternative types of service suppliers and foreign firms were not active in the Australasian pastoral agent industry.[46] However, agents were not entirely impervious to powerful forces operating outside the industry or smaller firms working on the margin of the industry which might chip away at particular services.

Contestability was greatest in financial services. Their extensive resource base and location in rural towns made the banks significant competitors to agents (see chapter 4). While they often preferred to lend via agents in recognition of the agent's specialist expertise and trading connections, this still placed banks in a strong position to influence individual and collective behaviour within the industry. As the wool market shifted back to Australasia, banks were gradually squeezed out of the consignment business, but their financial influence over agents and farmers and their connections in Britain maintained the credible threat of increased London sales. The 'external' threat also came from firms which had quit agreements or chose not to participate in them. This included the cooperatives which were a powerful influence on competition. Small local agents which specialised in private wool and livestock sales were also a threat. Since the cooperatives and smaller agents rarely lent on mortgages they had greater financial flexibility to initiate price-cutting wars.[47] In spite of weakening the market power of the agreement, participating firms sometimes excluded others with which they were reluctant to work.[48] Entry fees were generally not intended to be exclusive but to reflect and protect the benefits for members that had been built up over many years.[49]

Horizontal alliances among agents could be perceived as a threat to the traditional vertical network linking an agent to his farmers, shipowners, woolbuyers, farming suppliers, and bankers. Attempts to regulate the wool market would risk incurring the wrath of woolbuyers and encourage collective buying (see chapter 6). Agent control of commissions and interest rates would anger farmers and risk driving them further into the hands of cooperatives. In 1959, for example, agents disagreed on whether to increase their charges to farmers; while AMLF and NZLMA were in favour, Dalgety opposed the move expressing concern at the likely reaction from the Graziers Association.[50]

COOPERATIVE ALLIANCES AND GROUPINGS

Reference was made in previous sections to the development of major groupings of agent firms that created crosscurrents and factionalism. This resulted in increased transaction costs of an agreement and reduced levels of trust. Although strong national associations had evolved in both countries, cooperation was damaged by the extent to which they splintered into different alliances.

The main industry bodies were the woolbrokers' and the stock and station agents' associations. Most began as regional associations in the late nineteenth century to organise the local wool and livestock auctions and then affiliated into national bodies in the early twentieth century.[51] For example, the New Zealand Woolbrokers Association was formed in 1907, the National Council of Wool-Selling Brokers (in Australia) in 1919, and the New Zealand Livestock Auctioneers and Agents Association in 1923.[52] The formation of national groups was a defensive response to actual or perceived threats. The NZWBA provided a united front against buyers' organisations and emerged after previous abortive attempts to establish a national organisation had ended in disagreements.[53] In Australia the State associations were meeting together in conference before World War One and in 1914 formed an interstate council to discuss limitations on wool disposals. This was also viewed as a defensive measure; they noted: 'attacks are being made from all sides . . . growers forming co-operative selling agencies, buyers demanding increasingly onerous concessions, labor more insistently aggressive, it is scarcely necessary to dwell upon the advantages to be derived from cohesion and united action'.[54] The NCWSB was formed at the end of the wartime wool appraisement scheme in order to deal with postwar wool-handling arrangements although doubtless the firms had in mind a broader remit.[55] The formation of the NZLAAA three years later was precipitated by a proposed change to the sale of goods legislation to confer greater requirements on stock agents to investigate the financial position of purchasing farmers.[56]

These organisations included most significant players but internal divisions were common and led to periodic withdrawals.[57] Tensions existed between the different regional associations. It was mentioned earlier that differences in policies such as rebating led to disagreements between north and south island firms in New Zealand. The fear that national organisations would be dominated by northern associations with different interests and greater voting power from their larger wool sales made Canterbury agents reluctant initially to participate and led to subsequent threats of secession.[58] In Australia disputes between regional associations often resulted from trade diversion as States battled to attract more of the wool clip to their auctions. Sydney and Melbourne brokers competed for Riverina clips while, within Victoria, Melbourne and Geelong battled over their common hinterland. Rail freight rebates to divert clips became a source of conflict between associations. In 1921, for example, the Geelong association proposed rebating to farmers the difference between the cost of sending their wool to Adelaide and the additional cost of bringing it to Geelong.[59] While shared hinterlands were rarely a problem in New Zealand, border disputes arose between the Wellington and Blenheim associations. The federal structure of the national organisations in both countries made it difficult to impose their will on local associations. The NCWSB, for example, appears to have had only the ability to make recommendations to State associations without powers of enforcement on most issues.[60] These geographic divisions affected alliances at the firm level. NMA was one of the last of the expanding firms to move from Dunedin to Wellington and conflicted with its northern competitors, for example, over the failed 1946 merger of the NZWBA and NZLAAA.[61] Elders was notable for its concentration in South Australia until well into the twentieth century. With the emergence of large national firms in both nations regional disputes lessened.

Geographical division between firms originating in Britain or Australasia was also evident. Although diversification lessened differences in service provision by the end of the nineteenth century, there were still distinctions between the two groups in terms of their financial structure, lending policies, and preferred auction location. Remote management from London also affected outlooks; the 'Anglos' had similar information problems, shared a common business culture, and were closely connected to each other within the geographical limits of the City of London. ('Anglos' was a frequently used term for companies that were located in England.) As early as 1882 the London companies were meeting jointly and sharing information.[62] In 1896 Australian Estates received weather reports for New South Wales and Queensland from AMLF and Dalgety, and in the following year UMA received much-needed news of rains from AMLF.[63] Among the Australian firms Goldsbrough Mort and Harrison, Jones & Devlin regarded each other as friendly rivals and by the 1920s were all part of the same firm.

In the early twentieth century these geographic differences also blurred. The forces shaping this included the movement of managerial authority in the Anglos to Australasia, the establishment of London offices by the larger local firms, national expansion, and the relocation of the wool market. By 1939 Goldsbrough Mort noted: 'AML & F approximates most closely to our own company in the method of financing and general conduct of the business' in contrast to their very different views on market location at the turn of the century.[64] Tsokhas suggests that by the interwar period the interests of the two groups of major companies had coalesced.[65] This appears to be a largely accurate interpretation although some residual areas of dispute continued. The Anglos regarded Goldsbrough Mort as having dragged them into 'precipitate and dangerous' rate-cutting in New South Wales and Victoria in 1934. Elders had also broken rank in South Australia and Western Australia. In fact, Goldsbrough Mort played a go-between role connecting the smaller Australian companies like Commonwealth Wool and Produce, which initiated rate-cutting, with the more conservative Anglos. In response the leading Anglos met in London to discuss developing closer cooperation amongst themselves and with Younghusband in order to counteract Goldsbrough Mort's over-assertiveness.[66]

By 1953 Dalgety still referred to 'an Anglo-Australian block, whose interests would be contrary to those of purely Australian companies'.[67] Firms like Dalgety maintained an open mind about the London market, and kept on good relations with the Committee of London Woolbrokers.[68] Newspapers also picked up on this, the *Advertiser* noting rather polemically in 1962 that:

> the history of the Australian wool-broking industry has been an intense and dramatic struggle between Australians, determined to handle and market the nation's greatest exportable commodity here in Australia . . . and the merchant and banking interests of the United Kingdom . . . acquiring overseas products which could be marketed in, or from, the United Kingdom.[69]

When the major mergers took place in the Australian industry in the early 1960s it was the two leading Australian firms (Elders and Goldsbrough Mort) and the two leading Anglos (Dalgety and NZLMA) which merged with each other. The latter two firms merged in New Zealand, as did Wright Stephenson and NMA which by the postwar period strongly identified with New Zealand rather than Britain.

In the post-World War Two period alliances have been increasingly based on functional and size differences between large national firms, medium-sized regional firms, and cooperatives. Differences have appeared on questions of private and country wool sales, rebates for wool forwarding, and the establishment of new wool selling centres (see chapter 6). In recent years attempts have been made to improve cooperation within national and local organisations through closer relations between and complementary roles for the NZWBA and NZSSA, and through joint meetings of their local bodies in each region.[70] In the case of the NZSSA its executive was restructured in 1966 to create a federal structure of national, local, and cooperative firms to recognise the existence of these different interest groups within the industry.[71]

THE COOPERATION CONTRACT

Industry associations were constituted on the basis of a formal and detailed written contract, signed by its members and fixed for a particular period of normally three to five years. A legally enforceable contract was viewed as desirable since it replaced, or at least supplemented, reliance on memory and goodwill. This minimised misunderstanding on specific points and facilitated enforcement against breaches of contract. Such a contract was the basis for the SWBA although AMLF regarded the terms of the constitution of the Melbourne association as 'less effective and precise' than that of the Sydney assocation.[72] This comment suggests different local practices and an implied view that a detailed formal contract was preferable. The contract set out the objectives of the association, and then detailed the nature of its constitution and specified its areas of responsibility. The NZSSA stated its objectives as 'the supervision of all matters affecting the interests and general welfare of the stock and station agents'. It then detailed constitutional matters such as membership and voting rights, and set out specific responsibilities such as observing the interests of the industry in relation to the changing legal and statutory environment. The association clarified standard practices on matters such as the sale of wool and livestock as a code of conduct for the industry.[73] Additional supplementary documents covered specific practices in more detail: the NZWBA produced a document, the 'Conditions of sale of wool', outlining nineteen points of agreement dealing with each individual procedure.[74]

The existence of written agreements, which were fixed for a specific period, also enabled associations to codify learning experiences by embodying changes into new contracts. As the industry developed, business became more diverse and complex, networking declined, and firms looked inwards to develop their competitive advantages, all of which required carefully specified and defined terms for interfirm agreements. On the important question of avoiding intrusion into internal competitive strategies which was heavily disputed in the 1890s, later contracts included clauses that agreements were 'not to extend to or interfere with the control of business' of any firm.[75] Other evidence of learning relates to changes in enforcement clauses, voting rights, and the setting of entry fees.

Bilateral agreements between several firms normally included a written contract where particular details, for example, the sharing of commission, employees, or capital equipment required specification. Thus, for example, a deed of association governed an understanding between NMA and Matson from 1889 whereby the latter was to serve as NMA's representative in Christchurch in return for a loan, salary, and rental payment. To avoid any misunderstanding that might lead Matson to claim a share of the profits, the deed specified that 'nothing herein contained . . . shall be construed to create a partnership'.[76] This proved sensible since the agreement appears to have broken down although NMA ultimately acquired the firm. A similar style of agreement in 1874 between NZLMA and Driver Stewart, providing for the latter to be the larger firm's Dunedin representative, was notable for specifying in detail the division of management and control rights between the two firms.[77] Reciprocal selling agreements between AMLF, Australian Estates, and Goldsbrough Mort were covered by written memoranda of agreement setting out the precise responsibilities and tasks of each firm, such as cataloguing, selling, collecting the proceeds, and sending market and sales reports.[78]

Written contracts, however, appear to have been rare for collusive agreements, such as the fixing of interest rates or selling commissions where secrecy from graziers, governments, and public opinion was important. A study of the 1906 Australian Industries Preservation Act has concluded that while it was defective in many aspects of its attempt to outlaw collusive practices, by questioning their legality it forced many agreements underground.[79] In New Zealand the 1910 Commercial Trusts Act was similarly framed. Therefore, many formal written agreements were relinquished in favour of informal understandings, making them more difficult to monitor and enforce. A similar explanation may account for the apparent absence of formal agreements on price fixing in the stock and station agent industry and, as a result, some loss of effectiveness. While the written constitution of the local or national association brokering the particular agreement could be used as a point of reference to govern behaviour between parties, its terms were too broad and general for each specific agreement.

CONCLUSION

Stock and station agents have shown great awareness of the importance of interfirm relations to their and the industry's success. They have cooperated well together so long as this promoted their common interests and did not intrude far into their internal business. Thus, they have cooperated more in the sharing of resources than capabilities. Lower costs, improved coordination, and greater protection of mutual interests have emerged from cooperation on market infrastructure, technical change, and industry representation. However, cooperation has been less extensive and successful where it impinged more closely on the competitive advantages of individual firms, such as in the areas of wool canvassing and advertising. Because of the long-term building up of competitive advantages, such as goodwill, and the need to defend valuable information asymmetries, the more successful firms have been reluctant to risk these benefits. Smaller and newer firms, with less fixed capital, have also seen an opportunity to undercut them. Collusive behaviour designed to raise or maintain charges to farmers has largely failed because, again, some firms preferred competition, and all were sensitive to the need to avoid alienating farmers.

This chapter has revealed the range of crosscurrents of interest in the stock and station industry which manifested in different groupings of firms. Geographic and functional differences between firms were especially important in forming these shifting and divisive alliances which made cooperation more difficult by raising the costs of collusion and reducing levels of trust. With the threat of individual firms or groups leaving an agreement, developing effective punishment of transgressors was difficult. Written agreements provided some scope for cohesion, certainty and improved terms, but these were mostly used for national associations to develop the common interests of the industry. Collusive behaviour was rarely formalised in a written contract. Probably this was due to the threat from competition law and the goodwill loss; either way it mitigated the prospects of success. Overall, the pastoral industry has benefited from cooperation that promotes coordination and lower overhead costs without the losses associated with collusive price-fixing.

CHAPTER TEN

Business Intermediation and Rural Entrepreneurship: The Role of the Stock and Station Agent Industry

This work has sought to answer a question and fill a lacuna in the study of modern Australasian economic and business history. The question is how a farming community distant from its markets, lacking large-scale finance, susceptible to volatile fluctuations, and short on appropriate experience, spearheaded export-led economic development. The lacuna is the absence of studies of an industry, the stock and station agencies, which generated many of Australasia's largest, most advanced and successful business enterprises. The lack of research in this area is the more surprising given the remarkably large amount of archival material that survives for all of the leading firms. The need to fill this historiographical gap is emphasised by the industry's probable uniqueness to the region and its special nature as a quintessential Australasian institution embodied in local culture and society.

The question and the lacuna are addressed jointly by arguing that the stock and station industry filled the 'entrepreneurial gap' in Australasian farming. If entrepreneurs are those individuals who take the judgemental decisions required because of environmental uncertainty, then the agents fulfilled this role by acting as business intermediaries to farmers in three key areas, notably finance, marketing, and business advice. They fulfilled this role through three styles of transaction: undertaking the service themselves, negotiating on behalf of the farmer with a third party provider, and advising the farmer how best to complete the transaction himself. In the nineteenth century they were aided in this role by British finance, entrepreneurship, and connections to the London market, together with their embeddedness in local social and economic networks. In the twentieth century the dominant national agent firms drew heavily on their internalised resources and capabilities to provide farming services. They yielded both scale and scope economies by specialising in the pastoral sector and providing a diverse range of functional services.

Their organisational structures were designed with a view to developing effective information-handling processes, management control systems, and human capital resources.

This concluding chapter seeks to summarise the main findings of the investigation and provide an overall analysis of the role of stock and station agents.

GROWTH STRATEGIES AND PATTERNS

The initial growth of the pastoral industry attracted firms into wool marketing and finance in the mid-nineteenth century. Several soon began to specialise in this area gaining scale economies, expertise, and reputation in the process. By the later decades of the nineteenth century there was a move towards service diversification in the industry. Firms provided finance, marketing, and technical advice to farmers and in the process gained scope economies, especially in the use of information and physical assets. Diversification also recognised the linked and interdependent nature of these services, finance and technical advice, for example, attracting new wool-selling clients. Finally, national expansion was pursued by the leading firms as a competitive tool to gain prime-mover advantages in newly settled districts and to benefit from closer proximity to new farmers emerging from land subdivision. These growth processes were facilitated by the additional financial resources generated by the move towards incorporation in the 1880s. The leading five firms accounted for half of the local wool sales by the beginning of the twentieth century, which was a high concentration level for the time.

LOCAL AND INTERNATIONAL NETWORKS

British sources of finance, entrepreneurship, and commercial information were vital for agents. Some firms, such as AMLF and NZLMA, were established in London as free-standing multinational companies. Firms established locally, such as Goldsbrough Mort, still recognised the importance of British connections, which they enhanced by the establishment of a London office. Local connections within Australasia helped all firms in the daily operations of their business. Many firms were established or developed by leading settlers and benefited from the social and geographic cohesion of early settler society. These embedded bonds were fostered by the firms through social activities, community investments, and local recruitment as the basis of powerful business networks. Firms benefited from networking by the trust it generated and the spawning of reputations. This encouraged business relationships which were long-term and wide-ranging, and particularly emphasised a reciprocal exchange of information and honest behaviour. Such a relationship between agent and farmer was particularly important. As a focal point in the farming network, however, the agent also reduced the number of bilateral trading transactions between parties unknown to each other, such as farmer, shipowner, and wool importer. In effect, they provided a one-stop service for the busy and distant farmer.

CORPORATE CAPABILITIES

In the twentieth century network bonds began to break down, partly because of the changing nature of settler society where personal and social contact in business has become less important. However, the decline was also the product of changing policies by the leading agent firms which replaced their external links and role as a conduit between different groups with an emphasis on building up the corporate capabilities associated with large-scale, enduring business organisations. This led them to pass through institutional development stages not dissimilar from those identified by Chandler for leading American enterprises. The financial crisis of the 1890s and the decision to diversify services led to centralised management structures operating through departments specialised by pastoral service by the early twentieth century. The subsequent geographical expansion together with the interwar crisis generated decentralised divisions in an effort to overcome problems of control and performance measurement. These divisions were geographically (State-) based rather than based on the product orientation that is associated with United States multidivisionals. In turn, this produced the strategic decision-making central office by the 1940s so as to divide long-term planning from operational management at the divisional level.

Innovations in organisational design provided the background for improvements in operational procedures. Thus, a natural concomitant to the multidivisional was the development of management accounting and control systems, initially for performance evaluation in the interwar years and then for long-term planning after World War Two. Rationalised tiers of authority helped establish effective chains of command and communication, and standardised rules and procedures, both vital for mitigating coordination costs in a large professional bureaucracy and making some decisions routine. Accurate specification of duties encouraged investment in well-directed human resource management, something vital for a service industry. This was part of a strategy of encouraging lifetime employment with the firm or at least viewing it as a long-term career. Policies included the keeping of personnel records, business methods training for employees, performance appraisal, and the development of pension schemes. Thus, competitive advantage by large-scale firms was built on the original comparative advantage of the rural sector.

FINANCIAL SERVICES

Agents played a vital role in pastoral finance. Their expertise in the pastoral sector and their close network links helped them to make accurate risk assessments and fill a probable credit gap. As well as lending their own money they also intermediated for banks, which lacked their expertise and regular trading connections with many farmers. This mediation was often undertaken at a loss but the difference was made up through the farmer's wool commissions. The agents' close understanding of the highly cyclical nature of the industry and their reliance on trading commissions made them loyal and continuous supporters of the farmer. Agents also learnt how to design pastoral loan contracts in a way that would elicit further risk-sensitive information from the borrowing farmer. The willingness to accept a higher price (rate of interest), for example, might reveal a risk-loving farmer. Agents used their network connections, and later their corporate power, to monitor and enforce the loan contract.

MARKETING SERVICES

The intermediation of the agents overcame the problems faced by the farmer of long distances, high cost, and a lack of knowledge and contacts. Agents undertook or arranged a series of linked marketing functions including transport, insurance, storage, classification, sale, and collection of the proceeds. In playing their part agents exploited their network connections, locally and internationally, their organisational resources and corporate muscle, and their knowledge of agricultural commodity markets. By handling the work of a large number of farmers and marketing different needs, particularly produce, livestock and land, with similar resources and techniques, the firms yielded economies of scale and scope.

Agents spearheaded significant developments in agricultural marketing, including the move to a local auction system that reduced the number of intermediaries, the realisation time on sales, the shipping costs for the rising number of non-British buyers, and facilitated feedback to attending farmers on quality and presentation. The agents additionally improved coordination between selling centres and refined selling practices. While agents never exercised output fixing they helped to smooth some market fluctuations by periodic controlled release of wool on to the market through advice to client farmers. The livestock market was even more volatile and farmers looked to agents for advice, especially as a result of droughts when decisions to cull or restock had to be taken. In the property market the agents played a central role in land development and subdivision.

ADVISER AND SPOKESPERSON

The isolated and industrious farmer faced problems of the scarcity and high cost of information. The agent had many advantages as information provider, including network connections, geographical reach, and internal systems, which supported efficient information processing. The long-term trust-based relationship between the agents and many of their clients permitted the honest exchange of information that overcame the basic difficulties of trying to establish a normal market in information. They also used company magazines to broadcast new ideas in a way that filtered and synthesised new scientific developments for practising farmers. Their expertise, born of experience and specialisation in the industry, enabled them to transform information into the higher value of advice. Here we see the innovation and leadership aspects of entrepreneurship in their advocacy of many new innovations including refrigeration, machine shearing, and improved livestock breeding. Finally, the agents used their position as large and powerful corporations with influential leaders to act as an advocate or arbitrator for individual farmers in their dealings with other farmers or other groups inside and beyond the network, and as spokespeople for the industry as a whole on many matters.

NATIONAL DIFFERENCES

While the agents conducted largely the same business in Australia and New Zealand, their overall significance may have differed. The need for agents and their ability to operate effectively appears to have been greater in Australia. Geology and climate presented greater difficulties in Australia than New Zealand. The extended droughts and then floods in Australia in the 1890s meant enormous challenges for agents and farmers that had no parallel in New Zealand. Australia's larger land mass presented farming challenges of accessibility and geology away from the coast. An effective land settlement policy was required to develop larger, more remote areas, and decide where the boundaries of reasonable inland expansion lay. On the other hand, from a national perspective, the smaller and less diverse New Zealand economy relied more heavily on effective rural entrepreneurship for economic development and the mitigation of cyclical instability.

The operational efficiency of firms in the two nations is not easy to calculate precisely. Wool auctions were much larger in Australia than New Zealand suggesting one aspect of scale economies. New Zealand agents also faced more competition from the stronger cooperative movement that in turn reflected a larger dairying sector in which agents rarely held a significant market share. The greater political influence of farmers in the more specialised New Zealand economy also meant a greater role for, and the support of, government. On the other hand, Australian agents, like farmers, had to endure much greater distances and therefore coordination difficulties.

CORPORATE LEADERSHIP

This work has emphasised a convergence of corporate strategies and structures between firms from differing backgrounds which pursued a common approach. However, it is evident from chapter 2 that there have been differences in the progress and market share of individual firms, and from chapter 9 that they acknowledged variations in service bundles and competitiveness. The other chapters have alluded to some differences in the timing and nature of policy implementation between the leading firms. Overall, Dalgety was the market leader in both countries from the late nineteenth century until after World War Two. Elders and Wrightson have since caught up and, in many ways, surpassed it. Among other leaders NZLMA, AMLF, NMA and Murray Roberts lost their way to some degree. A possible deduction from this evidence is that the London companies had an initial advantage in access to British finance and entrepreneurial expertise. As the industry became repatriated to Australasia in terms of finance, marketing, technology and farming inputs, this competitive advantage waned. Dalgety was quick to recognise this change particularly with its local wool auctions, corporate structure, and the management of information and human resources. It may have benefited from its hybrid nature, being initially established as a colonial business in Melbourne before the head office was located in London following the breakdown of trading partnerships in London.

Why Dalgety has recently relinquished its leadership is more difficult to explain. Clearly, it regarded Elders as a dynamic competitor if a little risky in its expansionism. Policy disagreements within Dalgety in the 1960s between London and Australasia might suggest that the disabilities of distance remained a residual problem when faced with a particularly strong local competitor. The changes in ownership of Dalgety, Wrightson, and Elders gave each company a freer rein in the 1990s and revealed strategy differences whose relative effectiveness will only be worked out in the third century of the industry.

AN ASSESSMENT OF PASTORAL SERVICES

How vital were the pastoral agents to the success of Australian farming and how well did they fulfil their role? The share of farming services provided by agents is not easy to calculate precisely. The agents dominated wool sales especially after the relocation of the market to Australasia. Their share of finance markets, as lender or intermediary, also appears to have been impressive. Their information, advisory, and advocacy role is not so easily quantifiable but the qualitative evidence is suggestive of their importance. The agents played a lesser role, however, in some other products, most notably wheat and dairying. Because of its greater susceptibility to drought, agents tended to limit their interest in those products. Dairying was particularly appropriate for the cooperative structure since it required very close monitoring and specialised capital and technology which small-scale farmers could share. While already operating in a highly risky industry, agents judged, probably correctly, that extensive commitment to these areas would have raised the uncertainty of their business to unacceptable levels.

The limited and belated penetration of the agents into Western Australia, because of its later and smaller settlement, may help to give some indication of the benefits they provided elsewhere. The relocation of the London wool market to Western Australia occurred much later than for the other States. Significantly, wool from Western Australia was said to be badly presented particularly in terms of washing, packing and grading. It was also described as being of poor quality which reflected a failure to improve the quality of livestock through breeding programs.

The nature and extent of agent services was sensitive to cyclical and secular trends in agriculture. In economic upturns the agents tended to concentrate on efficient marketing and shared with banks the provision of finance for additional investments. In downturns the onus of support more often fell on a combination of agents and government, and the role of advice and advocacy came to the fore. In secular terms, agents expanded their range of services from the later decades of the nineteenth century to accommodate the rapid pastoral development but had little share in the dairy and arable expansion. After World War Two the agents' role expanded initially in light of intense competition but then gradually declined with the expansion of large independent agri-businesses, and the activities of government agencies. The return to private market control and individual responsibilities among smaller farmers in more recent years may enhance the agent role once more.

An alternative form of assessment is to compare the appropriateness of the agent with competing forms of service provision. Both in terms of efficiency (scale economies) and market power (negotiation and advocacy) the agents were preferable to individual farmers undertaking these functions themselves. The agents' sectoral specialisation gave them an advantage over functional specialists such as banks or government agencies in terms of scope economies, expertise, information about, and loyalty or constancy towards, farmers. Subdivision and the relocation of the market served to strengthen the hand of agents through their superior ability to provide more brokering services and assess the creditworthiness of smaller farmers. Loyalty was also an unavoidable imperative; with heavy sunk costs in industry-specific assets, the agents were not as well placed as banks to diversify into other industries. ('Sunk costs' refers to previously incurred expenditures which cannot be redeemed easily.) Farmers' cooperatives possessed all these features but often lacked vital connections and knowledge outside the immediate industry and overseas. Moreover, management problems emerged from the election of farmers with limited and narrow business experience to key positions. Conflicts of interest also surfaced; unlike producer cooperatives, agents could boast that they had become genuine intermediaries after discarding station ownership in most cases and replacing original farmer partners with professional managers. Moreover, since agents served as produce brokers rather than dealers and received their main income stream as a percentage of the price, their trading interests coincided with those of their farmer clients.

It was the breadth and length of term of the agents' approach that are critical for understanding their importance. Breadth enabled them to cross-subsidise between services to ensure vital matters of affordable finance and technical research were maintained. Since neither the market for loans nor information conforms well to the price mechanism, providing them as part of a bundle of synergistic services overcame these transactional obstacles. Broad relations with farmer clients and survival in the industry were vital for building up trust and establishing a strong reputation. Such trust mitigated the other potential conflict of interest where agents acted as local representatives of other groups such as shipowners, or even made strategic investments in such companies to increase their leverage over services.

It was only through long-term commitment to the industry that the agents could provide a high level of service. In particular, it enabled them to cross-subsidise between clients and between time periods using accumulated assets. The building up of large reserve and contingency funds, which has sometimes been viewed as indicative of unduly conservative accounting, was in fact well-founded. Thus, 'cooperative pricing'[1] enabled new farmers, especially smallholders, to get on to the land. It also smoothed the volatile cyclical fluctuations particularly associated with Australasian farming for the community as a whole. The long-term commitment also affected the quality of advice because expertise developed from an accumulated memory, witnessed, for example, by the different reactions to the 1890s and 1930s crises. Agents were better able to understand critical aspects of farming including volatility, climate, technology, and economics. It helped them to segment their clientele into, for example, risk levels, and free or tied, and thereby provided more directed and appropriate advice and support. It also affected their perspective by suggesting solutions to farmers which would bear short-term costs but maximise long-term benefits; for example, using slumps and droughts to achieve policy improvements such as reducing overstocking tendencies and improving stock quality through animal culling. This sacrifice of assets would not suit the interests of a short-term entrant to the industry. The agents' support for long-term infrastructural development was a further benefit.

Overall, length and breadth of approach tied the agents' interests closely to that of the long-term secular development of the farming industry as a whole, as well as its shorter-term seasonal and cyclical vicissitudes. This made them good 'social accountants' since they financed farmers who wished to build up a strong, enduring business rather than make a quick temporary profit, and so an agent took as much interest in a farmer's long-term plans as in his ability to pay off the loan under the precise contract terms.

While many highly successful long-term relationships existed between farmers and their agents, the 'man on the land' was not always convinced

of the service he received. Some objected, for example, to loan contracts
that tied their choice of consignor and therefore restricted competition
between agents. In practice, farmers could and did move between agents
for financial support, or borrowed from several firms simultaneously, but
had to balance such a change against the loss of long-term benefits from
single-firm trading.

Farmers might also be concerned at possible restrictive practices
amongst agent firms. This study has argued that most collusion among
agents was beneficial since it improved coordination and reduced infrastructure and development costs for the industry, particularly in marketing
and technical progress. Most firms were reluctant to extend that cooperation into more detailed areas of operation since they valued their separate
reputation and profile, and feared undermining farmer trust or that of other
industry stakeholders. The slight variations in service bundles provided by
each firm, and therefore different competitive advantages, made it difficult
to gain cooperation on any particular issue. These factors made the cost of
negotiating and enforcing secret collusion prohibitively high in many cases.
In addition, while market contestability may have been limited by the need
to build up expertise and connections, there was plenty of opportunity for
short-term entrants to chisel away at wool commissions, the main source of
company profits.

The central importance of the rural industries to the long-term
economic progress of both nations was clearly recognised by the agents;
as Wright Stephenson observed in 1932: 'you must keep the grass growing
in the country, or it will grow in the streets of your cities'.[2] The evidence
presented in this study can leave no doubt that, over the last 150 years,
stock and station agents have played a central and guiding role in the
success of the farming sector in Australia and New Zealand.

Appendix: Principal Mergers

Figures A1 to A6 indicate the principal mergers of companies in the industry. They are confined largely to intra-industry mergers except for a few conglomerations of the late 1990s. The date in parentheses specifies the earliest known date of operation of the acquired agent firm or its former constituent businesses. Inevitably, judgements have been made about which were the principal firms, and data on their origins is incomplete.

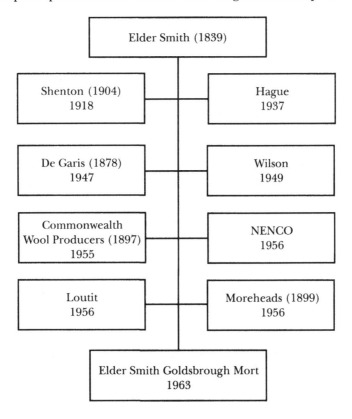

Figure A1 Elder Smith

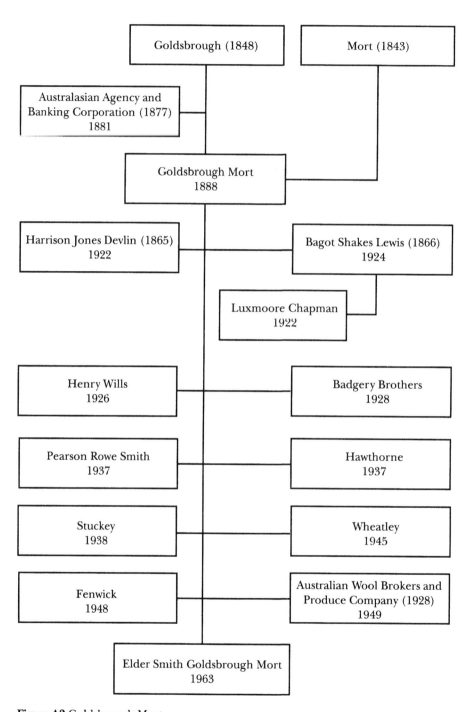

Figure A2 Goldsbrough Mort

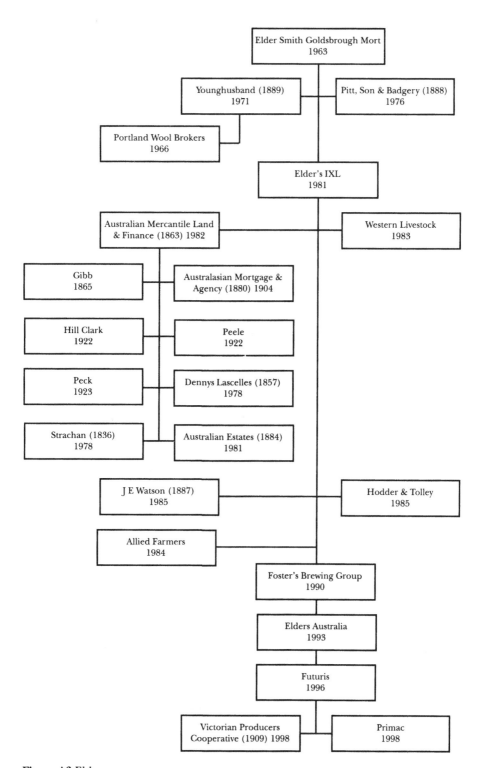

Figure A3 Elders

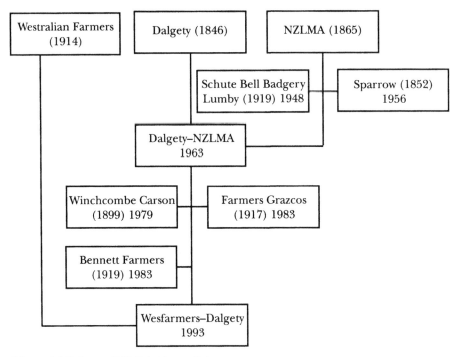

Figure A4 Dalgety–NZLMA (Australia)

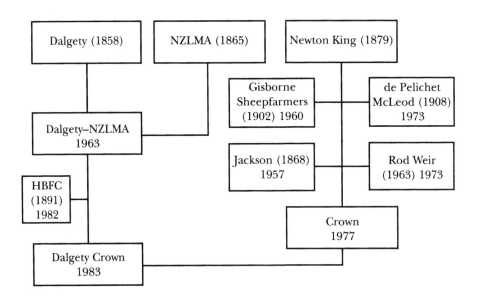

Figure A5 Dalgety–NZLMA (New Zealand)

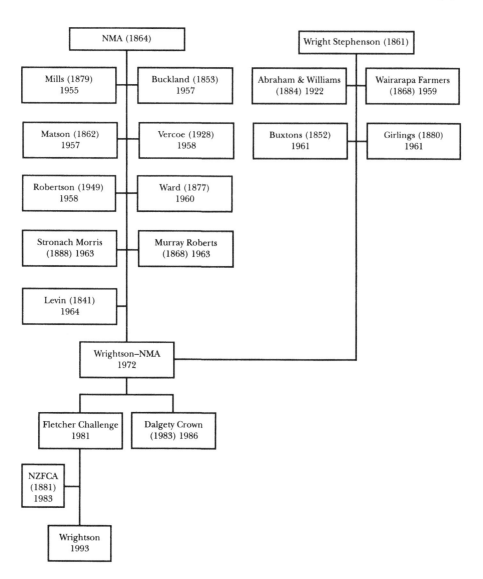

Figure A6 NMA–Wright Stephenson

Notes

CHAPTER ONE: A QUINTESSENTIALLY AUSTRALASIAN INSTITUTION

1   A. Maddison, *Dynamic Forces in Capitalist Development*, pp. 49–50; G. R. Hawke, *The Making of New Zealand. An Economic History*, p. 76; K. Rankin, 'New Zealand's Gross National Product: 1859–1939', pp. 54, 61; J. D. Gould, *The Muldoon Years*, p. 11.

2   N. G. Butlin, *Forming a Colonial Economy*, p. 34; Hawke, *Making*, pp. 9–10. Estimates of the size of the Aboriginal and Maori economies are more difficult to make and need not concern us here since this study deals with economic activities predominantly associated with European settlement.

3   Butlin, *Colonial Economy*, pp. 201, 222; Hawke, *Making*, p. 11.

4   R. V. Jackson, *Australian Economic Development in the Nineteenth Century*, pp. 13–16. The ratio of investment to GDP rose to the exceptionally high levels of about 20 per cent by the late 1880s.

5   Hawke, *Making*, pp. 77–9; Rankin, 'Gross National Product', p. 50.

6   Jackson, *Australian Economic Development*, p. 23.

7   N. G. Butlin, 'Some perspectives of Australian economic development, 1890–1965', pp. 281–6. Also, see W. Vamplew (ed.), *Australians. Historical Statistics*, pp. 133, 141 for details of trends in GDP in current prices. Hawke, *Making*, pp. 123–4; Rankin, 'Gross National Product', p. 61; Gould, *Muldoon Years*, p. 11.

8   Jackson, *Australian Economic Development*, p. 21; G. J. R. Linge, *Industrial Awakening. A Geography of Australian Manufacturing, 1788 to 1890* provides quantitative and geographical dimensions of expansion, State by State, while N. G. Butlin, *Investment in Australian Economic Development, 1861–1900* provides a sectoral analysis.

9   Butlin, *Investment*, pp. 240–1; Hawke, *Making*, p. 12.

10   Vamplew (ed.), *Australians*, pp. 133, 187, 191; Rankin, 'Gross National Product', pp. 58–61.

11   Jackson, *Australian Economic Development*, p. 71; E. A. Beaver, 'The Australian wool clip, 1861–1900' and N. G. Butlin, 'A problem in prices and quantities' disagree over the share of wool exports although they agree on the time trend of wool's declining share. Butlin, *Colonial Economy*, p. 192 provides more recent estimates, suggesting that pastoral exports may have accounted for more than 90 per cent of New South Wales exports in the 1840s. For the first half of the twentieth century see K. Tsokhas, *Markets, Money and Empire. The Political Economy of the Australian Wool Industry*, p. 2, who shows that wool still accounted for 30 to 50 per cent of export value.

12 J. B. Condliffe, *New Zealand in the Making*, p. 309; Hawke, *Making*, p. 38; M. Lloyd Prichard, *An Economic History of New Zealand to 1939*, p. 209.

13 Butlin, *Investment*, pp. 27–31.

14 Lloyd Prichard, *Economic History*, p. 217 shows the dominance of the London capital market in total New Zealand public debt by the early twentieth century.

15 Jackson, *Australian Economic Development*, p. 20; Hawke, *Making*, p. 72.

16 For example, see Gould, *Muldoon Years*, pp. 38–40 on the diversification of export commodities and markets in both nations.

17 Butlin, *Colonial Economy*, pp. 140, 142; Vamplew (ed.), *Australians*, p. 133; Hawke, *Making*, pp. 43–5, 77, 102; Condliffe, *New Zealand*, p. 247; W. H. Oliver & B. R. Williams (eds), *The Oxford History of New Zealand*, pp. 378, 471.

18 Vamplew (ed.), *Australians*, pp. 133, 134, 149; Hawke, *Making*, p. 70; E. A. Boehm, *Twentieth-Century Economic Development in Australia*, p. 104.

19 W. W. Rostow, *The Stages of Economic Growth: a Non-Communist Manifesto*.

20 See J. W. McCarty, 'Australia as a region of recent settlement in the nineteenth century', and the criticism by N. G. Butlin, 'Growth in a trading world: the Australian economy, heavily disguised'.

21 Tsokhas, *Australian Wool Industry*, p. 206.

22 These ideas are similar to the notion of a 'shared harvest' invoked to explain the wide-ranging effects of the postwar wheat industry. See G. Whitwell & D. Sydenham, *A Shared Harvest. The Australian Wheat Industry, 1939–1989*, p. 1. On the postwar industrial linkages of the wool industry see B. Cameron, 'New aspects of Australia's industrial structure', p. 69.

23 Jackson, *Australian Economic Development*, p. 16.

24 Condliffe, *New Zealand*, pp. 247–8; Hawke, *Making*, pp. 52–3.

25 T. A. Coghlan, *Labour and Industry in Australia*, vol. III, p. 1408; Butlin, *Investment*, ch. 6; Hawke, *Making*, pp. 70–1. Condliffe, *New Zealand*, pp. 245–6 also believes that increasing overseas indebtedness was not a problem since it came cheaply relative to the resulting value added through rising exports.

26 A. O. Hirschman, *The Strategy of Economic Development*, ch. 5 refers to this as a form of unbalanced development by shortage of social overhead capital; Jackson, *Australian Economic Development*, p. 16.

27 P. A. Petri, 'The interdependence of trade and investment in the Pacific', pp. 29–55; 'All's cool, calm on debt mountain', *Weekend Australian*, 8–9 March 1997, p. 60.

28 C. B. Schedvin, *Australia and the Great Depression: a Study of Economic Development and Policy in the 1920s and 1930s*, pp. 62–3. E. A. Boehm, 'Australia's economic Depression of the 1930s', pp. 607–8, 615–17; E. O. G. Shann, *The Boom of 1890 – and Now*.

29 Rankin, 'Gross National Product', p. 65.

30 C. G. F. Simkin, *The Instability of a Dependent Economy, Economic Fluctuations in New Zealand, 1840–1914*.

31 For example, W. B. Sutch, *Colony or Nation? Economic Crises in New Zealand from the 1860s to the 1960s*, p. 173. More recently G. T. Crocombe, M. J. Enright & M. E. Porter, *Upgrading New Zealand's Competitive Advantage*, pp. 147–9 have argued that New Zealand's traditional role as 'Britain's fertile farm' has contributed to a misaligned economic system.

32 M. Porter, *The Competitive Advantage of Nations*.

33 A. Chandler, *Scale and Scope: The Dynamics of Industrial Capitalism*. On Japan's postwar competitive advantages, see W. M. Fruin, *The Japanese Enterprise System: Competitive Strategies and Cooperative Structures*.

34 D. W. Meinig, *On the Margins of the Good Earth: the South Australian Wheat Frontier, 1869–84* notes the expansion of farming settlement too far into low rainfall areas due to recent good returns.

35 Some definitions treat pastoral and dairy separately. Terminology varies

between countries. This study distinguishes between agriculture and pastoralism but calls all producers 'farmers' rather than distinguish them from graziers, remembering that some farms were involved in both types of production. Farming is taken to cover all forms of pastoral and agricultural production.

36 Jackson, *Australian Economic Development*, p. 53.
37 Butlin, *Colonial Economy*, pp. 185, 195. G. J. Abbott, *The Pastoral Age: A Re-examination*, pp. 118–24.
38 Butlin, *Colonial Economy*, p. 181. S. Morgan, *Land Settlement in Early Tasmania*, pp. 57–64; D. May, *Aboriginal Labour and the Cattle Industry: Queensland from White Settlement to the Present*, pp. 29–38.
39 Wright Stephenson, 0001, Annual Report, 1932.
40 G. Raby, *Making Rural Australia: an Economic History of Technical and Institutional Creativity, 1788–1860*, p. 2.
41 Abbott, *Pastoral Age*, p. 104.
42 Jackson, *Australian Economic Development*, p. 59.
43 Hawke, *Making*, p. 32.
44 The drought of 1966 was reported as the worst on record with stock losses of around 10 per cent, though much higher in western New South Wales: J. B. Were Newspaper Collection, Elders file.
45 Elders N102/392, seasonal journal, 1903.
46 Hawke, *Making*, p. 34; May, *Aboriginal Labour*, ch. 3. There was some Aboriginal labour on the larger pastoral stations although farmers of smaller holdings rarely used them: N. G. Butlin, *Economics and the Dreamtime. A Hypothetical History*, pp. 207–11.
47 Hawke, *Making*, pp. 31–5.
48 Butlin, *Investment*, pp. 67–86.
49 Butlin, *Investment*, pp. 100–1, 108.
50 Hawke, *Making*, p. 95; S. Eldred-Grigg, *A Southern Gentry*, p. 135; J. D. Gould, 'The twilight of the estates, 1891–1910', pp. 2–3.
51 Tsokhas, *Australian Wool Industry*, p. 204.
52 In 1890 New Zealand exported 1.56 million carcasses of mutton and lamb, compared with Australia's 211 000: *APR*, 15 April 1891, p. 41.
53 Hawke, *Making*, pp. 85–7.
54 Hawke, *Making*, pp. 88–9.
55 The Babcock test to measure milk fat accurately was not invented until 1892 and the earliest milking machines in the same decade. Transport difficulties and disagreements between farmers and factory owners may also have caused delays: Hawke, *Making*, pp. 88–90; Schedvin, *Great Depression*, p. 66.
56 E. A. Boehm, *Twentieth-Century Economic Development in Australia*, pp. 68, 74; Schedvin, *Great Depression*, p. 66.
57 Hawke, *Making*, p. 99.
58 The average annual fluctuation in Australian wool prices between 1921 and 1939 was 24 per cent, and the difference between the highest and the lowest was 75 per cent: Tsokhas, *Australian Wool Industry*, p. 160. The year of 1921 was a particularly bad one in New Zealand with low wool prices and most output unsold.
59 NZLMA, 76-291, Head Office confidential files, 1940.
60 Hawke, *Making*, pp. 129–30.
61 Hawke, *Making*, pp. 132, 136; Boehm, *Economic Development in Australia*, p. 68.
62 Whitwell & Sydenham, *Shared Harvest*, p. 35.
63 B. L. Evans, *A History of Agricultural Production and Marketing in New Zealand*, pp. 39–40; Schedvin, *Great Depression*, p. 64.
64 Boehm, *Economic Development in Australia*, p. 70; Hawke, *Making*, p. 231.
65 Dalgety, 100/1/55/6, Correspondence of Melbourne Manager, 'Wool marketing', article from *Review of Bank of New South Wales*.

66 Hawke, *Making*, p. 238; Evans, *Agricultural Production*, pp. 170–1.
67 Tsokhas, *Markets*, p. 204. Examples of these are frequently seen in the media, for example, *Weekend Australian*, 15–16 February 1997, Weekend Review section, pp. 1, 6. Whitwell & Sydenham, *Shared Harvest*, ch. 8 discuss similar issues.
68 The term 'stock and station agent' is variously defined as the buying and selling of rural properties and stock or dealing in land, products and supplies, *Macquarie Dictionary* (2nd edn, Sydney, 1988), p. 985, *Australian Concise Oxford Dictionary* (2nd edn, Melbourne, 1992), p. 1141. However, the business of most leading agents was much wider than this. The terms 'pastoral' or 'farming' agent might better convey the broad meaning. The three terms are used interchangeably in this book, as was the practice of the firms themselves.
69 K. J. Forrest, 'Diversification and expansion in large diversified New Zealand companies'.
70 In E. Jolley, *The Well* (Ringwood, Vic.: Viking, 1986), Mr Bird the stock and station agent is a key figure in the area; H. Lawson, 'Peter Anderson and Co' in R. Burrows & A. Barton (eds), *Henry Lawson. A Stranger On the Darling* (Sydney: Angus & Robertson, 1966), pp. 297–305; T. Harvey noted: 'The last people to go under in a flood are the emus and the stock and station agent', *Sydney Morning Herald*, 23 October 1965, p. 92; an agent is mentioned in a poem about a squatter published in *Punch* magazine, S. Murray (ed.), *Dictionary of Australian Quotations* (Port Melbourne: Heinemann, 1992), pp. 259–60.
71 WWBA, MSY 4124, minutes.
72 Evans, *Agricultural Production*, p. 150.
73 They also noted the financial and technical assistance provided by agents. *The Australian Wool Industry. Report by the Commonwealth Wool Enquiry Committee*, Australian Parliamentary Papers, 4, p. 816.
74 Butlin, *Investment*, p. 421. He uses the phrase, 'particular set of institutions'. A. Barnard, *The Australian Wool Market 1840–1900*, p. 51; R. Gore, *Levins, 1841–1941*, p. 168. Also see G. R. MacDonald, *The Canterbury Frozen Meat Company Ltd, 1882–1957*, p. 138 and *Economist*, 20 January 1923, p. 92.
75 For example, Barnard, *Wool Market*; A. Barnard (ed.), *The Simple Fleece*. Typical of this genre of company history are: L. Anderson, *Throughout the East Coast: the Story of Williams and Kettle Ltd*; G. Parry, *NMA. The Story of the First Hundred Years of the National Mortgage Agency Company of New Zealand Ltd, 1864–1964*; W. Vaughan-Thomas, *Dalgety. The Romance of a Business*. One notable exception is J. D. Bailey, *A Hundred Years of Pastoral Banking: A History of the Australian Mercantile, Land and Finance Company, 1863–1963*. Tsokhas, *Markets*, contains some useful analysis of the strategies of several leading Australian firms in the interwar period.
76 G. Austin & K. Sugihara (eds), *Local Suppliers of Credit in the Third World, 1750–1960*; L. C. Gray, *History of Agriculture in the Southern United States to 1860*, vol. II, p. 713; J. T. M. Van Laanen, 'Between the Java Bank and the Chinese moneylender: banking and credit in colonial Indonesia', pp. 244–66.
77 Hawke, *Making*, p. 65.

CHAPTER TWO: THE DEVELOPMENT OF THE STOCK AND STATION AGENT INDUSTRY

1 S. Ville, 'Business development in colonial Australia', pp. 26–9; S. R. H. Jones, 'The establishment and operation of European business', in J. Deeks & P. Enderwick (eds), p. 46. NMA, UN 28, box 8, correspondence of Russell, Ritchie and Company of Dunedin, 1870, cites increased competition from British loan companies as the motive for their pastoral specialisation. Some agents were former station managers and farmers.

2 Dalgety, N8/20, F. G. Dalgety Letterbook, 1852–54.

3 A. Barnard, *The Australian Wool Market, 1840–1900*, pp. 60–5.

4 Some colonial 'financial agents', drawing on private English capital, lent extensively to settlers seeking to purchase farm properties: H. Mortimer Franklyn, *A Glance at Australia in 1880*, pp. 210–12.

5 See M. Wilkins, 'The free-standing company'.

6 J. D. Bailey, *A Hundred Years of Pastoral Banking. A History of the Australian Mercantile Land and Finance Company, 1863–1963*, pp. 3–5; R. C. J. Stone, *Makers of Fortune, A Colonial Business Community and Its Fall*, pp. 22–4.

7 R. Gore, *Levins, 1841–1941*, pp. 19, 38.

8 NMA was established in 1877 but acquired local New Zealand businesses that had been trading since 1864.

9 In its simplest form, the costs of specifying, negotiating, and monitoring a business contract or agreement are its transaction costs.

10 In a reflective Dalgety manager's report in 1943 it was noted that 'the Company has opened and closed Branch stock offices at various points, but it has found, without exception, that with the closure, the wool business disappears automatically': 100/1/35/20, Geelong Manager's Report. Elders, for example, diversified into livestock sales in 1884: N102/1, Board minutes of Elders Wool and Produce Company.

11 Bailey, *Pastoral Banking*, pp. 14–15, 70–3, 224–5. He points out that in 1874 AMLF had rejected Richard Goldsbrough's proposal for a merger that would have brought AMLF into local woolbroking much earlier.

12 In 1901 Dalgety was discussing how to relinquish its pastoral stations valued at £750 000: N8/5, Board minutes.

13 This might involve improving their general condition and management and waiting for an upturn in the market: P. G. Stevens, *Pyne, Gould, Guinness Ltd*, p. 25. N. G. Butlin, 'Company ownership of NSW pastoral stations, 1865–1900', pp. 89–110 notes that the rising share of pastoral leases in agent hands from 1 to 2 per cent in the mid-1870s to 15 per cent in 1889–90 reflected the operation of mortgaged stations, not the emergence of company ownership. Lending institutions became lessees simply by holding the firm's mortgage, foreclosure was not required: N. G. Butlin, *Investment in Australian Economic Development, 1861–1900*, pp. 134–6.

14 Barnard, Q50, box 10, file 4, balance sheet notes.

15 Dalgety, N8/69, correspondence, 1904.

16 Barnard, Q50, box 10, file 4 balance sheet notes; Bailey, *Pastoral Banking*, p. 157. However, AMLF continued to own a number of station properties in New South Wales and Queensland: Report from J. B. Were in 1937; AMLF, 97/21/37/1, correspondence, 1937.

17 Barnard, Q50, box 3, Goldsbrough Mort Board minutes.

18 Elders, N102/38, Board memoranda, 1949–52, undated document.

19 Butlin, *Investment*, p. 134.

20 NMA, UN 28, box 3, reports & accounts.

21 Elders noted these strategic investments as common practice by brokers in 1899: 8/57/4/5, correspondence. Elders bought shares in Spencer's Gulf Stevedoring Company in 1915: Elders, N102/6, Board minutes.

22 The analogy of investing in individual farms was remarked on by Dalgety as 'preference shareholders': 163/27, Managers' Conference, 1960.

23 For example, land sales by AMLF in 1917 and 1937, the latter in cooperation with government policy to develop western New South Wales: Barnard, Q50, box 10, file 4, balance sheet notes.

24 NZLMA was commended for being exclusively an agency firm whose farmer clients 'secure the undivided interest of the company': Franklyn, *Glance*, p. 206.

25 A. Barnard, *Visions and Profits: Studies in the Business Career of Thomas Sutcliffe*

Mort, pp. 132–6. H. Holt, *An Energetic Colonist. A Biographical Account of the Activities of the Late Hon. Thomas Holt, MLC*, p. 115.

26 Australian Estates, 165/301, company properties, 1930.

27 The 1860 Companies Act in New Zealand, the 1864 Act in Victoria and 1874 Act in New South Wales.

28 An Act of 1896 in Victoria specifically distinguished the 'private company' as a separate category of corporation with limited disclosure requirements. The Salomon Judgment of 1897 in Britain decided in favour of the private company. When Elders was floated in 1888 the owners and their associates controlled most of the equity: T. Hewat, *The Elders Explosion: One Hundred and Fifty Years of Progress from Elder to Elliott*, p. 32.

29 NMA, UN 28, box 8, letterbooks, 1877.

30 Others included UMA in 1886, Elders and Goldsbrough Mort both in 1888, Australian Estates in 1894, Levin in 1896, Wright Stephenson and Murray Roberts in 1896, and Winchcombe Carson in 1899. Currencies in this book are quoted in local Australasian unless otherwise stated. The British, Australian and New Zealand pounds were at virtual parity with each other until 1929.

31 Dalgety, N8/23, Doxat's letters, various 1876–82.

32 Dalgety, N8/23, Doxat's letters, various 1876–82. This appears to refer to 'financing' of the company through incorporation.

33 See J. H. Angus, *Donald Reid Otago Farmers Ltd: A History of Service to the Farming Community of Otago*, pp. 43–4, 50–2. The decision of Williams & Kettle to convert to a cooperative in 1891 inhibited its ability to follow other pioneers in becoming a national organisation. Murray Roberts' loss of ground may be linked to its equivocation, converting back from public to private in 1935, then to public again in 1963, and private once more in 1970.

34 The 1890s market share of the top five Australasian agent firms exceeded that for ten of fifteen British industries surveyed in 1919, which was subsequent to the consolidating effects of the 1890s merger movement and World War One: L. Hannah, *The Rise of the Corporate Economy*, p. 98. A frequently used modern benchmark would put the industry in the medium concentration bracket of 40 to 70 per cent for the leading four firms: D. W. Carlton & J. M. Perloff, *Modern Industrial Organisation*, pp. 344–6.

35 *Report of the Royal Commission on the Monetary and Banking System*, Australian Parliamentary Papers, 5, 1936, p. 1717, suggests there were twenty 'main' agents in Australia.

36 For example, its 529 181 bales of wool sold in Australasia and London in 1928–29 was the largest of any woolseller in the world: Barnard, Q50, box 10, file 4, balance sheet notes.

37 Dalgety, 100/1/66/3, Managers' Conference, 1951.

38 The Melbourne manager of Dalgety referred to Elders in 1950 as 'a most progressive company': 100/1/31/6, correspondence.

39 At the turn of the century Dalgety and NZLMA were also the leading importers supplying the declining London wool auctions: see chapter 6.

40 Goldsbrough Mort 2/145/18/437, General Wool File, 'The Co-operative Companies', 1926.

41 This information is taken from the *APR* and would appear to be less complete than the data on wool sales.

42 The full company lists are reproduced in S. Ville & D. Merrett, 'The development of large scale enterprise in Australia, 1910–64'.

43 This is confirmed by a cursory analysis of Australian sources such as *AIBR* and *JID*, which have featured many New Zealand firms.

44 The Wright Stephenson figure is based on the nearest estimates of 1907 and 1912.

45 Taken from the annual reports of the two companies.

46 At the 1905 annual general meeting of NMA William Soltau Davidson noted

that as a result of subdivision, 'the risks of the company are very much more scattered': UN 28, box 3, annual reports and accounts; D. Pope, 'Banks and banking business, 1860–1914', pp. 306–7 makes a similar point for bank branching in Australia.

47 AMLF, 97/36/16/1, Letters, 11 and 16 January 1899.
48 AMLF, 97/36/27/1, correspondence, 11 May 1898.
49 Elders, 8/57/2/40, correspondence.
50 Winchcombe Carson, K8190, correspondence. AMLF had similar plans: 133/5/1, correspondence, 25 June 1937.
51 NZLMA at their 1891 annual general meeting: Butlin, *Investment*, p. 437.
52 Elders, N102/5, Board minutes, 1907.
53 C. Fyfe, *The Bale Fillers: Western Australian Wool, 1826–1916*, pp. 233, 240–3.
54 AMLF, 97/36/27/2, correspondence 29 June 1898. Similar influences were at work in other industries, S. R. H. Jones, 'The establishment and operation of European business', p. 49.
55 A. L. Christensen, 'Structural and functional evolution in the New Zealand stock and station industry', p. 59.
56 Winchcombe Carson, K8228, correspondence, 1910.
57 Pitt Son & Badgery, N32/56, Board minutes; a Dalgety report in 1936 emphasised the value of cars in 'retaining old and securing new connections': 100/1/30/33, branch reports.
58 H. Y. Braddon, *Business Principles and Practice*, pp. 50–2.
59 Winchcombe Carson, K8189, correspondence, 16 September 1930.
60 Bailey, *Pastoral Banking*, p. 241 draws attention to AMLF's battle for free clients with the cooperative companies.
61 Elders, 8/106/1, correspondence.
62 Dalgety, N8/24, letterbook of Doxat.
63 Dalgety, N8/4, 5, Board minutes.
64 W. Vaughan-Thomas, *Dalgety. The Romance of a Business*, pp. 69–71.
65 For example, deciding against expansion into Western Australia in 1929: AMLF, 162/627, correspondence, 1929. Winchcombe Carson concentrated on New South Wales, frequently heading the sales list in both Sydney and Newcastle: J. B. Were Newspaper Collection, Winchcombe Carson file.
66 Dalgety, 100/1/55/13, correspondence. Goldsbrough Mort also considered Tasmania in 1885: 2/28/A(1), correspondence.
67 Dalgety, 163/1, NZLMA merger.
68 Wright Stephenson, 0001, annual reports.
69 NMA, UN 28, box 3, reports and accounts.
70 Figures taken from the *Australian Pastoralists Directory* concentrate on the eastern States and neglect the expansion in Western Australia.
71 Dalgety 163/26: Sydney Managers' conference 1959.
72 Bailey, *Pastoral Banking*, p. 261.
73 Dalgety N8/20, F. G. Dalgety letterbooks, 1853. Having a London, or Edinburgh, office also helped to sustain the confidence of British investors: N. Cain, 'Capital structure and financial disequilibrium: pastoral companies in Australia, 1880–1893', pp. 2–3.
74 P. Buckley, 'New theories of international business: some unresolved issues'.
75 Barnard, Q50, box 10, file 4, balance sheet notes.
76 J. B. Were Newspaper Collection, Wright Stephenson file.
77 'Recalling the Past. AML & F Centenary', *Pastoral Review and Graziers' Record*, 17 January 1964, p. 67.
78 Barnard, Q50, box 10, file 4, balance sheet notes.
79 Dalgety had been considering setting up an office in Buenos Aires as early as 1901: N8/5, Board minutes.
80 Barnard, Q50, box 10, file 4, balance sheet notes.
81 A subsidiary problem may have been the cost and difficulties of foreign

exchange transfers between overseas branches, a point made by both AMLF and NZLMA: Barnard, Q50, box 10, file 4, balance sheet notes.

82 Formally, this is referred to as reducing agency costs, or the principal–agent problem. Firms also found solutions to the problem of controlling their own increasingly distant workforce as the company expanded (see chapter 8).

83 AMLF, 97/36/41/1, correspondence, 12 November 1924.

84 Barnard, Q50, box 6, file 17.

85 For example, this was the case in Bagot Shakes & Lewis' acquisition of Luxmoore in 1922: Goldsbrough Mort, 98/1/3, Board minutes.

86 Dalgety, 100/1/55/12, Melbourne manager's correspondence; Elders N102/375, 'History of Elder Smith'.

87 Dalgety, 100/1/55/13, Melbourne correspondence. Banks also proffered advice. In 1935 the Bank of New South Wales used its broader geographical base to advise Elders of the opportunities provided by the economic expansion of Victoria but its more limited knowledge of the pastoral sector led it to advise incorrectly that Hague would not be interested in a takeover: N102/306, 312, correspondence.

88 Pearson Rowe, 46/6, acquisition correspondence.

89 Wright Stephenson, 0001, 1962 annual report.

90 Elders, N102/319, correspondence.

91 Goldsbrough Mort, 2A/30/35, correspondence, 1937.

92 NMA, UN 133, J. G. Ward papers.

93 Goldsbrough Mort, 2A/30/18, correspondence 1930.

94 Goldsbrough Mort, 2A/30/35; Pearson Rowe 46/6, acquisition correspondence.

95 'Wild Cat' Monthly, 6 February 1932, p. 77; JID, 1 November 1926, p. 693.

96 Westralian Farmers Ltd, Annual Report, 1918, pp. 17–18.

97 Elders, 103/4, 'Postwar development'.

98 Dalgety, 100/1/55/8, correspondence.

99 Dalgety, 100/1/55/14, correspondence, 24 March 1961. NZLMA noted of merchandise in 1946, 'in times of depression this department will prove the backbone': 76-291, HO confidential files. This idea had long been popular; at the end of the long drought of the 1890s Dalgetys suggested diversification as a way of countering future shocks: N8/69, correspondence, 1904.

100 Elders, 89/11, London reports, 1931.

101 Dalgety, 100/1/29/22, 100/1/50, correspondence.

102 Goldsbrough Mort, 2A/30/10,15,35 correspondence, 1913–38.

103 Dalgety, 100/1/29–32, Melbourne annual reports, 1914–61.

104 Goldsbrough Mort, 2A/30/10,15,35; Barnard, Q50, box 10, file 3.

105 NZLMA, 76-291, HO confidential files.

106 Wool and stock/station accounted for around 50 per cent of Dalgety's profits in Australia, 1946–55: 100/1/66/6, Managers' conferences.

107 NMA, UN 28, box 3, annual reports and accounts; Bailey, Pastoral Banking, pp. 258, 267; Jones, 'European business', pp. 58–61; P. Denton, Elliott. A Biography of John D. Elliott, p. 229.

108 Dalgety, 163/26, managers' conference; 100/1/30/18, Melbourne report.

109 In 1966, 60 per cent of mergers in the United States were of the conglomerate type: M. G. Blackford, The Rise of Modern Business in Britain, the United States, and Japan, p. 121.

110 Elders, 102/34, Board minutes, 1945.

111 Dalgety, 163/26, managers' conference; 100/1/30/18, Melbourne report.

112 By 1983 Elders accounted for 30 per cent of scouring and about 20 per cent of wool purchases: Bureau of Agricultural Economics, Wool Situation and Outlook 1984, p. 18.

113 Dalgety, 100/1/55/4, correspondence, 1957.

114 Dalgety, 100/1/55/6, correspondence, 1958.

115 Dalgety, 100/1/55/16, correspondence, 1961.

116 J. B. Were Newspaper Collection, NZLMA file.
117 J. B. Were Newspaper Collection, Elders file: Elders falling earnings rate in the 1950s. Barnard calculated that Goldsbrough Mort's earnings rates had been falling since the 1920s from 4s 2d in the pound to 2s 8d by the 1950s. He attributes one-third to a half of this to taxation: Q50, box 10.
118 Dalgety, 163/1, NZLMA merger.
119 Dalgety, 100/1/55/71, correspondence, 11 September 1961. The *Sydney Morning Herald*, 12 September 1961, p. 14 cited years of cooperation between the two firms and suggested Dalgety may have seen it as an opportunity to wrest national leadership back from Elders.
120 J. B. Were Newspaper Collection, Elders file. Recent mining mergers had also been motivated by the desire to control global output but this does not appear to have been a motive for the pastoral agents.
121 In 1972/73 the average four-firm concentration ratio in Australian manufacturing was 0.53 compared with 0.61 among the pastoral agents. It was also well above concentration levels in British manufacturing: Bureau of Industry Economics, *Mergers and Acquisitions*, pp. 33, 35.
122 Dalgety had specifically turned its face against the expansionism of the two Australian companies, believing in 1955 that 'it is in good times that bad debts are made'. Two years later Dalgety's Managing Director, G. S. Hunter, was explicitly critical of Elders as over-extending its turnover: 100/1/55/4, 100/1/66/6, Managers' conferences.
123 Bureau of Agricultural Economics, *Wool Situation and Outlook 1984*.
124 NMA, UN 28, merger papers.
125 Denton, *Elliott*, p. 159.
126 Denton, *Elliott*, p. 229.
127 Jones, 'European business,' pp. 58–61; I am grateful to Dr Steve Jones for his research notes on acquisitions taken from the *New Zealand Stock Exchange Yearbook*.
128 Bureau of Agricultural Economics, *Wool Situation and Outlook 1984*, p. 17. This report also expressed some concern that the conglomerates might use their financial leverage over farmers to restrict competition: p. 18.
129 *AFR*, 17 May 1995, p. 19 although the two firms have since cooperated in a joint wool-handling venture.

CHAPTER THREE: THE FARMING COMMUNITY NETWORK

1 O. Williamson, *The Economic Institutions of Capitalism*, pp. 216–27; A. Chandler, *The Visible Hand*, p. 7.
2 A. Godley & D. Ross (eds), *Banks, Networks and Small Firm Finance*.
3 W. W. Powell, 'Neither market nor hierarchy: network forms of organisation', p. 323.
4 Powell, 'Neither market', p. 303.
5 M. Alvesson & L. Lindkvist, 'Transaction costs, clans and corporate culture'.
6 Powell, 'Neither market', pp. 301–4, 323; W. G. Ouchi, 'Markets, bureaucracy and clans', p. 137.
7 Powell, 'Neither market', pp. 303–5, 325; R. G. Eccles & D. B. Cranes, 'Managing through networks in investment banking', pp. 177–81; M. J. Piore & C. F. Sabel, *The Second Industrial Divide: Possibilities for Prosperity*.
8 M. Casson, *Information and Organisation: A New Perspective on the Theory of the Firm*, pp. 131–41.
9 In production, buyers and sellers can delay decisions by drawing on or building up stocks.
10 Cross-sectoral service providers, such as banks and shipping companies did, of course, transact directly with each other on various other business matters

but relied heavily on the agent's expert intermediation on farming matters.

11 J. H. Angus, *Donald Reid Otago Farmers Ltd: A History of Service to the Farming Community of Otago*, pp. 15, 37, 57; J. C. Irving, *A Century's Challenge. Wright Stephenson and Co. Ltd, 1861–1961*, p. 18; Wright Stephenson, 0001, Annual Report, 1920.

12 Donald Stronach's local activities included serving as a major in the Otago Hussars, President of Carisbrook Cricket Club, and President of the Otago Agricultural Society: Stronach Morris, UN 14 letterbooks, 15 April 1911, and typescript history.

13 G. Carnegie, *Pastoral Accounting in Colonial Australia: A Case Study of Unregulated Accounting*, p. 68.

14 Wright Stephenson, 0585, Special Report, 1906.

15 Wright Stephenson, 0585, Special Report, 1906.

16 AMLF, 133/5/1, correspondence, 1937.

17 Elders, N102/35, Board memoranda.

18 Elders, N102/38, Board memoranda, 1936.

19 Dalgety, N8/24, Doxat's letters; Dennys Lascelles, 62, 12, Conran In-letters, 1894.

20 Angus, *Reid*, pp. 31, 89, 91–2.

21 G. Parry, *NMA. The Story of the First Hundred Years of the National Mortgage and Agency Company of New Zealand, 1864–1964*, pp. 67, 73.

22 Dalgety, N8/24, Doxat's letters, 9 December 1887.

23 AMLF, 97/36/30/2; 97/36/16/1.

24 Elders, N102/38, Board memoranda, 1950.

25 AMLF, 97/36/17/1, correspondence, 1904; 97/36/26/46, correspondence, 1913.

26 Angus, *Reid*, p. 83.

27 Robert Douglas of Pitt, Son & Badgery at Goulburn regularly received clients in his home before a local company office was established: Pitt, Son & Badgery, N32/59, Directors' Minutes, 1915.

28 AMLF, 97/36/26/42, letter of 31 August 1912.

29 Hepburn Leonard, 62, 12, correspondence of William Turner, 1864.

30 NBAC, Pitt, Son & Badgery, Directors' minutes, 1918.

31 R. H. Webster, *A Century of Service*, p. 13.

32 Angus, *Reid*, p. 85.

33 Webster, *Century*, p. 13.

34 Wright Stephenson, 0585, noted in 1906 that its land and stock business brought it into 'close touch with their customers and their places'. Winchcombe Carson fostered social contact at business meetings by supplying food and drink at livestock sales: K8235, Board minutes, 1912.

35 H. Mortimer Franklyn, *A Glance at Australia in 1880*, p. 205.

36 AMLF, 162/377, letter, 23 November 1926.

37 Elders was the local agent for a number of major shipping companies in the 1920s including P & O, Ellerman and Bucknall.

38 The Bank of New South Wales, for example, kept a tight central rein on the lending policies of its branches: K. Sinclair & W. F. Mandle, *Open Account. A History of the Bank of New South Wales in New Zealand, 1861–1961*, p. 50.

39 NMA, UN 28, J. M. Ritchie letterbooks, 1865.

40 NMA also had an enduring connection with the Albion, and later Shaw Savill Albion, Shipping Company, serving as their agent and consigning many produce cargoes on their vessels.

41 NMA, UN 28, correspondence, 1946.

42 Stronach Morris and sheep dip producer, Ness & Company, entered into a joint arrangement to hire a traveller who would sell the dip and acquire new business for Stronach Morris simultaneously. Stronach Morris was a small firm

and this provided a useful means to reduce its costs: Stronach Morris, UN 14, letterbooks, 25 October 1897.

43   NMA, UN 28, correspondence, 1948.

44   NMA, UN 28, correspondence, 1926.

45   Parry, *NMA*, pp. 139, 152, 160.

46   NMA, UN 28, correspondence, 1924.

47   Parry, *NMA*, pp. 103, 110–12. R. C. J. Stone, *Makers of Fortune, A Colonial Business Community and Its Fall* provides a detailed study of business networks in Auckland that included the NZLMA.

48   Bureau of Industry Economics, *Beyond the Firm. An Assessment of Business Linkages and Networks in Australia*, deals with modern networks in Australia and emphasises the economic cooperative motive.

49   Dalgety, 163/27, Managers' Conference, 1960.

50   Bureau of Industry Economics, *Beyond the Firm*, p. xxiii emphasises lack of trust as a major reason for the breakdown of modern business networks in Australia.

51   Dalgety, 100/1/35/20, Manager's report, 30 June 1942.

52   A very detailed agency agreement was drawn up between NZLMA and Dunlop in 1940: 76-291 HO confidential files. The New Zealand agents and banks signed a contract of agreement in 1918 dealing with key issues such as canvassing clients and rebate commissions: WWBA, MSY 4123, minutes.

53   Otago Farmers, AG 728, Board Minutes, vol. 6, September 1930.

54   Otago Farmers, AG 728, Board Minutes, vol. 6, 20 March 1930.

55   However, the agent companies of Australasian origin made game of their domestic shareholders, many of whom were farmers. In 1927 Wright Stephenson claimed that 80 per cent of its capital came from farmers and staff members, although this would have been taken from across New Zealand, not solely a local or regional community: Irving, *Century's Challenge*, p. 107.

56   Otago Farmers, AG 728, Farmers Board Minutes, vol. 9, 1936; Stronach Morris, UN 14, letterbooks for 1890s: although this structure had also helped to create the conflict of interest in the first place.

57   Otago Farmers, AG 728, Board Minutes, vol. 8, February 1935.

58   J. B. Condliffe, *New Zealand in the Making*, p. 243.

59   Angus, *Reid*, p. 31.

60   Otago Farmers, AG 728, Board Minutes, vol. 7, April 1933.

61   Winchcombe Carson, K8189, correspondence.

62   Farmers & Graziers, Z278, 'The First 50 Years', pp. 1–2 and Westralian Farmers' Ltd 334.683051, Annual Report 1917, p. 5, and 1918, pp. 17–18.

63   F. Capie, 'The first Export Monopoly Control Board', pp. 133–41.

64   H. Belshaw, *The Provision of Credit with Special Reference to Agriculture*, p. 273.

65   Although firms still recognise the importance of building trust and developing a 'reliable reputation': K. Emms & A. Squires, *Stock and Station Agents Handbook*, p. 12.

66   Dalgety, 100/1/30/9, Melbourne Department Reports, 1944; 100/1/55/6, London Conference, June 1958.

67   Dalgety, 100/1/66/6, Managers' Conference, 1955.

68   The role of one of these, Fran Rowe, is highlighted in 'Bush farmers shielded by a sheila', *Independent*, 29 August 1998, p. 17.

CHAPTER FOUR: FINANCIAL SERVICES

1   N. G. Butlin, *Investment in Australian Economic Development, 1861–1900*, pp. 122–4.

2   J. D. Bailey, *A Hundred Years of Pastoral Banking: A History of the Australian Mercantile, Land and Finance Company, 1863–1963*, p. 31.

3   Dennys Lascelles, 62, 12, Conran correspondence from Donald brothers, 1892.

4   A. Trollope, *Australia and New Zealand, vol I*, p. 97.

5   F. G. Jarrett, 'Agricultural credit – pastoral finance companies', pp. 190–1.

6   R. Powell & N. Milham, 'Capital, investment, and finance', p. 230. Cyclical indebtedness rose again in the 1990s.

7   R. J. Edgar & F. G. Jarrett, 'Finance for agriculture: pastoral finance companies', pp. 422–3.

8   S. J. Butlin, *Foundations of the Australian Monetary System, 1788–1851*, pp. 258–74.

9   S. J. Butlin, *The Australian Monetary System, 1851–1914*, pp. 93–7.

10 R. F. Holder, *Bank of New South Wales: A History*, p. 363.

11 Rural advances constituted 19 to 24 per cent of bank lending in the 1950s: Jarrett, 'Agricultural credit', p. 197.

12 AMLF, 97/36/26/46, correspondence, 28 February 1913.

13 AMLF, 97/36/26/41, correspondence, 15 April 1920.

14 Elders, N102/31, Board memoranda. The remainder included several fertiliser companies and government departments.

15 Wright Stephenson, 0001, 1949.

16 Barnard on 1950s, Q50, box 10, drafts; H. C. Coombs, 'Rural credit developments in Australia', p. 58; Jarrett, 'Agricultural credit', pp. 206–10, 222. Year-to-year fluctuations in rural lending was also greater among the banks than the agents: p. 194. But anti-inflationary monetary policy by the central banks, particularly in relation to their reserve assets ratios, affected the trading banks' provision of pastoral finance.

17 The Rural Bank sought the NZSSA's advice on foreclosure in 1988: NZSSA, MSY 4144.

18 Powell & Milhan, 'Capital, investment', pp. 242–5.

19 K. Emms & A. Squires, *Stock and Station Agents Handbook*, p. 82; Powell & Milhan, 'Capital, investment', p. 233, table 15.4 lists the range and importance of rural lending by different Australian financial institutions, 1960–88.

20 Butlin, *Foundations of the Australian Monetary System*, pp. 508–9.

21 D. Pope, 'Private finance', pp. 251–2.

22 L. J. Hume, 'Wool in the Australian economy, 1946–58', p. 622. The withdrawal of bank services from farming communities in crisis is again a topical concern.

23 Goldsbrough Mort, 2A/30/37, correspondence, 2/136/15, General Manager diary notes.

24 AMLF, 97/36/26/41, correspondence, 15 April 1920.

25 This is explained more formally and in greater detail by J. Stiglitz & A. Weiss, 'Banks as social accountants and screening devices for the allocation of credit'.

26 H. Mortimer Franklyn, *A Glance at Australia in 1880*, p. 212. In his autobiographical *The Ways of Life*, Evan Bain noted that a bank rejected a loan application and 'had never seen a square of the country'.

27 *Royal Commission into the Monetary and Banking Systems*, Australian Parliamentary Papers 5, 1937, p. 1589.

28 NZLMA, MSY 1385, Board minutes.

29 *AFR*, 22 December 1998, p. 20.

30 NZLMA, MSY 1383, Board minutes, 1866–73.

31 Hepburn and Leonard, 69, 10, out-correspondence of William Turner.

32 Dennys Lascelles, 62, 12, Conran in-letters from Perpetual Executive Trustees Agency, 21 November 1894.

33 Dennys Lascelles, 62, 12, Conran out-letters, 1889; Elders, N102/38, Board memoranda, 1950.

34 The first series, chronologically, is taken from the balance sheets of NZLMA,

Dalgety, Elders, AMLF, and Goldsbrough Mort, and includes New Zealand for the first two; Pope, 'Private finance', pp. 251–2 and Powell & Milham, 'Capital, investment', p. 233 for the second; and the third is taken from *AIBR* and Reserve Bank of Australia data; the lenders are unspecified.

35   For example, Dalgety, NZLMA, Elders, and Goldsbrough Mort, accounted for 62 per cent of advances by agents in 1961, which was slightly larger than their Australian woolbroking share but may have included some New Zealand loans: Dalgety, 100/1/55/17, correspondence; Dalgety, 163/1, NZLMA merger. Dalgety, Goldsbrough Mort, and Elders dominated livestock mortgages at Adelaide in 1934: Elders, N102/31, Board memoranda.

36   NMA, UN 28, box 3, Annual reports and accounts, 1894.

37   Another relevant comparison is the average debt per bale owed to Goldsbrough Mort as a fraction of the wool price which rose from 0.44 in 1923 to 1.83 in 1930 before dropping back in the late 1930s: Barnard, Q50, box 4, folder 3.

38   Goldsbrough Mort, 2A/30/37, 38, 1937 takeover of Stuckey's.

39   A central theme in P. Denton, *Elliott. A Biography of John D. Elliott.*

40   Wright Stephenson, 0001, annual report, 1911; Dalgety, 100/1/224/1, Australian Wool Annual 1927–28; Barnard, Q50, box 3, Board minutes.

41   Dalgety noted in 1903 that banks were taking over some mortgages: N8/68, correspondence; and in 1931 Goldsbrough Mort approached Australian Mutual Provident to take over some of its pastoral mortgages: 2/658B, correspondence.

42   NZSSA, MSY 4143, 4144, minutes 1957–78, 1979–91. At the time of writing, Elders appear to be moving further into rural lending once more.

43   Elders, 8/57/1, correspondence. It lost around £40 000 on one account: N102/3 Board minutes, 1893. On a smaller scale, Stronach Morris was almost bankrupted by concentrating too much capital in a single loan to a family member: UN 14, correspondence, 1890s.

44   AMLF, 97/36/27/2, correspondence.

45   Dalgety, 11/1/55/8, correspondence, 1958.

46   Wright Stephenson, 0585, Special Report, 1906.

47   Pitt, Son & Badgery, 10/2/1, Board minutes, 1892; NZLMA, MSY 1385, Board minutes, 1878; Murray Roberts, 0575, reports and accounts. More unusually, Goldsbrough Mort donated £15 000 to Fairbridge Farm School at Molong to provide homes for fifty-six British migrant orphans although this was presented as a charitable act to celebrate the centenary of Richard Goldsbrough's business rather than a direct contribution to pastoralism: Barnard, miscellaneous files box 6, file 6.

48   Dalgety, 100/1/55/11, correspondence, 1959.

49   R. C. J. Stone, *Makers of Fortune, A Colonial Business Community and Its Fall,* pp. 55, 85.

50   Murray Roberts, 0575, reports and accounts.

51   For further comparisons, see N. Cain, 'Capital structure and financial disequilibrium: pastoral companies in Australia, 1880–93'.

52   Pope, 'Private finance', p. 251.

53   Wright Stephenson, 0585, 1906.

54   Pastoralism had been the major sector for British funds in Australasia in the nineteenth century accounting, for example, for £53 million of £129 million of non-government investment in 1893: *AIBR*, 19 September 1893, p. 848.

55   NZLMA, MSY 1384, Board minutes.

56   Bailey, *Pastoral Banking*, p. 43.

57   Cain, 'Capital structure', p. 5. The leading Australian companies had largely converted to perpetuals by 1898 although it may have been unusual in New Zealand before about 1912: *AIBR*, 19 October 1898, p. 660; Wright Stephenson, 0001, 1912.

58 Australian Estates, 165/47, correspondence, 16 October 1924. Also Cain, 'Capital structure', pp. 14–16.

59 AMLF, 97/36/26/42, 46, correspondence, 31 August 1912, 28 February 1913; Dalgety, 100/1/66/6, Managers' conference.

60 Dalgety, 100/1/55/9, correspondence, 16 January 1959.

61 Otago Farmers, AG 728, Board minutes 7, 1931.

62 N. Cain, 'Pastoral expansion and crisis in New South Wales, 1880–93: the lending view', p. 196.

63 Wright Stephenson, 0585.

64 For example, see the extensive lending details in the Board minutes of NZLMA.

65 The example of Norman Bourke: Australian Estates, 165/142, correspondence.

66 Pitt, Son & Badgery, 10/2/21, Directors' Minutes, 1905.

67 Goldsbrough Mort, 2B/36, Board minutes.

68 AMLF, 97/36/14/5; 97/36/26/46, correspondence.

69 In 1921 Australian Estates believed 1200 sheep was insufficient for a loan of £1500 and 1800 for £4000: 165/144, correspondence.

70 The occasional charging of an establishment fee of several per cent of the value of the loan was an additional insurance for agents: NZLMA, MSY 1384, Board minutes, 26 June 1878.

71 NMA, UN 28, box 5, correspondence, 1921.

72 NMA, UN 28, box 5, correspondence, 1921. In some areas the tradition of moral security took longer to die out, most notably South Australia: Barnard, Q50, box 6, folder 5.

73 Taking evidence from a variety of companies and periods, there was a variance from 66 to 80 per cent. For example, Pitt, Son & Badgery, 10/2, Board minutes, 1890s; Winchcombe Carson, K8228, correspondence, 1909, 1927; Elders, N102/15, 16, Board minutes, 1951 and 1954.

74 Goldsbrough Mort, 2/124 Board Minutes, 18 May 1894. It was one of several firms which offered lower rates of interest where good margins existed: Barnard, Q50, box 3, 1899.

75 For example, Otago Farmers' client Hugh Blaikie took up a great deal of time and money in legal costs, board discussions, interviews, and the preparation of reports including a 33-page question enquiry completed by Blaikie: Otago Farmers, AG 728, Board Minutes, 6, 1929.

76 Murray Roberts, 0575, reports and accounts; Pitt, Son & Badgery, 10/2/9, Board minutes, 1897.

77 Elders, N102/35, Board memoranda.

78 Dennys Lascelles, 62, 12, Conran in-correspondence, 21 June 1906.

79 Otago Farmers, AG 728, Board Minutes, 7, 11 February 1932; Murray Roberts, 0575, balance sheets and reports.

80 Otago Farmers, AG 728, Board Minutes, 5, 1928. However, in 1940 AMLF was confident that 'the keenness of our competitors' would allow it to offload some accounts: 162/396, correspondence, 11 January 1940.

81 Winchcombe Carson, K8229, Board minutes, action taken against Dalgety in 1937.

82 Australian Estates, 165/141, correspondence.

83 Goldsbrough Mort, 2/123/7, Board minutes.

84 Elders, N102/32, Board memoranda, 1939.

85 NZLMA, 76-291, Confidential HO files, 1956.

86 Wright Stephenson, 0585.

87 Dennys Lascelles, 62, 12, in-correspondence, 1895.

88 Wright Stephenson, 0585.

89 Dennys Lascelles, 62, 12, in-correspondence, 1897.

90 Bailey, 'Pastoral banking', p. 255. Williams & Kettle claim not to have

dispossessed a single client in the 1930s: L. Anderson, *Throughout the East Coast: the Story of Williams and Kettle Ltd*, p. 138.

91 Winchcombe Carson, K8229, 1933.

92 Goldsbrough Mort, 2B/36/15, Board minutes.

93 K. Tsokhas, *Markets, Money and Empire. The Political Economy of the Australian Wool Industry*, pp. 6–7, 128–9, argues that 'the key consideration was to continue to lend in a way that made possible an equilibrium between the market value of assets and the value of debts for as many clients as possible'.

94 Tsokhas, *Markets, Money*, pp. 121–2, 129.

95 AMLF, 133/5/1, correspondence, 1937.

96 Tsokhas, *Markets, Money*, pp. 149–50.

97 NZLMA, 76-291, HO confidential files.

98 Pyne Gould Guinness, for example, wrote off £0.5 million of irrecoverable loans from its balance sheet in the 1930s in an effort to keep farmers on the land: P. G. Stevens, *Pyne, Gould, Guinness Ltd*, p. 90.

99 Barnard, Q50, box 4, file 4.

100 NMA, UN 28, box 10, correspondence.

101 UMA, 165/42, correspondence, 7 November 1892. Occasionally agents allowed the lure of good commissions to obscure the basic unsoundness of the loan, Murray Roberts despairing in 1896, '[we have] perhaps let our desire to obtain the business outweigh our discretion': Murray Roberts, 0575, accounts and reports.

102 Dalgety, 163/27, Managers' conference, 1960.

103 Australian Estates, 165/301, client statements.

104 Butlin, *Investment*, pp. 126, 421.

105 NMA, UN 133, Glenconner memoranda. Australian Estates was also losing market share through lack of specialisation.

106 Barnard, Q50, box 10, file 3.

107 Dalgety, 163/27, 1960.

108 Barnard, Q50, box 10, file 3.

109 Stiglitz & Weiss, 'Banks as social accountants', p. 100.

CHAPTER FIVE: MARKETING SERVICES: LIVESTOCK, LAND,
AND PRODUCE

1 H. Mortimer Franklyn, *A Glance at Australia in 1880*, p. 211.

2 Also 63, 62, 60 and 55 per cent respectively for Sydney, Adelaide, Perth, and Brisbane: Barnard, Q50, box 10. Also see Dalgety, 100/1/32/6, Melbourne report 1956; 100/1/66/5, Managers' conference, 1954 for whom 57 per cent of net profit in Australia in 1953 came from wool, and Elders for whom 69 per cent came from wool and livestock in 1960–61: J. B. Were Newspaper Collection, Elders file.

3 A point made by Dalgety in 1921: 100/1/35, Geelong reports.

4 Known as the 'accelerator' effect.

5 For example, Goldsbrough Mort noted, 'We are . . . hampered in our wool trade owing to having no fat stock dept': Barnard, Q50, box 4, correspondence, 1930.

6 Dalgety, 100/1/70/1, 2, wool conference report, 1953; 100/1/35/20, Geelong report, 1943.

7 Dalgety, 100/1/35/20, 1943.

8 NMA, UN 28, London special letterbooks. The previous year Dalgety had also attributed, in part, its postwar loss of market share in wool selling to inadequate livestock sales: 100/1/70/1, 2, 1953.

9 Goldsbrough Mort, 2A/42/1, 2A/30/10, correspondence, 1939, 1927; Elders, N102/391, pocket compendium, 15 October 1931.

10 This three-way segmentation is noted by Dalgety: 100/1/55/8, correspondence, 1958.
11 Winchcombe Carson, K8189, correspondence, 1932.
12 Goldsbrough Mort complained in 1896 that it had lost as much as 50 per cent of its wool clients since the previous year as a result of such a rate war: 2/174/587a, correspondence.
13 See F. Gruen, 'The case for the present marketing system', pp. 496–506.
14 In 1925 at the Midland and State saleyards 473 881 sheep and lambs, 32 728 pigs, and 34 528 cattle were sold: Goldsbrough Mort, 2A/87, stock statistics. Similar patterns are indicated from the Adelaide livestock sales: Elders, N102/252, stock register, 1913. Horse bazaars declined with the advent of the motor vehicle except for a temporary revival in World War One.
15 The accounts of Pearson, Rowe bear testimony to the range of services: paying rail freights, dealing with shipping companies like Union Steamship Company, reimbursing the Melbourne Harbour Trust Company for receiving cattle, and paying Hill & Sons of Wodonga for unloading and paddocking.
16 K. Tsokhas, *Markets, Money and Empire. The Political Economy of the Australian Wool Industry*, p. 137.
17 Although in 1940 the New Zealand Department of Agriculture wrote to the NZLAAA citing complaints from butchers that 'large numbers of ewes in an advanced state of pregnancy are being offered for sale as fat sheep', and requesting that auctioneers ensure only ewes guaranteed 'empty' should be offered for sale: NZLAAA, 96-223-13, correspondence 1940.
18 Elders, N102/97, correspondence, 1908.
19 NZLMA mediated when several ewes and rams died en route to their new owner and on another occasion when a traded cow proved to be pregnant: 76-291, HO confidential files, 1904.
20 Pitt, Son & Badgery, 10/2/2, Directors' minutes, 1893.
21 Similar trends can be found in livestock auctions at Midland and State saleyards: Goldsbrough Mort, 2A/87, 1925–44.
22 Hepburn Leonard, 69, 10, correspondence of William Turner.
23 Goldsbrough Mort, 2A/87, 1925–44.
24 Bennett & Fisher was an important firm in South Australia but not one of the leading national firms.
25 Goldsbrough Mort, 2A/87, 1925–44 and *Dalgety's Annual Wool Review*, 1925.
26 Elders, 8/57/2/36, 40, miscellaneous papers of W. J. Young.
27 Elders, N102/6, Board minutes, 1913.
28 NZLAAA, 96-223-16, correspondence, 1939.
29 Elders, N102/6, Board minutes, 1913.
30 UMA, 165/135, Board correspondence.
31 Elders, N102/97, 1907.
32 For example, Bagot Shakes & Lewis in 1922 and Murray Roberts and Goldsbrough Mort: 98/14, papers regarding Bagot Shakes Lewis; Murray Roberts, 0015, Board minutes.
33 NMA, annual report 1966.
34 Dalgety, N8/67, correspondence, 1903.
35 N. G. Butlin, *Investment in Australian Economic Development, 1861–1900*, pp. 109–10.
36 Goldsbrough Mort, 2/174/355, correspondence, 14 August 1895.
37 UMA, 165/136.
38 Elders, N102/97, 1909–14.
39 Dalgety, N8/67, 68, correspondence.
40 Agents complained about the high rail charges of State and Commonwealth governments: Goldsbrough Mort, 98/14.
41 Elders, N102/97.

42   Elders, N102/197, newspaper cuttings. Goldsbrough Mort was doing likewise: 2/210, correspondence.

43   J. C. Irving, *A Century's Challenge. Wright Stephenson and Co. Ltd, 1861–1961*, pp. 126–45. Pyne and NMA also showed a periodic interest in bloodstock: P. G. Stevens, *Pyne, Gould, Guinness Ltd*, p. 40.

44   There was a big rise in tallow exports in the 1890s: *AIBR*, 19 March 1896, p. 160.

45   *AIBR*, 20 February 1905, p. 114.

46   Goldsbrough Mort, 2/210.

47   Elders, N102/97; Barnard, Q50, box 4.

48   Winchcombe Carson, *Annual Wool Review*, 1898.

49   See H. Munz, *The Australian Wool Industry*, p. 63.

50   NZLAAA, MSY 4142, minutes.

51   Figures are taken from a variety of sources including Elders, N102/1, 5, 6, Board minutes, 1882–1916; Goldsbrough Mort, 2A/41/4, correspondence, 1933–44; Hepburn Leonard, 69, 10, correspondence of William Turner, 1863–6; Murray Roberts, 0566, HO ledgers, 1910–36; NZLAAA minutes; Pearson Rowe, 46/6/2, correspondence, 1936–39.

52   Stronach Morris, UN 14, typescript history.

53   Although Goldsbrough Mort initially believed selling fat stock in saleyards would increase the company's business 'at no cost to the company': Barnard, Q50, box 4.

54   NZLAAA, 96-223-16, correspondence, 1939.

55   Otago Farmers, AG 728, Board minutes, 6.

56   NZLAAA, MSY 4142, 1932; *JID*, 1 December 1932, p. 503.

57   A. Barnard, *Visions and Profits: Studies in the Business Career of Thomas Sutcliffe Mort*, p. 30.

58   Franklyn, *Glance*, pp. 211, 220–1.

59   Elders, N102/98, correspondence, 1912.

60   Wright Stephenson, 0585, 1906 Special Report.

61   Dennys Lascelles, 62, 12, Conran correspondence, 1892. The company was also active in the development of local infrastructure such as the Hopetoun Railway.

62   Dalgety, 100/1/55/6, correspondence, 1958. Murray Roberts and NMA also regarded dairying accounts as yielding only limited commissions: Murray Roberts, 0575, reports and accounts, 1894; NMA, UN 28, box 5, correspondence, 1918.

63   H. G. Philpott, *A History of the New Zealand Dairy Industry, 1840–1935*, p. 397.

64   Dalgety, N8/69, correspondence, 1904.

65   F. B. Stephens, 'Co-operation in New Zealand', p. 749; see also H. Belshaw, *The Provision of Credit with Special Reference to Agriculture*, pp. 272, 276.

66   Winchcombe Carson, K8228, Board minutes; AMLF, 97/36/26/46, correspondence, 1913.

67   Dalgety, annual reports, 1929, 1939; NZLMA, 76-291, 1904. In New Zealand, Murray Roberts also regarded wheat accounts as yielding little profit: 0575, reports and accounts, 1880.

68   G. Whitwell & D. Sydenham, *A Shared Harvest. The Australian Wheat Industry, 1939–89*, pp. 38–9; B. D. Graham, 'Graziers in politics, 1917–29', p. 594.

69   NMA, UN 28, correspondence, 1952.

70   NMA, UN 28, box 10. In several cases a larger firm, or several agents in cooperation, produced farm materials. Wright Stephenson was renowned for its seed dressing plant and NMA for its fertiliser production.

71   NMA, UN 28, box 5, correspondence.

72   Dalgety, 100/1/66/3, Managers' conference, 1951.

CHAPTER SIX: MARKETING SERVICES: WOOL CONSIGNMENT AND BROKERAGE

1   The latter point was noted by Elders in 1905: N102/97, correspondence.
2   A. Barnard, *The Australian Wool Market, 1840–1900*, pp. 7–8.
3   Known as skirting and rolling.
4   Some shipments were sold in Liverpool.
5   Barnard, *Wool Market*, p. 47.
6   Barnard, *Wool Market*, p. 47.
7   Direct shipment was especially common amongst the large settlers in southern New Zealand, such as Canterbury runholder Cracroft Wilson: ARC.1990.7, correspondence, 1868–78.
8   Barnard, *Wool Market*, pp. 47, 63.
9   Dennys Lascelles, 62, 12, Conran in-Letters; UMA, 165/136, Board letterbook.
10 For example, Dalgety, 100/1/30/12, Melbourne reports, 1923.
11 Elders, N102/97.
12 L. Anderson, *Throughout the East Coast: the Story of Williams and Kettle Ltd*, pp. 33–4.
13 Dennys Lascelles, 62, 12, Conran in-letters.
14 Dennys Lascelles, 62, 12, Conran in-letters, 1900.
15 Elders, 8/57/4/7B, correspondence, 1899. Dalgety installed a hydraulic dump at its Carnarvon store in Western Australia in 1910 to avoid a repeat of the problem of insufficient shipping space for the clips in the previous year: C. Fyfe, *The Bale Fillers: Western Australian Wool, 1826–1916*, p. 229.
16 Dennys Lascelles, 62, 12, Conran in-letters, 1889. Lighters are small riverboats which can help to speed up the loading or unloading of an ocean-going vessel. Marcel Conran of Dennys Lascelles noted in 1891, 'Considering the large stake my firm has in Geelong; and that the nature of the business is such that the condition of the harbour is of the greatest importance': Dennys Lascelles, 62, 12, Conran's out-letters.
17 See Dennys Lascelles, 62, 12, Conran's correspondence to Federal Steam Navigation Company in 1897.
18 Dennys Lascelles, 62, 12, Conran's correspondence to Federal Steam Navigation Company in 1897.
19 Dennys Lascelles, 62, 12, Conran in-letters.
20 Dennys Lascelles, 62, 12, Conran in-letters, 1893.
21 Elders, 102/97.
22 Barnard, *Wool Market*, p. 217.
23 *APR*, 15 March 1897, p. 43.
24 Fyfe, *Bale Fillers*, pp. 246–7, 253–4, 260; Dalgety, 100/1/29/3, Melbourne reports, 1916.
25 G. Parry, *NMA. The Story of the First Hundred Years of the National Mortgage and Agency Company of New Zealand Ltd, 1864–1964*, p. 24; J. C. Irving, *A Century's Challenge. Wright Stephenson and Co. Ltd, 1861–1961*, p. 24; R. Gore, *Levins, 1841–1941*, pp. 26–7.
26 R. T. Appleyard & C. B. Schedvin (eds), *Australian Financiers: Biographical Essays*, p. 102. The dates vary according to source. Barnard, *Wool Market*, p. 68 suggests that entry to the major market of Melbourne was in 1880 for NZLMA, 1887 for Dalgety, and 1888 for UMA. Several primary sources, however, suggest Dalgety was selling locally by 1886 but NZLMA not until 1887: Barnard, Q50, box 4, correspondence of General Manager; Dalgety N8/24, Doxat's letters, 1887. Since early sales, if not very successful, could be intermittent, commencement dates are not always clear.
27 Goldsbrough Mort, 2/28/A(1), correspondence.
28 UMA, 165/103, 135, Board minutes and letterbook, 1888–1900.
29 J. D. Bailey, *A Hundred Years of Pastoral Banking: A History of the Australian Mercantile, Land and Finance Company, 1863–1963*, pp. 174–5.

30 A. Barnard, 'A century and a half of wool marketing', pp. 486–7.
31 Fyfe, *Bale Fillers*, pp. 120–1.
32 AMLF, 97/36/26/17, correspondence 1903; Barnard, Q50, box 10. NZLMA observed in 1878 that many small sheep farmers in the Manawatu preferred local sales but that the company did not offer this option: MSY 1384, Board minutes. Goldsbrough Mort observed in 1884, 'growers are becoming more alive to the advantages of offering their produce in the local market': 2/40/1, Board minutes.
33 AMLF, 97/36/26/6, correspondence.
34 In *APR*, 15 September 1894, pp. 353–7.
35 New Zealand currency, NZWBA minutes.
36 Elders, N102/97.
37 Barnard, *Wool Market*, pp. 33–9.
38 Barnard, *Wool Market*, p. 219, table 10; Barnard, 'A century', p. 478; *APR*, 15 March 1902, p. 7.
39 Dennys Lascelles, 62, 12, Conran out-letters. The company also advised a client in 1892 that it was better for United States firms to buy in Australia since direct shipment was cheaper. A similar point was made in relation to Japan, United States and Continental Europe by the New Zealand Woolbrokers Association in 1932: NZWBA, MSY 4137, minutes.
40 *AIBR*, 20 July 1901.
41 Contemporaries noted the large proportion of wool which was sold in both countries on reaching London: *AIBR*, 19 July 1902, p. 547.
42 *AIBR*, 21 July 1908, p. 557.
43 Dennys Lascelles, 62, 12, Conran correspondence, 1908.
44 Fyfe, *Bale Fillers*, p. 256.
45 AMLF, 97/36/26/31, 97/36/16/10, correspondence, 1903, 1906.
46 In 1952 NMA reported that it had consigned little to London in recent years because of buoyant prices but lower prices in that year had caused more growers to opt for sale in London: UN 28, London letterbooks.
47 Dalgety, 100/1/55/15, correspondence.
48 Elders, 89/11/2, London reports, 1950.
49 NZLMA, 76-291, HO confidential files, 1947.
50 Dalgety, 100/1/66/4, Managers' conference, 1953; Fyfe, *Bale Fillers*, p. 257.
51 AIBR, 17 October 1899, pp. 699–700.
52 Goldsbrough Mort, 2A/206, wool, miscellaneous figures on consumption.
53 Barnard, 'A century', p. 485 draws attention to converging prices. In 1932 the NZWBA noted the absence of speculative reselling by this time: MSY 4137.
54 Barnard, *Wool Market*, pp. 110, 154–5; Dennys Lascelles, 62, 12, Conran out-letters, 1892; J. H. Angus, *Donald Reid Otago Farmers Ltd: A History of Service to the Farming Community of Otago*, pp. 27–8. Sydney had periodically held central wool sales from the 1860s.
55 WWBA, MSX 4324, correspondence 1918.
56 Dalgety, 100/1/55/13, correspondence, 1960; WWBA, MSX 4324, 1916 notes private sales by agents.
57 WWBA, MSY 4136; although in 1953 the NZWBA noted that the season had recently been extended to twelve months: minutes, MSY 4140.
58 Dalgety, 100/1/66/6, Managers' conference.
59 Barnard, 'A century', p. 482.
60 NZWBA, MSY 4137, 1932, MSY 4141, minutes, 1966.
61 H. Munz, *The Australian Wool Industry*, pp. 103, 133.
62 Turnbull Library, Dalgety, 032-0785, correspondence. Companies also compared their practices favourably with those firms outside the national organisation which were included in the wartime system of wool selling: WWBA, MSY 4123, minutes, World War One.

63 For example, NZWBA, MSY 4141, 1966; NZSSA, MSY 4143, minutes, 1967; Dalgety, 100/1/55/16, correspondence, 1961.

64 F. Gruen, 'The case for the present marketing system', pp. 496–506; Munz, *Australian Wool Industry*, pp. 131–3 *passim.*

65 Elders, 8/57/3, correspondence, 1898; Dalgety, 100/1/55/15, 1961.

66 Goldsbrough Mort, 2A/208/8, Canadian wool market report, 1937.

67 Fyfe, *Bale Fillers*, 271–2.

68 For example, in the Dalgety and NZLMA merger rising selling costs and salaries were cited as outstripping revenues: Dalgety, 163/1, merger papers, 1961–2.

69 Dalgety, 100/1/30/36, Melbourne reports.

70 Goldsbrough Mort, 2A/55A/13, correpondence; Dalgety, 100/1/55/13, 1960.

71 The shift in location did reduce their activities negotiating shipping freights but there were few fixed costs in this work.

72 Elders, N102/4, Board minutes.

73 Dalgety, 100/1/55/13, 1960.

74 Elders, 102/4, Board minutes, 1907; Dalgety, 100/1/30/25, Melbourne reports, 1930.

75 Elders, N102/33, Board memoranda.

76 It was also noted that spare capacity was advisable to plan more effectively for periodic modernisation of handling methods: Dalgety, 100/1/32/9, Melbourne reports, 1961. Wartime expansion and bottlenecks also obliged firms to invest in additional wool storage, for example, NZLMA in 1918: Barnard, Q50, box 10, file 4.

77 Goldsbrough Mort noted in 1960, 'Our wool and stock business is so closely related . . . that it would be impossible to give up any department or area': Q50, box 10, file 3.

78 Dalgety, 100/1/35/20, Geelong reports.

79 Goldsbrough Mort, 2A 202, correspondence, 1939.

80 De Garis, for example, favoured private buying: 8/10/6/21, correspondence, 1924.

81 Dalgety, 100/1/30/32, Melbourne report, 1935; Barnard, 'A century', p. 480.

82 NZSSA, MSY 4143, 1966.

83 WWBA, MSY 4131, minutes.

84 NZSSA, MSY 4144, 1991; K. B. Nicholson, *Marketing of Agricultural and Horticultural Products*, p. 83.

85 Goldsbrough Mort, 2A/208-2, miscellaneous wool files, 1941; Elders, N102/99, correspondence, 1915; Dalgety, 100/1/55/15, correspondence, 1961.

86 Elders, N102/99, 1915.

87 AMLF, 162/687, correspondence, 1934.

88 Dalgety, 100/1/66/1, correspondence, 100/1/55/6, correspondence 18 August 1961.

89 Dalgety, 100/1/55/16, correspondence, 1965.

90 WWBA, MSY 4123, minutes.

91 NZWBA, MSY 4137.

92 Goldsbrough Mort considered reducing commission rates to 1.5 per cent in 1924 to counter competition from cooperatives while the cooperatives initiated a 20 per cent rate reduction in Australia in 1934: Barnard, Q50, box 3, file 5; University of Melbourne Archives, Stock Exchange box 592, Dennys Lascelles Annual Report.

93 Evidence on consignment and brokerage rates are taken from a wide range of the sources used in this study.

94 Detailed in *The Australian Wool Industry. Report by the Commonwealth Wool Enquiry Committee*, Australian Parliamentary Papers, 4, p. 870.

95 L. J. Hume, 'Wool in the Australian economy, 1946–58', pp. 617–21.
96 Hume, 'Wool', p. 619.
97 WWBA, MSY 4125, minutes 1920.
98 Barnard, Q50, box 10, chapter drafts.
99 Goldsbrough Mort, 2A/55A/13, 1922; Dalgety, 100/1/55/13, correspondence, 1960.
100 WWBA, MSX 4323 correspondence, 1910.
101 NZWBA, MSY 4135, 1918.
102 Goldsbrough Mort, 2A/202, 1939.
103 Goldsbrough Mort, 2A/208-2, 1941.
104 Dalgety, 100/1/55/16, 1960.
105 Barnard, 'A century', p. 480; *JID*, 1 September 1928, p. 409.
106 This depends on the price elasticity of demand for wool. Some agent charges were fixed and commission rates were lower on larger volumes.
107 Elders, N102/15, 1951.
108 AMLF, 97/36/26/32, correspondence; Elders, N102/97, 98.
109 K. Tsokhas, *Markets, Money and Empire. The Political Economy of the Australian Wool Industry*, ch. 4.
110 At the 1931 Empire Wool Conference. A futures market was established in Sydney in 1960: Barnard, *Fleece*, p. 480; Dalgety, 100/1/55/15 in 1960.
111 Elders, N102/9, Board minutes, 1925.
112 Tsokhas, *Markets, Money*, ch. 4.
113 Gruen, 'Present marketing system', pp. 492–5.
114 Munz, *Australian Wool Industry*, p. 133; Goldsbrough Mort, 2A/208-4, wool files, 1939.
115 Tsokhas, *Markets, Money*, pp. 25–30.
116 Elders, N102/7 in 1917.
117 These issues are detailed in Tsokhas, *Markets, Money*, ch. 3.
118 Some growers believed that greater stabilisation of wool selling was needed while Sir John Higgins, chairman of BAWRA, believed its operations should be made permanent.
119 A. Barnard, 'Wool brokers and the marketing pattern, 1914–20', p. 14.
120 NZWBA, MSY 4138, minutes 1944. Wool was sold but often left in Australia and New Zealand rather than being shipped to Britain.
121 Dalgety, 100/1/55/15; Elders annual report, 1968.
122 655 000 bales by February 1991: *Wool Report* (February 1996), p. 5
123 Elders, N102/9, 15, Board minutes, 1924–29, 1950–52 and annual report 1966.
124 R. Mauldon, 'Price policy', p. 318.
125 *Sydney Morning Herald*, 26 May 1990, p. 27 and 2 February 1991, p. 22; K. Emms & A. Squires, *Stock and Station Agents Handbook*, pp. 7–8. The Australian Wool Realisation Commission was created in 1991 to dispose of the stockpiles.
126 Although unhelpful political influence is still apparent; at the time of the 1998 general election a moratorium on reducing the stockpile ended up costing farmers dearly.
127 *Diversity and Innovation for Australian Wool. Report of the Wool Industry Taskforce*, pp. 20, 27.
128 Goldsbrough Mort, 2A/208-3, wool files, 1930; 2A/36, correspondence, 1930.
129 *Sydney Morning Herald*, 2 August 1997, p. 93 and 8 June 1998, p. 35; *AFR*, 11 June 1998, p. 24.
130 Elders, N102/9, 1925.

CHAPTER SEVEN: INFORMATION, ADVISORY, AND ADVOCACY SERVICES

1   G. Stigler, 'The economics of information'.
2   K. Arrow, *Essays in the Theory of Risk-Bearing*, p. 152.
3   O. E. Williamson, *The Economic Institutions of Capitalism.*
4   I. McLean, 'The demand for agricultural research in Australia, 1870–1914', p. 1. Until recent decades, patent laws applied only to agricultural machinery and not plant or animal biology: G. Raby, *Making Rural Australia: an Economic History of Technical and Institutional Creativity, 1788–1860*, p. 14.
5   See Raby, *Rural Australia*; McLean, 'Agricultural research'.
6   Dalgety, 100/1/30/37, correspondence, 30 June 1940.
7   AMLF, 162/377, correspondence, 23 November 1926.
8   Winchcombe Carson, K8228, Board minutes.
9   Dalgety, 100/1/55/14, correspondence, 24 March 1961.
10   Dalgety, N8/23, Doxat's correspondence, 6 June 1876.
11   NMA, UN 28, box 3, annual reports and accounts, 1940, box 5, correspondence, 1920.
12   NMA, UN 28, merger papers, 1972.
13   It also permitted CSIR to conduct experiments on its stations. H. Mortimer Franklyn, *A Glance at Australia in 1880* confirms that Australian Estates' experience as a farmer meant it possessed accurate information suitable for diffusion to other farmers: pp. 220–1. The industry may have benefited from one firm adopting this alternative growth path.
14   Australian Estates, 165/139, 140, 141, correspondence.
15   *Pastoral Review*, 16 September 1936, p. 1002.
16   For example, they gave their views on new tractor types in 1952: NMA, UN 28, box 3, annual reports and accounts, box 10, correspondence.
17   Dennys Lascelles, 62, 12, Conran correspondence, 1891.
18   Dennys Lascelles, 62, 12, Conran correspondence, 1891.
19   Dalgety, 100/1/55/6 correspondence, 27 December 1957.
20   *Pastoral Review*, 16 September 1935, p. 269.
21   16 January 1937, p. 30. Also see Australian Estates, 2200/Box 7, Pastoral Department minutes.
22   WWBA, MSY 4128, minutes, 1927.
23   For example, Goldsbrough Mort sent out a questionnaire about livestock breeds to its tied clients in 1895: 2/210, correspondence.
24   Dennys Lascelles, 62, 12, Conran in-letters.
25   Goldsbrough Mort, 2A/30/16, correspondence.
26   Dalgety, 100/1/51, correspondence, 1960; 100/1/30/37, correspondence, 30 June 1940.
27   R. Gore, *Levins, 1841–1941*, pp. 130–3.
28   J. H. Angus, *Donald Reid Otago Farmers Ltd: A History of Service to the Farming Community of Otago*, p. 25.
29   Wright Stephenson, 0280.
30   Elders, 103/4, postwar development file, 1944.
31   *Pastoral Review*, 16 September 1936, p. 1002.
32   Winchcombe Carson, K8189, correspondence, 1920.
33   NZLMA, 76-291.
34   Stronach Morris, correspondence.
35   16 September 1935, p. 969.
36   NZLMA, 76-291, Gore correspondence.
37   NZLMA, 76-291, Gore correspondence, 1904.
38   Dennys Lascelles, 62, 12, Conran correspondence.
39   All three examples are technological issues since evidence of the use of marketing and financial information is contained in the previous three chapters.

40 AMLF, 97/36/14, correspondence, 1893.
41 AMLF, 97/36/14, correspondence, 1893.
42 Dennys Lascelles, 62, 12, Conran in-letters.
43 AMLF, 97/36/14, 1893. He was especially critical of the mail steamers which already made profits from the postal subvention: *APR*, 16 October 1893, pp. 399–400.
44 AMLF, 97/36/14, 1893.
45 Trust & Agency Company of Australasia, annual report, 1879.
46 AMLF, 97/36/14/5, 7, 1893. Also Goldsbrough Mort: N. Cain, 'Pastoral expansion and crisis in New South Wales, 1880–93: the lending view', p. 195.
47 Australian Estates, 165/138, Melbourne correspondence.
48 Australian Estates, 165/136, correspondence, 24 December 1897.
49 Elders, N102/97, 98, correspondence.
50 *APR*, 15 March 1899, p. 167.
51 Australian Estates, 165/136; *Australian Pastoral Directory*, 1903.
52 Gore, *Levins*, pp. 130–3. The two companies also cooperated in the development of the cream separator.
53 Stronach Morris, UN 14, letterbooks.
54 Murray Roberts, 0575, reports and accounts.
55 Winchcombe Carson, K8228, 8229, Board minutes.
56 UMA, 165/136, correspondence, 1895–1900.
57 Pastoralist members of the New South Wales Legislative Assembly fell from 44 to 15 per cent in 1856–89: A. W. Martin, 'Pastoralists in the Legislative Assembly, 1870–90', pp. 578–9.
58 Martin, 'Pastoralists', p. 590.
59 K. Tsokhas, *Markets, Money and Empire. The Political Economy of the Australian Wool Industry*, p. 9.
60 Tsokhas, *Markets, Money*, pp. 41, 58–61. These ideas are discussed extensively throughout the study.
61 WWBA, MSY 4124, minutes, 1920.
62 Elders, N102/11, Board minutes.
63 He noted, 'I think it is about time we had a big war as an antidote to excessive luxury and too much wealth . . . the French are not improving as the centuries advance and for them too another war would do no harm'! UN 28, box 5, J. M. Ritchie correspondence, 1898.

CHAPTER EIGHT: ORGANISATIONAL STRUCTURES AND ADMINISTRATIVE PRACTICES

1 A. D. Chandler, Jr, *Strategy and Structure: Chapters in the History of American Industrial Enterprise*; E. T. Penrose, *The Theory of the Growth of the Firm*.
2 Chandler, *Strategy and Structure*.
3 The principal–agent problem deals with the idea that the manager (agent) acts in a manner inconsistent with the best interests of the owner (principal). This is made possible by concealed information or actions.
4 For example, see J. Yates, *Control Through Communication. The Rise of System in American Management*.
5 Dalgety, 163/26, Managers' conference.
6 Wright Stephenson, 0585, Special Report, 1906.
7 Dalgety, N8/1, Board minutes, 1884–89.
8 The migration of one of the leading Auckland figures, Thomas Russell, to Britain in 1894 provided a trusted go-between linking the management structures in both countries: C. J. R. Stone, *Makers of Fortune, A Colonial Business Community and Its Fall*, p. 24.
9 H. Y. Braddon, *Business Principles and Practice*, p. 42 cites Dalgety as a typical

firm with this structure and contrasts it with the lack of departmental delegation in the banks.

10 Dalgety, N8/23, Doxat's correspondence.
11 Dalgety, N8/21, Board minutes, 1892.
12 Dalgety, N8/24, Doxat's correspondence.
13 In New Zealand some firms continued to use the term 'superintendent' well into the twentieth century but recognised that it was synonymous with 'general manager': NZLMA, 76-291, HO confidential files, box 68, 1937.
14 AMLF, 162/627, correspondence, 1929. Also NZLMA, 76-291, HO confidential files, 1 December 1937.
15 NMA, UN 28, box 5, correspondence.
16 Wright Stephenson, 0585.
17 Chandler, *Strategy and Structure*, ch. 1.
18 AMLF, 162/630, correspondence, 1935: Dalgety, 100/1/32/7, Melbourne reports, 1959.
19 AMLF, 97/36/40/2, correspondence, 1924.
20 Dalgety, 163/1, NZLMA merger, 1962.
21 Elders, N102/312, correspondence, 1935.
22 J. B. Quinn, H. Mintzberg & R. M. James, *The Strategy Process. Concepts, Contexts and Cases*, pp. 582-3.
23 In the smaller or emergent State divisions some tasks were shared with a neighbouring State or head office.
24 Dalgety, 163/1, 1962.
25 Barnard, Q50, box 10, drafts.
26 Elders, N102/39, Board memoranda, 1953.
27 In relation to forecasting future conditions and on the dangers of rumoured takeovers: NZLMA, 76-291, HO confidential files.
28 NZLMA, 76-291, HO confidential files, correspondence, 3 December 1947.
29 NZLMA, 76-291, HO confidential files, correspondence, 3 December 1947.
30 Dalgety, 100/1/55/10, correspondence, 1959.
31 NMA, UN 28, box 10, General Manager's out-letters.
32 NMA, UN 28, box 3, annual reports and accounts.
33 NMA, UN 133, subject file 27, Lord Glenconner's memoranda.
34 Dalgety, 100/1/55/4, correspondence.
35 Dalgety, 100/1/55/6, correspondence, 1957.
36 NZLMA, 76-291, HO confidential files, correspondence, 1946.
37 Elders, 103/5, 'Postwar developments', 1944.
38 Quinn, Mintzberg & James, *Strategy Process*, p. 584.
39 Dalgety, 100/1/55/16, correspondence, 1961.
40 Elders Wool and Produce Company (1882–88) and Elder Shenton and Company (1904–18) (for their Western Australian operations). In each case the experiment had failed and the firm reversed the decision within a few years.
41 http://www.wrightson.co.nz, Wrightson Home page, 16 July 1999.
42 *AFR*, 14 August 1996, p. 29. By contrast, Elders has been expanding its capital base.
43 Yates, *Control Through Communication*.
44 Pitt, Son & Badgery, N32/62, Board minutes.
45 Quinn, Mintzberg & James, *Strategy Process*, pp. 547-58, 638-49.
46 AMLF, 97/36/30/2, correspondence.
47 Yates, *Control Through Communication*, p. xvii.
48 Goldsbrough Mort, 2/156, Manager's correspondence, 1926.
49 NMA, UN 28, special London letterbook.
50 These arguments were used by Dalgety, 100/1/55/16, 'Review of Administrative Aspects', n.d., c. 1960.
51 Elders, N102/323.

52 NMA, UN 28, box 5, correspondence, 1918.
53 NMA, UN 28, Special London letterbook.
54 These interwar forces for increased management accounting provision offset any negative tendencies of the manner referred to by Johnson & Kaplan in terms of conservative external reporting and misguided academic research: H. T. Johnson & R. Kaplan, *Relevance Lost: the Rise and Fall of Management Accounting*.
55 A. Atkinson, et al., 'New directions in management accounting research', pp. 79–108; R. H. Chenhall & K. Langfield-Smith, 'Adoption and benefits of management accounting practices: an Australian study', pp. 1–19.
56 NMA, UN 28, box 7, private letterbooks 1910–43.
57 Goldsbrough Mort, 2A/30/12, private letters, 1930.
58 For example, the practice of Elders by 1935: N102/31, Board memoranda.
59 Barnard, Q50, box 5, folder 8, 'Comments on accounting and cost controls', 1968.
60 Winchcombe Carson, K8229, Board minutes, 1937.
61 Barnard, Q50, box 5, folder 8.
62 Barnard, Q50, box 5, folder 8.
63 Dalgety, 100/1/55/16.
64 Elders, N102/39.
65 Dalgety, 100/1/55/3, correspondence, 1957.
66 Dalgety, 100/1/67, Managers' conference, 1953.
67 In 1935 BHP's assets per employee were £825, in 1939 Goldsbrough Mort's ratio was £8562: *JID*, 1935, p. 397; Barnard, Q50, box 10, file 12.
68 Dalgety, 100/1/66/3, Managers' conference, 1951.
69 J. B. Were Newspaper Collection, NZLMA file, 1956.
70 On their appointment of John Earwaker in 1910 Winchcombe Carson observed that he would be bringing with him various accounts: K8228, Board minutes.
71 D. Pope, 'Banks and banking business, 1860–1914', p. 311.
72 Elders, N102/262, accounting procedures, and N102/391, pocket compendium, 1931.
73 AMLF, 97/36/27/2, correspondence, 1898.
74 NMA, UN 28, Special London letterbook.
75 Elders, N102/12, Board minutes; Goldsbrough Mort annual report.
76 Elders, N102/36, Board memoranda, 1941.
77 Elders, N102/375, typescript history of Elders by J. G. Dobs, 1962.
78 AMLF, 162/627, correspondence, 1929; Barnard, Q50, box 6; Goldsbrough Mort, 2/28/A (2), correspondence, 1888.
79 Goldsbrough Mort, 2/158/1, correspondence, 1927.
80 C. Wright, *The Management of Labour. A History of Australian Employers*, Part 3, provides an excellent discussion of the adoption of human resource management policies.
81 Dalgety, 100/1/66/1, conference report, 1947.
82 Dalgety, 100/1/66/3, conference report, 1951.
83 Dalgety, 100/1/55/14, correspondence, 1960.
84 Dalgety, 100/1/55/16. A 1950s survey of Australian firms across a range of sectors found that only 14 per cent had formal training schemes: Wright, *Management of Labour*, p. 56.
85 Dalgety, 100/1/55/16; 100/1/66/3, 1951.
86 Barnard, Q50, box 10, file III.5.
87 Dalgety, 100/1/55/6, correspondence, 1958. On early management and administrative education see D. Cochrane, 'Business administration at the University of Melbourne'; M. Brown, 'The Australian Administrative Staff College: the first decade'.
88 NMA, UN 28, box 10, General Manager outward letters, 1946.

89 Dalgety, 100/1/66/1, 1947.
90 Elders, N102/375.
91 NMA, UN 28, box 3, annual reports. Several agent companies had in-house publications before 1939 predating their main growth in many sectors since the 1950s: Wright, *Management of Labour*, pp. 60–1.
92 Winchcombe Carson, K8228. N. Quigley, *Private Superannuation in the Banking Industry*, ch. 2 discusses the early development of pension funds amongst banks in the late nineteenth century and highlights their supersession of earlier loyalty guarantee funds.
93 NMA, UN 28, Special London letterbook, 1920.
94 G. Patmore, *Australian Labour History*, pp. 141–5.
95 NMA was critical of Levins' failure to introduce a pension scheme: UN 133, subject files 12, Report on Levins, 1954–60.
96 NMA, UN 28, box 7, private letterbooks, 1940.
97 Dalgety, 100/1/55/3.
98 T. Hewat, *The Elders Explosion: One Hundred and Fifty Years of Progress from Elder to Elliott*, pp. 35–6.
99 A. D. Chandler, *Scale and Scope: The Dynamics of Industrial Capitalism*, contrasts personal and managerial capitalism.
100 G. Parry, *NMA. The Story of the First Hundred Years of the National Mortgage and Agency Company of New Zealand Ltd, 1864–1964*, pp. 229–31.
101 R. H. Chenhall, 'Some elements of organisational control in Australian division-alised firms', pp. 1–36; N. Capon, C. Christodoulou, J. U. Farley & J. M. Hulbert, 'A comparative analysis of the strategy and structure of United States and Australian corporations', pp. 51–74. Also see K. Sheridan, *The Firm in Australia: a Theoretical and Empirical Study of Size, Growth and Profitability*, pp. 132–6. '

CHAPTER NINE: INTER-ORGANISATIONAL RELATIONS: COMPETITION, COOPERATION, AND COLLUSION AMONG AGENCY FIRMS

1 The terms 'cooperation' and 'collusion' are sometimes used interchangeably. However, in line with dictionary definitions, 'cooperation' is distinguished as joint operation or action from 'collusion' as a secret undertaking or conspiracy: *Macquarie Concise Dictionary* and *Australian Concise Oxford Dictionary*.
2 For an excellent parallel study of interfirm relations see G. Boyce, *Information, Mediation and Institutional Development. The Rise of Large-Scale Enterprise in British Shipping 1870–1919*.
3 Goldsbrough Mort, 2A/30/37, correspondence, 1937.
4 Dennys Lascelles, 62, 12, Conran out-letters. Also, in 1899 Dalgety, Goldsbrough Mort and NZLMA were considering organising separate auctions: Goldsbrough Mort, 2/124/23, Board minutes, 1897.
5 Goldsbrough Mort, 2A/30/20, correspondence.
6 NZSSA, MSY 4143, minutes.
7 Goldsbrough Mort, 2A/30/11, correspondence. Similar relationships developed between AMLF, Dalgety, Australian Estates and Goldsbrough Mort in the 1930s: AMLF, 133/5/2, correspondence, 1937.
8 Winchcombe Carson, K8228, Board minutes, 1902.
9 Dalgety, 100/1/55/17, correspondence, 1961.
10 NZSSA, MSY 4143, minutes.
11 Pitt, Son & Badgery, N32/57, Board minutes; Dalgety, 100/1/30/39, reports.
12 Winchcombe Carson, K8235, Board minutes, 1913.
13 NMA, UN 28, box 10, correspondence, 1930.
14 Elders, N102/97, correspondence, 1908.
15 For example, AMLF, 133/6/2, correspondence, 1939; NZWBA, MSY 4135, 4140, minutes, 1917–22, 1951–65.

16   Goldsbrough Mort, 2/174/42, correspondence, 1893; Barnard, Q50, box 3, Board minutes.
17   Stronach Morris, UN 14, miscellaneous papers.
18   Winchcombe Carson, K8228, Board minutes.
19   Barnard, Q50, box 3, Board minutes.
20   Goldsbrough Mort, 2A/41/4, correspondence.
21   H. L. Wilkinson, *The Trust Movement in Australia*. The closest mention is of the artificial manure manufacturers combine in which several pastoral agents had an interest through investment in the Mount Lyell or Wallaroo companies: pp. 92–4.
22   Dennys Lascelles, 62, 12, Conran out-letters.
23   Goldsbrough Mort, 2/174/296, correspondence.
24   Goldsbrough Mort, 2/174/587a, correspondence.
25   Goldsbrough Mort, 2A/208-5, correspondence, 1930.
26   A. Barnard, 'Wool brokers and the marketing pattern, 1914–20', pp. 2–6.
27   Barnard, Q50, box 10, file 12.
28   NZWBA, MSX 4330, minutes.
29   G. Fleming & D. Terwiel, 'What effect did early Australian anti-trust legislation have on firm behaviour? Lessons from business history', pp. 47–56 show that the need for secrecy to avoid detection under the Australian Industries Preservation Act (1906) raised the costs of collusion amongst the Newcastle coal companies.
30   K. Tsokhas, *Markets, Money and Empire. The Political Economy of the Australian Wool Industry*, p. 150.
31   Tsokhas, *Markets, Money*, pp. 150–2.
32   Goldsbrough Mort, 2/174/239, 587a, correspondence.
33   A 1903 rate agreement among the Dunedin agents encouraged reporting of breaches: NMA, UN 14, miscellaneous papers.
34   Dennys Lascelles, 62, 12, Conran out-letters.
35   Otago Farmers, AG 728, Board minutes 7, 1933.
36   Otago Farmers, AG 728, Board minutes 9, 1939; J. H. Angus, *Donald Reid Otago Farmers Ltd: A History of Service to the Farming Community of Otago*, p. 41.
37   The Otago Farmers Board noting their past opportunism when discussing current strategies: AG 728, Minutes 6, 1930.
38   WWBA, MSY 4121, Rules and Regulations, 1915.
39   WWBA, MSY 4135, Rules and Regulations of NZWBA, undated.
40   WWBA, MSY 4131, minutes.
41   Winchcombe Carson, K8228, Board minutes, 1920.
42   WWBA, MSX 4326, correspondence.
43   WWBA, MSX 4324, correspondence.
44   Wright Stephenson left the Otago Woolbrokers Association in 1897 but was readmitted by 1900: Angus, *Reid*, p. 41.
45   For example, a 1926 resolution of the Dunedin Stock Brokers Association stated that any agent buying livestock should withdraw from the organisation: Otago Farmers, AG 728, Board minutes, 5, 1925.
46   Foreign firms here means those active in overseas markets who might expand into Australasia. The English-owned firms such as AMLF were, of course, established for the purpose of doing business in Australasia.
47   Tsokhas, *Markets, Money*, p. 150.
48   In 1922 Winchcombe Carson, Harrison, Jones & Devlin, and Schute Bell even resigned in protest against a motion admitting new members to the NCWSB: Winchcombe Carson, K 8228, Board minutes.
49   Including substantial assets in which new members would have a share: NZSSA, MSY 4144, minutes, 1991.
50   Dalgety, 100/1/55/10, correspondence.
51   For example, a local association was formed in Dunedin in 1890–91: Angus,

Reid, pp. 28, 41. The Stock and Station Agents Association of New South Wales was formed in 1890: R. H. Webster, *A Century of Service*, p. 20.

52   The Federated Wool Selling Brokers of Australia was its forerunner in 1918–19 but had limited aims and was bureaucratic, 'a tiresome waste of time', according to one historian: Barnard, 'Wool brokers', p. 18.

53   NZWBA, 96-223-01, correspondence, 1910.

54   Elders, 8/106/1, correspondence, 1914.

55   Discussed in various places including Winchcombe Carson, K8228, Board minutes, 1914–22. Its stated objective was to safeguard the interests of brokers, growers and the trade in general: Barnard, 'Wool brokers', p. 19.

56   NZLAAA, MSY 4142, minutes, 1924.

57   In 1924 the NCWSB claimed to have all of the brokers in Australia among its fifty-one members: Elders, 8/106/1, correspondence.

58   NZWBA, 96-223-01, 1910; WWBA, MSY 4126, minutes, 1923.

59   Goldsbrough Mort, 2A/55A/12, minutes of MWBA and correspondence from NCWSB.

60   AMLF, 162/687, correspondence, 1934.

61   NMA, UN 28, box 10.

62   Dalgety, N8/23, correspondence.

63   Australian Estates, correspondence 165/136.

64   Goldsbrough Mort, 2A/202, wool store costs.

65   Tsokhas, *Markets, Money*, p. 202.

66   Tsokhas, *Markets, Money*, p. 152.

67   Dalgety, 100/1/67, conference report.

68   Elders' relations with the London committee, by contrast, were not good in 1954: 100/1/55/9, correspondence.

69   J. B. Were Newspaper Collection, Elders file.

70   The NZSSA appears to have emerged from the NZLAAA in 1933. In recent years it has taken on the role of the executive body for the industry with the NZWBA acting as an administrative organ: NZSSA, MSY 4143, 4144.

71   NZSSA, MSY 4143.

72   AMLF, 162/687, correspondence 1934.

73   The Stock and Station Agents Association of New South Wales noted that this was designed to distinguish its members from 'pocket book agents', 'street corner operators', and other marginal businesses: Webster, *Service*, p. 25.

74   NZWBA, 96-223-09, miscellaneous papers, 1939.

75   Post-1983 rules and regulations of NZSSA, MSY 4144.

76   NMA, UN 28, papers relating to Matson.

77   NZLMA, MSY 1384, Board minutes.

78   AMLF, 133/5/2, 1937.

79   Fleming & Terwiel, 'Lessons from business history', pp. 52–3.

CHAPTER TEN: BUSINESS INTERMEDIATION AND RURAL ENTREPRENEURSHIP: THE ROLE OF THE STOCK AND STATION AGENT INDUSTRY

1   This involves providing concessional rates in the short term to build up long-term cooperation: G. Boyce, *Information, Mediation and Institutional Development. The Rise of Large-Scale Enterprise in British Shipping 1870–1919*, pp. 201–2.

2   Wright Stephenson, 0001, Annual Report.

Bibliography

PRIMARY SOURCES

Canterbury Museum, Christchurch
Cracroft Wilson
Trust & Agency Co. of Australasia

Canterbury Public Library, Christchurch
Henry Matson

Fletcher Challenge Archives and Records Centre, Auckland
Murray Roberts
Wright Stephenson

Hocken Archives, University of Otago
National Mortgage Association
Otago Farmers Cooperative Association of New Zealand
Stronach Morris & Co. Ltd

Menzies Library, Australian National University, Canberra
Australian Parliamentary Papers

Mitchell Library, State Library of New South Wales
Westralian Farmers
Winchcombe Carson

Donald Cochrane Library, Monash University
J. B. Were Newspaper Collection

New Zealand Wool Board Statistical Handbook

Noel Butlin Archives Centre, Australian National University, Canberra
Australian Estates
Australian Mortgage (later Mercantile) Loan & Finance
Barnard papers
Dalgety
Elders
Farmers & Graziers
Goldsbrough Mort (including annual reports of most companies)
New Zealand Loan & Mercantile Agency
Pearson Rowe Smith
Pitt, Son & Badgery

Union Mortgage & Agency
Younghusband

University of Melbourne Archives
Dennys Lascelles
Hepburn Leonard
Strachan

Turnbull Library, National Library of New Zealand
Dalgety
New Zealand Livestock Agents and Auctioneers Association
New Zealand Loan & Mercantile Agency
New Zealand Stock and Station Agents Association
New Zealand Woolbrokers Association
Wellington Woolbrokers Association

SECONDARY SOURCES

Abbott, G. J. *The Pastoral Age: a Re-examination*, Melbourne: Macmillan and Dalgety Australia, 1971.
'All's cool, calm on debt mountain', *Weekend Australian*, 8–9 March 1997, p. 60.
Alvesson, M. and Lindkvist, L. 'Transaction costs, clans and corporate culture', *Journal of Management Studies*, 30, 1993, 3.
Anderson, L. *Throughout the East Coast: the Story of Williams and Kettle Ltd*, Hastings: Pictorial Publications, 1974.
Angus, J.H. *Donald Reid Otago Farmers Ltd: A History of Service to the Farming Community of Otago*, Dunedin: Donald Reid Otago Farmers, 1978.
Appleyard, R. T. & Schedvin, C. B. (eds) *Australian Financiers: Biographical Essays*, Melbourne: Macmillan, 1988.
Arrow, K. *Essays in the Theory of Risk-Bearing*, Chicago: Markham, 1971.
Atkinson, A., Balakrishnan, R., Booth, P., Cote, J. M., Groot, T., Malmi, T., Roberts, H., Uliana, E. & Wu, A. 'New directions in management accounting research', *Journal of Management Accounting Research*, 9, 1997.
Austin, G. & Sugihara, K. (eds) *Local Suppliers of Credit in the Third World, 1750–1960*, Houndmills, Basingstoke: Macmillan, 1993.
Bailey, J. D. *A Hundred Years of Pastoral Banking: A History of the Australian Mercantile, Land and Finance Company, 1863–1963*, Oxford: Clarendon Press, 1966.
Bain, E. *The Ways of Life*, Perth: Elder Smith Goldsbrough Mort, 1976.
Barnard, A. 'A century and a half of wool marketing' in Barnard (ed.) *The Simple Fleece*, 1962.
—— *The Australian Wool Market, 1840–1900*, Carlton: Melbourne University Press, 1958.
—— *Visions and Profits: Studies in the Business Career of Thomas Sutcliffe Mort*, Carlton: Melbourne University Press, 1961.
—— 'Wool brokers and the marketing pattern, 1914–20', *Australian Economic History Review*, 11, 1971, 1.
Barnard, A. (ed.) *The Simple Fleece. Studies in the Australian Wool Industry*, Carlton: Melbourne University Press, 1962.
Beaver, E. A. 'The Australian wool clip, 1861–1900', *Economic Record*, 39, 1963.
Belshaw, H. *The Provision of Credit with Special Reference to Agriculture*, Cambridge: W. Heffer & Sons, 1931.
—— 'The financing of land purchases and of farming operations', in H. Belshaw, D. Williams & F. Stephens (eds) *Agricultural Organisation in New Zealand*, Carlton: Melbourne University Press, 1936.
Blackford, M. G. *The Rise of Modern Business in Britain, the United States, and Japan*, Chapel Hill, NC: University of North Carolina Press, 1900.

Boehm, E. A. 'Australia's economic Depression of the 1930s', *Economic Record*, 49, 1973, 128.

—— *Twentieth-Century Economic Development in Australia*, Camberwell, Vic.: Longman, 1971.

Boyce, G. *Information, Mediation and Institutional Development. The Rise of Large-Scale Enterprise in British Shipping 1870–1919*, Manchester: Manchester University Press, 1995.

Braddon, H. Y. *Business Principles and Practice*, Sydney: William Brooks, 1914.

Brown, M. 'The Australian Administrative Staff College: the first decade', *Personnel Practice Bulletin*, 22, 1966, 3.

Buckley, P. 'New theories of international business: some unresolved issues', in M. Casson (ed.) *The Growth of International Business*, London: Allen & Unwin, 1983.

Bureau of Agricultural Economics *Wool Situation and Outlook*, Canberra: AGPS, 1990.

Bureau of Industry Economics *Beyond the Firm. An Assessment of Business Linkages and Networks in Australia*, Canberra: AGPS, 1995.

—— *Mergers and Acquisitions*, Research Report 36, Canberra: AGPS, 1990.

Butlin, N. G. 'A problem in prices and quantities', *Economic Record*, 40, 1964.

—— 'Bush farmers shielded by a sheila', *Independent*, 29 August 1998.

—— 'Company ownership of NSW pastoral stations, 1865–1900', *Historical Studies*, 4, 1950.

—— *Economics and the Dreamtime. A Hypothetical History*, Cambridge: Cambridge University Press, 1993.

—— *Forming a Colonial Economy: Australia 1810–1850*, Cambridge: Cambridge University Press, 1994.

—— 'Growth in a trading world: the Australian economy, heavily disguised', *Business Archives & History*, 4, 1964.

—— *Investment in Australian Economic Development, 1861–1900*, Cambridge: Cambridge University Press, 1964.

—— 'Some perspectives of Australian economic development, 1890–1965', in C. Forster (ed.) *Australian Economic Development in the Twentieth Century*, London: Allen & Unwin, 1970.

Butlin, S. J. *Foundations of the Australian Monetary System, 1788–1851*, Carlton: Melbourne University Press, 1953.

—— *The Australian Monetary System, 1851–1914*, Sydney: J. F. Butlin, 1986.

Cain, N. 'Capital structure and financial disequilibrium: pastoral companies in Australia, 1880–93', *Australian Economic Papers*, 2, 1963, 1.

—— 'Pastoral expansion and crisis in New South Wales, 1880–93: the lending view', *Australian Economic Papers*, 2, 1963, 2.

Cameron, B. 'New aspects of Australia's industrial structure', *Economic Record*, 34, 1958.

Capie, F. 'The first Export Monopoly Control Board', *Journal of Agricultural Economics*, 29, 1978.

Capon, N., Christodoulou, C., Farley J. U. & Hulbert, J. M. 'A comparative analysis of the strategy and structure of United States and Australian corporations', *Journal of International Business*, Spring 1987.

Carlton, D. W. & Perloff, J. M. *Modern Industrial Organisation*, New York: Harper Collins, 1994.

Carnegie, G. *Pastoral Accounting in Colonial Australia: a Case Study of Unregulated Accounting*, New York: Garland, 1997.

Casson, M. *Information and Organisation: A New Perspective on the Theory of the Firm*, Oxford: Clarendon Press, 1997.

—— 'Institutional economics and business history: a way forward?', *Business History*, 39, 1997, 4.

—— *The Entrepreneur: an Economic Theory*, Oxford: Robertson, 1982.

Chandler, A. D. *Scale and Scope: The Dynamics of Industrial Capitalism*, Cambridge, MA: Belknap Press, 1990.

—— *Strategy and Structure: Chapters in the History of American Industrial Enterprise*, Cambridge, MA: MIT Press, 1962.

—— *The Visible Hand*, Cambridge, MA: Belknap Press, 1977.

Chenhall, R. H. 'Some elements of organisational control in Australian division-alised firms', *Australian Journal of Management*, 4, 1979.

Chenhall, R. H. & Langfield-Smith, K. 'Adoption and benefits of management accounting practices: an Australian study', *Management Accounting Research*, 9, 1998.

Christensen, A. L. 'Structural and functional evolution in the New Zealand stock and station industry', MA thesis, University of Auckland, 1986.

Cochrane, D. 'Business administration at the University of Melbourne', *Personnel Practice Bulletin*, 12, 1957, 6.

Coghlan, T. A. *Labour and Industry in Australia*, Oxford: Oxford University Press, 1918.

Condliffe, J. B. *New Zealand in the Making*, 2nd edn, London: Allen & Unwin, 1959.

Coombs, H. C. 'Rural credit developments in Australia', *Australian Journal of Agricultural Economics*, 3, 1959.

Crocombe, G. T., Enright, M. J. & Porter, M. E. *Upgrading New Zealand's Competitive Advantage*, Auckland: Oxford University Press, 1991.

Denton, P. *Elliott. A Biography of John D. Elliott*, St Peter's, NSW: Little Hills Press, 1986.

Dunsdorfs, E. *The Australian Wheat-Growing Industry, 1788–1948*, Carlton: Melbourne University Press, 1956.

Eccles, R. G. & Cranes, D. B. 'Managing through networks in investment banking', *California Management Review*, 30, 1987, 1.

Edgar, R. J. & Jarrett, F. G. 'Finance for agriculture: pastoral finance companies', in R. R. Hirst & R. H. Wallace (eds), *The Australian Capital Market*, Melbourne: Cheshire, 1974.

Eldred-Grigg, S. *A Southern Gentry*, Wellington: Reed, 1980.

Emms, K. & Squires, A. *Stock and Station Agents Handbook*, Chatswood, NSW: Butterworth-Heinemann, 1995.

Evans, A. L. *A History of Agricultural Production and Marketing in New Zealand*, Palmerston North: Keeling & Mundy, 1969.

Fleming, G. & Terwiel, D. 'What effect did early Australian anti-trust legislation have on firm behaviour? Lessons from business history', *Australian Business Law Review*, 27, 1999, 1.

Forrest, K. J. 'Diversification and expansion in large diversified New Zealand companies', MA thesis, Massey University, 1976.

Franklyn, H. Mortimer *A Glance at Australia in 1880*, Melbourne: Victorian Review Publishing Co., 1881.

Fruin, W. M. *The Japanese Enterprise System: Competitive Strategies and Cooperative Structures*, Oxford: Clarendon Press, 1992.

Fyfe, C. *The Bale Fillers: Western Australian Wool, 1826–1916*, Nedlands, Western Australia: University of Western Australia Press, 1983.

Godley, A. & Ross, D. (eds) *Banks, Networks and Small Firm Finance*, London: Frank Cass, 1996.

Goldsbrough Mort *A Practical Treatise on Wool and Sheep Breeding, Edible Scrubs, The Economical Use of Tank Water, Station Book-Keeping*, Sydney: Goldsbrough Mort, 1897.

Gore, R. *Levins, 1841–1941*, Wellington: Whitcombe & Tombs, 1956.

Gould, J. D. *The Muldoon Years*, Auckland: Hodder & Stoughton, 1985.

—— 'The twilight of the estates, 1891–1910', *Australian Economic History Review*, 10, 1970.

Graham, B. D. 'Graziers in politics, 1917—29', in Barnard (ed.), *The Simple Fleece*, 1962.

Gray, L. C. *History of Agriculture in the Southern United States to 1860*, vol. II, New York: Smith, 1941.

Gruen, F. 'The case for the present marketing system', in Barnard (ed.), *The Simple Fleece*, 1962.

Hannah, L. *The Rise of the Corporate Economy*, 2nd edn, London: Methuen, 1983.

Hawke, G. R. *The Making of New Zealand. An Economic History*, Cambridge: Cambridge University Press, 1985.

Hewat, T. *The Elders Explosion: One Hundred and Fifty Years of Progress from Elder to Elliott*, Sydney: Bay Books, 1988.

Hirschman, A. O. *The Strategy of Economic Development*, New Haven: Yale University Press, 1962.

Holder, R. F. *Bank of New South Wales: A History*, Sydney: Angus & Robertson, 1970.

Holt, H. *An Energetic Colonist. A Biographical Acccount of the Activities of the Late Hon. Thomas Holt, MLC*, Melbourne: Hawthorn Press, 1972.

Hume, L. J. 'Wool in the Australian economy, 1946–58', in Barnard (ed.), *The Simple Fleece*, 1962.

Irving, J. C. *A Century's Challenge. Wright Stephenson and Co. Ltd, 1861–1961*, Wellington: Wright, Stephenson & Co., 1961.

Jackson, R. V. *Australian Economic Development in the Nineteenth Century*, Canberra: Australian National University Press, 1977.

Jarrett, F. G. 'Agricultural credit—pastoral finance companies' in R. R. Hirst & R. H. Wallace (eds), *Studies in the Australian Capital Market*, Melbourne: Cheshire, 1964.

Johnson, F. T. & Kaplan, R. *Relevance Lost: The Rise and Fall of Management Accounting*, Boston, MA: Harvard Business School Press, 1977.

Jones, S. R. H. 'The establishment and operation of European business' in J. Deeks & P. Enderwick (eds), *Business and New Zealand Society*, Auckland: Longman Paul, 1994.

Langlois, R. N. & Robertson, P. L. *Firms, Markets and Economic Change. A Dynamic Theory of Business Institutions*, London: Routledge, 1995.

Linge, G. J. R. *Industrial Awakening. A Geography of Australian Manufacturing, 1788 to 1890*, Canberra: Australian National University Press, 1979.

Lloyd Prichard, M. *An Economic History of New Zealand to 1939*, Auckland: Collins, 1970.

MacDonald, G. R. *The Canterbury Frozen Meat Company Ltd, 1882–1957*, Christchurch: Whitcombe & Tombs, 1957.

Maddison, A. *Dynamic Forces in Capitalist Development*, Oxford: Oxford University Press, 1991.

Martin, W. 'Pastoralists in the Legislative Assembly, 1870–90', in Barnard (ed.), *The Simple Fleece*, 1962.

Mauldon, R. 'Price policy', in D. B. Williams (ed.), *Agriculture in the Australian Economy*, Sydney: Sydney University Press with Oxford University Press, 1990.

May, D. *Aboriginal Labour and the Cattle Industry: Queensland from White Settlement to the Present*, Cambridge: Cambridge University Press, 1994.

McCarty, J. W. 'Australia as a region of recent settlement in the nineteenth century', *Australian Economic History Review*, 13, 1973.

McLean, I. 'The demand for agricultural research in Australia, 1870–1914', *ANU Working Papers in Economic History*, 2, 1982.

Meinig, D. W. *On the Margins of the Good Earth: the South Australian Wheat Frontier, 1869–84*, London: John Murray, 1963.

Morgan, S. *Land Settlement in Early Tasmania*, Cambridge: Cambridge University Press, 1992.

Munz, H. *The Australian Wool Industry*, 3rd edn, Melbourne: Cheshire, 1964.

Nicholson, K. B. *Marketing of Agricultural and Horticultural Products*, Lincoln: Agribusiness and Economics Research Unit, Lincoln University, 1990.

Oliver, W. H. & Williams, B. R. (eds), *The Oxford History of New Zealand*, Auckland: Oxford University Press, 1981.

Olsson, M. *The Rise and Decline of Nations*, New Haven: Yale University Press, 1982.

Ouchi, W. G. 'Markets, bureaucracy and clans', *Administrative Science Quarterly*, 25, 1980.

Parry, G. *NMA. The Story of the First Hundred Years of the National Mortgage Agency Company of New Zealand Ltd, 1864–1964*, Dunedin: National Mortgage Agency Company, 1964.

Patmore, G. *Australian Labour History*, Melbourne: Longman, 1991.

Penrose, E. T. *The Theory of the Growth of the Firm*, 2nd edn, Oxford: Oxford University Press, 1980.

Petri, P. A. 'The interdependence of trade and investment in the Pacific' in E. K. Y. Chen & P. Drysdale (eds), *Corporate Links and Foreign Direct Investment in Asia and the Pacific*, Pymble, NSW: Harper Educational, 1995.

Philpott, H. G. *A History of the New Zealand Dairy Industry, 1840–1935*, Wellington: Government Printer, 1937.

Piore, M. J. & Sabel, C. F. *The Second Industrial Divide: Possibilities for Prosperity*, New York: Basic Books, 1984.

Pope, D. 'Banks and banking business, 1860–1914' in D. Pope & L. Alston (eds), *Australia's Greatest Asset. Human Resources in the Nineteenth and Twentieth Centuries*, Annandale, NSW: Federation Press, 1989.

—— 'Private finance' in Vamplew (ed.), *Australians. Historical Statistics*, 1987.

Porter, M. E. *The Competitive Advantage of Nations*, New York: Free Press, 1990.

Powell, R. & Milham, N. 'Capital, investment and finance' in D. B. Williams (ed.), *Agriculture in the Australian Economy*, Sydney: Sydney University Press and Oxford University Press, 1990.

Powell, W. W. 'Neither market nor hierarchy: network forms of organisation', *Research in Organisational Behaviour*, 12, 1990.

Quigley, N. C. *Private Superannuation in the Banking Industry. A Centennial History of the Bank of New Zealand Officers' Provident Association*, Wellington: Bank of New Zealand Officers' Provident Association, 1988.

Quinn, J. B., Mintzberg, H. & James, R. M. *The Strategy Process. Concepts, Contexts and Cases*, Englewood Cliffs, New Jersey: Prentice Hall, 1988.

Raby, G. *Making Rural Australia: An Economic History of Technical and Institutional Creativity, 1788–1860*, Melbourne: Oxford University Press, 1995.

Rankin, K. 'New Zealand's Gross National Product: 1859–1939', *Review of Income and Wealth*, 38, 1992, 1.

'Recalling the past. AML&F Centenary', *Pastoral Review and Graziers Record*, 17, 1964, January.

Report of the Wool Industry Taskforce *Diversity and Innovation for Australian Wool*, Adelaide: Wool Industry Taskforce, 1999.

Rostow, W. W. *The Stages of Economic Growth: a Non-Communist Manifesto*, Cambridge: Cambridge University Press, 1990.

Schedvin, C. B. *Australia and the Great Depression: a Study of Economic Development and Policy in the 1920s and 1930s*, Sydney: Sydney University Press, 1970.

Shann, E. O. G. *The Boom of 1890—and Now*, Sydney: Cornstalk, 1927.

Sheridan, K. *The Firm in Australia: A Theoretical and Empirical Study of Size, Growth and Profitability*, Melbourne: Thomas Nelson, 1974.

Simkin, C. G. F. *The Instability of a Dependent Economy, Economic Fluctuations in New Zealand, 1840–1914*, London: Oxford University Press, 1951.

Sinclair, K. & Mandle, W. F. *Open Account. A History of the Bank of New South Wales in New Zealand, 1861–1961*, Wellington: Whitcombe & Tombs, 1961.

Stephens, F. 'Co-operation in New Zealand' in H. Belshaw, D. Williams & F. Stephens (eds), *Agricultural Organisation in New Zealand*, Carlton: Melbourne University Press, 1936.

Stevens, P. G. *Pyne, Gould, Guinness Ltd*, Christchurch: Pyne Gould Guinness, 1970.

Stigler, G. 'The economics of information', *Journal of Political Economy*, 69, 1961.

Stiglitz, J. & Weiss, A. 'Banks as social accountants and screening devices for the allocation of credit', *Greek Economic Review*, 12, 1990.

Stone, R. C. J. *Makers of Fortune, A Colonial Business Community and Its Fall*, Auckland: Auckland University Press, 1973.

Sutch, W. B. *Colony or Nation? Economic Crises in New Zealand from the 1860s to the 1960s*, Sydney: Sydney University Press, 1966.

Trollope, A. *Australia and New Zealand*, vol. I, London: Chapman & Hall, 1873.

Tsokhas, K. *Markets, Money and Empire. The Political Economy of the Australian Wool Industry*, Carlton: Melbourne University Press, 1990.

Tsokhas, K. A. *Class Apart? Business and Australian Politics 1960–80*, Melbourne: Oxford University Press, 1985.

Vamplew, W. (ed.) *Australians. Historical Statistics*, Broadway, NSW: Fairfax, Syme & Weldon, 1987.

Van Laanen, J. T. M. 'Between the Java Bank and the Chinese moneylender: banking and credit in colonial Indonesia' in A. Booth, W. J. O'Malley & A. Weidemann (eds) *Indonesian Economic History in the Dutch Colonial Era*, New Haven: Yale University, Southeast Asia Studies, 1990.

Vaughan-Thomas, W. *Dalgety. The Romance of a Business*, London: Henry Melland, 1984.

Ville, S. 'Business development in colonial Australia', *Australian Economic History Review*, 38, 1998, 1.

—— 'The coastal trade of New Zealand in the nineteenth century', *New Zealand Journal of History*, 27, 1993, 1.

Ville, S. & Merrett, D. T. 'The development of large scale enterprise in Australia, 1910–64', in *Business History*, 42, 2000.

Webster, R. H. *A Century of Service: A Memorial to the Stock and Station Agents of New South Wales*, North Richmond, NSW: Stock and Station Agents Association of New South Wales, 1991.

Whitwell, G. & Sydenham, D. *A Shared Harvest. The Australian Wheat Industry, 1939–89*, Melbourne: Macmillan, 1991.

Wilkins, M. 'The free-standing company', *Economic History Review*, 2nd ser., 41, 1988.

Wilkinson, H. L. *The Trust Movement in Australia*, Melbourne: Critchley Parker, 1914.

Williamson, O. E. *The Economic Institutions of Capitalism*, New York: Free Press, 1985.

Wright, C. *The Management of Labour. A History of Australian Employers*, Melbourne: Oxford University Press, 1995.

Yates, J. *Control Through Communication. The Rise of System in American Management*, Baltimore: Johns Hopkins University Press, 1989.

Index

Note: The major themes are indexed for each main agent (AMLF, Dalgety, Elders, Goldsbrough Mort, NMA, NZLMA, Wright Stephenson), the arguments being applicable to all of them even where specific evidence is not sourced for each. The references to each of these companies are too numerous to index individually.

Aborigines 216
Abraham and Williams 48
accounting 154
    auditing 180
    branch 183
    budgeting 182
    capital 13
    control 180
    costing 181
    financial 179–80
    management 179–83
    performance measures 181–2
    planning 182–3
    standardisation 181
Adelaide 44, 77, 105–7, 127, 130, 134, 181, 191, 197
agri-business 13, 15, 72, 76, 208
agriculture – *see* farming
Aitchison, David 19
Albany 142
Allied Farmers Cooperative 46
Alvesson, M. & Lindkvist, L. 56–7, 60
Argentina 12, 13, 46, 137
Arrow, K. 151
Associated Livestock Auctioneering Company 113
Auckland 12, 42, 44, 48, 127, 129
Australian Administrative College 186
Australasian Mortgage & Agency Company 27, 38–9
Australia
    capital formation 3–4, 5–6
    indebtedness 6
    economic growth 1–3
    foreign trade 2–3, 13
    investment 2–3, 7

    manufacturing 2, 3
    market size 7
    migration, population, work force 1, 2, 3, 9
    comparisons with New Zealand 10–11, 46, 76, 133–4, 206
Australian Agricultural Company 8
Australian Airways 50
Australian Estates
    acquisition by CSR 54
    advice 151–2
    big business 36, 38–9
    establishment 23
    financial services 91, 96
    information conduit 157
    interfirm relations 190, 193, 197, 200
    marketing services 102–3
    profitability 99–100
    publications 157
    scientific and technical experiments 154, 155, 160, 161
Australian Institute of Management 186
Australian Mortgage Loan & Finance
    accounting practices 179–83
    establishment 19
    financial services 205
        contracting 78–9, 91–9
        lending strategies 81–6
        profitability 99–100
        share of loans market 76–81
    financial structure 86–91
    growth 203
        big business 36, 38–9, 53
        branches 33–6, 44–5
        diversification 20–3, 50–2
        international 45–6

Australian Mortgage Loan & Finance (*cont.*)
    national 39–45
    vertical 21–2
    wool broking 27–31, 53
  incorporation 23–4
  information services 206
    acquisition and dissemination 153–8
    farmers' advocate 161–2
    technical examples 158–61
  interfirm cooperation
    alliances 196–9
    contracts 47, 199–200
    limits 192–6
    strategies 189–92
  labour policies 139, 170, 183–8
  marketing services 102–3, 205
    farm equipment 116
    household goods 116–17
    land 114–15
    livestock 105–14
    non–wool produce 115–16
    wool 119–49
  mergers 47–50, 53–5, 213
  networks 203–4
    decline 71–2
    economic 67–71
    social, kinship 60–5
  organisational structure
    hierarchical development 166–76
    operational development 176–9
  rationalisation 52–3
Australian Wheat Board 116
Australian Wool Board 147
Australian Wool Council 147
Australian Wool Corporation 147
Australian Wool Exchange 148
Australian Wool Services Ltd 147
automobiles
  accounting 181
  company fleets 41, 191
  competitive tool 41
  costs of 181, 191
  motor trade 50–1

Bagot Shakes & Lewis 38–9, 48, 107
Bailey, J. D. 75, 98
Bank of Australasia 80, 86, 89, 121, 122–3
Bank of New South Wales 65, 99, 121, 122–3
Bank of New Zealand 19, 65, 79, 80, 89, 91,
    122–3, 166
banks
  internal labour markets 183, 187
  relations with agents 16, 42, 79–80, 111,
    196, 209
  relations with farmers 64
  rural lending 76–81
  wool trade 121–3, 130, 133, 142
Barnard, Alan 16
Bendigo Bank 79
Benelux 174
Bennett Fisher 106
Bennett Farmers 39, 53
Bethune & Hunter 130

BHP 183
Birt & Company 125
Blenheim 197
Boston 138
Brierley, Ron 54
Brisbane 40, 44, 127, 190
British Australian Wool Realisation
    Appraisement 146, 162
British Columbia 132
British New Zealand Mortgage and Agency
    Company 122–3
Broken Hill 107
Brooks, Robert & Company 80, 122–3, 154
Buckland, Alfred 48
Butlin, Noel 3, 5, 7, 15, 75, 100

Cain, N. 91
Campbell, W. E. M. 172
Canada 132, 137–8
Canterbury 10, 42, 44, 129
Casson, Mark 57
Challenge Corporation 54
Chandler, Alfred 6–7, 164–5, 170, 188, 204
Christchurch 127, 180
Coghlan, T. A. 5–6
Colman, G. 155
Commercial Banking Company of Sydney 122–3
Commercial, Pastoral and Agricultural
    Association of New South Wales 162
Committee of London Wool Selling Brokers
    142
Commonwealth Development Bank 77
company structure
  departments 166–7, 168
  divisions 170–2, 176
  head office 172–4
Commonwealth Wool and Produce Company
    48, 192, 198
competitive advantages 6–7
conglomeration 51–2, 54,
Conran, Marcel 161
Cooke, John 158
Cooper's 152
cooperatives
  dairying 69, 115
  employment 69
  evolution of 20
  financial structure and lending policies
    89–91
  managerial, financial weaknesses 20, 69
  network role 68–70
  relations with agents 16, 20, 28, 29, 42, 50,
    68–70, 111, 199, 208
CSIR 71, 155, 158
Crown 54
CSR 23, 54

dairying 2, 11, 12, 13, 69, 70, 85, 115, 207–8
Dalgety
  accounting practices 179–83
  corporate memory 153
  establishment 19, 20
  financial services 205

contracting 78–9, 91–9
  lending strategies 81–6
  profitability 99–100
  share of loans market 76–81
financial structure 86–91
franchising 176
future directions 54–5
growth 203
  big business 36, 38–9
  branches 33–7, 44–5, 139–40
  diversification 20–3, 50–2
  international 45–6
  national 39–45
  vertical 21–2
  wool broking 27–34, 53, 148
incorporation 23–4
information services 206
  acquisition and dissemination 153–8
  farmers' advocate 161–2
  technical examples 158–61
interfirm cooperation
  alliances 196–9
  contracts 47, 199–200
  limits 192–6
  strategies 189–92
labour policies 139, 154, 174, 183–8
management 46
marketing services 102–3, 205
  farm equipment 116
  household goods 116–17
  land 114–15
  livestock 105–14
  non-wool produce 115–16
  wool 119–49
mergers 47–50, 53–5, 199, 214
networks 203–4
  decline 71–2
  economic 67–71
  social, kinship 60–5
organisational structure 165
  hierarchical development 166–76
  operational development 176–9
profits & earnings 46, 51, 52–3, 103
rationalisation 52–3
Dalgety New Zealand Loan – see Dalgety
Dalgety, Frederick 24
Dalgety Trading Company 176
Danysz, Dr 160
Davidson, William Soltau 65
De Dion 41
De Garis 49, 192
Denmark 12, 13, 16
Dennys Lascelles
  financial services 80, 95, 96, 98
  information services 154, 155, 158, 159, 161
  interfirm relations 192, 194
  marketing 114, 121, 124, 125
  merger with AMLF 53, 54
  networks 62
Devonport 48
Donald Reid 20, 24, 60, 62, 69, 156
Doxat, E. T. 24, 43, 169
Driver Stewart 200

droughts 10, 11, 39–40, 75, 83, 107, 108–9, 115–16
Dunedin 44, 46, 60–1, 65–7, 127, 130, 135, 157, 170, 173, 191, 194, 195, 197, 200
Dunedin Savings Bank 60

East Africa 46
East Coast (NZ) 42, 129
Elder Smith – see Elder's
Elder Smith Goldsbrough Mort – see Elders
Elders
  accounting practices 179–83
  establishment 19
  financial structure 86–91
  financial service 205
    contracting 78–9, 91–9
    lending strategies 81–6
    profitability 99–100
    share of loans market 76–81
  future directions 54–5
  growth 203
    big business 36, 38–9
    branches 33–6, 44–5, 53, 139–40
    diversification 20–3, 50–2
    international 45–6
    national 39–45
    vertical 21–2, 22, 52, 54–5
    wool broking 27–31, 48, 53, 148
  information services 206
    acquisition and dissemination 153–8
    farmers' advocate 161–2
    technical examples 158–61
  interfirm cooperation
    alliances 196–9
    contracts 47, 199–200
    limits 192–6
    strategies 189–92
  labour policies 139, 183–8
  marketing services 102–3, 205
    farm equipment 116
    household goods 116–17
    land 114–15
    livestock 105–14
    non-wool produce 115–16
    wool 119–49
  mergers 47–50, 53–5, 199, 211, 213
  networks 203–4
    decline 71–2
    economic 67–71
    social, kinship 60–5
  organisational structure
    hierarchical development 166–76
    operational development 176–9
  profits and earnings 52–3, 103
  rationalisation 52–3
Elder, David 63
Elders IXL 54
Electrolux 174
Elliott, John 54
employees – see human resource management

Falconer (AMLF) 131
Farmers & Graziers Cooperative 27, 29, 38–9, 49–50, 70

254 INDEX

farmers
    'free' or 'tied' 40, 42, 100, 104
    banks 64
    closeness to market 131
    feedback 63
    indebtedness 75–6, 108
    reputation 92–3
farming
    capital intensity of 5, 75
    economic development 2, 3–7
    equipment 116
    geographic expansion 40
    income 13
    investment 3–4, 5–6, 7, 75
    mixed 11, 40, 109, 131
    output 3, 7–8, 13
    postwar 51
    sectoral linkages 4–5
    small scale 11, 12, 13, 14, 16, 40, 75, 85,
        131, 135, 139
    technology 8, 10, 11, 12–13, 16, 109
    uncertainty 8–9, 58
Federal Steam Navigation Company 124
Fergus, Thomas 60
Firth, Josiah Clifton 19
Fletcher Challenge 54
Ford 185
Foster's 54
Fraser, Malcolm 141
Fremantle 127, 148
Futuris 54

Geelong 48, 124, 125, 135, 192, 194, 197
General Motors 51, 185
Gibbs, Richard 21
Global Wool 148
gold 2, 65, 126
Goldsbrough Mort
    accounting practices 179–83
    establishment 19
    financial services 205
        contracting 78–9, 91–9
        lending strategies 81–6
        profitability 99–100
        share of loans market 76–81
    financial structure 86–91
    growth 20
        big business 36, 38–9
        branches 33–6, 53, 139–40
        diversification 20–3, 50–2
        national 39–45
        vertical 21–2
        wool broking 27–31, 44–5, 48, 53
    incorporation 23–4
    information services 206
        acquisition and dissemination 153–8
        farmers' advocate 161–2
        publications 156
        technical examples 158–61
    interfirm cooperation
        alliances 196–9
        contracts 47, 199–200

        limits 192–6
        strategies 189–92
    labour policies 49, 139, 183–8
    marketing services 102–3, 205
        farm equipment 116
        household goods 116–17
        land 114–15
        livestock 105–14
        non-wool produce 115–16
        wool 119–49
    mergers 47–50, 53–5, 199, 212
    networks 203–4
        decline 71–2
        economic 67–71
        social, kinship 60–5
    organisational structure
        hierarchical development 166–76
        operational development 176–9
    profits & earnings 51, 52–3, 103
    rationalisation 52–3
    suspension 39–40, 89
Goldsbrough, Richard 19, 23, 130
Gollin & Company 176
goodwill 49
Goodwin & De Lisle 86
Gore 62
Gore R. 16
Goulburn 142, 145
Gould 19, 21
government
    finance 70–1, 77
    legislation 11–12, 23, 70, 75, 76, 77, 162,
        200
    research 155
    role in networks 70–1
    wool market 141, 146–7
graziers – see farmers
Great Southern Railway 41
Gross Domestic Product 1–3, 5
Growers Alternative Selling System 140

Hague 48, 49
Hallett, H. E. 48
Harrison Jones & Devlin 27, 38–9, 48, 191–2
Hawke 5, 12
Hawke's Bay 10, 42, 44, 124, 129
Hawke's Bay Farmers Cooperative Association
    20
Henry Jones IXL 54
Henry Wills 49
Hepburn & Leonard 63, 80, 105–6
Hobart 127
Holt, Henry 23
Hong Kong 6
Hughes, William (PM) 162
Human Resource Management
    bureaucracies 177
    company assets 183
    impact of war 184
    incentives 182, 184–5, 187
    internal labour markets 183, 184–5, 185,
        186
    job classification 179

lifetime employment 184–5
  pension funds 186, 187
  personnel officers 186
  professional management class 187–8
  recruitment 185
  skills 183–4
  training 185, 186, 186–7
  women 186
Hunter, M. D. 99–100
Hutchinson, Alexander 161

Imperial Airways 50
Imperial Chemical Industries 157, 185
incorporation 23–6
Industrial Equity Limited 54
information
  competitive tool 151–2, 191
  correspondence 153, 154, 156
  feedbacks 158
  financial 78–9, 92
  network 57, 152
  paradox 151
  public goods 15, 151
  publications 153, 155, 156–7
  reciprocal 151
  social events 156
  synergies 20, 22
  technical 154, 158
  zero-priced 151, 152
inter-firm strategies
  alliances
    Anglo–Australian 197–8
    associations 196–7
    regional 193, 195, 197, 200
    size 196, 198, 199
  cooperation
    costs 193–4, 200
    enforcement 194, 195
    industry interests 190
    market infrastructure 135, 148, 189–90
    marketing 148, 191
  collusion
    charges 191, 191–2
    entry barriers 195, 196
    external competitors 195, 196
    other industries 192
  competition
    efficiency levels 192–3
    over clients 91, 96, 191
    service bundles 190–1, 193, 199
  contracts 47–8, 199–200
Invercargill 92

James Turner 19, 23
Japan 1
John Bridge & Company 27, 49, 91

Kenya 46
Kidd, James 40

land
  disputes 12
  ᴜᴀʟ 104

tenure 75
  improvement, legislation 11–12, 75
  settlement 11, 13, 75, 91, 114, 114–15
  sub-division 11–12, 22, 40, 75, 114–15
Levins
  acquisition by NMA 49, 54
  establishment 19
  interfirm relations 195
  marketing services 103, 130
  shearing technology 161
  wool broking 27, 32
Liberal Association of New South Wales 162
Lister's 161
livestock
  auctions 103, 104, 105–7
  bloodstock 109–10
  breeding 9–10, 11, 107, 109–11
  capital stock 108,
  dual function 110–11
  market volatility 107–9
  numbers 10
  private sales 105–7
  saleyards 107, 111–13
  slaughter 108
loans – see individual companies
Logan Campbell, John 19
Longburn Freezing works 65–6
Longreach 104, 157

Mallee 114
Maoris 11, 12, 161, 216
marketing
  challenges 102
  commissions 111, 142–3
  computer-assisted 113–14
  different methods 104, 107
  functions 105
  international comparisons 137–8
  remote 114
  segmentation 104, 111
  synergies 103–4, 139
marketing boards 12, 70
Marlborough 10
Marlborough East Coast Settlers Association
    142
Massey Agricultural College 71, 155
Massey, William (PM) 162
Matson, Henry 200
McBain, Sir James 161–2
Melbourne 63, 120, 124, 126–7, 130, 133, 134,
    135, 148, 166, 197
Melbourne Woolbrokers Association 199
Mills, James 65–6
Mintzberg, H 177
Montevideo 124
Moreheads 48
Morris Little & Son 63, 152
Morrison 122–3
Mort, Thomas 19, 23, 114, 130
Mortimer Franklyn, H. 114
Murray Roberts
  establishment 20
  mergers 47–50, 54

Murray Roberts (*cont.*)
   organisational structure 166, 169
   financial structure 86–91
   financial services 85, 86
   marketing services 124
   farmers' advocate 161
   growth 21, 27, 32–4, 39–45, 207
Murrumbidgee 127
Myer 52

National Bank of New Zealand 65–6, 80
National Council of Wool-Selling Brokers 141,
   195, 196, 197
National Country Party 162
National Mortgage & Agency
   accounting practices 179–83
   establishment 20
   financial services 205
      contracting 78–9, 91–9
      lending strategies 81–6
      profitability 99–100
      share of loans market 76–81
   financial structure 86–91
   growth 203
      national 39–45
      big business 39
      wool broking 27, 32–4
      international 45–6
      diversification 20–3, 50–2
      vertical 21–2
   incorporation 23–4
   information services 206
      acquisition and dissemination 153–8
      farmers' advocate 161–2
      technical examples 158–61
   interfirm cooperation
      alliances 196–9
      contracts 47, 199–200
      labour policies 139, 183–8
      limits 192–6
      strategies 189–92
   marketing services 102–3, 205
      farm equipment 116
      household goods 116–17
      land 114–15
      livestock 105–14
      non-wool produce 115–16
      wool 119–49
   mergers 47–50, 53–5, 199, 215
   networks 203–4
      case study 65–7
      decline 71–2
      economic 67–71
      social, kinship 60–7
   organisational structure
      hierarchical development 166–76
      operational development 176–9
   rationalisation 52–3
National Insurance Company 65–6
Native Land Court (NZ) 161
Nelson Brothers 159
networks 15, 203–4
   agents 58–60

   dairying 115
   decline 71–2
   growth of 60–71
   information 57, 152
   lending 64, 96
   political influence 63
   rural counsellors 72
   settler society 60–1
   theories 56–7
   trade and finance 63
   types 58–60
New England and North-West Producers
   Cooperative 142
New South Wales 42, 45, 48, 50, 70, 77, 91–2,
   98, 108, 126–7, 128, 134, 198
New Zealand
   capital formation 3–4, 5–6
   comparisons with Australia 10–11, 46, 76,
      133–4, 206
   economic growth 1–3
   foreign trade 2–3
   investment 2–3, 7
   manufacturing 2, 3
   market size 7
   migration, population, work force 1, 2, 3
New Zealand and Australian Land Company
   122, 186
New Zealand Farmers Cooperative
   Association 195
New Zealand Livestock Agents and
   Auctioneers Association 111, 196, 197
New Zealand Loan & Mercantile Agency
   accounting practices 179–83
   establishment 19, 20
   financial services 205
      contracts 78–9, 91–9
      lending strategies 81–6
      profitability 99–100
      share of loans market 76–81
   financial structure 86–91
   growth 203
      big business 36, 38–9
      branches 33–6, 44–5
      diversification 20–3, 50–2
      international 45–6
      national 39–45
      vertical 21–2
      wool broking 27–34, 53
   incorporation 23–4
   information services 206
      acquisition and dissemination 153–8
      farmers' advocate 161–2
      technical examples, 158–61
   interfirm cooperation
      alliances 196–9
      contracts 47, 199–200
      limits 192–6
      strategies 189–92
   labour policies 139, 183–8
   marketing services 102–3, 205
      farm equipment 116
      household goods 116–17
      land 114–15

livestock 105–14
  non-wool produce, 115–16
  wool 119–49
mergers 47–50, 53–5, 199, 215
networks 203–4
  decline 71–2
  economic 67–71
  social, kinship 60–5
organisational structure
  hierarchical development 166–76
  operational development 176–9
  profits and earnings 51, 52–3
  rationalisation 52–3
  relations with Bank of New Zealand 19,
    79, 80, 166
  suspension 39–40, 89
New Zealand Stock and Station Agents
  Association 199
New Zealand Trust & Loan 23
New Zealand Wool Board 140, 147
New Zealand Wool Commission 146–7
New Zealand Wool Marketing Corporation
  147
New Zealand Woolbrokers Association 131,
  143–4, 162, 194, 195, 196, 197, 199
Newcastle, NSW 44, 142, 144
Nicholson, Charles 19
Northern Territory 43
Northland 12

office technology 41, 155–6
Otago 42, 44, 60, 65–7, 111, 129
Otago Farmers Cooperative 68–9, 86–91, 111
Ottawa Conference 13

Pearson Rowe 48, 49
Peninsular & Oriental Shipping Company 159
Penrose, Edith 164
Perpetual Executors Trustees Association 80
Perth 44, 134
Pick, J. E. 95
Pitt Son & Badgery
  acquisition 54
  financial services 85, 92, 93, 99
  growth 41
  interfirm relations 191–2
  networks 63
  organisational structure 177
  wool marketing 142, 144
Porter, Michael 6
Portland 141
Portland Woolbrokers 142, 144
primary producers – see farmers
Pyne Gould Guinness 21, 27, 32–4, 39–45

Queensland 40, 42, 43, 45, 48, 50, 70, 79, 128,
  198
Queensland Investment Land Mortgage &
  Agency Company 23, 39
Queensland Primary Producers' Cooperative
  Association 41, 50

rabbits 5, 11, 150–60, 100

railways 2, 41, 85, 126, 197
Rankin, Keith 2, 6
Redfern Alexander 122
refrigeration 2, 4, 5, 11, 12, 13, 64, 115, 158–9
Reid & Gray 65–6
Renault 51
Richardsons 22
Ritchie, G. R. 65–6, 173–4
Ritchie, J. M. 169
Riverina 126–7, 197
Rockhampton 44
Ross and Glendinning 22
Rostow, Walt 4
Rural Banking and Finance Corporation 77
rural finance
  demand 74–6
  fluctuations in, risks of 39–40
  infrastructural 75
  intermediation 79–80, 99
  long term 39–40, 74–5
  short term 74–5
  supply 22, 76–86
Rural Industries Bank of Western Australia 79
Russell Ritchie & Company 24
Russell, George Gray 60

Sanderson Murray 20, 21, 122
Scottish Australian Investment Company
  122–3
Scottish Widows' Fund 79
Shaw Savill Albion 67, 124
sheep 8
  comebacks 111
  Corriedale 110
  merinos 8, 110, 111
  numbers 8, 10
  Polwarth 110
  shearing 11, 160–1
Sheep and Wool New Zealand Ltd 140
shipping 126
  contractual power of agents 124, 125
  disputes 125
  freight rates 124, 127, 132
  navigation 124–5
  sail, steam 5, 121
  stowage 124–5
ships: *Cornwall* 124, *Timaru* 125, *Port Stephens*
  125
Simkin, C. G. F. 6
Singapore 6
South Africa 46
South America 46
South Australia 42, 43, 48, 50, 83, 107, 128,
  149, 172, 178, 198
South Australian Farmers Cooperative 39
South Australian Land & Mortgage Company
  39
Southland 42, 129
Stanley, Arthur 162
staple theory 4
State Advances Corporation 77
Stigler, G. 150–1
Strachan 58

Stronach Morris 54, 61, 68, 157, 161
Stuckeys 47–8
Sutch, W. B. 6
Sydney 44, 120, 126–7, 130, 134, 135, 148,
    166, 190
Sydney Woolbrokers Association 191, 192,
    194, 199
Synott, M. D. 23

Tanganyika 46
Tara 40
Tasmania 42, 43, 79, 128
taxation 59
telegrams 41, 132, 153, 169
Timaru 65
Toronto 138
Townsville 44
travel agencies 50
Trollope, A. 75
Tsokhas, Kosmas 162, 193, 198
Turner, William 63
Tyser 124

Union Bank of Australia 122–3
Union Mortgage & Agency 23, 107, 108–9,
    120, 121, 130, 198
Union Steamship Company 65–7
United Kingdom (or Britain) 1, 3, 6, 7, 9, 12,
    13, 14, 16, 19, 65, 85, 120, 133, 166,
    169, 196, 197–8, 199
United States of America 1, 3, 7, 14, 15, 51–2,
    107, 132, 137–8
University of Melbourne 85, 155, 186
urbanisation 2
Uruguay 137

Victoria 42, 43, 48, 50, 110, 126–7, 128, 134,
    159, 198
Vogel, Julius (PM) 3

Wagga Wagga 126
Waikato 12
Wairarapa 10
Wallaroo Phosphate Company 116
Ward, J. G. 49
Watt, W. 62
Weaver & Perry 49
Webster, A. G. 48
Wellington 42, 44, 49, 127, 129, 142, 197
Wellington Woolbrokers Association 193, 194,
    195
Wesfarmers 50, 54
Western Australia 40, 41, 42, 43, 48, 50, 62,
    107, 127, 128, 133, 134, 138, 142, 198,
    208
Westralian Farmers' Cooperative 38–9, 50, 70
wheat 12, 115–16
White Star 67
Whittingham, A. H. 62
William, S. 155
William Sloane 23
Williamson, O. 151
Williams & Kettle

establishment 19–20
    competition with cooperatives 20
    growth 22, 28, 44, 124
    marketing services 124
Wincombe Carson
    accounting 182,
    acquisition by Dalgety 54
    big business 38–9
    financial services 91
    information services 153
    interfirm relations 191, 191–2
    marketing services 104, 111, 115
    national growth 39–45
    network links 61
    political donation 162
    wool broking 27–30
Wolseley Shearing Machine Company 161
wool 103, 104
    artificial fibres 12, 143, 145
    demand 131–2
    handling and dumping 137
    manufacture 9, 132
    output 8, 18–19
    relative prices 132–3
    scouring 52
    stockpiles 146, 147
wool auctions
    classing 136
    competition between centres 140, 142, 144
    costs 134, 137–42
    extended season 135–6
    inspection 136
    interlotting 136
    national rosters 135
    order of sale 144
    pies 145
    presentation 136, 139
    salerooms 135, 139
    sampling 136
    warehouses 135, 13
wool buyers 120, 131–2, 133
wool exports 4–5, 8, 10–11, 126
wool growers – see farmers
wool market 9
    alternative locations 120, 126–34
    control 143–8
    costs 131, 133–4
    country and private sales 22, 120, 126,
        135, 138, 140, 143–4
    dealers 142
    economic stimulus 149
    efficiency criteria 132–3
    electronic 147–8
    futures 145
    Imperial Wool Purchase 12, 145–6
    Joint Disposals Organisation 146
    overseas consignment 120–5
    reserve prices 146–7
Wright Stephenson
    accounting practices 179–83
    establishment 19
    financial services 205
        contracting 78–9, 91–9

lending strategies 81–6
  profitability 99–100
  share of loans market 76–81
financial structure 86–91
growth 203
  national 39–45
  big business 39
  wool broking 27, 32–4, 36
  international 45–6
  diversification 20–3, 50–2
  vertical 21–2
incorporation 23–4
information services 206
  acquisition and dissemination 153–8
  farmers' advocate 161–2
  technical examples 158–61
interfirm cooperation
  alliances 196–9
  contracts 47, 199–200
  limits 192–6
  strategies 189–92
labour policies 139, 183–8

marketing services 46, 102–3, 205
  farm equipment 116
  household goods 116–17
  land 114–15
  livestock 105–14
  non-wool produce, 115–16
  wool 119–49
mergers 47–50, 53–5, 199, 215
networks 203–4
  decline 71–2
  economic 67–71
  social, kinship 60–5
organisational structure
  hierarchical development 166–76
  operational development 176–9
rationalisation 52–3
Wrightson–NMA – *see* Wright Stephenson

Yates, J. 176–7
Young, Henry 19
Young, Walter 188
Younghusband 38–9, 53, 198